Infernal Traffic:
Excavation of a Liberated African Graveyard in Rupert's Valley, St Helena

Infernal Traffic:
Excavation of a Liberated African Graveyard in Rupert's Valley, St Helena

Andrew Pearson, Ben Jeffs, Annsofie Witkin
and Helen MacQuarrie

CBA Research Report 169
Council for British Archaeology
2011

Published in 2011 by the Council for British Archaeology
St Mary's House, 66 Bootham, York, YO30 7BZ

British Library cataloguing in Publication Data
A catalogue record for this book is available from the British Library
ISBN 978-1-902771-89-2

Typeset by Archétype Informatique, www.archetype-it.com
Printed and bound by Charlesworth Press

The publisher acknowledges with gratitude a grant from the Department for International Development
towards the cost of publication

*From the very nature of the means used to
extirpate it, this infernal traffic becomes armed with
new horrors, and continues to tear out, year after year,
the very bowels of the African continent – that scene of
the greatest sufferings which have ever scourged
humanity – the worst of all crimes ever
perpetrated by man.*

Henry Brougham, House of Lords, 1838

Contents

List of figures

Picture credits

The photographs and figures within this report are the work of the project team, with the exception of the following images, which are reproduced courtesy of several individuals and organisations.

Within this printed volume: Figs 2.4 and 5.3 (Royal Naval Museum); Figs 2.5, 2.9 and 2.13 (UK National Archives); Figs 2.6 and 2.8 (Robin Castell/ The Castell Collection); Figs 2.10 and 2.14 (St Helena Government); Figs 5.17 and 5.27 (The Anglo-Saxon Laboratory). Within the digital volume: Figs D2.61, D2.64, D2.100 and D2.107 (The Anglo-Saxon Laboratory); Figs D6.5 and D6.28 (Ruth Mauritzen).

List of tables

List of contributors

Andrew Pearson BA MA PhD MIfA, Leverhulme Research Fellow, Department of Archaeology and Anthropology, University of Bristol, 43 Woodland Road, Clifton, Bristol, BS8 1UU. Director, Pearson Archaeology Ltd

Ben Jeffs BSc MA, Director, Blackfreighter Archaeology and Conservation, Netherfield House, Main Road, Claybrooke Magna, LE17 5AJ

Annsofie Witkin BA MSc, PhD, Department of Archaeology and Anthropology, University of Bristol, 43 Woodland Road, Clifton, Bristol, BS8 1UU. Formerly Project Officer, Oxford Archaeology

Helen MacQuarrie MA MPhil AIfA, Project Officer, AOC Archaeology Group, London. Formerly AHRC-funded postgraduate researcher, Department of Archaeology and Anthropology, University of Bristol

Penelope Walton Rogers FSA Dip Acc, The Anglo-Saxon Laboratory, Bootham House, 61 Bootham, York YO30 7BT. Proprietor of the Anglo-Saxon Laboratory

Quita Mould BA MA, Freelance finds specialist and a Director of Barbican Research Associates, Eastmoor Manor, Eastmoor, King's Lynn, Norfolk, PE33 9PZ

Isabella von Holstein BSc, The Anglo-Saxon Laboratory, Bootham House, 61 Bootham, York YO30 7BT. PhD student, BioArch Laboratory, University of York

Josie Sheppard, Dip AGMS, York Castle Museum, Eye of York, York YO1 9RY. Curator and freelance consultant

Natasha Ferguson BA MA, Centre for Battlefield Archaeology, University of Glasgow, The Gregory Building, Lilybank Gardens, University of Glasgow, Glasgow G12 8QQ

Foreword   *by His Excellency Andrew Gurr, Governor of St Helena*

Being Governor of a small island is an exciting and rewarding task, but when I accepted the role in 2007 I did not expect that a team of professional archaeologists uncovering fresh revelations about our colourful history – almost on an hourly basis – would become such a highlight of my tenure.

The island's heritage is at times obvious and at others subtle. There are colonial buildings that have remained unchanged for many decades, there is a profusion of ancient military defences, and there are the ghosts of Napoleon, Dinizulu, Boer War prisoners and East India Company employees. Much of this heritage is known and celebrated by those living on the island, even though it rarely receives the international attention that it deserves. However, when it comes to the important dimension of St Helena's role in bringing the slave trade to an end, it is almost too painful and solemn to rate as a tourist attraction, or even as a matter of island pride.

Before 2006, awareness of what lay beneath the surface of Rupert's Valley was sketchy to say the least, and in many ways it had been ignored. And yet the surprises unearthed by Dr Pearson and his team in Rupert's Valley shout to us down the ages not only of the incredible cruelty of the slave trade, of the immense mountain of human suffering, but also of the absolutely pivotal role that St Helena played in helping to alleviate and eradicate such inhumanity.

The sheer scale of the graveyards, allied with the extremely young age profile of the bodies, is both revealing and disturbing: standing by the excavated graves, it was not hard to imagine that this barren, steep-sided valley once contained a human conveyor belt that channelled relief and horror at the same time.

The archaeological team has drawn on material from unpublished archives, as well as a wealth of trowel-in-hand experience, to relate this amalgam of tragedy and rescue. It is important that we never forget what happened in Rupert's Valley and the island is taking steps to ensure that this is the case. As I write, the construction of an ossuary for the reburial of the human remains is being taken in hand, whilst the possibility of a permanent visitor centre is also being investigated.

The excavations described in this report only came about because of the need to build an airport – a move intended to secure St Helena's future in the 21st century. There are many telling lessons from the past, and it is to be hoped that they will remain with us as we address that future. This book will prove to be a cornerstone of that remembrance.

Plantation House, St Helena
September 2011

Acknowledgements

This project, the first archaeological study to be undertaken on St Helena, could not have been accomplished without the support of numerous individuals and organisations.

The work published in this report arose out of the Air Access project, which has been funded in its entirety by the Department for International Development (DFID). At the outset of the study the scale and significance of the archaeology that was ultimately discovered could not have been anticipated and thanks are due to Phil Mason, Nigel Kirby, Anna Ballance and Dick Beales of DFID for their ready support, particularly in mid-2008 when the true scale of the excavations became clear.

The cultural heritage chapter of the Air Access Environmental Statement was written by the author (Andrew Pearson – AP) whilst an employee of Faber Maunsell (now AECOM), and the main period of field work and the post-excavation programme has also been undertaken in collaboration with AECOM. Kath Thorp, Iain Bell and Ruth Mauritzen have all contributed from the outset of the study, most particularly during the writing of the Environmental Statement and the period of the 2008 excavation.

On St Helena our work received an enormous amount of support. Whilst this project was not community archaeology in a strict sense, it nevertheless came to involve numerous local residents without whose help our task would have been far more difficult. At an official level we received enthusiastic support from the governor, Andrew Gurr, from the island's Legislative Council and from Sharon Wainwright, the Air Access co-ordinator on St Helena. Thanks are also due to Clare Harris and Belinda Beard of St Helena Government for their administrative support throughout the period of field work.

The Legal, Lands and Planning Department and the Public Works and Services Department both provided essential support, including the initial consent to allow us to excavate on land owned by Crown Estates. During the course of the field work they also gave much practical help. Thanks are especially owed to Gavin George, Glynis Fowler, Len Coleman, Derek Richards and Alan Hudson. Within Rupert's Valley, we are grateful to Robert Scipio and the staff at the Mid Valley Fuel Farm and Power Station for their ready co-operation with our excavation, which at times caused them considerable disruption.

The St Helena National Trust (SHNT) played a key role, most notably recruiting volunteers for the excavation and helping with our programme of outreach. Vince Thompson, Rebecca Cairns-Wicks and Phyllis Coleman deserve particular thanks for the time and effort expended on our behalf. SHNT also allowed us to use the Pipe Building in Jamestown for storage of the human remains, and in doing so delayed their own plans for its conversion to a museum. Thanks are also due to the staff of the St Helena Government Archives and the Museum of St Helena, the St Helena Heritage Society, and to the Friends of St Helena.

The excavation team comprised staff from AOC Archaeology and Northampton Archaeology. Particular mention must be made of Adam Yates who, as part of the original team, supervised most of the machine stripping of the site and was continuously present at the excavation from its inception in May 2008 through to the end of August 2008. Paula Williams' management of the initial processing of the finds and skeletal remains was also invaluable. The 2008 osteological assessment was undertaken on-island by Annsofie Witkin (Bristol University), who returned the following year with Diana Mahoney Swales (Sheffield University) to carry out the full analysis. The 2009 analysis was aided by Sophie Thorpe.

In addition to the professional staff, a large number of volunteers became involved with our work during the 2008 season. Some were St Helenians, whilst others were long-term non-St Helenian residents. It is unfortunately not possible to name all of the volunteers here, but special mention is due to Helen Joshua, Murray Henry and Samara Isaac, students from Prince Andrew's School who worked as excavators on the site throughout most of the 2008 season. Similarly, both during the excavation and subsequently, Barbara George has tirelessly answered my questions about St Helenian history, following up lines of enquiry which could not be answered by UK-based sources. Thanks are also owed to Nick, Gail, Henry and Ed Thorpe, who not only showed a keen interest in the excavations, but who also allowed us the use of one of their properties for the osteological analysis.

The finds were stabilised and conserved by Phil Parkes of Cardiff Conservation Services. Their study has been co-ordinated by Helen MacQuarrie, who also carried out the analysis of some of the artefact types. Her work formed part of a broader research project investigating the assemblage, undertaken at Bristol University and funded by the Arts and Humanities Research Council. Other aspects of the finds analysis were undertaken by Natasha Ferguson, Quita Mould, Penelope Walton Rogers, Isabella von Holstein, Josie Sheppard, Paul Gates and Richard Evershed. Additional information and advice was provided by Christopher DeCorse, Peter

Gasson, Allan Hall, Roberto Portela Miguez and Marilee Woods.

Throughout the project we have benefited from the input of numerous individuals from the academic, commercial and amateur archaeological fields. In particular, David Shilston of Atkins, whose trial pitting in 2006 encountered several graves in Rupert's Valley, provided the project with valuable advance notice of the graveyards' existence, as well as much useful data. Other contributions have been made by: Richard Benjamin; Michael Blakey; Bob Conrich; Jerome Handler; Deborah Hodson; Patrick Manning; Ian Mathieson; Neil Maylan; Rob Philpott; Marcus Rediker; Hannes Schroeder; Edmund Simons; Stéphane Van de Velde; Jason Williams; and Jenny Wraight. The staff of the National Archives at Kew provided much advice about the records in their collections, whilst transcription of many of the original texts was undertaken by Kate and Sue Pearson. Advice on database and GIS analyses has been provided by Doerte Steup and Iona Pearson.

Kate Robson-Brown commented upon the initial text of this report, whilst the final manuscript was reviewed by Ken Nystrom (State University of New York) and James Walvin (University of York). Thanks are also owed to the Council for British Archaeology, both for their support of this unusual project, the first overseas project to be published in their Research Report series, and for their practical help in bringing this monograph to publication.

Finally, I would like to pay tribute to my co-authors, Ben Jeffs, Annsofie Witkin and Helen MacQuarrie. Ben and Annsofie became involved in the project during the writing of the Environmental Statement in 2007, and all three played a central role in the 2008 excavations and the subsequent analysis. Their inputs have extended far beyond the written contributions contained within this monograph, reflecting a project that has grown past any of our original expectations.

Andrew Pearson
Department of Archaeology and Anthropology,
University of Bristol

Summary

This report describes and discusses archaeological investigations of the 'Liberated African' graveyards in Rupert's Valley, on the island of St Helena in the South Atlantic. These works were undertaken between 2007 and 2008, and were funded by the British Government (Department for International Development). They arose from wider environmental studies initiated in response to proposals to build an airport on the island, which is presently only accessible by sea.

The graveyards as a whole belong to the middle decades of the 19th century, and relate to Britain's attempts to abolish the transatlantic slave trade. Between 1840 and 1872 a Vice-Admiralty court operated on St Helena, adjudicating cases of slave ships captured by the Royal Navy's West Africa Squadron. As a part of this process, the human cargo of these vessels, nearly all of whom had been transported in appalling conditions, were brought ashore on St Helena.

The records indicate that over 26,000 'Liberated' or 'recaptive' Africans were received by the 'Liberated African Establishment' on the island during this period. 'Depots' were set up in two valleys, acting as receiving centres, hospitals and quarantine zones. The first of these, Lemon Valley, was abandoned after 1843, but Rupert's Valley continued to receive and treat slaves into the late 1860s.

The majority of recaptives survived. Some became residents of St Helena but most were moved onwards to other British colonies, principally in the Caribbean. Nevertheless, the mortality rate on the slave ships and after landing was extremely high. The slave vessels arrived with corpses aboard, and many other Liberated Africans died in the days and weeks after landing. Periodic attempts were made to dispose of the bodies at sea, but this measure proved impractical. As a result, burial on land became necessary, and large areas close to the depots were given over to unconsecrated, institutional, graveyards. Over the Establishment's lifetime it is estimated that around 8000 Africans were buried in these graveyards, most in Rupert's Valley.

Burials in the valley have been encountered in the past, but the present report is concerned with discoveries made between 2006 and 2008. These began when geotechnical trial pitting in 2006 encountered a small number of burials, work which was followed by more formal archaeological investigations in 2007. Full open-area excavation of a part of the upper graveyard was undertaken during a four-month period in 2008.

The 2008 excavation took in an area that measured only *c* 100m x 30m. However, the density of burials was such that 325 articulated skeletons were recovered, as well as a considerable volume of disarticulated human bone from a series of discrete pits. The general level of preservation was high, with survival of organics such as hair and fingernails being common.

Rupert's Valley is narrow, and much of it is either too rocky to allow burial, or lies within the floodplain of a small stream. Suitable space for burial was clearly at a premium, and although a reasonable number of graves contained just a single body, multiple burials were prevalent. Up to seven individuals were deposited in graves that in normal circumstances would have been deemed suitable for just one person. Only five people were buried in wooden coffins: four still- or newborn babies, and a single adolescent male.

The osteological analysis reveals a population that was extremely young. Children aged up to 12 years accounted for one-third of the skeletons, with young and prime adult males also well-represented. Only seventeen people were in the age bracket of 36–45 years, and these were the oldest individuals. The proportion of the sexes was more difficult to determine, mainly due to the youth of this population. There is no doubt that they were of African origin: over one-third of the skeletons had teeth that had been modified into patterns by either filing or chipping, a clear indication of cultural practices.

These individuals were certainly also victims of the slave trade. However, there was little skeletal evidence for the physical abuse that they must have endured during captivity and transportation, other than a small number of protection injuries. The exact cause of death is also opaque, although scurvy was prevalent and must have been a major contributing factor. Given that these individuals had spent only a short time at sea, this evidence indicates that their diet prior to embarkation had been poor. Lead projectiles (ie musket balls) recovered from the graves of two older children suggest that these individuals had been shot.

Over 100 registered individual or group small finds were recovered, including coins, iron and copper alloy objects, glass ampoules and bottles, clay pipes, beads, buttons and textile fragments. Most of this assemblage has a European origin. Whilst a few of these items (notably jewellery) may have been owned by the Africans prior to their enslavement, the majority probably relate to the period spent in captivity or within Rupert's Valley.

In general the burials were of an institutional character. After the arrival of a laden slave ship burials were carried out hurriedly, and often in great numbers. For the most part the process was concerned with rapid disposal: human dignity or cultural practices were not a consideration. The coffin burials of the stillborn or newborn babies, on the other hand, appear to evince both European and African cultural influences.

The excavations revealed only a small portion of the upper of the two graveyards in Rupert's Valley. However, the discoveries are of very great signifi-

cance. Firstly, this site is unique: no other known burial ground contains solely the bodies of first generation Africans who died as a result of their transportation. On a cultural level, too, the site has a huge resonance, providing a stark physical reminder of the human consequences of the slave trade.

Resumen

Este informe arqueológico describe y debate las investigaciones llevadas a cabo en el cementerio 'Liberated African' ('Africanos liberados') localizado en Rupert's Valley, en la isla de Santa Helena en el Atlántico Sur. Estos trabajos tuvieron lugar entre 2007 y 2008, y fueron financiados por el Gobierno Británico (Departamento de Desarrollo International). Surgen a raíz de los estudios medioambientales iniciados en respuesta a la propuesta de construir un aeropuerto en la isla, a la que solo es posible acceder por mar.

El cementerio en su totalidad pertenece a las décadas centrales del siglo XIX y está relacionado con los intentos británicos de abolir el comercio de esclavos transatlántico. Entre 1840 y 1872, una corte del Vice-Almirantazgo operaba en Santa Helena, juzgando casos de barcos de esclavos capturados por el Escuadrón 'West Africa' de la Armada Real. Como parte de este proceso, el cargamento humano de estos navíos, que casi en su totalidad había sido transportado en condiciones horrendas, fue desembarcado en las orillas de Santa Helena.

Los archivos indican que más de 26.000 Africanos 'liberados' o 'recapturados' fueron recibidos por el 'Liberated African Establishment' ('Centro de Africanos Liberados') creado en la isla durante este periodo. Dos 'almacenes' fueron construidos en dos valles distintos con el fin de recibir a tan elevado número, funcionando como centros de acogida, hospitales y zonas de cuarentena. El primero de ellos, Lemon Valley, fue abandonado después de 1843, pero Rupert's Valley continuó recibiendo y atendiendo a esclavos hasta finales de la década de los 60 del Siglo XIX.

La mayoría de los 'liberados' sobrevivió. Algunos de ellos se convirtieron en residentes de Santa Helena pero la mayoría fueron trasladados a otras colonias Británicas, principalmente en el Caribe. A pesar de todo, la tasa de mortalidad en los barcos de esclavos y tras el desembarco era extremadamente elevada. Los barcos de esclavos atracaban con numerosos cadáveres a bordo y muchos otros 'Liberated Africans' ('Africanos liberados') morían en los días y semanas posteriores a su desembarco. Periódicamente se llevaron a cabo intentos para deshacerse de los cuerpos en altamar, pero esta técnica demostró ser poco práctica. Como resultado, la sepultura en

tierra se hizo necesaria y grandes áreas cerca de los centros de acogida fueron dedicadas a cementerios institucionales y no consagrados. Se estima que, durante el tiempo en que el 'Establishment' (centro de acogida) estuvo activo, alrededor de 8000 africanos fueron enterrados en estos cementerios, la gran mayoría en Rupert's Valley.

Ya se habían localizado enterramientos en el valle con anterioridad, pero el presente informe está dedicado a los descubrimientos hechos entre 2006 y 2008. Estos comenzaron en 2006 cuando un estudio geotécnico del terreno sacó a la luz un pequeño número de enterramientos; a este estudio siguió una investigación arqueológica más formal en 2007. En 2008 y durante cuatro meses, se llevó a cabo una excavación abierta y completa en un área de la parte alta del cementerio.

La excavación de 2008 tan solo abracaba un área de unos 100m × 30m. Sin embargo, la densidad de enterramientos era tal que 325 esqueletos completos fueron recuperados junto con un considerable número de huesos humanos desarticulados localizados en una zanja concreta. El nivel general de conservación era alto, siendo común incluso la presencia de materiales orgánicos tales como cabellos o uñas.

Rupert's Valley es estrecho y en su mayor parte, bien demasiado rocoso como para albergar enterramientos, bien parte del lecho de un pequeño arroyo. El espacio disponible para enterramientos era claramente escaso y, aunque un número razonable de tumbas contenían un solo cuerpo, los enterramientos múltiples eran frecuentes. Hasta siete individuos fueron depositados en tumbas que, en condiciones normales, hubieran albergado a una única persona. Tan solo cinco personas fueron enterradas en ataúdes de madera: cuatro mortinatos o neonatos y un único varón adolescente.

El estudio osteológico revela una población extremadamente joven. Niños en edades de hasta 12 años conforman un tercio de los esqueletos, con varones jóvenes y en adultez temprana también bien representados. Solo se contabilizaron diecisiete personas en edades comprendidas entre 36 y 45 años, y estos eran los individuos de mayor edad. La proporción de géneros fue más difícil de determinar, principalmente debido a la juventud de esta población. No hay duda de que eran de origen Africano: más de un tercio de los esqueletos presentaban una dentadura modificada en patrones por limaduras o cascajo, lo que claramente indica prácticas culturales.

Estos individuos fueron definitivamente víctimas del comercio de esclavos. Sin embargo, hay escasas evidencias en los esqueletos que evidencien abuso físico durante el periodo de cautividad y transporte, más allá de leves lesiones defensivas. Las causas exactas de la muerte permanecen también opacas, aunque el escorbuto estaba bastante extendido y muy probablemente fuera uno de los factores que más contribuyó. Suponiendo que estos individuos solo permanecieran cortos periodos de tiempo en altamar, la presencia de dicha enfermedad evidencia que su dieta antes de embarcar había sido muy pobre. Proyectiles de plomo (balas de mosquetón) recuperados en las tumbas de dos niños mayores sugieren que estos individuos fueron disparados.

Más de 100 de pequeños hallazgos fueron recuperados individualmente o en grupo, incluyendo monedas, objetos de hierro y aleación de cobre, ampollas y botellas de cristal, pipas de arcilla, abalorios, botones y fragmentos de material textil. Este conjunto de materiales arqueológicos es en su mayoría de origen Europeo. Mientras algunos de estos objetos (sobretodo joyería) podrían haber pertenecido a los Africanos antes de su esclavización es probable que la mayoría de ellos estén relacionados con su etapa en cautiverio o en Rupert's Valley.

En general los enterramientos tenían un carácter institucional. Tras la llegada de un barco de esclavos repleto, frecuentemente y de manera apresurada se llevaban a cabo un gran número de enterramientos. En su mayor parte dicho proceso tenía que ver con la rápida eliminación de los cuerpos: la dignidad humana o las prácticas culturales no se tenían en cuenta. Por el contrario, los ataúdes de mortinatos o neonatos parecen manifestar influencias culturales Europeas y Africanas.

Las excavaciones revelaron tan solo una pequeña parte de la parte alta de ambos cementerios en Rupert's Valley. Sin embargo, los hallazgos son de gran relevancia. En primer lugar, el yacimiento es único: ningún otro cementerio conocido contiene exclusivamente los cuerpos de esclavos Africanos de primera generación fallecidos como resultado de su transporte. De igual modo, el yacimiento tiene una gran repercusión cultural al proporcionar un crudo y palpable recuerdo de las consecuencias humanitarias del tráfico de esclavos.

Résumé

Les recherches archéologiques menées sur les cimetières des 'Africains libérés' dans la Rupert's Valley sur l'ile de Ste Hélène dans l'Atlantique Sud, entreprises entre 2007 et 2008 et financées par le gouvernement Britannique (Ministère du Développement International), forment le sujet de ce rapport. Elles font suite à une étude de l'environnement plus ample mise en œuvre en réaction à un projet de construction d'un aéroport sur une ile qui jusqu'alors n'était accessible que par voie de mer.

Les cimetières datent du milieu du 19ème siècle et appartiennent à l'époque de l'abolition par la Grande-Bretagne du commerce transatlantique d'esclaves. Une cour de la vice-amirauté fut établie sur l'ile de Ste Hélène entre 1840 et 1872, chargée de juger de cas de navires d'esclaves interceptés par le West Africa Squadron de la Royal Navy. La cargaison humaine que ces navires transportaient, la plupart dans des conditions atroces, fut ainsi débarquée sur l'ile.

Les documents indiquent que plus de 26 000 'Africains libérés' ou 'repris' furent accueillis par 'l'Etablissement des Africains libérés' pendant cette période. Des 'entrepôts' furent construits dans deux vallées; ils servaient de lieux d'accueil, d'hôpitaux et de zones de quarantaine. Le plus ancien des deux, Lemon Valley, fut abandonné après 1843, mais celui de Rupert's Valley continua de fonctionner juque vers la fin des années 1860.

La grande majorité des 'repris' survécût. Certains s'établirent sur Ste Hélène mais la plupart furent transférés vers d'autres colonies Britanniques, principalement dans les Antilles. Le taux de mortalité sur les navires d'esclaves ainsi qu'après débarquement était extrêmement élevé. Les navires arrivaient avec une partie des esclaves déjà morts, et un grand nombre d'Africain 'libérés' succombèrent dans les jours et semaines suivant le débarquement. On essaya de temps en temps de disposer des corps en mer, mais cette mesure ne fut pas efficace. Par conséquent, il fut nécessaire d'enterrer les morts sur terre ferme ; ainsi de vastes zones proches des entrepôts furent réservées à des cimetières institutionnels en terre non-consacrée. On estime qu'environ 8000 Africains furent ensevelis dans ces cimetières pendant la durée de l'Etablissement, la plupart dans ceux de la Rupert's Valley.

Des sépultures ont jadis été retrouvées dans cette vallée, mais ce sont les découvertes faites entre 2006 et 2008 qui forment le sujet de notre rapport. Les premières sépultures furent découvertes pendant des sondages géotechniques en 2006 ; ces travaux menèrent à des recherches archéologiques plus structurées en 2007. Des fouilles programmées sur une partie du cimetière supérieur furent entreprises pendant quatre mois en 2008.

Les fouilles de 2008 s'étendirent sur une aire mesurant 100 x 30m. La densité des sépultures était telle que l'on retrouva 325 squelettes articulés ainsi qu'un nombre considérable d'ossements humains non-articulés provenant d'une série de fosses distinctes. Les ossements étaient en bon état de conservation, et il était courant de rencontrer des matières organiques comme les ongles et les cheveux encore conservés.

La vallée de Rupert's Valley est étroite ; elle est en grande partie trop rocheuse pour permettre l'ensevelissement, ou alors elle se situe dans la zone d'inondation d'une petite rivière. Les endroits propices à la sépulture étaient donc une denrée rare, ce qui explique, malgré un nombre respectable d'inhumations simples, la prépondérance des sépultures multiples. Des tombes qui normalement n'auraient contenu qu'un seul corps reçurent jusqu'à sept individus. Des cercueils ne sont attestés que pour cinq personnes: quatre contenaient des mort-nés ou des nouveau-nés et un seul cercueil contenait un jeune adolescent.

Les examens ostéologiques ont mis en évidence une population extrêmement jeune. Un tiers des squelettes appartient à des enfants jusqu'à 12 ans ; les males jeunes et adultes sont également bien représentés. Seuls 17 individus âgés entre 36 et 45 ans ont été retrouves, et ceux-ci sont les plus âgés de l'échantillon. Il est plus difficile de déterminer le sexe des individus, étant donné qu'il s'agit d'une population très jeune. Il n'y a pas de doute qu'elle était d'origine africaine: les dents de plus d'un tiers des squelettes avaient été modifiées par écaillage et remplissage, ce qui indique clairement des pratiques culturelles autochtones.

Nous sommes clairement confrontés à des victimes du commerce d'esclaves. Cependant les squelettes exhibent peu de traces des rigueurs physiques que ces individus ont dû subir pendant leur captivité et leur transport, mis à part un petit nombre de blessures reçues quand la victime voulait se défendre. Il est également difficile d'établir les causes de mort ; le scorbut était répandu et a dû contribuer considérablement à la mortalité. Vu que ces individus n'avaient passé que très peu de temps en mer, il en ressort que leur alimentation avant embarquement était pauvre. Des projectiles de plomb (provenant de mousquets) retrouvés dans deux tombes d'enfant indiquent qu'ils avaient été exécutés.

Plus de 100 objets ou groupes d'objets ont été relevés : parmi eux on compte des monnaies, des objets de fer et d'alliage de cuivre, des ampoules et des bouteilles de verre, des pipes en terre, des perles, des boutons et des fragments de tissu. La plupart est d'origine européenne. La majorité de ces objets doit se rapporter a la période passée en captivité ou dans la Rupert's Valley, quoique quelques autres articles (les bijoux surtout) auraient pu être des possessions d'Africains acquises avant leur esclavage.

En général les sépultures étaient de caractère institutionnel. Apres débarquement, les corps étaient transportés en hâte et souvent en grand nombre. Il s'agissait, pour la plupart, de disposer des corps le plus rapidement possible ; on ne prenait en considération ni la dignité humaine ni les pratiques culturelles. Les inhumations en cercueil de mort-nés ou de nouveau-nés démontrent cependant certaines influences tant européennes qu'africaines.

Les fouilles n'ont mis à jour qu'une petite partie du cimetière supérieur des deux cimetières de la Rupert's Valley. Les découvertes sont cependant de grande importance. Tout d'abord ce site est unique : il n'existe pas d'autre cimetière contenant uniquement les corps d'Africains de première génération morts à la suite de leur transport. Du point de vue culturel il est également significatif, rappelant à l'humanité les conséquences terribles du commerce d'esclaves.

Zusammenfassung

Dieser Bericht enthält die Beschreibung und Auswertung von archäologischen Untersuchungen, die die ,befreiten Afrikaner' der Gräberfelder der Rupert's Valley auf der Insel Sankt Helena im Südatlantik betreffen. Sie wurden zwischen 2007 und 2008 durchgeführt und von der britischen Regierung (Amt für internationale Entwicklung) unterstützt. Die archäologischen Untersuchungen folgen eine umfangreiche ökologische Auswertung der Umgebung, die das Bauprojekt eines Flughafens auf der Insel (die bisher nur bei Boot erreicht werden konnte) verursachte.

Die Gräberfelder gehören zur Mitte des 19. Jahrhunderts, als Großbritannien versuchte, den transatlantischen Sklavenhandel abzuschaffen. Ein Gericht der Vize-Admiralität war zwischen 1840 und 1872 auf Sankt Helena tätig; dieses Gericht entschied über das Schicksal der Sklavenschiffe, die von dem West Africa Squadron der Royal Navy festgenommen wurden. In dieser Beziehung wurde die menschliche Fracht, die unter grausamen Bedingungen transportiert wurde, auf Sankt Helena abgeladen.

Die Belege zeigen, dass mehr als 26 000 ,befreite' oder ,wiedergefangene' Afrikaner im ,Liberated African Establishment' auf der Insel aufgenommen wurden. Lager wurden in zwei Täler gebaut und dienten als Auffanglager, Krankenhäuser und Quarantänezonen. Lemon Valley, die erste solche Anstalt, wurde 1843 aufgegeben, aber Rupert's Valley empfing Sklaven weiterhin bis spät in die 1860er Jahren.

Die Mehrzahl der ,Befreiten' überlebte. Einige niederließen sich auf der Insel, aber die meisten wurden nach anderen britischen Kolonien weitergeschickt, vor allem nach den karibischen Inseln. Dennoch war die Sterblichkeitsrate auf den Sklavenschiffen bevor und nach Landung sehr hoch. Die Sklavenschiffe erreichten Sankt Helena mit Leichen an Bord, und viele andere Sklaven starben kurz nach Ankommen. Es wurde periodisch versucht, die Leichen im See zu entsorgen, aber diese Maßnahme erwies sich als unpraktisch. Als Folge davon wurde es notwendig, auf Lande zu bestatten. Große Flächen in der Nähe der Lager wurden ungeweihten institutionellen Gräberfeldern übergegeben. Wahrend der Lebensdauer des Establishments wurden rund um 8000 Afrikaner in diesen Gräberfeldern bestattet, die meisten in der Rupert's Valley.

Schon früher hatte man Bestattungen in diesem Tal gefunden, aber der vorliegende Bericht betrachtet nur die Gräber, die zwischen 2006 und 2008 entdeckt wurden. Geotechnische Aufschlüsse in 2006 begegneten einige Gräber, und diese ersten Auffindungen führten zu geplanten archäologischen Ausgrabungen in 2007. Während vier Monate in 2008 wurde eine Flächengrabung in einem Teil des oberen Gräberfeldes der Rupert's Valley durchgeführt.

Die Ausgrabungen von 2008 dehnten sich über eine Fläche von nur c. 100 x 30m. Dennoch war die Dichte der Bestattungen so groß, dass 325 Skelette im anatomischen Verband ausgegraben werden konnten. Eine große Menge von Skelettresten, die anatomisch nicht verbunden waren, wurde auch in einer Serie von Gruben geborgen. Der Erhaltungszustand der Knochen war sehr gut, und sogar organische Stoffe wir Haar und Fingernägel waren oft gut erhalten.

Rupert's Valley ist eng: ein großer Teil ist zu felsig für Bestattungen, und andere teile befinden sich im Überschwemmungsgebiet von einem kleinen Bach. Geeignetes Gelände war eindeutig knapp, und, obschon eine angemessene Anzahl von Gräber nur eine Leiche enthielt, waren die Mehrfachbestattungen in der Mehrzahl. Bis sieben Leichen wurden in Gräber, die normalerweise nur eine Leiche enthalten sollten, gelegt. Nur fünf Bestattungen mit Sarg wurden geborgen: vier enthielten Totgeborene oder Neugeborene und eine einen Jugendlichen.

Die osteologischen Untersuchungen lassen eine Bevölkerung, die sehr jung war, erkennen. Ein Drittel der Skelette gehört zu Kindern bis zwölf Jahre alt und Jugendliche oder junge erwachsene Männer sind auch häufig. Nur siebzehn Individuen, die ältesten, gehörten zu der 36–45 Jahre Altersstufe.

Die Bestimmung der Geschlechter ist sehr schwierig, da die Bevölkerung so jung ist. Zweifellos war diese Bevölkerung afrikanischen Ursprungs: mehr als ein Drittel der Skelette hatte Zähne, die abgeändert waren: die Muster, die durch Feilen oder Abschaben erhalten wurden, zeigen, dass es sich um Kulturbräuche handelt.

Die gestorbenen waren auch zweifellos die Opfer des Sklavenhandels. Dennoch gab es, außer eine geringe Anzahl von Verletzungen, wenige Beweise körperlicher Gewalt, die die Sklaven sicherlich während der Gefangenschaft und des Transportes erlitten haben. Die Todesursache ist auch schwer zu bestimmen, obschon der Skorbut sehr verbreitet war und wahrscheinlich einen entscheidenden Faktor darstellte. Da die Sklaven nur eine sehr kurze Zeit au See verbrachten, können wir davon schließen, dass ihre Ernährung vor Einschiffung mangelhaft war. Die in zwei Kindergräber gefundenen Geschosse aus Blei (von einer Muskete) bedeuten wahrscheinlich, dass diese Kinder geschossen wurden.

Der Befund enthält über 100 Artefakte oder Artefaktgruppen, wie Münzen, Eisen- und Buntmetallfunde, Glasampullen und Flaschen, Tonpfeifen, Perlen, Knöpfe und Stoffresten. Diese Gegenstände kommen fast alle ursprünglich aus Europa. Obschon einige Artikel (zum Beispiel Schmuck) vielleicht in den Besitz von den Afrikanern vor ihrer Versklavung kamen, gehört die Mehrheit zu der Zeit ihrer Gefangenschaft oder Niederlassung in Rupert's Valley.

Im Allgemeinen war der Charakter der Bestattungen institutionell. Nach der Landung der Sklavenschiffe wurden die Leichen fluchtartig und oft in großer Anzahl begraben. Meistens sorgte man nur, dass die Leichen schnell entsorgt wurden, ohne die menschliche Würde oder Bräuche zu berücksichtigen. Die Sargbestattungen der totgeborenen oder neugeborenen Kleinkinder deuten jedoch auf europäische und afrikanische Einflüsse.

Die Ausgrabung hat nur einen kleinen Teil des oberen Gräberfeldes der Rupert's Valley aufgedeckt. Dennoch sind die Aussagen bedeutungsvoll. Es handelt sich um einen einzigartigen Fundort: kein anderes Graberfeld enthält nur die Leichen von afrikanischen Sklaven, die als Folge ihrer Gefangenschaft starben. Kulturell gesehen besitzt die Fundstelle auch große Bedeutung: eine wahre Erinnerung an die menschlichen Folgen des Sklavenhandels.

1 Introduction *by Andrew Pearson*

1.1 Aims and objectives

St Helena has a rich history and its cultural heritage is of international significance. Its well-known association with Napoleon disguises a longer and far more important contribution to British history, not least the key role that the island played in Britain's colonial development during its time as an East India Company possession.

The Liberated African Establishment on St Helena was in operation during the final years of the transatlantic slave trade and the island played a major, though largely overlooked, role in its suppression. Between the Establishment's foundation in 1840 and final closure nearly 30 years later, in excess of 26,000 Africans rescued from slave ships were brought to St Helena. Their story reaches out far beyond the Atlantic crossing: it began in Africa, and for most of the survivors ended in emigration to British colonies in the Caribbean. St Helena was a microcosm of Britain's Abolitionist campaigns, of its successes, failures and contradictions.

As discussed further in section 1.5, this research stems from a commercial archaeology project that pertained to the proposed airport on St Helena. To a large extent the layout and design of the airport defined the parameters of the desk-based assessment and subsequent field investigation, particularly in terms of the area of study. Certainly it is the case that the route of the haul road through Rupert's Valley dictated the location of the open-area excavation, the data from which form the core of this report.

The primary objective of the 2008 excavation in Rupert's Valley was to remove all burials that were within or near the footprint of the proposed airport

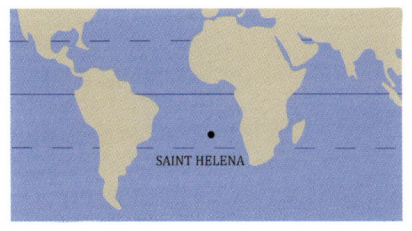

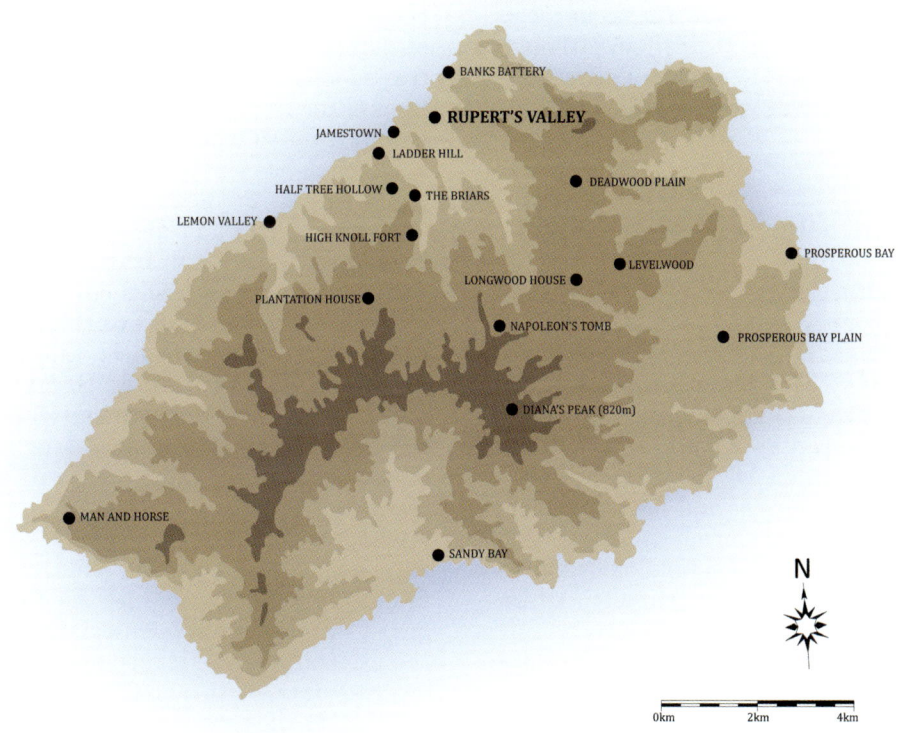

Figure 1.1 St Helena

haul road. The human remains were exhumed so as to enable respectful reburial, and in many ways the information gleaned from this assemblage is a secondary benefit: probably most St Helenians would take this view.

Nevertheless, the data relating to the archaeological discoveries in Rupert's Valley between 2006 and 2008 are of very great importance, and the objective of this report is to present this baseline information. The intention is to offer a structural account of the excavation, to set out the analysis of the human remains and the associated material culture, and to place these findings within an historical and archaeological context. It is, however, recognised that this report represents only a necessary first stage of study, and that there is great scope for further historical, osteological and artefactual lines of enquiry.

It is anticipated that longer-term research will alter some of the conclusions offered within this volume, as well as significantly widening the scope of discussion. For this reason the first six chapters of the report are intended to be entirely objective: it is hoped that subsequent study may refine the findings offered in these chapters, but not overtake them in any fundamental way. Subjective discussion is deliberately confined to Chapter 7, and here it is recognised that future scholarship may supplant some elements of the commentary.

Even with the present level of analysis, however, the value of this assemblage is clear. It offers a unique archaeological insight into the transatlantic slave trade, which is simultaneously fascinating and disturbing. Perhaps most importantly, it enables us to go beyond the historical statistics of the trade – which often involve numbers that are so large as to defy comprehension. Rupert's Valley, although itself a graveyard on a massive scale, shows the slave trade, its cruelties and its consequences, on a human scale.

1.2   The structure of the report

1.2.1   *The print/digital split*

The information about the Rupert's Valley excavations is presented in three parts: a printed volume; a digital volume; and digital appendices.

The printed volume contains the core narrative about the historical context of the site, the excavations, the human remains and the artefacts recovered. Its final chapters offer an interpretation of this information. The printed volume is designed to be read in isolation from any supplementary data.

The digital volume provides supporting data which were considered too detailed to merit publication in physical form (Appendices D1–D5). This information will enable detailed interrogation of the site, its features, finds and the skeletal remains. Appendix D6 comprises supplementary photographs of Rupert's Valley, and also a selection of images

of St Helena's natural environment and cultural heritage.

The digital appendices comprise an archive of primary information generated during the excavation and post-excavation phases of the project, in accordance with standard archive requirements.

The content of the digital volume and digital archive is set out in Appendix 2, at the end of this printed volume.

1.2.2   *Contents of the printed volume*

The remaining part of this chapter is given over to a description of Rupert's Valley and an outline of the project's background. Chapter 2 then turns to the historical context of the graveyards. Although this is a report about archaeological discoveries, one of the main outcomes of this project has been the emergence of an historical narrative which has largely been overlooked by modern scholarship. There has proved to be a wealth of primary and secondary source material which pertains to St Helena's Liberated African Establishment: this enables a detailed discussion of the overarching chronological framework and of various thematic aspects of life within Rupert's Valley.

Chapter 3 details the archaeological investigations within Rupert's Valley between 2006 and 2008. It includes a narrative on the graves and other archaeological features within the main area of excavation, although the full structural data are presented within the digital volume.

Chapter 4 contains the analysis of the human remains. In addition to being a standard discussion of demographic profile and metric and non-metric traits, this chapter brings forward many of the unusual aspects of this assemblage, from the cultural modification of teeth amongst many of the individuals to evidence for the violence associated with their enslavement.

Chapter 5 contains the catalogue of the artefacts that were recovered during the main period of excavation, and sets each of these in context. Chapter 6 offers a spatial analysis of the site, combining the archaeological, osteological and artefactual data. This approach has been adopted as a means of commenting in more detail about the development of the graveyard and the processes of burial. It also deals, albeit less satisfactorily, with possible cultural aspects of the site.

Chapter 7 offers a holistic discussion of the excavation findings. It addresses some purely archaeological issues, such as the location of the graveyards within the valley and the precise date of the excavated area. It also draws together the osteological data, with a particular focus on evidence relating to the period of enslavement, and to cause of death. The intention is to offer an archaeological counterpoint to historical studies which have been published in recent decades, most notably those dealing with demographics, epidemiology and the material culture of slavery. Some conclusions can be reached with reasonable certainty, but despite the wealth of historical evidence there is also much about this site and its material assemblage which remains an enigma. For example, little was actually written about the process of burial: although it was clearly an 'institutional' graveyard, the style of burial, and the artefacts present, raise questions about the extent to which European or African influences prevailed. The origin of the artefacts and the point at which they may have been obtained by their owner is another key question. Their provenance, whether in pre-slavery Africa, during the period of enslavement, or in Rupert's Valley, would have significantly altered their meaning to the owner. It is also central to the way in which we, as archaeologists, view them.

1.3 Rupert's Valley

Rupert's Valley is located in the north-west part of St Helena, adjacent to James Valley in which the island's capital, Jamestown, is situated. Rupert's is one of a number of deeply incised valleys running inland from the sea on this the lee side of St Helena (Fig 1.2).

At its mouth the valley is approximately 250m wide, the shallow-shelving bay extending several hundred metres out to sea. The floor of the valley, within 2km of the coast, is relatively flat, rising only 60m from sea level. The centre of the valley is occupied by a small stream, which meanders through the upper part and is canalised nearer to the sea. This represents the only natural source of water but at most times the stream bed is dry. Only after heavy rain is there any significant flow of water – and after particularly severe storms the valley has historically been prone to flash floods.

Historical descriptions of Rupert's Valley are generally unfavourable. They emphasise its hot, arid and wind-blown character: in the words of one commentator it was 'a desolate valley running down to the sea between bare and bleak hills approached only by a winding path cut in the rock' (Bishop Claugton, 1859; quoted in Schuler 2000). Such descriptions overstate the negative, and certainly since the provision of a permanent water supply in the mid-19th century the valley has proved perfectly habitable. One author went as far as to describe it as a 'pleasant and healthy place to dwell in', though even he conceded that from a distance the first impression was of a 'dreary wilderness' (Grant 1883, 9). Nevertheless, despite its proximity to James Valley and its populous and elegant colonial settlement, Rupert's Valley is a stark contrast and feels a world apart.

Habitable land is limited. The valley floor is commonly less than 100m wide, beyond which are gentle slopes that quickly give way to steep hillsides rising to heights of 260m to the west and over 400m to the east. At its landward (southern) end, the

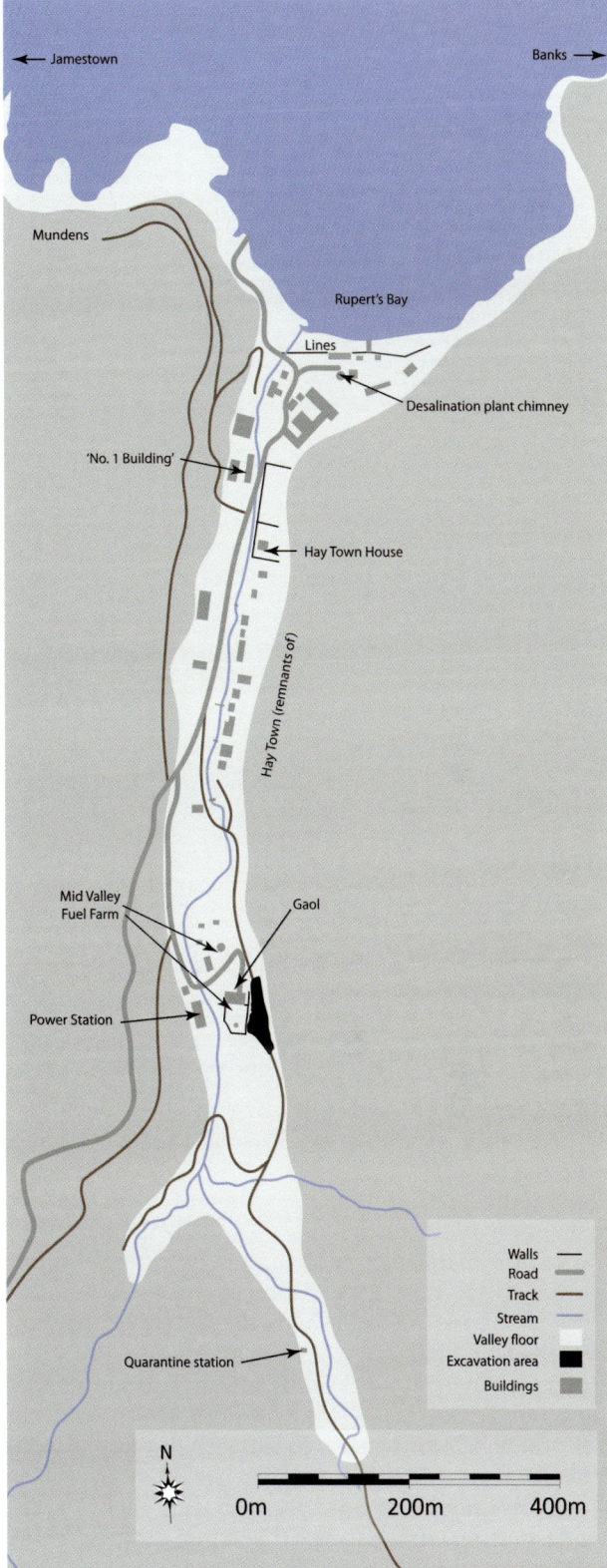

Figure 1.2 Rupert's Valley

valley becomes extremely constricted, ultimately terminating in steep terrain that rises up to meet Deadwood Plain.

Rupert's Valley is characterised by a mix of historic buildings and modern industrial structures, dispersed amongst the natural scrub vegetation. At

Figure 1.3   Rupert's Bay. View from the Shears, at the western edge of the bay. The defensive Lines, now broken in their central part, and the Boer War period chimney (standing behind the metal boom) are now the only historic elements to survive in what has become an industrial area

the bay, the dominant historic element is the massive masonry wall of the defensive Lines, originally built in the late 17th century though subsequently much altered (Fig 1.3). The defences once completely blocked the entrance to the valley, but they are now breached in their central part and occupied by the steel boom for a pipeline used by tankers replenishing island fuel supplies. A stone building that was originally part of the Liberated African Establishment and the chimney of a Boer War-period desalination plant are also present. Immediately behind the Lines and the adjacent wharf is a fuel storage depot, together with a number of metal warehouses, most associated with the fisheries industry.

The lower part of Rupert's Valley is also home to its small population. Attempts to create a settlement here in the mid-19th century (the so-called 'Hay Town') met with very limited success (see section 2.4.2), and indeed the only substantial population that has ever been present was that of the Liberated Africans. Nevertheless, a small group of single-storey dwellings dating to the early 1860s is present in the lower valley alongside the canalised

stream, whilst the somewhat larger Hay Town House stands in isolation a little nearer to the sea (see Fig 2.12).

The central part of the valley (in which the main excavation took place) is dominated by the island's power station, built in 1983. Adjacent to this is the Mid Valley Fuel Farm, a complex which includes the shell of the mid-19th century gaol, now used as a garage for its fuel tankers (see Figs 1.5 and 2.11). A little removed from the power station in the valley floor is a concrete-built church, dedicated in 1996. Beyond this point the only structures present are the medical incinerator and animal quarantine station, half a kilometre distant from the power station and reached by a small unmetalled track.

Vehicle access is by Field Road, which runs precipitously around the hillside, down from the junction with James Valley. Field Road is of comparatively recent construction, although the route itself is a historic one. Nevertheless, up until its completion in the late 1960s, the principal access to the valley was on foot, via the 17th-century military path around the coast, which followed the cliff edge from

Figure 1.4 (above) Rupert's Valley: view south from the old military path. In the left of the photograph are the cottages that make up the attempted settlement of 'Hay Town', whilst the lower of the two African graveyards occupies the sloping ground in the centre-right. The upper graveyard is just out of shot, above and to the left of the fuel silos

Figure 1.5 (left) The excavation site. View north from Bunker's Hill battery during the early stages of the excavation, after the completion of the initial soil-strip

Jamestown and Mundens to the west, before continuing eastwards from Rupert's Valley to Banks Battery.

1.4   The discovery of the graveyards

Any discussion about the discovery of the burial grounds in Rupert's Valley is to some extent misleading, because on St Helena their existence has never been forgotten. The population of the island is fairly static, in the sense that many people continue to live in the same locality as previous generations of their family. Whilst this trait has begun to erode since the middle of the 20th century, there remains considerable continuity. The Liberated African Establishment dominated Rupert's Valley for much of the mid-19th century and local knowledge of the graveyards has been preserved through to the present day. For most of the islanders this knowledge is retained only in very general terms: an awareness of the grave-yards' existence but not of their precise location (see Baker 2004, chapter 9). However, during the course of the archaeological field work and post-excava-tion, the authors have met a number of islanders who claimed to have discovered burials as far back as the 1960s. Moreover, two copies of G W Melliss' map of Rupert's Valley, surveyed in 1861 and which depict the graveyards in considerable detail, have been in plain sight for a number of years – one in the Museum of St Helena in Jamestown and the other in the offices of the Public Works and Services Department.

In contrast, after its closure in 1867 the Liberated African Establishment on St Helena was quickly forgotten by the wider world. With the effective suppression of the transatlantic slave trade, public attention in England shifted to other subjects, whilst the topic rapidly disap-peared from the official correspondence between St Helena and the Colonial Office. Despite this, the Establishment features in various histories of the island, for example those by Melliss (1875), Jackson (1902), and Gosse (1938). In these accounts the scale of the Establishment, the number of recaptive Africans received, and the high rates of mortality come across very clearly, but the grave-yards themselves are not mentioned.

Over recent decades the graves of Africans have occasionally been encountered during construc-tion work, and by chance discoveries. Burials were disturbed when a cable was laid through the lower valley in the 1960s or 1970s, in the area of the lower graveyard. There is also an unconfirmed report of bones having been found on the opposite, east, side of the valley, near to Hay Town House (R Castell, pers comm).

The largest discovery came about during the building of the Power Station and Mid Valley Fuel Farm in the early 1980s. The exact number of burials is not known but was significant (Gill and Teale 1999, 378).[1] The human remains were reburied at the Church of St Paul in the centre of the island, along with other skeletons exhumed during separate building operations in Half Tree Hollow (B George, pers comm). At around the same period a small quantity of human bone was found when a fuel pipe was laid between Rupert's Bay and the Mid Valley Fuel Farm, in the road verge adjacent to the lower of the two known graveyards. More recently, disarticulated bone is reported to have been found during the building of the church in the centre of the valley, although this was probably derived from burials further up the valley which had been washed out by heavy rains, as opposed to being from in situ inhumations. In the present day, a walkover of the valley will regularly reveal small fragments of human bone, particularly in the area of the two main graveyards.

1.5 Archaeological investigations, 2006–2008

The archaeological investigations described in this report arose out of proposals by the UK Government (Department for International Development – DFID) to build an airport on St Helena, which is presently only accessible by ship. These proposals prompted the compilation of an Environmental Impact Assessment (EIA), which included a study of the cultural heritage remains within the airport development area. This study encompassed much of the northern part of the island because, whilst the runway itself was to be located on Prosperous Bay Plain in the north-east, a 13km haul road linking the airport to port facilities in Rupert's Valley was also required.

The initial discovery of graves during the project came about during geotechnical trial pitting by David Shilston of Atkins in 2006. These encoun-tered burials at three locations, one within the compound of the Mid Valley Fuel Farm and two further up-valley (see section 3.3.1). In April 2007, as part of the research for the EIA, the author (AP) undertook a limited amount of trial trench evalua-tion in Rupert's Valley. Using the Melliss map as a guide, and drawing on the discoveries made in the 1980s and by the recent test pitting, the evalua-tion aimed to establish the location of the Liberated African graveyards and their approximate bounda-ries. The findings confirmed the general accuracy of the Melliss map, proving the existence of burials in the lower graveyard and demonstrating that the ground between there and the upper graveyard (ie in the central part of the valley around the modern church) was devoid of graves.

The Environmental Statement for the airport was published in April 2008. The cultural heritage chapter of this document demonstrated the need for further investigations and so a small team of archaeologists returned to St Helena in May 2008. Once again their work spanned the whole of the airport development area, ranging from structural recording of military remains on Prosperous Bay Plain, to site survey in Sharks Valley, as well as archaeological evaluation and excavation. The main focus, however, was Rupert's Valley. Here the work included building recording at Rupert's Bay – of the defensive Lines, of a desalination plant built to provide water for Boer Prisoners of War held on Deadwood Plain, and of the last surviving building of the Liberated African Establishment.

Evaluation trenching was also resumed, con-tinuing the work of 2007. A number of locations, particularly in the upper valley, had been identified as potentially being on the fringes of the graveyard shown by Melliss. A number of these lay close to, or coincided with, the alignment of the proposed haul road for the airport. The evaluation trenching eliminated all but one of these potential areas from the study. As described in Chapter 3 and shown on Figure 7.1, burials in the lower valley appeared to be

Figure 1.6   Excavation with St Helenian volunteers, July 2008

confined to the gentler slopes on its south-western side and did not extend into the valley floor. Further up the valley, most potential areas were generally found to be too rocky for them to have been a viable place for burials.

Full excavation was confined to a single area in which burials coincided with the haul road. This location was a small promontory in the middle part of the valley, on the northern slopes above the Power Station and Mid Valley Fuel Farm (section 3.4.1). The excavations were initially expected to be quite limited in scale. At this location the haul road was to adopt the line of the existing unmetalled track which leads to the island's medical incinerator and animal quarantine station. In order to create the haul road this track required widening and surfacing, but that widening could have been to either the left or right of the existing centreline. It was therefore hoped that the road could be extended to the north-east, that is to say slightly cut into the hillside and away from the known concentration of burials. In such a scenario it would have been necessary only to excavate graves along a narrow corridor adjacent to the existing track.

The discovery that numerous graves were present in the slopes above the track, however, made this approach unworkable. Engineering solutions to protect the burials in situ were discussed with

DFID but none proved to be feasible. The decision was therefore taken to excavate all the burials on this small promontory, both above and below the track. Although some graves lay outside the area of construction, these were on or near the edge of an actively eroding slope: their survival in even the medium term seemed unlikely and so the decision was taken to include these in the excavations.

The size of the new excavation area, coupled with the density of burials, necessitated a larger team of archaeologists being brought out from the UK to join the original group. The final team comprised fifteen professional archaeologists, supported throughout by a number of volunteers. Working conditions were not always ideal. For most of the time the weather in Rupert's Valley was extremely hot and windy, and so efforts had to be made to prevent the bones from desiccating during excavation. During some weeks, however, extremely heavy rain showers swept down the valley from Deadwood Plain, often inundating the site with little warning.

The logistical challenge was also considerable. All specialist equipment had to be brought from the UK, whilst even commonplace items such as finds bags could not be bought in bulk on the island. Since access to the island was only by ship, the needs of the project had to be anticipated many weeks in advance. Retrospectively the archaeology

Figure 1.7   The excavation's public open day, August 2008. Hundreds of St Helenians visited the excavation site – the first archaeological dig ever to be undertaken on the island

appears quite straightforward: the site belonged to a single phase and had few intercutting features; it contained only burials, lacking any other feature-type; and the number of artefacts was limited. At the time, however, all this was far from certain. Even the number of burials contained by the promontory was unclear until the later stages of the excavation. In particular, there were considerable doubts as to whether the thick spread of rock that covered the centre of the promontory post-dated the graveyard (and therefore sealed burials) or pre-dated it, in which case it would have precluded burials being dug.

The sheer number of skeletons recovered also posed difficulties, with the substantial room needed to dry, clean, analyse and store them having to be found in Jamestown. In its later stages the excavation required the closure of the track to the quarantine station, which necessitated the creation of an alternative track and bridge to the upper valley. There was inevitably a degree of improvisation throughout the project and, as is made clear in the acknowledgements at the start of this report, the excavations would never have succeeded without the help of numerous organisations and individuals, both on St Helena and in the UK.

The main excavation was carried out between June and September 2008. As a final stage of the work in Rupert's Valley the two main graveyards were fenced off, protecting them from accidental damage and demarcating them from the adjacent scrub, a landscape which is otherwise indistinguishable from the graveyards. At the time of writing the human remains are in secure storage in Jamestown, with discussion ongoing as to how and where they will be reinterred. No further excavations within the graveyards are anticipated.

Note

1   See also *Report of the Proceedings of the Commission of Enquiry into objections raised to the erection of a new power station at Rupert's Valley on part or parts of disused burial grounds.* Issued by proclamation on St Helena, 29 January 1985.

2   The historical context   *by Andrew Pearson*

2.1   Sources

St Helena's role in bringing about the extinction of the transatlantic slave trade, although discussed in some late 19th- and early 20th-century books about the island (Melliss 1875; Gosse 1938), appears to have been quickly forgotten by wider scholarship. The longest account of the Establishment is found in Emily Jackson's *St Helena: the historic island from its discovery to the present date* (1903), amounting to some 30 pages. Key histories of the West Africa Squadron only mention the island in passing or omit it altogether (eg Lloyd 1949; Ward 1969), choosing instead to emphasise the role of Sierra Leone. It is also rare even to find St Helena in the index of any of the formative narratives on slavery (eg Du Bois 1896; Mathieson 1929) or more recent overviews of the subject (eg Thomas 1997). The inclusion of St Helena within the recently published *Atlas of the Transatlantic Slave Trade* (Eltis and Richardson 2010) and its supporting database (Eltis *et al* 1999) is therefore a welcome development.

The narrative offered below is nevertheless mainly derived from primary sources held in the UK National Archives, Kew, and in the St Helena Government Archives. In the National Archives the main records are those of the Colonial Office, specifically the Original Correspondence contained within the CO 247 series. Also of relevance are the Entry Books (CO 248), Sessional Papers (CO 250) and the 'Blue Books' of statistics compiled annually for the colony (CO 252). Documents pertaining to emigration can be found in the original correspondence of the West Indian colonies, and these shed light on the final stages of the Liberated Africans' journey from St Helena: CO 101 (Grenada); CO 111 (British Guiana); CO 137 (Jamaica); and CO 295 (Trinidad). The records of the St Helena Vice-Admiralty court are included in the Foreign Office FO 84 series, although adjudications prior to 1846 and after 1865 are not present. Much of the Admiralty correspondence relating to St Helena is contained in the CO 247 volumes but further useful letters, particularly pertaining to logistics, are found in ADM 101 and 123. Detailed Audit Office records also survive within the AO 19 series.[1]

St Helena's archives in Jamestown comprise a small but highly valuable collection – records that date from the earliest years of English settlement through to modern times. The collection includes a great deal of documentation pertaining to the island's role in the abolition of the slave trade. There is an element of duplication of material held at Kew, most notably in terms of the high-level political dialogue between island's governor and the Colonial Office. However, much local-level correspondence was never transmitted to London, but was simply retained by St Helena's government. This material provides a wealth of detail about the Establishment that survives nowhere else. The Jamestown archives also preserve the Vice-Admiralty court proceedings, and although some of these volumes have been badly damaged by termites, they complement and expand on the material present in the UK National Archives. St Helena's archives also preserve collections of the island's early newspapers, almanacs and proclamations.

A small number of contemporary sources have also been identified which pertain to the Liberated African Establishment. Foremost of these are the writings of Dr George McHenry, surgeon in the depot at Lemon Valley from late 1840 to 1843. He first published a short account in the *Colonial Gazette*, but then wrote a far more extensive piece that was serialised in *Simmond's Colonial Magazine and Foreign Miscellany* during 1845 and 1846. These contributions, whilst clearly written with an anti-slavery (and to some extent an anti-establishment) agenda, are nevertheless a remarkable source. Another short account by McHenry, *Visits to Slave Ships,* was published by the British and Foreign Anti Slavery Society in 1863 and is reproduced in Appendix 1 of this report. A few other mid-19th-century accounts of Rupert's Valley appear in biographies and travel journals, adding a little extra detail and occasional anecdotes about the Africans and their life in the Establishment.

Other primary and secondary sources include: House of Commons Parliamentary Reports; East India Company records (held by the British Library); and a miscellaneous collection of published and unpublished material relating to St Helena in the Rhodes Library, Oxford.

2.2   St Helena's history: a brief overview

St Helena was discovered by the Portuguese in 1502, prior to which date there was no human habitation. As such, its history and archaeology belongs exclusively to the post-medieval period. For much of the 16th century the island remained the preserve of the Portuguese, although as early as the 1530s it had been visited by French vessels. During these early years, and indeed up to the middle of the 17th century, there was little by way of a permanent population, notable exceptions being an escaped political prisoner by the name of Dom Fernando Lopez (between 1515 and his death in 1546) and a group of slaves who escaped from a passing ship at some date prior to 1557 (Gosse 1938, chapter 1).

The more common use of the island was as a provisioning station and rendezvous point for ships on their return from the East Indies, a role that St Helena would continue to fulfil well into the 19th century. During the initial decades after its discovery, visits were more or less on an annual basis, most being by the yearly Portuguese trade fleet returning from the East Indies. Stores of food and water could be restocked, whilst sick sailors were temporarily left there to recuperate.

The English had become aware of the island's existence by around 1580, and their first visit was that of Thomas Cavendish in 1588. During the following year it was also revealed to the Dutch, through Jan Huyghen van Linschoten who was a Dutch pilot with a Portuguese fleet. In writing about his visit, Cavendish was able to describe a chapel and a small number of houses in Chapel Valley (now the site of Jamestown). These presumably represent some of the very earliest structures to be built in James Valley but no trace of them is now recorded. However, it is possible that physical remains of these buildings still survive, either as part of more recent structures or buried below ground.

From the 1580s there followed a period during which ships belonging to all the major European nations competing for Asian trade called at St Helena, as well as those of lesser players such as the French and the Danes. This era of disputed possession was accompanied by vandalism and minor damage to the few buildings that were present, fuelled by both national and religious divisions (Gosse 1938, chapters 1 and 2). By 1625 (the date of the so-called battle of Chapel Valley) these conflicts were becoming more serious in scale, and the same year saw the first attempt at fortification of the island, by the Portuguese. The Dutch formally annexed the island in 1633 but their ambitions for sovereignty were never realised. Instead it was the English, under the auspices of the East India Company, who established a permanent settlement in 1659.

In a sideshow to the Second Anglo-Dutch War, the island was briefly occupied by the Dutch between January and May 1673; it was then recaptured by the English and has remained in their possession ever since. In December of the same year Charles II granted the East India Company all rights of sovereignty over St Helena, which it retained for the next century and a half. During the early years of the settlement it numbered only a few hundred people but over the course of the 18th century it gradually climbed to a figure above 3000: the population comprised the garrison, settlers, freedmen and slaves, the latter group normally the most numerous.

The maritime and strategic advantages of St Helena rested on two factors: its location and its favourable climate. Sailing in the South Atlantic is dictated by the Benguela Current, which flows northwards up the coast of Africa, where it joins the South Equatorial Current (heading towards the Caribbean) and the Brazil Current (which flows south around the coast of Brazil and Argentina). These currents combine with the prevailing South-East Trade Winds and Westerlies to create a system in which the natural sailing routes follow an anti-clockwise direction (see Fig 2.2 below; Laurie 1799; Walvin 2006, maps 34–38). Ships crossing the South Atlantic would therefore usually take in St Helena, as would those returning from Asia, since St Helena lay in the direct route between the Cape of Good Hope and Cape Verde.

Climate was an equally important factor. St Helena is not the only island in the South Atlantic, but others (the Falklands aside) have never been home to a sizeable population. Ascension Island's arid environment does not lend itself well to settlement, nor does Tristan da Cunha's rugged mountain landscape, with no natural harbour and a harsh climate tending towards heavy rain and high winds. By contrast, early explorers of St Helena described an island paradise covered by dense woodland, with abundant fresh water and sheltered landing places (Edwards 1988; see also Gosse 1938, chapter 1). However, it did not take long for the environment to be radically altered, both by the mismanagement of the settlers and by the herds of goats that roamed loose, denuding the island of much of its vegetation (Ashmole and Ashmole 2000, chapter 7). Nevertheless, St Helena remained fertile, and a preferred port of call for passing vessels wishing to refit, reprovision and rest their crews.

In contrast to the preceding period, St Helena's 18th-century history is not defined by military events, but by the consolidation of settlement in this remote outpost. Correspondence between the island's governor and the directors of the East India Company follows a continuous theme: concern with profit and investment return from London, set against the practical reality of maintaining a settlement in so distant a location on the part of the governor (Janisch 1908). The latter difficulties should not be underestimated, historical records showing periodic epidemics, droughts and mutinies of the garrison throughout the century. These took place alongside continual concerns over day-to-day issues such as food supply and civil law and order.

The key event in St Helena's history is invariably considered to be Napoleon's exile between 1815 and 1821, his time on the island being discussed by numerous commentators (eg Blackburn 2000). In addition to becoming the temporary focus of European affairs, the island also found its population doubled by the additional garrison established there during these years. The existing barracks were inadequate to cope with such numbers and a new camp was therefore established on Deadwood Plain.

Following the death of Napoleon, the population fell back to its more usual level and the island once

Figure 2.1 Jamestown, view from the harbour

again slipped into obscurity. Worse was to come, as the British Government took over administration of the Island in 1833, it becoming an official Crown Colony in April 1834. This turn of events proved a body-blow to St Helena's fortunes, not least because it took place alongside the abolition of the East India Company's trading monopolies that included the India and China tea trade.

By the later 19th century the island's fortunes were in serious decline. The advent of the steamship, and of refrigeration, meant that it was no longer necessary for vessels to call at St Helena, whilst the opening of the Suez Canal in 1869 meant that much traffic from India and the Far East no longer used the Atlantic seaways. Where in the 1840s it was common for over 1000 ships to have called annually, by 1890 this figure had fallen to 200 (Gill and Teale 1999). Mail steamers to and from the Cape ceased to call at the island after 1889, further emphasising its isolation. As a whole, these developments undermined the island's long-standing strategic importance: this was most obviously signified by the withdrawal of its small remaining garrison in 1906, although a military presence was

re-established during both the First and Second World Wars.

The remoteness of the island led to its use as a concentration camp during the Boer War, over 4500 prisoners being held on camps at Deadwood Plain and Broad Bottom between 1900 and 1902 (George 1999; Jackson 1903). The need to supply such large numbers of people with fresh water led to the construction of a desalination plant at Rupert's Bay, the chimney stack of which still survives in the compound behind the Lines. The presence of the Boer prisoners brought with it an improvement in communications, as the island was provided with a submarine telegraph cable, first to Cape Town in 1899 and subsequently to Britain via Ascension Island (Denholm 1994).[2]

After the decline of the Atlantic sailing routes, the island's subsequent economic history is one of attempts to address the issue of its financial dependency. It has certainly made significant strides forward from the nadir of the 1930s, when social and economic conditions were extremely poor. Initiatives have included whaling, flax production, tourism, forestry and fishing, although only the latter has proved truly successful. The airport proposals which gave rise to this archaeological project are, in many ways, a continuation of this process.

2.3   The history of the Liberated African Establishment

2.3.1   Early years, 1840–44

During the initial decades after Abolition, St Helena played only an indirect, supporting, role in the suppression of the slave trade. Its location did not render it particularly relevant, because most naval activity was focused close to the African coast in areas to the north of the equator. Sierra Leone acted as the main base for the West Africa Squadron and the principal location for the adjudication of slave ships and the emancipation of their cargo (Bethell 1966; Helfman 2006; Martinez 2007). Ascension Island, first garrisoned in response to Napoleon's exile on St Helena in 1815, also served as a naval base for the squadron (Hart-Davis 1972). Nevertheless, St Helena was sometimes used as a place for the reprovisioning of the patrolling cruisers and as early as 1815 the embryonic squadron visited St Helena for supplies (Rees 2009, 33). It was recognised that when cruisers patrolled south of the equator or returned from the Cape, St Helena was advantageously positioned. In addition, Sierra Leone's poor climate (which rightly had a reputation for being fatal to European visitors) made it unpopular with naval commanders as a place for resting their crews (Fyfe 1993).[3] Despite its distance from the main cruising areas St Helena was therefore occasionally used as a place for shore leave, along with Ascension Island and the Canaries (Lloyd 1949, 69).

These practices continued throughout the 1820s and 1830s, but the direct role of St Helena began as a consequence of the 1839 *Act for the Suppression of the Slave Trade* (2 and 3 Vict. c. 73) which provided authorisation for British warships to detain Portuguese vessels equipped for the slave trade, and for Vice-Admiralty courts to condemn them. At a stroke, this act removed the limitations of earlier failed treaties with Portugal, including the immunity of its vessels when sailing south of the equator. On 18 September 1839 the Foreign Office issued instructions to the Lords Commissioners of the Admiralty signifying that naval vessels were to detain Portuguese slave vessels, vessels hoisting no flag, and those without papers proving their nationality. British courts of Vice-Admiralty were to be established for the adjudication of such vessels and Africans found on board were to be landed at the nearest British settlement and placed under the care of the governor.[4]

These instructions were duly transmitted to St Helena's governor, Major-General George Middlemore, together with orders to establish a Vice-Admiralty court on the island and letters patent appointing him as Vice-Admiral. The process of

establishing the court did not prove straightforward. The island's Chief Justice, William Wilde, expressed the opinion that the governor was not empowered to form such a court and refused to swear in the judge or other officers. Although Wilde made his objections on the basis of a fine point of law, his subsequent petty obstruction of its operation suggests that this issue may have had a more personal dimension. However, the island's council disagreed with Wilde and the court's judge, Charles Hodson, and the other court officers were sworn in on 8 June 1840. It nevertheless seems probable that the court proceeded with a certain lack of confidence: writing in October 1841, Hodson stated that in taking on his role as judge of the Vice-Admiralty court, 'there was not any competent person of whose advice in such a proceeding I could avail myself, nor any books to which I could refer for guidance.' One might surmise from this that he had little help from Wilde.

From the outset, Middlemore expressed concerns to the British Government about St Helena's ability to cope with any significant number of 'liberated' or 'recaptive' Africans.[5] The reasons he cited were economic, namely that the island's resources were barely sufficient for the existing population and that any additional demand would create serious shortages and drive up prices. The view in London was complacent: in July 1840 Lord John Russell, Secretary of State for War and the Colonies, replied to Middlemore stating that 'it is, I trust, highly improbable that any Africans who may be captured by her Majesty's cruisers will be landed at St Helena'.

By that date, however, events were already proving Lord John Russell's assumptions to be false. On 14 March HMS *Waterwitch* seized the Portuguese brig *Cabacca* off Ambriz. The vessel carried two slaves – a woman and her son. Finding the slaver to be unseaworthy, *Waterwitch's* crew destroyed her by fire and, after a further period of cruising, brought them to St Helena, reaching the island on 9 June. *Cabacca* was the first vessel to be condemned by the Vice-Admiralty court, on 11 June 1840. She carried only two slaves (a woman and a child) and other early prizes also brought either very few slaves or none at all. Indeed, up until the end of November 1840 only 22 slaves were received, and all survived to be placed as servants to various inhabitants of the island.[6]

The first months of St Helena's anti-slavery role were, therefore, comparatively quiet, and the bickering about the legality of the Vice-Admiralty court must have seemed somewhat pointless. However, this situation changed radically from December 1840, by which time the West Africa Squadron was taking full advantage of the 1839 Act to make captures at sea, and in addition pursued aggressive tactics on the coast, most notable being those of the Sierra Leone division under the command of Joseph Denman.

The location of St Helena, which during the early decades of the 19th century had precluded a major role in the anti-slavery campaign, now brought it

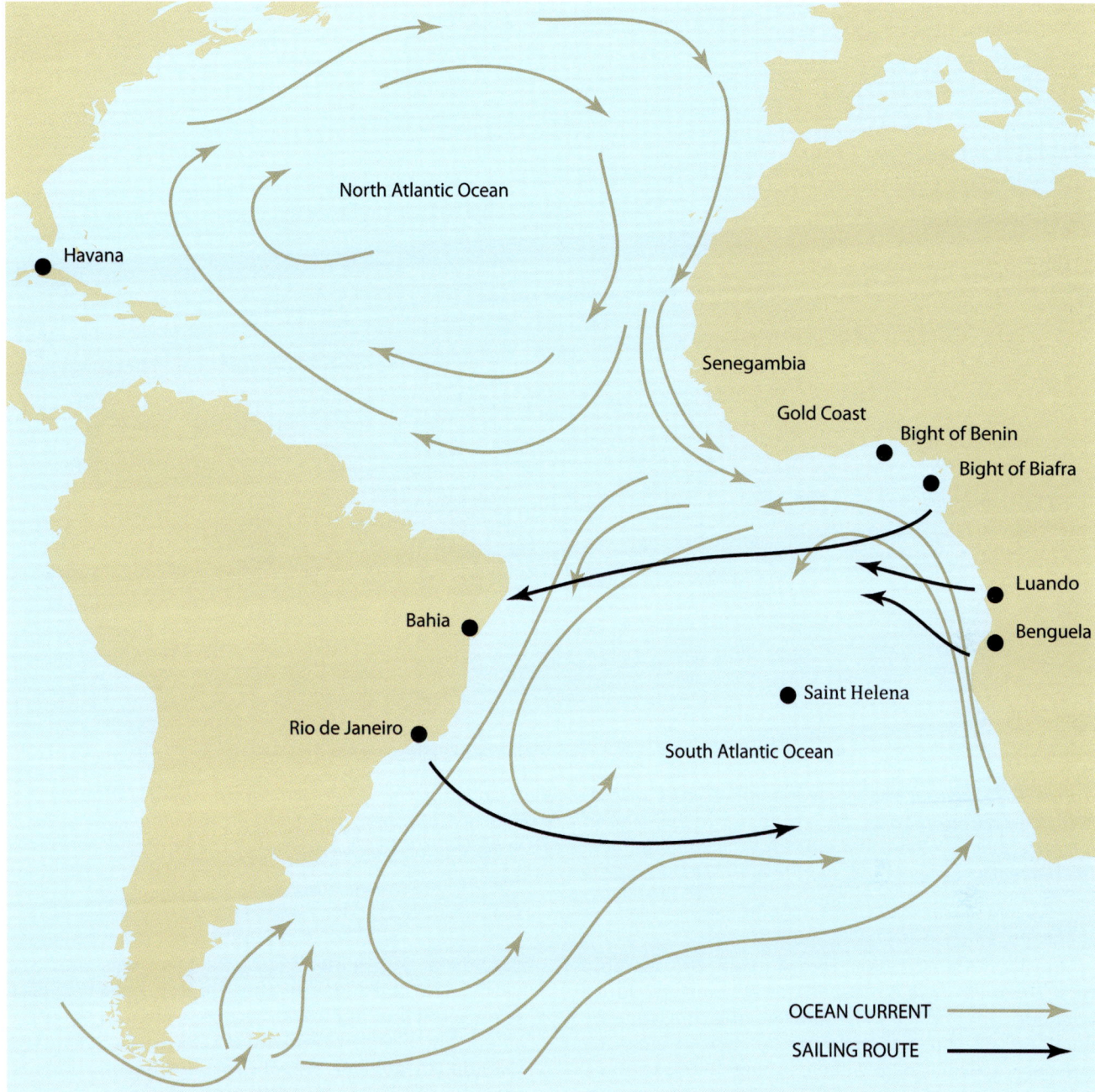

Figure 2.2 Atlantic shipping routes, ocean currents and trade winds, based on Miller (1988)

to the fore. From the 1840s military and diplomatic pressure first reduced and then extinguished the traditional slave-trading entrepôts on the Windward and Gold Coasts and the Bights of Benin and Biafra. Instead, the principal slave-exporting zones shifted south of the equator to modern-day Congo and Angola on the West African coast, and to Mozambique on the east. Slave ships now adopted a direct route across the South Atlantic to the main markets in Brazil and Cuba, following the South-East Trade Winds (Fig 2.2).

When a slave vessel was captured south of the equator this usually took place at or near the West African coast. Under these circumstances it was impractical for the Royal Navy to use Sierra Leone, because such a route ran counter to prevailing currents and winds. Above the equator these operate in a clockwise direction, and so a ship heading northwards is opposed by both the Guinea Current and the North-East Trade Winds. To add to this problem, sailing conditions around the Senegambia and Guinea coasts were also notorious for their unpredictable storms, calms and adverse currents, and it could sometimes take many weeks to travel even short distances. To take one example, the slave ship *Dores* under the command of a Royal Naval prize crew took 146 days to travel between Accra and Freetown, a journey which under favourable circumstances should have taken less than three weeks (Murray 1845). Similarly, the 1854 log

Figure 2.3   Lemon Valley, view north, taking in the area occupied by the Liberated African Establishment between 1840 and 1843. The ruins in the foreground are those of Chamberlain's Cottage, which was used as a hospital for the recaptives and later became the house of Dr McHenry. The white roof of the barracks behind the defensive Lines is just visible against the sea

of the USS *Constitution* records that the warship took thirteen days to travel the 60 nautical miles between Mayumba and Loando: during this time she anchored 31 times to prevent the current carrying her back over her own wake (Canney 2006, 169).

By contrast, St Helena offered a very predictable landfall. The Vice-Admiralty court records show that it rarely took more than two weeks to reach the island from the central or southern part of the African coast – and indeed, modern yachts continue to make this journey rapidly and on a single tack (T Meakins, pers comm; Admiralty 2004). When a prize was laden with slaves this was a vital consideration, since every day at sea invariably led to more deaths. The fatal consequences of delayed landfalls were often emphasised by naval commanders.

Even when captures were not taking place, St Helena was a far more efficient option for the reprovisioning of the squadron. The lengthy voyage up the coast to Sierra Leone reduced the time that a vessel could actively patrol the slaving grounds to the south of the equator, whereas a warship touching at St Helena could be back on station within two to three weeks. This situation does much to explain the relative ineffectiveness of the United States Africa

Squadron. For many years its base was at Cape Verde, 1800km north of the equator, resulting in a situation where its warships spent virtually no time on station. Only in 1859 did it relocate to St Paul de Loando (in modern Angola), whilst negotiations in 1860 finally led to the designation of St Helena as the official location for the crews' rest and relaxation (Canney 2006, 219).[7]

The first major capture sent to St Helena was in December 1840, when HMS *Waterwitch* dispatched the Portuguese vessel *Julia* to the island carrying 215 slaves, many of whom were afflicted by smallpox. Next came prizes to HMS *Brisk*, arriving between mid-February and late March 1841. First of these was the *Louiza*, carrying 420 slaves of whom 82 had died during the passage to St Helena from smallpox and dysentery. Arriving soon after was the *Marcianna*, a vessel of less than 80 tons but nonetheless carrying 256 slaves, once again including smallpox victims. She was followed on 16 March by the *Minerva* with her contingent of 316 slaves whilst the *Euro*, seized by HMS *Waterwitch*, brought 305 Africans to the island on 3 May.

The initial location chosen for the reception and quarantine of recaptives was Lemon Valley (Fig

2.3).[8] Situated on the lee side of the island, 3km to the south-west of Jamestown, the valley had been occupied since the early years of the English colony but had become virtually uninhabited by 1840 (Jeffs and Pearson 2011). The mouth of the valley, as with virtually all potential landing places around the island, was blocked by a defensive Line, but this and the adjacent barracks were disused. The East India Company had use of some small buildings there to house invalid retirees, whilst a few mulatto fishermen also lived nearby in huts close to the sea. All were swiftly evacuated, and these buildings became the basis of the 'depot' for the reception of recaptives, whilst the hulk of the small slave ship *Andorinha* was retained to provide additional accommodation, usually for those sick with transmissible diseases, in particular smallpox.

Several factors recommended the use of Lemon Valley: the climate was pleasant, it had a regular supply of natural water, and buildings already existed which could be converted to a hospital and accommodation. It was, up until the end of 1843, the primary base for the reception, quarantine and treatment of the island's recaptives. Only with time did its disadvantages become apparent, leading in the long term to the adoption of Rupert's Bay as the primary depot for the Liberated African Establishment.

Between January and August 1841 St Helena's Vice-Admiralty court adjudicated about twenty cases, most merely equipped for the trade but several actually carrying slaves. On 2 April there were 885 recaptive Africans present, and by August the island had taken in a total of 1824 recaptives. Of these 467 had died, 136 had been placed as servants, whilst the remaining 1221 continued to be in the charge of the governor, under the auspices of the Collector of Customs. St Helena was clearly ill prepared to deal with such an influx. The activities of the Vice-Admiralty court and the maintenance of the Liberated African Establishment dominate the island's official correspondence during this year, and behind the diplomatic language there is a pervading sense of crisis.

When the Vice-Admiralty court was established there were only three medical practitioners on the island: the Colonial Surgeon, the surgeon for the 91st Regiment, and the Health Officer. These individuals were already responsible for a standing population of over 4000 people. In response to this problem, and specifically to the arrival of HMS *Waterwitch's* prize in December 1840, the governor recruited a new surgeon to care for the recaptives. The man in question was Dr George McHenry, who was returning from service in India and whose ship happened to call at St Helena. He took over the administration of Lemon Valley from the Colonial Surgeon, at which time there were 162 Africans in the valley itself and a further 42 quarantined in the *Andorinha*, anchored in the bay. Although his appointment was supposed to be temporary, McHenry was in fact to spend nearly three years in

this role, most of it in quarantine with his African charges in Lemon Valley.

The existing facilities afforded by Lemon Valley and the *Andorinha* were not adequate for the number of recaptives who arrived in the early months of 1841. The hulks of both the *Louiza* and the *Julia* were therefore procured, to be used for the quarantine of those suffering from smallpox. In Lemon Valley itself, the numbers far exceeded the capacity of the four small buildings behind the Lines: as a temporary measure the Africans were housed in eighteen stiflingly hot tents, made from the timber and sails of captured slave vessels.

With so many deaths, the task of burial became overwhelming. Little is written about the measures adopted in Lemon Valley but attempts had clearly been made to dispose of corpses at sea. However, as early as 24 December 1840 Dr McHenry wrote to the Colonial Secretary in Jamestown to inform him that this was no longer feasible:

> I beg to call your attention to the circumstances of Lieut. Wilcox's having refused to allow his boat and men any longer to heave the dead bodies into the sea, in consequence of which we will be obliged for the future to sink close to the vessel the bodies of such as may die. As the vessel is not very distant from the beach, the probability is that the bodies will be driven ashore and what the result may be I leave to yourselves to judge ... The sole reason for refusing his boat is, I believe, because his men are too much worked. No less than three of them have been laid up lately by hard labour.

St Helena's administration was forced to look for more satisfactory solutions. Lemon Valley was proving too small and, in addition to being an inconvenient distance from the provisions held at Jamestown, it was proving difficult to supply by sea on account of the regular heavy swell in the bay. Rupert's Valley was therefore pressed into service.

Rupert's Valley had probably been occupied since formal settlement of St Helena began in the 17th century. The first direct evidence comes from 1678 when several archive references mention repairs to houses for twelve soldiers stationed in the valley, although no physical evidence of this early settlement period survives. The defence of Rupert's Valley was seen as essential, though no mention is made of significant fortifications until 1702 when Captain Richards, a 'very ingenious' visitor, suggested a plan to fortify the valley. The works at the valley mouth, in spite of regular flooding, continued through to 1707 when they were described as 'almost finished' in a letter to the Court of Directors of the East India Company. These works do not seem to have been very satisfactory: by 1717 they were 'much decayed' and the battery was expected to be quite inadequate to repel an enemy landing. Flood damage was a constant problem. High surfs are reported to have undermined parts of the defences at Rupert's Bay in 1755, whilst flash flooding in 1787 reduced them to 'a state of ruin, the repairs equal [in cost] to building a new fortification'. Nevertheless, these works were undertaken and the present Lines across the mouth of the bay mainly belong to this phase of construction.

In 1840 Rupert's Valley was essentially uninhabited. The Lines were only nominally garrisoned and except for two sheds used as ammunition stores, the barracks and ancillary buildings at the bay were not in use. Despite its proximity to Jamestown there were no other structures in the valley and no inhabitants. The buildings, property of the Ordnance Department, were rapidly brought back into repair so as to accommodate Africans who had passed their quarantine period in Lemon Valley – the first occupants were intended to be those who had been survivors of the *Louiza*. The governor also proposed the use of the redundant barracks behind Banks Battery (in the bay to the north-east of Rupert's) but this idea was rejected by the island's Board of Officers.

The administration also sought long-term solutions. St Helena was required to find food, clothing, medicine and myriad other provisions to support its new African community (see section 2.4.7). Existing stores on the island were completely inadequate, and therefore most of the supplies had to be imported from England. St Helena's treasury was expending large sums of money on these items and on staff salaries, but it was by no means certain that it would be able to recover these sums from the British government, particularly if they arose from the court's condemnation of a slave ship which was later deemed to be an illegal judgement. Moreover, the island was put to the expense of supporting a number of Portuguese seamen who had crewed the slave ships. Not liable to prosecution under the 1839 Act, their food, accommodation and onward passage had to be met out of government funds. As early as February 1841 Governor Middlemore wrote to the Secretary of State for the Colonies, pointing out the ongoing costs of maintaining the Africans on St Helena and the need for additional buildings (and attendant expense) should any more arrive at the island. He also pointed out that the 470 present were already too numerous for all of them to be employed as apprentices amongst the inhabitants.

The response of the Colonial Office was to sanction the expenses already incurred, although internal letters at the Treasury complained of the 'ruinous' sums of money involved and expressed concerns about future expense. In response, the governor was informed that:

> ... he may avail himself of any opportunity that may offer for embarking these Negroes either to the Cape of Good Hope or to any other British colony from which offers may come for paying the expense of their passage thither, assuring always that due precautions are taken for the health and comfort of the people and that they shall consent to their own removal from St Helena.

The implementation of these instructions represented the first attempt to 'normalise' St Helena's anti-slavery role, and of what was increasingly being called in official correspondence its 'Liberated African Establishment'. The measures were only supposed to address a short-term crisis, but in fact they would be the blueprint for the Establishment up until its final closure nearly 30 years later.

Lemon Valley and its fleet of hulks, for the moment, continued to serve as the principal receiving depot for new arrivals. For a short time there was an attempt to house the women and children in Lemon Valley, and the adult males in Rupert's Valley. However, this system unravelled with the next major influx of recaptives; after this point, the sick were sent to Lemon Valley, whilst the healthy and convalescents were placed in Rupert's Valley. Little was done to improve or augment the facilities in Lemon Valley, or to add to its limited staff. By contrast, a little money was spent on Rupert's Valley whilst High Knoll Fort, above Jamestown, was also pressed into service but played a lesser role than either of the two main depots.

Measures for the 'disposal' of the survivors were also pursued (see section 2.5). A significant number were taken on as apprentices and so became long-term additions to the island's population, but this was only a partial solution. The strain on the island's resources caused by the presence of so many recaptives was emphasised by Middlemore in numerous communications to England during 1840 and 1841. He petitioned both the Colonial Office and the Admiralty, requesting that no more slavers be sent to his colony. These requests, presumably supported by the Treasury, bore fruit in December 1841 when instructions were issued by the Admiralty to the commodore of the West Africa Squadron that prizes were to be taken to courts other than that on St Helena.

These orders had an immediate and appreciable effect, the number of slave ships arriving for adjudication falling markedly in 1842 and 1843. The expectation in Jamestown and London alike was that St Helena's role as an anti-slaving station would shortly come to an end, and by December 1843 the Treasury confidently stated that 'very few, if any, captured Negroes will in future be carried to that colony'.

On 1 January 1844 the Establishment was officially decommissioned by the incumbent governor, Hamelin Trelawney. Dr McHenry and his staff were discharged, leaving only 45 Africans remaining on the island who were not employed, apprenticed or otherwise supporting themselves. Unfortunately, hopes that this situation would be permanent were quickly dashed. On 27 January HMS *Thunderbolt* arrived at Jamestown: accompanying her was a prize containing 72 Africans, some with smallpox. The commander, Lt Ashton, stated that the slaver was unseaworthy, leaving him no option but to escort it to St Helena. The governor was, to say the least, unsympathetic: the depot had been broken up, the buildings and makeshift tents were in a severe state of dilapidation, and he had lost most of his staff (including the doctor) to other colonies. He refused to land the slaves and demanded that Ashton go elsewhere. In the event, however, the slaver proved impossible to repair and eventually Trelawney accepted reality and allowed the slaves into Rupert's Valley.

The *Thunderbolt* incident was a turning point for the Establishment. Although the British government reiterated its instruction to naval commanders to avoid St Helena, this order now came with a qualification: under exceptional circumstances captains should have the discretion to bring prizes to the colony. These events epitomise the divisions between the St Helenian administration and its colonial masters in England, and within London between the various agencies of government. The Treasury was opposed to the use of St Helena as a receiving station for recaptives, on the grounds that it was more expensive to maintain than any other colony which possessed a Vice-Admiralty court. Conversely, the Foreign Office under Palmerston was pursuing a vigorous anti-slavery agenda and the island had proved to be an invaluable asset. The Colonial Office appears to have been more ambivalent to the question, but ultimately accepted Palmerston's arguments – a decision that was doubtless welcomed at the Admiralty, which had found St Helena to be far more viable in both strategic and logistical terms.[9]

The number of prizes brought to St Helena remained low during 1844 and 1845, such that the governor found it possible to purchase a slave hulk to accommodate the recaptives, rather than refitting the depot at Rupert's Bay. Emigration continued and at the close of 1844 only nine Africans remained, these being the remnants of the cargo brought by *Thunderbolt* in January. Nevertheless, this disguised a longer-term trend. As the traditional slave-exporting zones in West Africa such as the Bight of Benin came under increasing military and diplomatic pressure, the balance of the trade shifted ever more to areas south of the equator, to Congo, Angola and Mozambique. St Helena became an increasingly practical place to bring prizes, whilst Sierra Leone became less and less accessible. The 'exceptional' circumstances of 1844 would soon become the norm, and within only a few years the default of using St Helena would go largely unquestioned.

2.3.2 The Brazilian slave trade, c 1845–53

The history of the Establishment entered a new phase in the middle of 1845. In 1841 the bilateral treaty of 1826 between Britain and Brazil that outlawed the slave trade had lapsed and attempts to replace it met with failure. Instead, in 1845, Britain opted for unilateral action in the form of the *Act to carry into execution a Convention between His Majesty and the Emperor of Brazil, for the Regulation and final Abolition of the African Slave Trade* (8 and 9 Vict. c. 122). Better known as the Aberdeen Act,

it authorised British cruisers to capture Brazilian slavers both north and south of the equator and to bring them for adjudication before Vice-Admiralty courts.

Despite Brazilian outrage at this measure, there followed a period of aggressive tactics by the Royal Navy. From late 1845 up until the effective suppression of the Brazilian trade in 1851, significant numbers of captured vessels once again arrived at Jamestown. Most slave vessels were intercepted off Central Africa but some were taken from the South American coast, including two commandeered in the harbour of Rio de Janeiro itself in 1850 and 1851. Many were merely equipped for slave trading, but others carried hundreds of recaptive Africans.

Lemon Valley is no longer mentioned in the correspondence and it appears that it was never revived as a quarantine depot after 1844. Although its climate was far superior to that of Rupert's Valley there were numerous disadvantages to its use. It was a considerable distance from Jamestown, and the sea conditions often made landing provisions (and recaptive Africans) awkward or impossible. The valley itself was very narrow, which restricted settlement to a small area and meant that the burial grounds had to be placed near to the buildings. The small stream quickly became muddied and unusable when significant numbers of people were present, whilst rock fall from the steep slopes of the valley posed a frequent hazard.

Instead, the entire Establishment was located in Rupert's Valley. In 1846 the existing buildings and tents were refitted at a cost of £1000, but because the tents were not considered suitable for the weak or sick a further £3478 was spent on the construction of sixteen 'sheds', each to provide accommodation for up to 38 people.[10]

The period began with a massive influx of recaptives: 2110 were landed between 26 December 1845 and 31 March 1846. There then appears to have been another hiatus, probably arising from a repeat of the instructions issued to naval officers to use any port except St Helena. Nevertheless, vessels continued to be brought to the island, although between November 1846 and April 1847 none carried slaves. On St Helena expectations veered from one extreme to the other: during April and May of 1846 Acting Governor Fraser felt able to discharge over half of the Establishment's staff, leaving only a surgeon, clerk, dispenser of medicines, superintendent and overseer. Only a year later, Fraser's successor Patrick Ross appears to have been left with the impression that *all* captured slave vessels were to be brought to St Helena. In fact, the truth lay somewhere between these extremes, the critical document being an order by Charles Hotham, commodore of the West African Squadron, in which he instructed his officers that:

When a full slaver is captured to the southward of the line [ie the equator] the commanding officer will duly consider whether the probability of a speedy passage is in favour of Sierra Leone

CAPTURE OF A BRAZILIAN SLAVER BY H.M.S. "RATTLER," OFF LAGOS.

Figure 2.4   HMS Rattler *capturing the* Andorinha. *The* Andorinha *(one of several vessels of this name to be taken as a prize) was captured off Lagos, present-day Nigeria, on 5 July 1849. She was destroyed at sea on account of her unseaworthy condition and condemned in St Helena's Vice-Admiralty court during the following September. Whilst equipped for the trade, she had not embarked any slaves at the time of her capture. Image from the* Illustrated London News *(29 December 1849, Volume 15, 440)*

or Saint Helena and he will send the detained vessel to which ever port can be most speedily reached.

From 5 April 1847 to 1 December 1849 a further 6258 recaptives were received on St Helena. The number held within the Establishment fluctuated wildly. At times the depot was virtually empty, for example in March 1847 when only six people remained, all of whom were too sick to embark for the West Indies. By contrast, at its maximum over 3000 recaptives were present in Rupert's Valley. Emigration was vigorously pursued as a means of moving the Africans on from St Helena. In certain cases the recaptives transferred directly from the slave ship onto a vessel bound for Britain's Caribbean colonies without ever touching land. The mortality on these onward voyages was usually extremely low but certain vessels experienced high death rates. Correspondence from the receiving colonies shows that some who embarked were still sick, whilst the immediate transfer from slave ship to emigrant vessel often precluded their vaccination against smallpox.

The 1850 'Blue Book' for the colony presented a summary of the statistics for the Establishment between its inception in 1840 and the end of 1849.[11] These figures, reproduced in Table 2.1, give a clear impression of the huge numbers of recaptives living and dying on St Helena, and emigrating from its shores.

The Brazilian slave trade did not long survive Palmerston's aggression and its demise, when it came, was remarkably swift. In 1850 the Brazilian Chamber of Deputies passed legislation banning the foreign slave trade, although the institution of slavery itself was not completely abolished until 1885. British official estimates suggest that slave imports to Brazil were 54,061 in 1849, 22,856 in 1850, 3,287 in 1851 and 800 in 1852. In 1853 it was officially announced that there had been no imports (Parliamentary Papers 1865, Volume V p 465; summarised in Lloyd 1949, appendix A).

The influx of recaptives into St Helena directly reflected this trend: St Helena received 3124 recaptives in 1850, falling to 134 in 1851 and 66 in 1852. The Establishment's future once again became a subject of debate during 1853, with recommendations made

Table 2.1 Census of Liberated Africans received on St Helena, 1840–49

Received …	
9 June 1840 to 30 June 1843	6638
on 27 January 1844	70
26 December 1845 to 31 March 1846	2110
5 April 1847 to 1 December 1849	6258
Total	**15076**
Born …	
from 9 June 1840 to 30 June 1843	14
26 December 1845 to 31 March 1846	5
5 April 1847 to 1 December 1849	12
Total	**31**
Emigrated to Jamaica from 9 June 1840 to …	
27 January 1844	625
31 March 1846	468
1 December 1849	1682
Total	**2775**
Emigrated to British Guiana from 9 June 1840 to …	
27 January 1844	1287
31 March 1846	818
1 December 1849	923
Total	**3028**
Emigrated to Trinidad from 9 June 1840 to …	
27 January 1844	800
31 March 1846	100
1 December 1849	1566
Total	**2466**
Emigrated to Cape of Good Hope from 9 June 1840 to …	
27 January 1844	1332
31 March 1846	34
1 December 1849	38
Total	**1404**
Emigrated to Grenada	**91**
Settled on the island from 9 June 1840 to …	
27 January 1844	391
31 March 1846	34
1 December 1849	118
Total	**543**
Deceased from 9 June 1840 to …	
27 January 1844	2287
31 March 1846	593
1 December 1849	1880
Total	**4760**
[Grand] Total	**15067**
Remaining on charge 1 December 1849	40

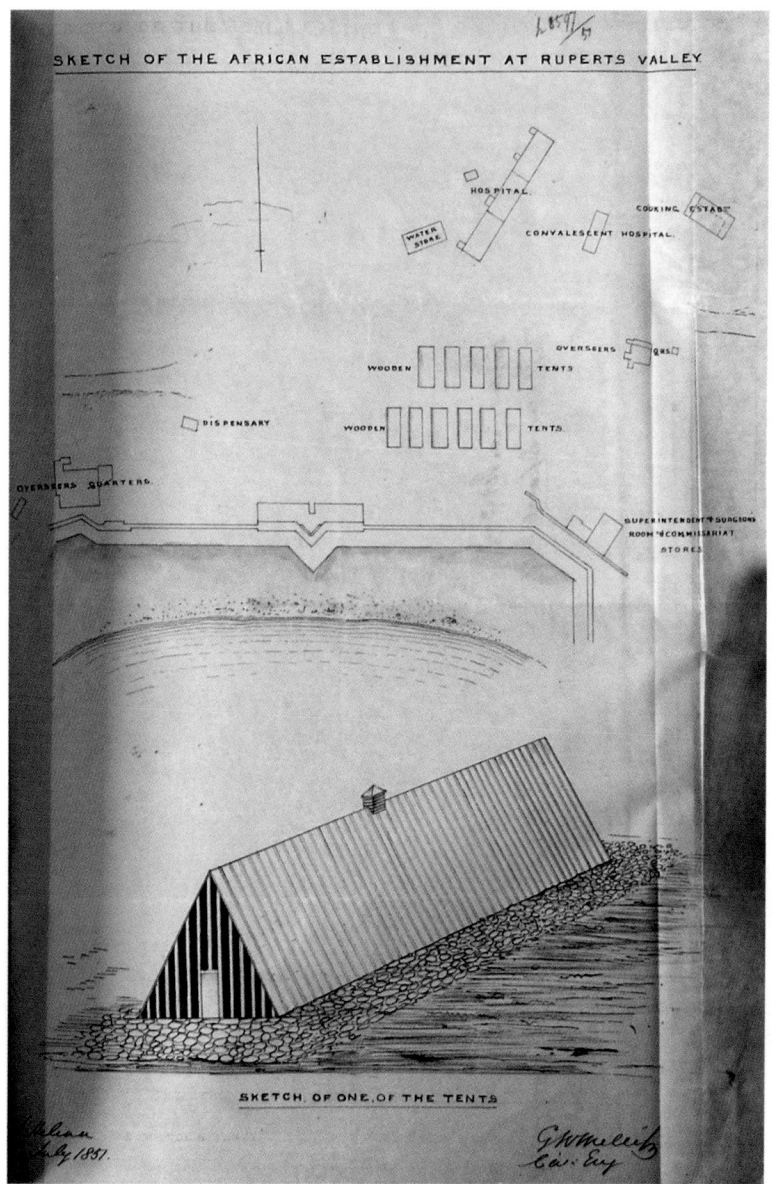

Figure 2.5   Sketch plan of Rupert's Bay, 1851. Source: TNA CO 247/77

for it to be closed. On 3 January 1854 instructions were duly given to disband the African Establishment at St Helena, coincident with renewed orders from the Admiralty for the West Africa Squadron to take its captures elsewhere, namely to Sierra Leone, Loanda, and Havana, unless in exceptional circumstances. Most of the staff in the depot were reassigned or pensioned off, although the Superintendent was retained in case the lull in the Brazil trade turned out to be only temporary. He also took responsibility for the small number of Africans remaining in Rupert's Valley until employment could be found for them. The post of Emigration Officer, responsible for the onward transport of recaptives to the West Indian colonies, was also abolished. Its incumbent, Lieutenant Rowlatt, was instead offered the post of Emigration Agent in Belfast, a position which would have involved him in another great diaspora, that of the Irish to the New World.

2.3.3   The Cuban slave trade, c 1854–72

The middle years of the 1850s were a quiet period for the anti-slavery campaign in the Atlantic. The Brazilian slave trade proved to have been permanently extinguished, whilst that of Cuba remained largely dormant. In addition, the Crimean War (1853–56) led to a temporary reduction in the number of British cruisers assigned to the West Africa Squadron and the fall in slave ship captures during this period is partly a consequence of this situation.

St Helena's role was very limited during this time. Its Vice-Admiralty court adjudicated on just eight cases between 1853 and 1855: seven of these vessels were merely equipped for slaving, but the last brought a contingent of 90 slaves, who were received into the depot at Rupert's Bay in November 1855. No prizes arrived at all in 1856 and for a time the

Figure 2.6 Contemporary photograph of Rupert's Bay. An undated image, but one clearly taken during the lifetime of the Establishment. The Africans are mustered in two lines in front of the tents (bottom left)

depot stood completely empty. The receiving stations at Sierra Leone, Cape Town, and Liberia also experienced a lull during this period.

The hiatus did not last, however, due to the revival of the Cuban slave trade in the later 1850s. In part this was due to the passing of the *Sugar Duties Act* (1846) which opened up British markets to foreign sugar, so promoting the growth of the Cuban plantations at the expense of those in the West Indies: by 1860 Cuba produced over a quarter of the world's sugar (Corwin 1967, 131; Scott 1985, table 8). In addition, a cholera epidemic at the start of the decade had killed off a significant part of the island's slave population, but Cubans' fear of revolts by the remaining unfree population resulted in a situation where many were not immediately replaced. However, by the later 1850s these fears had receded, demand for slaves rose, and their price in the Havana markets rocketed, at times reaching $1000 per head (Bergad *et al* 2003, appendices A and B). Cuba's demand was so great that a new slave-trading company was formed, with agents representing its interests as far afield as Mozambique and New York (Thomas 1997, 771). Steamships, including some British-built vessels, could achieve quicker Atlantic crossings and invariably carried

greater numbers than in the age of sail, in some cases as many as 1500 on a single voyage.

The 19th-century slave trade to Cuba had always been of a lesser volume than that to Brazil, but the numbers involved in its final stage were still extremely large. British sources in Havana reported that more slaving expeditions left Cuba between 1859 and 1861 than at any time since the 1820s, some 80,000 slaves being imported into the island during this brief period. The increase in the volume of the trade also coincided with the end of the Crimean War and the reinforcement of the West Africa Squadron: captures increased, aided considerably by the greater proportion of steam warships assigned to the patrol. These factors were reflected on St Helena by a renewed influx of captured slave vessels and their human cargo, and to a revival of the dormant Establishment.

The calm in Rupert's Valley came to an end following the capture of a slaver by HMS *Alecto*. The vessel carried 450 slaves, virtually all of whom were sick from dysentery or diarrhoea. They arrived at St Helena at the end of November 1857, but as had been the case after previous interludes of disuse, the Establishment was found to be entirely unprepared. Unusually high surf prevented the Africans being

Figure 2.7 'No. 1 Building' of the Liberated African Establishment. This structure is the sole surviving element of the depot. Located a little inland from the bay, it is now occupied by the Fisheries Department

landed at Rupert's Bay: the recaptives therefore had to be disembarked at Jamestown and either walked or were carried around to the depot. When they finally arrived in the valley, they found the depot completely unstaffed and with no supplies whatsoever. Moreover, after several years of neglect the buildings were in a state of severe dilapidation. A subsequent report by the Colonial Engineer was damning: the tents were infested by termites and were considered unserviceable, whilst many of the other buildings had serious defects. Roofs leaked, and the boilers used for cooking filled the kitchen with smoke. Essential repairs were estimated at £600, whilst proposals for a new hospital and accommodation blocks were submitted, with a predicted cost of £5000.

Needless to say, these events provoked a response from London, with Downing Street demanding to know precisely where *Alecto* made her capture, and the exact reasons for taking the prize to St Helena. However, as in previous instances, these objections (once again based on financial concerns) were overruled, so ushering in the final phase of the Establishment's operation.

The volume of slave traffic was never as great as that in previous decades, when both the Cuban and Brazilian slave markets were flourishing. Nevertheless, the total number of recaptives received by St Helena during this period was considerable – over 7000 between 1858 and the final closure of the depot in 1867 – with a rate of arrivals that sometimes matched that seen in the late 1840s.

Despite the unpreparedness seen in late 1857, a degree of order seems to have been established fairly swiftly. Although most of the staff were entirely new to the task (including the medical personnel), the reception, treatment and onward transport of recaptives had been a well-practised routine only a few years before, and the same process was rapidly put back into place. Nevertheless, the arrival of a slave ship with its sick, dead and dying would have been no less harrowing than at previous times. Indeed, in some cases the scenario is likely to have been worse, since it was during this later period that prizes carrying the greatest numbers of slaves were received. Probably the most extreme case was a vessel captured by HMS *Pluto*: although reasonably large by slave ship standards (453 tons), 146 out of her cargo of 874 slaves died during their three-week journey to St Helena. Also notable is an unnamed vessel brought to St Helena in November 1861: a mere 243 tons, she carried 870 slaves at the time of capture, of whom 25 died en route to the island. The average cargo of laden slave ships brought to St Helena between 1859 and 1865 exceeded 450 individuals.

Figure 2.8 Rupert's Valley in the area of the lower graveyard. Although the photograph is undated, it must have been taken at some point in the later 19th century after the Establishment was finally broken up. It looks southwards up the valley, from an elevated viewpoint on the military path. In the foreground is the shell of the cook-house (evidently converted into a stock pen), behind which is No. 1 Building and the walled compound of the Establishment's garden. The lower graveyard is just visible: it lies immediately beyond the last cottage on the western side of the valley (the white building in the centre-right of the photograph). At this distance, however, no details of the burial ground can be discerned

In spite of this huge influx of people, little was done to improve the depot in Rupert's Valley. The proposals for new buildings were not taken up, except for a single accommodation block, sanctioned in 1862 and completed in 1865, long after the last major consignment of recaptives arrived. The tents remained in place, described in 1861 as 'badly constructed, badly ventilated, and long since condemned as unfit for habitation'. Moreover, the number of permanent staff remained fairly low, and in contrast to earlier episodes there was a fairly fast turnover of medical personnel. The impact of this situation on the quality of care afforded to the Africans is not known but it surely cannot have been positive.

Prizes were brought to St Helena with reasonable (if unpredictable) frequency from 1858 through to 1863 – all of which had been destined for Cuba. However, these arrivals ended abruptly after this date, as the Cuban slave trade suddenly and unexpectedly collapsed. Already under pressure from both the British and United States navies, the final blow to Cuba's trade was dealt by the Lincoln

administration's grant of a mutual right of search in 1862, enabling Royal Navy vessels to intercept American-flagged slavers. Anglo-American Mixed Commission courts were established at Cape Town, Sierra Leone, and New York to condemn the captured vessels. Following this agreement, and despite strenuous Spanish objections, Britain placed a number of warships in Cuban waters, a move that did much to choke off the trade. Meanwhile in both Spain and Cuba there was also a genuine change of attitude towards slavery, such that the Spanish senate passed a bill banning the trade in April 1866, which was promulgated in Cuba in September of the following year (Thomas 1997, 783). The last verified import of slaves to Cuba was in 1870, when a cargo of 900 Africans was illegally landed.

2.3.4 *Closure*

With the demise of the Cuban slave trade, St Helena's role in the suppression of the slave trade soon became obsolete. The last vessel carrying a large number of slaves was received in August 1863, this being the *Haydee*, a ship of 161 tons into which 584 individuals had been crammed. HMS *Griffon* carried the last six freed slaves to the island in June 1864, originally the cargo of a felucca that had been destroyed off the African coast for being unseaworthy. Two more prizes were brought between then and September 1865, but both were merely equipped for the trade.

The familiar process of down-scaling and decommissioning had already begun by this date. Since 1864 the Superintendent had been retained on a permanent salary, but all other staff were employed only when there were Africans present in the depot; by the end of 1867 the Establishment had been completely disbanded. The buildings at Rupert's Bay and the remaining stores were placed under the charge of the Commissariat and a certain Mr Gillespie was retained in case of the unexpected arrival of any more slave ships. Concerns were raised about the possibility of a revival of the slave trade (and therefore the wisdom of breaking up the depot) but in contrast to previous episodes this was no false dawn. The last case adjudicated by the Vice-Admiralty court was concluded on 6 July 1868, the verdict being the condemnation of an unnamed brig captured by HMS *Speedwell*. The registrar of the court continued to send quarterly reports back to London, but these only stated that no cases had been heard. The duty to try slave ships finally ceased in 1872.

After these events the Establishment, which for many years had been so prominent in St Helena's communications with London, quickly faded out of the official correspondence. From 1868 there are a number of letters relating to African emigration (see section 2.5), but even references to this subject are scant after the early 1870s. The last letters to mention the Establishment date to 1885: they record the transfer of the buildings behind the Lines at Rupert's Bay to the War Office, and the sale of the remaining stores.

With the break-up of the depot at Rupert's Bay, the valley reverted to its former character. By 1885 the depot's tents had been dismantled and the permanent structures behind the Lines reclaimed for military use. At this time the dispensary, the hospital, and No. 1 Building remained in place, but of these only the latter now survives, used as offices by the Fisheries Department.

The sole access to Rupert's Valley remained the military path leading around Munden's Point to Jamestown, and the valley stayed isolated well into the 20th century. There continued to be some military occupation of the Lines, whilst the remoteness of St Helena led to its use as a concentration camp during the Boer War (George 1999; Jackson 1902; Royle 2006). The need to supply large numbers of people with fresh water led to the construction of a desalination plant at Rupert's Bay.

The valley remained sparsely populated. In 1938 it was reported that:

There is only one person on the island suffering from leprosy. To be thoroughly isolated, he lives all alone at Rupert's Bay, a God-forsaken hot, stony valley next to James Valley. There the wretched creature lives in solitude, and he will continue to live there until death comes and releases him.

(Gosse 1938, 364)

A visitor in the 1960s commented that 'virtually nobody lived there, and half the handful of cottages were empty ... up the valley were the ruins of three or four buildings which had been part of the slave village, and, I was told, unmarked in all this desolation, were burial grounds' (Baker 2004, 90).

The situation has changed considerably over the last half-century, mostly due to the industrialisation of the valley. Nevertheless, the essential truth remains the same as in 1960: other than No. 1 Building, there is now nothing above ground in Rupert's Valley that serves as a reminder of the Liberated African Establishment.

On a wider stage, St Helena also faded from international attention. In the 1850s and 1860s its anti-slavery role had featured quite prominently in British and United States newspapers, in the latter case particularly in the northern states immediately prior to the Civil War. Following the end of the Cuban slave trade, however, international attention shifted elsewhere. Within only a short time, St Helena was remembered for being the place of Napoleon's exile, but for little else. Its role in the extinction of Atlantic slavery, without doubt a far more significant contribution to world history, soon became an all but forgotten story.

2.4   The operation of the Establishment

In addition to providing a chronology for the Liberated African Establishment, the historical sources give considerable insight into its daily operation, and of life within the Rupert's Valley depot. The information is somewhat unbalanced, in the sense that some subjects were exhaustively discussed, whilst others barely received comment. Medical matters, for example, were a focal point of much of the correspondence, but the graveyards and the task of burial pass largely unremarked. As a whole, the portrait of the Establishment is almost exclusively transmitted by European commentators: the voices of the Africans themselves are rarely heard.

2.4.1   The physical form of the depot

A number of written commentaries, plans, sketches, and photographs enable a precise understanding of the physical form of the depot at Rupert's Bay. The literary evidence does not paint a particularly attractive picture: in 1849, for example, Dr Rawlins,

Figure 2.9 Drawing of Rupert's Valley, c 1858. This hand-drawn sketch is included in the Colonial Office's correspondence volume for 1858. Unfortunately the bottom half of the sketch has been torn away and lost; nevertheless, the surviving portion offers a very true, detailed record of the depot. Source: TNA CO 247/90

surgeon (and permanent resident) in Rupert's Valley for the previous two years, described the depot in the following way:

> Rupert's Valley ... is a most bleak and dreary spot; below the battery is a large flat surface, on which are erected the tents for the Africans; in the rear of these is the building (of wood) occupied as the hospital.

Rawlins' description combines with other contemporary and slightly later comments, such as that reported in *The Times* (10 November 1858):

> The negro houses, considerable in size, neat within and without, and made like the sharp roof of a house let down upon the ground; the long one-storey hospitals, the shops of the apothecary and physician ...

Various writers described the climate of the valley, and once again, their comments were generally unfavourable. In particular, they concentrate on the arid conditions and on the 'cutting winds' that sweep from inland areas down to the sea.

The pictorial evidence confirms these commentaries, although all of this visual material dates to the 1850s or later and so it is this period, rather than the 1840s, where we are best informed. The Lines, whilst structurally intact, appear to have become disused by 1850, the Establishment having taken over buildings formerly occupied by the military garrison.

An 1851 plan (see Fig 2.5) shows that the most prominent features of the depot were the eleven large wooden tents, arranged in two rows immediately behind the Lines. These tents are also shown in a sketch dating to 1858 and an undated photograph of roughly the same period (see Figs 2.6 and 2.9). Overseers' quarters occupied the buildings adjacent to the Lines, formerly used as the garrison barracks or as storerooms and magazines. A dis-

pensary building stood nearby. Immediately inland from the tents was the narrow wooden hospital building, next to which was another tent used for convalescing patients, along with a cookhouse and water store.[12] Also next to the hospital was a small structure only a few metres square: its function is not specified on any map drawn during the depot's operation, but interestingly it is labelled as a 'dead house' on a plan of 1885. A small garden occupied the ground a little up-valley from the hospital.[13] This arrangement essentially represents the depot's final layout, which stayed unchanged until it was physically broken up in the 1880s.

The key piece of cartographic evidence is G W Melliss' map of 1861 (Fig 2.10). In many respects this has been the single most significant document for the investigations of Rupert's Valley, because it provides the only detailed overview of the whole valley, including the precise position of the graveyards – the latter being a subject which is discussed below in section 7.1. Melliss depicted an identical layout for the depot to that on the 1851 plan; the only addition after Melliss' survey was the long stone building on the east side of the road leading from the bay. This structure is now the only surviving element of the depot, and local tradition identifies it as a hospital (see Fig 2.7). However, on a survey of 1885 it is simply labelled as 'No. 1 Building' and its precise function is not specified.

This 1885 survey offers the final detailed view of the Establishment (see Fig 2.13). It was drawn up to show the buildings that were to be taken over by the War Office and demonstrates that most were still in existence, although the tents had been removed by that point.

Despite there being such good evidence for the depot, there is comparatively little information about the graveyards. Melliss' map provides the only plan of their location, whilst two comments in an 1850 Parliamentary report describe the active

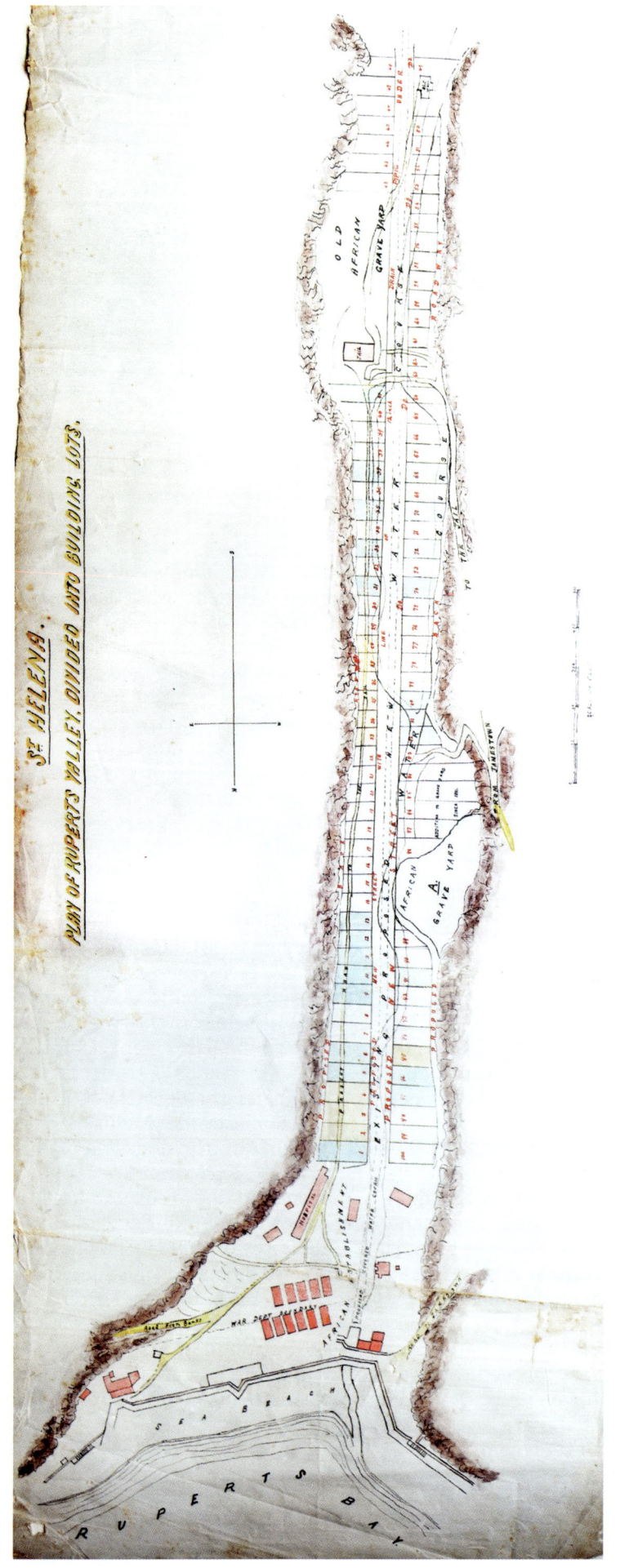

Figure 2.10 G W Melliss' map of Rupert's Valley, 1861

Figure 2.11 Rupert's Valley gaol, showing the east wall, the highest-surviving element of a compound that used to be closed on all four sides. The excavation site lay immediately to the east (just out of view to the left of the photograph), on the sloping terrace above the gaol

burial ground as being about a quarter of a mile up the valley from the hospital and tents next to the bay. This subject, and by implication the date of the area excavated in 2008, is discussed in detail below (section 7.2).

2.4.2 The development of Rupert's Valley, 1850–72

The early 1850s saw the beginning of significant changes to Rupert's Valley. Prior to the advent of the Establishment there had been no occupation of the valley other than the military garrison at the bay. The climate at Rupert's Valley was tolerable, if not particularly favourable, but the main hindrance to settlement was the lack of any reliable source of fresh water.[14] However, during the early 1850s measures were taken to rectify this situation and although prompted by the needs of the Liberated African depot, these were to have longer-term consequences.

The 1851 correspondence contains the first references to a permanent solution, this being the diversion of a stream into a 'covered drain' (culvert), so as to bring fresh water into the lower valley. At the time it was recognised that such a basic measure

might not be adequate and this quickly proved to be the case; a more complex solution was devised instead, the water being carried by iron pipes leading from the Briars over Rupert's Hill. The scheme was carried into effect by 1852, by which time certain private individuals were apparently interested in buying land in the upper valley.

The introduction of water resulted in the siting of the island's new gaol in Rupert's Valley. The location, size and condition of the existing gaol in Jamestown had long been considered unsatisfactory, and had been the subject of correspondence between St Helena and London for many years. Various proposals for a replacement had been put forward, including for a larger building in James Valley or above the main settlement, at Ladder Hill. All had been rejected, not least because of the astonishing cost of the schemes and the small number of prisoners held in the gaol at any one time.[15]

Eventually the administration settled for a fairly modest gaol in the upper part of Rupert's Valley. Its location is shown on the Melliss map of 1861, immediately next to the 2008 excavation area. The gaol was designed (or based on designs) by Colonel Joshua Jebb, a leading figure in the prison reform movement who had a major input into such buildings as Pentonville and Broadmoor Prisons

Figure 2.12   Hay Town House

and, in the colonies, Freemantle Prison. The site for the gaol in Rupert's Valley was selected in 1852, with the building completed in late 1855. It was occupied until 1867, when it was completely gutted by fire and subsequently abandoned. The shell of a building still exists at this location, currently used as a depot for the nearby fuel farm (Fig 2.11).

During the 1860s attempts were also made to establish a large urban settlement in Rupert's Valley. Jamestown was becoming overcrowded and Rupert's Valley, newly supplied with fresh water, was considered to be a logical place for expansion. The plans were promoted by governor Gore-Browne and his successor Edward Drummond Hay, from whom the settlement took its name – Hay Town. The ambition was for an extensive settlement that would take up most of lower Rupert's Valley. Its extent can be seen on Melliss' 1861 map: the rectangular enclosures are notional land parcels. Occupation was anticipated to be quite dense, and indeed there was concern expressed that some of the building lots being put up for sale were actually within the African graveyards; the government gave the rather unconvincing response that these lots would be the last ones to be sold.

The reality was less impressive. Relocation to Rupert's Valley was not a popular idea, and in any case the island's economy was beginning to decline and elements of its population were seeking to emigrate. In the event only a few structures were built: the elegant Hay Town House (dated 1862) and some cottages on the north-east side of the lower valley, also built during the 1860s (Fig 2.12). These buildings are now home to Rupert's modern population. The other legacy of Hay Town is the culvert that runs through the centre of the lower valley, retaining the stream which previously had a tendency to destructive flash floods. The culvert was completed around 1862, and was almost completely the work of the Africans who occupied the depot at that time; the total cost of its construction was £6, expended on tools.

2.4.3   Administration

Staffing of the Establishment appears to have been fairly low. From 1840 to 1850 the responsibility for the Liberated Africans and for the running of the depot as a whole rested with St Helena's Collector of Customs. This must have been an onerous post: the Collector was responsible for the upkeep of the buildings within the depots at Lemon Valley and Rupert's Valley, for the supply of food, clothing and other provisions, and he was the signatory for the Establishment's quarterly accounts. He was involved with the Africans' employment on the island and, in the early years of the 1840s, with their emigration. The Collector's role was gradually farmed out to others: from the mid-1840s emigration agents were appointed, whilst in 1850 a full-time Superintendent's position was created to take over the day-to-day running of the depot at Rupert's.

The depots in Lemon Valley and Rupert's Valley were both placed in charge of a surgeon, whilst the Colonial Surgeon also appears to have taken a role in the care of the recaptives. The Collector (or after 1850, the Superintendent) and the surgeon were a permanent fixture of the Establishment, but the number and make-up of other staff within the depot changed over its lifetime. In 1846 it consisted of a surgeon, dispenser of medicines, two matrons, a hospital dresser, a clerk and book-keeper, a superintendent of stock, four overseers, two cooks and a messenger. Three years later it was said to comprise 'a surgeon, a dispensing chemist and compounder of medicines, a hospital dresser or ward-master, with as many assistants (exclusive of negro assistants) as are required in proportion to the number of sick in hospital'.

Relations between the medical men, and between them and the Collector of Customs, were often strained. In large part this arose because of their differing remits and responsibilities, and when the recaptives died in significant numbers accusations of failure of care came from both quarters.

This situation comes across very well in the House of Commons Parliamentary Paper on emigration (No. 643; 1850). Here, assertions in a report written by the Colonial Surgeon Dr Vowells about affairs within Rupert's Valley were commented on, and often rebutted by, the Collector of Customs John Young. For instance, Vowells claimed that the number of medical staff was insufficient; Young responds that 'no motives of economy have operated at any time to restrict the expenditure of what has been required by the medical officers in the Hospital Depot'. Elsewhere in the same document the two disagree as to whether 'effluvia' was leaking from the graveyard near to the tents that accommodated the Africans. Other tensions may have arisen for more personal reasons. Certainly Dr Rawlins, the surgeon at Rupert's Valley, evoked antipathy in a number of quarters: during his tenure he was accused of everything from medical malpractice to an illegal elopement.

2.4.4 *The arrival of a slave ship*

The historical narrative shows the operation of the Establishment to have been characterised by the ebb and flow of recaptive Africans passing through the depot. There was essentially a cyclical process. Freed slaves arrived aboard captured prizes, were disembarked and treated; those that survived were then moved onwards as swiftly as was practicable – a subject discussed in more detail in section 2.5. At times the depot stood virtually empty, often for several months and, at one stage in the 1860s, for a year and a half. However, at any point it could receive many hundreds of Africans, usually with little or no warning.

The defining event in Rupert's Valley was the arrival of a slave ship. When a prize brought a significant cargo of slaves the depot would be changed beyond recognition, from a scene of abandonment or quiet order, to one of horror. Given the unpredictability of slave ship captures throughout the lifetime of the depot, it is unlikely that the authorities ever truly coped with an influx of any scale.

The most detailed accounts of such an event are given by George McHenry (1845–46; 1863; see Appendix 1). A number of other visitors to Rupert's Valley also witnessed the arrival of a slave ship and some left vivid accounts of their experiences. In March 1849 the bishop of Cape Town, Robert Gray, went aboard a newly arrived vessel that he did not name but which must have been the *Astucio*. It had been twelve days at sea since its capture off the West African coast by HMS *Philomel*:

> She was a schooner of about 100 tons, and had 560 slaves on board ... The cargo was a particularly healthy one, the number of deaths being only about one-a-day. Two were lying dead upon the deck, and one had the day before jumped overboard ... They had a worn look and a wasted

appearance, and were moved into the boats like bales of goods, apparently without will of their own ... I never beheld a more piteous sight.

> (Gray 1849, 109)

Another, later, narrative is that by John Charles Melliss:

> A visit to a full-freighted slaveship arriving at St. Helena is not easily to be forgotten; a scene so intensified in all that is horrible that it almost defies description. The vessel, scarcely a hundred tons burthen at most, contains perhaps little short of a thousand souls, which have been closely packed, for many weeks together, in the hottest and most polluted of atmospheres. I went on board one of these ships as she cast anchor off Rupert's Valley in 1861, and the whole deck, as I picked my way from end to end, in order to avoid treading upon them, was thickly strewn with the dead, dying, and starved bodies of what seemed to me to be a species of ape which I had never seen before. One's sensations of horror were certainly lessened by the impossibility of realizing that the miserable, helpless objects being picked up from the deck and handed over the ship's side, one by one, living, dying, and dead alike, were really human beings. Their arms and legs were worn down to about the size of a walking-stick. Many died as they passed from the ship to the boat, and, indeed, the work of unloading had to be proceeded with so quickly that there was no time to separate the dead from the living.

> (Melliss 1875, 30)

Such commentators were not without fault and to modern eyes their attitudes towards the Africans was at best patronising, and often bigoted in the extreme. On their recovery, for example, Melliss had nothing good to say about the Africans who remained on St Helena. Nevertheless, and similarly to the naval personnel involved in suppression, the experience of the slave ship invariably left the visitor with a hatred of the slave trade that bordered on the evangelical.

2.4.5 *Disembarkation*

The embarkation of slaves at the African coast is a process that is described in numerous sources, and is known to have been a complex operation (see Rediker 2007). However, the unloading of the human cargo of a slaver in Rupert's Valley must have entailed equal difficulties, albeit for different reasons.

As McHenry, Gray, Melliss and other commentators make clear, by the time of the slaver's arrival at St Helena there would be dead on board the ship, whilst many of the living were too sick to walk: John Young, Collector of Customs, commented that 'in every gang [ie ship-load of recaptives] a large number of human skeletons are debarked'. All of these had therefore to be carried off the ship, though some corpses proved inaccessible until items such as casks were removed from the ship. Rupert's Valley is shallow-shelving, so seagoing vessels would not have been able to dock at the small wharf next to the Lines, which meant that both the living and the dead had to be transhipped into rowing boats and brought ashore in small contingents. The time and effort involved in unloading some of the largest cargoes (in excess of 800 individuals) is self evident.[16]

Once on land, the dead were presumably buried immediately, although this part of the unloading process is not discussed by any of the sources. More is said of the procedure for the survivors. The ideal was for each to be examined by the depot's surgeon, the healthy separated from the sick, and all to be placed in some form of accommodation within the depot, either the hospital or the tents. However, as the Collector of Customs pointed out, this was simply not practical when the depot already housed, or was receiving, a large number of recaptives, 'the wards being all required, and seldom sufficient for the sick' (House of Commons Parliamentary Papers 1850 [No. 643], 75). Nevertheless, despite these constraints, enough references to such inspections occur within the correspondence to indicate that they were undertaken whenever circumstances permitted, both at the point of reception and as a normal part of hospital activities.

2.4.6 Medical treatment

The recaptive Africans disembarked at St Helena suffered from numerous diseases and injuries. The main afflictions recorded by the medical staff comprised yellow fever, smallpox, measles, pneumonia, catarrh, dysentery, diarrhoea and opthalmia. Scurvy, beri-beri and cachexia, all conditions caused by malnutrition, were also recorded. Onchocerciasis ('river blindness' or 'craw craw'), and ulcers and skin irritation, caused by parasites, were common. Venereal disease was also identified, but the records suggest that its occurrence was relatively infrequent. Added to these afflictions were the impacts of the terrible ship-board conditions: broken bones, seasickness, dehydration and severe cramp. The traumatic effect of the transition into slavery was also identified – a 'melancholy' that could commonly lead to suicide. Although smallpox was prominent during the first years of the Establishment, by far the greatest killer appears to have been dysentery. Dr McHenry, for example, recorded that the number of recoveries from this condition did not exceed one in twelve, and that convalescents were very liable to relapses.

Treatment regimes evolved during the lifetime of the Establishment and were extensively documented. It is a subject that merits further detailed

study, but is one that falls beyond the scope of this report. It is clear that a holistic approach to treatment was taken: discussion of sanitation, diet, clothing, living conditions and the environment all feature prominently in the correspondence from the Governor, Collector of Customs and the medical staff. Advice was also sought from experts abroad: for example, the Portuguese Head Surgeon of the Province of Angola offered advice on a suitable diet for African patients, and on methods for curing dysentery and scurvy.

The medical staff learnt from hard experience which approaches were successful, and which failed. As they themselves admitted, many approaches did not yield results:

> Every plan that has been suggested to me, or recommended by others, has had a fair and just trial, all, alas, to end in the one result: death. The remedies recommended on the coast, and by the slavers, have with me proved quite inadequate; yet being perfectly in the dark as to the best remedies, I have been led to try empirical ones.
>
> (Report by Dr Rawlins, 25 May 1849, reproduced in House of Commons Parliamentary Papers 1850 [No. 643], 93)

Despite this, there does not appear to have been any lack of effort on the part of the senior staff – indeed the correspondence indicates the opposite. A significant number of letters by the Establishment's surgeons indicate that they were extremely sensitive to criticisms of their conduct, and at times both Drs McHenry and Rawlins went to great lengths to rebut accusations of failure in their duties. On the other hand, McHenry was highly critical of the care afforded to the Africans by the overseers appointed to Lemon Valley in 1841, although the quality of such staff must surely have improved over the long term (see section 7.4.2).

Ultimately, the medical staff and colonial authorities recognised that their efforts could, at best, be only partially successful. Rupert's Valley was far from ideal as a place for a hospital, and its crude facilities were woefully inadequate when a fully laden slaver arrived. Expediency often replaced best practice in these circumstances. To some extent the Africans appear to have obstructed the efforts of the medical staff, either rejecting the treatment offered, or adopting their own self-healing methods. Added to these difficulties, of course, was the fact that contemporary medical practices were simply not sufficiently advanced to cope with sicknesses of these types, and on such a scale. Perhaps the most telling statement is that by John Young, who commented in 1849 that, 'the application of European remedies will always prove more injurious than beneficial'.

The mortality rate, although variable, was often very high: the statistics given for the period from 1840 to 1849 indicate that 32% of all recaptives received into Lemon Valley and Rupert's Valley did not survive (a total of 4760 deaths; see Table 2.1).

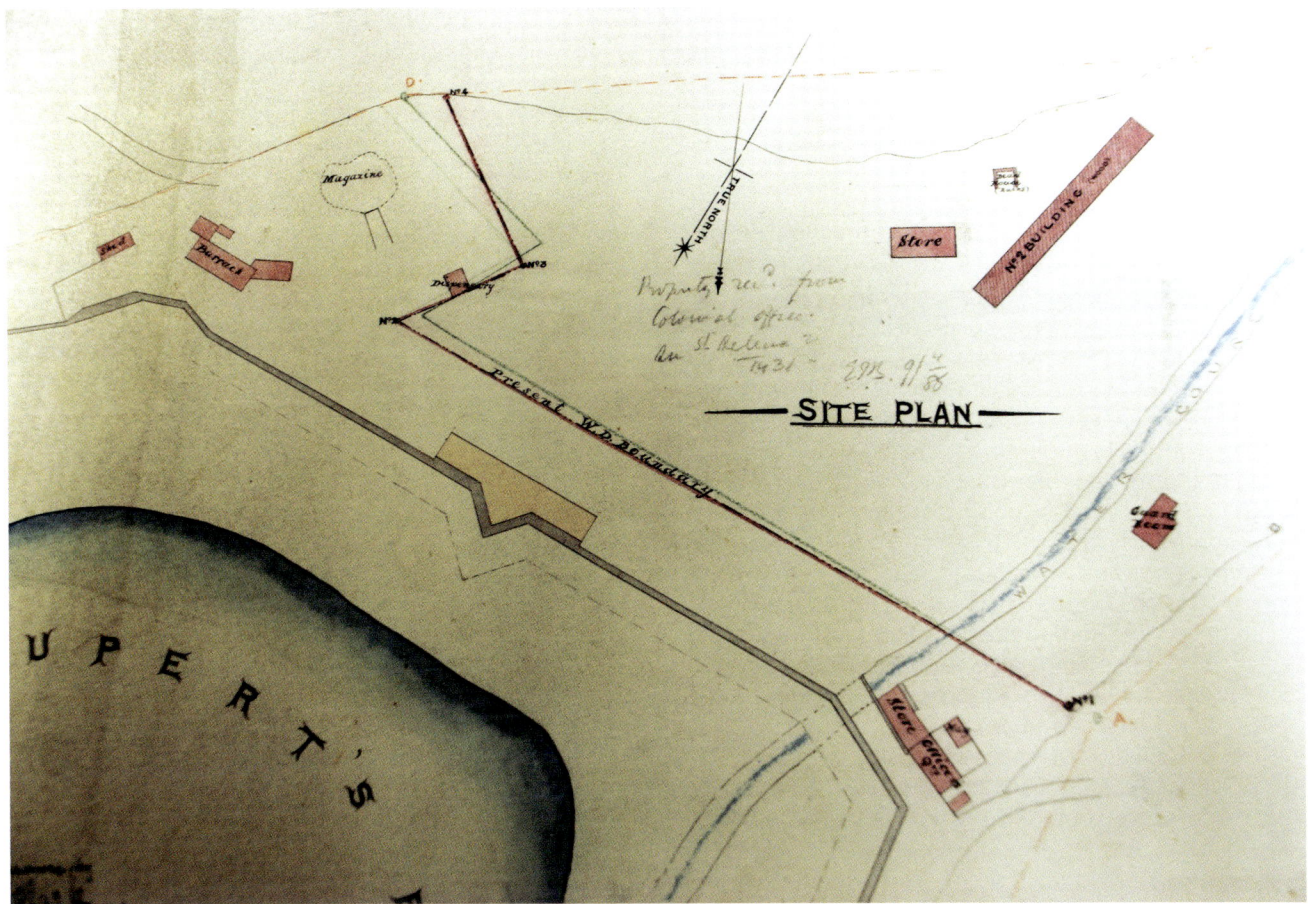

Figure 2.13   Plan of Rupert's Bay, 1885: 'Buildings taken over from the Liberated Africans Establishment'. Source: TNA WO 78/2344

Statistics for the period from 1850 onwards were not compiled in such an accessible way, but there is little reason to assume that mortality rates improved to any great extent. There appears to have been a decline in deaths during 1850 and 1851, but later reports show that deaths were once again at high levels. Enquiries were untaken into episodes of unusually high mortality, but the surgeons always rejected any accusation of poor practice. At the end of the day, colonial officials and other commentators laid the blame, quite rightly, with the slave traders and the conditions which the Africans had endured during their capture and transportation.

A different aspect of medical work was the use of autopsies. These are only very occasionally mentioned in the historical records, the most complete description being the post-mortem examination of a 40-year-old African who died suddenly during convalescence (House of Commons Parliamentary Papers 1850 [No. 643], 92). The autopsies appear to have taken place in the depot: a passing comment in a letter recommended that they be carried out elsewhere, because the practice upset the African inmates. The most likely location for these procedures was the 'dead house', marked on an 1885 plan of the depot. This very small square structure stood next to the wooden hospital block (Building No. 2) and was ruinous by 1885; it can just

be discerned on the plan of Rupert's Bay shown as Figure 2.13.[17]

2.4.7   Logistics and supply

The logistics required to support the Liberated Africans were very considerable. Essentially, a system had to be put in place that was capable of sustaining a community which at times numbered several thousand – and all this on a remote South Atlantic island. The unpredictability of prize captures exacerbated the situation, making it impossible to anticipate when supplies would be needed and in what volumes. The problem was most acute with regard to perishable foodstuffs and medicines.

The requirements of the depot are set out in minute detail by the historical sources. Every item had to be listed and quantified, and this information survives in the Establishment's accounts. The lists embraced all aspects of life in the depot, from food, clothing and medicine to domestic utensils and rat traps.

During the formative years of the Establishment these supplies were obtained from a variety of places – in short, from any source from which they could be quickly procured. The slave vessels themselves provided some items, notably fuel and food, although the farina, which was usually the staple on board ship, offered a diet for the Africans that was far from ideal. Other goods came from the stores of the Commissariat and Ordnance departments, with the remainder bought from local merchants (often at exorbitant prices).

In the longer term most goods appear to have been procured from private contractors, although government stores were still drawn upon in cases of emergency. There is a reasonable amount of evidence for this practice, mostly in the form of invitations to tender for new contracts, which appeared periodically in St Helena's newspapers. A few pieces of official correspondence also relate to this subject, notably the governor's statement in 1852 that he 'made it an unavoidable rule to advertise everything which can be offered to public competition'. Tenders were apparently awarded on the basis of samples or 'sealed patterns', which subsequently acted as a benchmark for the quality of the articles concerned.

The origin of the supplies was undoubtedly very varied, and is a discussion that goes beyond the scope of this report. However, this subject does hold a particular interest, given the survival of textiles within the excavated graves (see section 5.9). The historical sources indicate that most of the blankets and clothing were new: the garments given to any recaptives suffering from dysentery or diarrhoea were written off, whilst there were frequent complaints from Establishment staff that the healthy Africans took little care of their new outfits and destroyed them through neglect.

There are enough references in the correspondence to infer that a good deal of the clothing came from Britain. In 1841, for example, the governor recommended that 'suitable clothing in sufficient quantity be supplied from England', whilst in a subsequent letter he wrote to the Colonial Secretary in London stating that 'the clothing which your Lordship has mentioned as being about to be forwarded for the use of the Africans has not yet arrived'. In 1842 the island's Colonial Secretary mentioned the purchase of a 'large supply [of clothing] shortly expected in a ship from England' but such references are infrequent, and it is quite likely that other clothing (or the textiles with which to manufacture it) was imported from locations other than England. Indeed, given the hand-to-mouth operation of the depot at times of crisis, and St Helena's position at a maritime crossroads, it is hard to see the situation having been otherwise. Some clothing may have been manufactured on St Helena itself (though maybe using imported fabric), but it seems improbable that its domestic industry could have supplied blankets and clothing in the volumes necessary to meet the entire needs of the depot.

There is good evidence for the types of clothing issued to the Liberated Africans. In 1842 Dr McHenry reported that:

the clothing furnished to the slaves consisted of a pair of trousers and calico shirt or duck smock for

each, besides which Guernseys were provided for the sick and convalescents and during two or three months red woollen or scotch caps were given, one to each individual. The women and girls were clothed in a calico undergown and a printed calico gown; flannel undergowns were likewise provided but mostly for the sick. During a short time, two or three months only, a very coarse cotton handkerchief was allowed to each female to be used for covering the head.

Formal supply lists also survive. The majority relate to clothing issued to the Africans prior to emigration, when their old garments were replaced, but the following estimate from October 1841 details the items needed to support the 1700 Africans then living on the island:

145	Men's shirts of stout coloured cotton	£16
145	Smock frocks of duck	£40
290	Trousers of duck	£65
145	Guernseys or woollen shirts	£54
207	Boys shirts of stout coloured cotton	£18
207	Smock frocks of duck	£54
414	Trousers of duck	£72
207	Guernseys or woollen shirts	£51
62	Women's gowns of stout coloured cotton	£14
31	Women's undergarments of flannel or woollen	£12
31	Shifts of white calico	£3
120	Girls' gowns of stout coloured calico	£18
60	Girls' undergarments of flannel or woollen	£19
60	Girls' shifts of white calico	£4
91	Handkerchiefs of coloured cotton	£2
1	1 bale woollen caps	£89

Interestingly, in all of these lists there is not a single mention of shoes. To some extent this may reflect the fact that most of these inventories pertained to supplies for emigration ships: shoes would be unnecessary (and quite possibly ruined) on board, and the expectation was that the Africans would be re-equipped on arrival at the colonies. It is equally possible that shoes represented items which were thought to be too problematic, given the difficulties encountered in persuading the recaptives to wear any form of European clothes on first arrival. However, perhaps the explanation is still more straightforward: that these Africans, in common with many poorer groups of European society, simply did not wear them.

Attempts were made to ensure that the clothing and blankets were of good quality, but some does seem to have been sub-standard. One letter from the depot's superintendent, for example, rebuts an accusation that emigrant Africans were clothed with 'second hand articles, probably "part of the

Numb. 32.

The St. Helena Gazette.

Published by Authority.

☞ *It is requested that Notifications for the St. Helena Gazette, of any length, may be sent to the Printer early in the Week, and those of a few lines on Fridays, by* **12** *o Clock, A. M.*

SATURDAY, JANUARY 17TH, 1846.

GOVERNMENT NOTIFICATION

THE Queen has been graciously pleased to approve of SAUL SOLOMON, Esquire, to be Consul for the Free Hanseatick Republicks of Hamburgh and of Lubeck, in and for this Island.

By command of his Excellency the Governor,

(signed)   R. C. PENNELL,
Colonial Secretary.

⁂ NATHANIEL SOLOMON, Esquire, has been nominated Vice-Consul for the above named Free Hanseatick Republicks.

HIS Excellency the Governor has been pleased to make the following promotion and appointment in the Local Militia of this Island, dated 12th December, 1845.

Ensign GEORGE ALEXANDER to be Lieutenant, vice SOLOMON resigned,

MATTHEW TORBETT, Gent. to be Ensign, vice ALEXANDER promoted.
13th January,

LADIES' BAZAAR,

IT is requested that those Ladies who so kindly intend to contribute Work to the Bazaar, in aid of repairing the Country Church, will send their contributions to the Castle, by the 10th of February, as it is proposed to hold the Bazaar on the 14th.

ON THURSDAY the 22d Instant, will be sold by Public Auction, on the Wharf, the following Stores from the Condemned Vessel

"ISABELLA,"

Consisting of Masts, Yards, Sails, Standing and Running Rigging, Beans, Farina, Firewood, Water Casks, Lumber, &c., and the HULL.

Also the Cargo, consisting of Beans, Farina, Masts, Yards, Sails, Standing and Running Rigging, Water Casks, Firewood, &c., of the Condemned Vessel,

UNKNOWN—19TH.

FOR READY MONEY.

Sale to commence at Eleven o'Clock in the Forenoon,

By Decree of the Vice Admiralty Court,

EDW. GULLIVER. R. N.
Marshal V. A. Court.

St. Helena, 16th January, 1846.

G. BAXTER

BEGS most respectfully to return his sincere thanks to his Friends and the Public in general of St. Helena, for the liberal support he has met with since his commencing business; and informs them, that in addition to his usual Stores, he has made extensive purchases from the well-known Bark, "*INDUS*," in every description of

FANCY PERFUMERY,

Baskets, Ladies' Boots, Straw and Silk Hats, Bran, Fruits, &c. &c., and will be most happy to supply them with every article on the most reasonable terms.

The smallest order thankfully received.

Figure 2.14   Excerpt from the St Helena Gazette, *advertising the auction of a slave ship, 17 January 1846. The* Isabella *was seized by HMS* Cygnet *in late October 1845 and arrived at St Helena on 24 November. She was condemned by the Vice-Admiralty court three weeks later*

clothing of some deceased seaman", and that the trousers were not made from "condemned bread bags from the commissariat stores or some such stuff"'. The actual appearance of the clothes is not known – the one photograph showing the recaptives is not of sufficient detail (see Fig 2.6). However, one visitor to Rupert's Valley did make a passing reference to the African children's ill-fitting European clothes, describing a rough game in which 'the boys tumble over in a confused mass of woolly heads and striped cotton' (Anon 1865, 72).

2.4.8   Ship-breaking

A very different aspect of the economics of the Establishment took the form of ship-breaking. By the 1840s it had become the practice to destroy captured slave vessels, rather than to sell them intact. The advent of the Vice-Admiralty court on St Helena therefore created an entirely new sector of the economy. A broken slave ship yielded many tons of timber and iron, and these on an island where both commodities were scarce. If Sierra Leone offers an analogy, minor personal fortunes could be made from the purchase and resale of such items. Bill posters still survive that advertised the auction of captured slave ships on Jamestown wharf: at busy periods several vessels could be sold off during the course of a single week (Fig 2.14). Even in 1852 – a very quiet year for prize captures – the value of this activity to the island's economy was estimated at over £1000.[18]

Whilst the legal condemnation and auction of slave ships took place in Jamestown, the actual breaking appears to have been undertaken in Rupert's Bay. Little is said about this process, but given that several hundred vessels were destroyed in this way it must have been a major enterprise and one of the defining characteristics of the bay. Although no timbers from slave ships can definitely be identified within the fabric of modern Jamestown, much of this wood must still be present. It is also tempting to suggest that a proportion of the island's historic ironwork began its existence as the fittings of slave ships and as items such as shackles.

Unfortunately, there was an unexpected consequence of this ship-breaking industry, which was to have far-reaching consequences for the island. In 1840 a slaver was dismantled in Rupert's Bay, but her timbers contained white ants (or termites). The introduction of these insects proved disastrous. Although some masonry structures existed on St Helena at that time, many buildings were of timber; by 1860 the termites had reduced much of Jamestown to ruins and were beginning to spread across the island. The problem has never entirely gone away, and there are records of termites having rendered Plantation House uninhabitable by 1928, and the Church of St Paul was condemned as unsafe in 1939 (Gill and Teale 1999). St Helena is now characterised by an almost complete absence of timber buildings, and generally only hardwood features survive for any time within the termite areas.

2.4.9   Life in Rupert's Valley

During periods when no slave ships arrived, the depot took on a very different aspect. Although deaths continued to occur, they usually did so at a decreasing rate, with the number of healthy and convalescent recaptives far outweighing the sick and dying.

The question inevitably arose of how to occupy these people prior to settlement or emigration and a strict daily regime was enforced. Occupations were sought for the recaptives, many of which directly contributed to the running of the Establishment, for example collecting and delivering stores and growing food in the gardens. Beyond the depot the men were at times set to tasks such as fishing, stone-breaking, the repair of roads, and the clearing of blackberry and furze (gorse) from government lands. In 1851 they were used as labour during the building of the country church in the island's interior. This work in fact represented unpaid exploitation.

However, perhaps more interestingly in the context of the finds recovered from the 2008 excavation, are the pastimes by which the depot's management sought to keep the Africans occupied. In one account of Lemon Valley the women are recorded as 'stringing beads', whilst elsewhere it was suggested that the inhabitants of Rupert's Valley might be given 'a parcel of iron hoops' which they could convert into knives. The Colonial Surgeon, writing in August 1848, considered this employment to be 'a moral and physical preventive of disease' (House of Commons Parliamentary Papers 1850 [No. 643], 79).

The scene in Rupert's Valley was usually comparatively orderly, as described by *The Times* in 1858:

> ... the Africans [were] drawn up in three rows, according to age and sex, for muster and inspection. The superintendant [*sic*] of the establishment had the roll-call in his hands, from which he called the names in the language of the Africans ... All were decently and comfortably dressed ... they are fed as well as the soldiers of the garrison.

Other accounts describe a similar situation, but also note some of the less formal aspects of the depot: a visitor who published under the pseudonym of 'a Bird of Passage' described some of the children at play (Anon 1865, 72), whilst another recorded a boat race in which the Africans soundly beat their European competitors (Lefroy 1895, 54). The situation was not always so harmonious, however: in 1861 it was reported that for two months the Liberated Africans at Rupert's had been behaving in a 'mutinous and rebellious manner' and had become quite unmanageable. On at least one occasion there had been a small armed uprising against the overseers. Given the trauma suffered by the recaptives whilst on board the slave ship, their cultural disorientation within the depot, and the general difficulties of communication, this was probably not an isolated event.

Some element of education was pursued, although this was only possible for those Africans who stayed in the depot for a reasonable period, or who became long-term residents of the island. There are records in 1845 of a Sunday School for the Liberated Africans having been set up at High Knoll fort, whilst there were also periodic attempts to appoint a teacher in Rupert's Valley. In 1863 a small grant was finally obtained from the British government for just this purpose, but it came too late to benefit any but the very last arrivals at the depot.

These attempts at education were not particularly successful, perhaps unsurprisingly given the attendant obstacles of language and culture. The bishop of St Helena complained of problems with the Africans' intellectual capacity, and of their extreme ignorance. Few seemed to gain any benefit from the attempts to teach them, most (in his opinion) leaving the island as 'lamentably ignorant' as when they had first landed.

Education inevitably went hand-in-hand with

a Christianising agenda (eg Bertram 1852). The various teachers who spent time in the depot were usually religious ministers, one example being the Reverend Frey, a Protestant missionary who spent a short time on St Helena in 1846, whilst returning to his native Germany from Malabar. The extent to which such missionary work bore fruit is not clear. Baptisms are known to have taken place, and at least a few of the recaptives appear to have become eager converts. One of the very few primary sources that derives from the Africans themselves (albeit through the filter of a colonial officer) is a letter addressed to Queen Victoria in 1848 from three individuals naming themselves Benjamin Vemba, John March and James George. In it, they offer 'praises to God, for His merciful guidance in bringing us into the hands of Christian people, from whom we have been taught to love and serve God'. In similar vein in 1851, the governor submitted a request to London from 'certain Liberated Africans praying to be sent back to their own country with a view to converting their heathen brethren'.

Other baptisms, however, may have been imposed on people who did not wish to be converted, or who had no concept of what this rite signified. Certainly the practice of mass baptism prior to the sailing of an emigration vessel (adopted between 1859 and 1863; see Anon 1862) was singularly unsuccessful: the Africans came to associate baptism with forced migration, and on at least one occasion ran away from the bishop when he came to visit the depot.

Burial rites are not discussed in the historical sources. Many interments must have been too hurried to allow any type of ceremony, but what happened at times of lesser crisis is not known. The only pertinent comment yet to be found in the records comes from the *St Helena Herald* (25 January 1854). Here, an anonymous St Helenian signing himself 'A Christian' urged the Africans to become baptised, so they could have a Christian burial and not be interred in Rupert's Valley 'like dogs'. However, in publishing this piece the editor observed that none of the recaptives bought the newspaper, and so were unlikely to read this plea. Such limited evidence, written with so clear an agenda, cannot be used to infer that all burials in the depot were of a 'pagan' or entirely irreligious institutional character. Nevertheless, it affords an interesting insight into the islanders' perception of the goings-on in Rupert's Valley and of practices in its graveyards.

2.5 Settlement and emigration

The question of what to do with the recaptive Africans was one which occupied the British and St Helenian administrations from the earliest years of the Establishment. From its 16th-century beginnings the island had always relied on immigrant labour, both voluntary and forced, to support its economy; over the centuries it has drawn on peoples of Malagasy, Indian, Chinese and Boer ethnicities, as well as African and European peoples.

It appears that the original solution for the recaptives, applied to the survivors of the slave ships brought to St Helena in late 1840 and early 1841, was to integrate them into St Helena's population. A few hundred were employed as servants, whilst the children were apprenticed: the conditions of their service were eventually formalised by the island's Ordinance *For the Protection and Care of such Liberated Africans as shall become Servants or Apprentices in the Island of St Helena* (No. 3 of 1842; 27 July). Others were taken on by members of the local bureaucracy or militia: one boy is found in Manchester in 1845, servant to a lieutenant of the 46th Regiment. These people accounted for only a minority of the recaptives, however. A few were recruited into the British Army, but most emigrated – some to the Cape of Good Hope but the majority to the West Indian colonies of Jamaica, Trinidad and Guiana.

The Colonial Office made it clear from the outset that it would not provide funds to pay for the onward transportation of recaptive Africans from St Helena. Instead, the onus was placed upon the importing colonies, and to some extent private individuals, to meet this expense. As early as December 1841 a plantation owner offered to fit out a ship to take Africans from St Helena to his properties in Jamaica. About the same time Middlemore was entering into negotiations with his counterpart in Cape Town about the possibility of that colony receiving freed slaves.

The first emigrant vessel to depart from St Helena was the *Mary Hartley*, which left the island for British Guiana on 21 December 1841 carrying 111 male and 29 female passengers. She was not dedicated to this task, simply being a ship carrying rice from Calcutta which happened to have additional capacity. *Mary Hartley* was followed by several other vessels in the first half of 1842, which between them took 2675 Africans to Cape Colony, Demerara, Jamaica, Trinidad, and British Guiana. These departures were the forerunner of many such journeys over the next three decades. Approximately 18,000 Africans left St Helena for other colonies between 1840 and the early 1870s, a part of the last stage of the slavery-driven diaspora from Africa to the Americas (Adderley 2006). British Guiana alone received 5812 emigrants from St Helena, in a process that saw its existing West African population supplanted by one that was largely of Central African origin (Schuler 2000; 2002).[19]

Emigration was no panacea. The St Helenian recaptives fell prey to the same ambiguities and muddled concepts of freedom experienced by earlier liberated slaves, for example those brought to Sierra Leone in the years after 1807. Their freedom was of the most limited type, as apprenticeship, army service or emigration to other colonies as indentured labourers all entailed a lengthy period of compulsory service, and one which they were not guaranteed to survive. The wishes of the Africans

SLAVERY.

(Africans still living on St. Helena who were captured by H.M. Cruisers and freed.)

Figure 2.15   Liberated Africans on St Helena, c 1900. From Jackson 1903, 264

themselves are also an open question. It was a common view amongst British officials that few of the Africans desired to return to their homeland, and to a certain extent this may have been true: many recaptives came from conditions of actual or effective slavery within Africa, whilst others' homes had been destroyed by warfare. For some, a return to their place of origin was simply untenable: the very young in particular had no concept about where, within the vast African continent, they had

been brought from. Nevertheless, for many Africans their initial capture, transport on the slave ship, incarceration on St Helena, and onward transport to the colonies formed part of a single linear experience. These components of their journey, frequently rigidly separated by modern scholars, were often conflated in post-abolition empirical and allegorical enslavement narratives (Schuler 2000; 2002). It appears that many recaptives did not accept the British explanation of indenture as a legitimate reimbursement of transportation costs to the colonies, but instead considered their acquisition as a sale.

The initial good intentions of the Colonial Office, namely that only those Africans who volunteered should be made to emigrate, quickly foundered on St Helena, as indeed was also the case at Sierra Leone (see Schuler 1980). It was soon discovered that many were simply not willing to leave, the women being particularly reluctant. As early as 1842 matters had come to a head and the governor adopted the expedient of cutting off all support to those who refused to emigrate. By the late 1840s any pretence at voluntary emigration had been abandoned, the governor having 'standing orders to send them away whenever he can find opportunities.'

The fate of the Africans who were initially settled on St Helena is unclear. The Blue Books record that in the 1842 the number settled ('denizened') on the island was 238, this figure rising to 543 in 1849. Unfortunately after this date the census lacks detail and it is impossible to determine the size of the African population.

Eventually, however, most probably left the island. Correspondence during the late 1860s and early 1870s, virtually the last to deal with the Liberated African question, refers to the emigration of unemployed families of 'African birth'. Some left the colony for the West Indies, whilst others went to Sierra Leone and Lagos. These emigrants numbered several hundred in total, which probably accounted for most of the recaptives settled on the island in the 1840s and their descendants. Of those that remained, commentators such as Melliss (1875, 31) were damning: 'a poverty-stricken, dependent portion of the population'.

Some of the Africans on St Helena survived into old age. Emily Jackson's book of 1903 contains a photograph of five aged Africans, taken around the turn of the century (Fig 2.15). The text accompanying the photograph reads:

> [HMS] Cyclops is spoken of by one of the old men still living, and there were five I was able to photograph who came in her – two men and three old women, who are now in the poorhouse. The men, although over seventy, are still able to earn a little, but the women are helpless, and almost blind, being all of good age. The taller man is named Duke Wellington, the other Blinker.

HMS *Cyclops* brought prizes to St Helena within a concise period between 1849 and 1850, so these Africans had been resident on the island for over half a century. An Arthur Wellington is recorded as having died a pauper in 1909 whilst Charlotte Harper, 'an African', died on 26 August 1929 aged 100. Within the Deaths Register, the term 'African' appears to be reserved for recaptives, as distinct from emancipated slaves or others of African descent living on the island. If, as seems likely, Charlotte Harper was a Liberated African, then her story was indeed remarkable – a life that began in Africa in the early 19th century and ended on a remote South Atlantic island at the eve of the Great Depression. Her death marked the passing of an era. Whether the descendents of Liberated Africans still live on St Helena is not known.

2.6 Conclusion

Any judgement about the success of the Liberated African Establishment on St Helena is at best subjective, and at worst entirely meaningless. Even at the time, the implementation of Britain's abolitionist policies was widely criticised, and these faults do not diminish when viewed from a longer historical standpoint (see for example Asiegbu 1976). Best intentions foundered on the practical reality of enforcing the anti-slavery campaign, whilst many of the measures adopted, particularly with regard to education and religious conversion, are now considered as bigoted in the extreme. Emigration from St Helena was mostly enforced rather than voluntary, with social effects in the Caribbean that reach into the modern day.

Moreover, Atlantic slavery was to a large extent brought to an end by diplomacy, rather than by the efforts of the West Africa Squadron. The number of slave ships captured by the Royal Navy is in many respects a mark of the failure of abolitionist policies, since there was no better indication that the trade remained active. If one takes this view, then the thousands of Africans received on St Helena must also be seen in a similar light. Furthermore, given that most of the slaves arrived at the island alive, the graveyards in Rupert's Valley are a tangible reminder of the thousands for whom medical treatment was unavailing. The historical record does not enable a precise estimate to be made of the total number of deaths after 1849; however, if the mortality rates reported in the 1840s continued over the next two decades, then approximately 8000 recaptive Africans were buried on St Helena or around its coast.

Nevertheless, if examined in other terms, St Helena's contribution was very significant. Between 1840 and 1867 the island received over 26,000 Liberated Africans. This represents about 16% of the 160,000 African slaves liberated by the West Africa Squadron and, more importantly, nearly half of those freed between 1840 and the final extinction of the trade. Sierra Leone undoubtedly played a pivotal role in the suppression of slavery throughout the 19th century, but in the dying years of slavery the use of its Vice-Admiralty court was much diminished.

The outcomes for St Helena itself were mixed. The cost to the colonial administration and the British government was very large, and their struggle to meet the logistical challenge comes across strongly in the correspondence between St Helena and London. On the other hand, away from Lemon and Rupert's Valley, the picture for many individuals was rather different. The British (and later the American) Navy's use of the island for provisioning of their ships and resting of crews brought in considerable revenue to St Helena, revitalising an economy that was heading towards decline after its transition from East India Company possession to Crown Colony.

These benefits did not outlast the closure of the Establishment and the withdrawal of the West Africa Squadron, however. Writing in 1875, J C Melliss summed up the bitterness felt by the island's inhabitants: they had played a major part in the suppression of the slave trade, but had not benefited. Indeed, the ravages of the white ant had caused widespread damage, resulting in misery and impoverishment for many. No financial support from England was perceived to have been offered. Melliss concludes:

> The place, once so gay with naval men and ships, now knows them no more. But the negroes, who could have been best spared, still remain.

Notes

1   A discussion of these sources is given by Smith (1995). In addition, there exist a number of unpublished articles pertaining to the island. Those pertaining to slavery and the Liberated African Establishment include Schulenburg (2003), Teale (1974; 1979) and Van de Velde (nd; 2007).

2   Rupert's Bay was chosen as the landing point for the cable, with No. 1 Building of the Liberated African Depot being adapted as the cable house. The Eastern Telegraph Company's depot also included several buildings immediately behind Rupert's Lines, together with a narrow gauge railway for the landing of supplies. All of these features have now gone, but the cable itself was never removed and was encountered during the archaeological evaluation undertaken for this project.

3   Until Ascension and St Helena were used as bases for cruisers, Freetown was the one place where naval officers could go ashore for spells of leave. Sierra Leone, however, was universally despised by naval personnel. One captain commented that 'I never knew, nor heard mention of, so villainous, miserable or sickly abode' (Chamier 1832), whilst another called it 'a pestiferous charnel house ... a detestable spot with no one good-quality to recommend it' (quoted from Lloyd 1949, 15).

4   The Act also had the effect of pushing virtually all slave cases to the Vice-Admiralty courts – principally at Sierra Leone and St Helena. By contrast, the mixed commission courts were of comparatively little importance: that at Cape Town, for example, only brought eight cases

between 1843 and 1864, with a mere three vessels actually condemned (Lloyd 1949, 221).

5   The term 'recaptive' is frequently found in contemporary correspondence when describing slaves taken from illegal ships. It arises from the 1807 Abolition Act, in which not only the slave ship but also the slaves became the prizes of their Royal Navy rescuers. In this monograph 'recaptive' is used interchangeably with 'Liberated African', although it is recognised that neither term is particularly satisfactory.

6   The statistics quoted within this report for the numbers of prizes, and of recaptives landed on St Helena, have been assembled from several sources. The *Transatlantic Slave Trade Database* (Eltis *et al* 1999) provides a large list of captures, but for the purposes of the Rupert's Valley project a separate database has been used, assembled from partially different source material. This principally comprises Vice-Admiralty court records from the FO 84 series of the UK National Archives, and the remnants of the Vice-Admiralty records held in the St Helena Government Archives. Discrepancies between these data and the *Transatlantic Slave Trade Database* are extremely minor.

7   The advantages of St Helena for the anti-slavery squadrons persisted even when the majority of warships were powered by steam. A telling illustration of this can be found in letters by Commodore Phipps Hornby in 1866, in which he quantifies average voyage durations between St Helena, Ascension Island and various points on the African coast. The same correspondence also emphasises the benefits of St Helena's climate over that of Ascension (UK National Archives ADM 123/74).

8   This was not the first time that Lemon Valley had been used for this purpose. On 18 June 1716 it was reported that 'Small pox has broken out amongst the last Slaves from Madagascar and they are sent to Lemon Valley for Quarantine'. During Napoleon's incarceration on the island it also served as the hospital and burial ground for naval personnel suffering from dysentery.

9   This question was revisited once again in 1849. The Foreign Office cited 'almost unanswerable grounds of humanity' in support of the strategy of taking ships carrying slaves to St Helena, when it was closer than either Sierra Leone or the Cape. This view was supported by the Colonial Secretary Earl Grey and by the Admiralty, but the Treasury complained that it had not been consulted.

10   In 1840, £1 0s 0d would have the same spending worth of £44.10 in today's money. (For an online currency converter see http://www.nationalarchives.gov.uk/currency/results.asp#mid).

11   Comparable statistics for the reception of recaptives and of mortality/emigration were not

compiled for the years after 1850. In general, the reporting of statistics for the colony is most rigorous during the years immediately following its transition to Crown rule (ie the 1830s and 1840s). For reasons that are not entirely clear, the period after 1850 is markedly less well documented in many respects – a fact that comes across strongly when the Blue Books are examined.

12 On a slightly earlier map this structure is labelled as a 'rush store'.

13 Although not shown on any plan or drawing, correspondence in the early 1850s continues to mention the use of one or more hulks anchored in Rupert's Bay. These housed recaptives with transmissible diseases and provided extra accommodation when there was not enough space in the tents.

14 References to this problem are found in correspondence as early as 1715, when East India Company administrators commented that 'with more labour we could carry a good run of water into Rupert's Valley which is almost a plain and though not very wide is above two miles long and with a good run of water might be turned into garden ground'. Some solutions had already been attempted: a well was sunk near Rupert's Bay to provide fresh water for mortar during construction of the defences in 1744, whilst in 1832 there is a record of a 'pump sent out for the well sunk 80 feet deep in Rupert's'.

15 In 1838 a proposal was put forward costing £10,000. At that time the number of prisoners averaged between 40 and 50.

16 Notionally, let us assume that a rowing boat was able to carry ten Africans and required half an hour to reach the slave ship, load, return to shore and unload its cargo. On this basis, 80 such round trips would be required for 800 recaptives, equating to 40 'boat hours' of continuous operation.

17 Such procedures were probably quite common practice as a means of establishing cause of death. McHenry carried out an autopsy on the wife of one of the overseers who died in Lemon Valley. Another autopsy is recorded in 1847, carried out on four members of the crew of HMS *Kingfisher*. Another 'dead house' is mentioned as existing at Lemon Valley in 1842.

18 A correspondent to the *St Helena Herald* (30 June 1853) wrote how 'each capture gave employment to a considerable number of persons, demolishing the vessel, etc'. He went on to bemoan the lack of recent prizes. The value of individual prizes varied considerably, depending on their size, condition and the amount and type of stores that they carried. Some raised very little at auction, but others proved lucrative: the brig *Newport*, of 106 tons, was sold at auction for £688 (*St Helena Herald*, 1855).

19 Schuler estimates that between 1841 and 1865 chartered vessels supplied 13,172 Africans to British Guiana, from Rio, Sierra Leone and St Helena.

3 The excavations *by Ben Jeffs*

3.1 Introduction

Following the discovery of graves during geotechnical works in 2006, archaeological evaluation was undertaken throughout Rupert's Valley during 2007 and 2008, extending from the bay to the quarantine station (see section 3.3). However, the main excavations took place in the central part of Rupert's Valley, immediately adjacent to the Mid Valley Fuel Farm (Fig 3.1).

3.2 Cartographic evidence

At the outset of the excavations knowledge of the graveyards was framed by the cartographic evidence, the principal data coming from G W Melliss' map of 1861, entitled: 'St Helena. Plan of Rupert's Valley. Divided into building lots' (see Fig 2.10). This map arose from proposals to develop a new town within the valley, and as such its primary purpose was to show land boundaries. However, in so doing it also depicted the main structures of the African Establishment and key topographic features of the valley, such as its watercourse and paths.

Presumably as a means of avoiding development on the burial grounds the map shows two graveyards, both of which are explicitly described as 'African'. The most defined graveyard is shown in the north of the valley, against its western wall, and is drawn with hard boundaries. This burial ground is marked in two phases: to the north as the 'African

Grave Yard', with a similarly sized area to the south labelled as 'Addition to graveyard since 1851'.

To the south of the valley, against the eastern wall, the map marks an 'Old African Grave Yard'. The boundaries of this area are not marked and the extent indicated is not clear. It is this second area within which the 2008 excavations fell.

The only other cartographic source that shows the position (or even the presence) of the graveyards was produced in 1872 as a revision of Edmund Palmer's survey of the island, first published in 1852 (Fig 3.2). Here, the graveyard is marked as being to the south of the well house (visible as 'Old Well' on Melliss' map, but now demolished). This places the 'Old Burial Ground (Liberated Slaves)' a good deal further up the valley, half way between the modern quarantine station and the gaol. In this respect the Palmer revision is at odds with both the Melliss map and the findings of the archaeological evaluations; certainly no burials were discovered here during the 2007 and 2008 trial trenching exercise. This subject is discussed further in section 7.2, which considers the dates and location of all the known burials within the valley.

3.3 Trial pits and evaluation trenches

Between 2006 and 2008 a total of 37 trial pits and evaluation trenches were dug in Rupert's Valley during the course of the Air Access project (Fig 3.4). Thirteen trial pits were undertaken by Atkins

Figure 3.1 The excavation site: view east from Field Road. The site was close to completion at the time of this photograph, with the full extent of burials nearly apparent, except in its central part

Figure 3.2 Detail from the 1872 revision of Palmer's map of St Helena

'Old Gaol', Mid Valley Fuel Farm and upper cemetery

Lower cemetery

'No. 1 Building'

Area occupied by Liberated African Depot

Figure 3.3   Overview of Rupert's Valley showing the location of the Liberated African depot and the graveyards

in 2006, as part of the geotechnical study of the whole airport development area. Seven evaluation trenches were dug in 2007 during the initial archaeological survey.

The process was completed in 2008 with the excavation of a further nineteen trenches by the archaeology team. These were cut in areas displaying any depth of talus, fluvial or colluvial deposits. The trenches were cut by mechanical excavator, under close archaeological supervision, to a depth of at least 0.85m from existing ground level. All trenches were cut to the top of very open talus and alluvial deposits, ground which evidently precluded the presence of burials.

These investigations encompassed the whole of Rupert's Valley, from the bay to the quarantine station. The majority of the pits and trenches did not encounter burials. Instead, they provided valuable negative evidence, demonstrating that many parts of the valley were not only devoid of graves but also that, in most places, the ground was entirely unsuitable for use as a graveyard. However, burials were found in four locations: three during 2006 and one in 2007. None of the 2008 trenches encountered any burials or features of archaeological interest.

As a whole, the works have established the location of the burial areas in reasonably precise terms – which were proven to be broadly coincident with the graveyards depicted by Melliss. This is discussed further in section 7.1, with the graveyard locations being shown on Figure 7.1.

3.3.1   Atkins Trial Pits (2006)

Three trial pits, TP/R5, TP/B1 and TP/B3 revealed burials.

TP/R5 was dug inside the compound of the Mid Valley Fuel Farm, 2m from the wall of the old gaol. The pit exposed a single inhumation, buried with the head to the east, the feet at a depth of 550mm and the chest at 800mm below the gravelled surface. A vertical slab of stone was present at the foot end of the grave, but this is likely to be a natural feature. No further information was recorded about this burial.

TP/B1 and TP/B3 were dug in the upper valley, on the floodplain to the south of the power station and fuel farm. TP/B1 revealed a single inhumation, buried with the head to the north, at a depth of 550mm. From the photographic evidence it appears that the skeleton was that of an adult, and judging from the angle of the mandible and the smoothness of the frontal bone it can tentatively be suggested that it was female.

TP/B3 revealed part of two skeletons at a depth of 1.2m, aligned north–south and lying parallel but head-to-toe. The head, torso and pelvis of one skeleton, and the legs and pelvis of the second, were within the footprint of the trial pit. It was not determined whether they occupied a single grave, but this seems likely. The exposed femurs measured 450mm, which indicates that they belonged to a tall, mature adult.

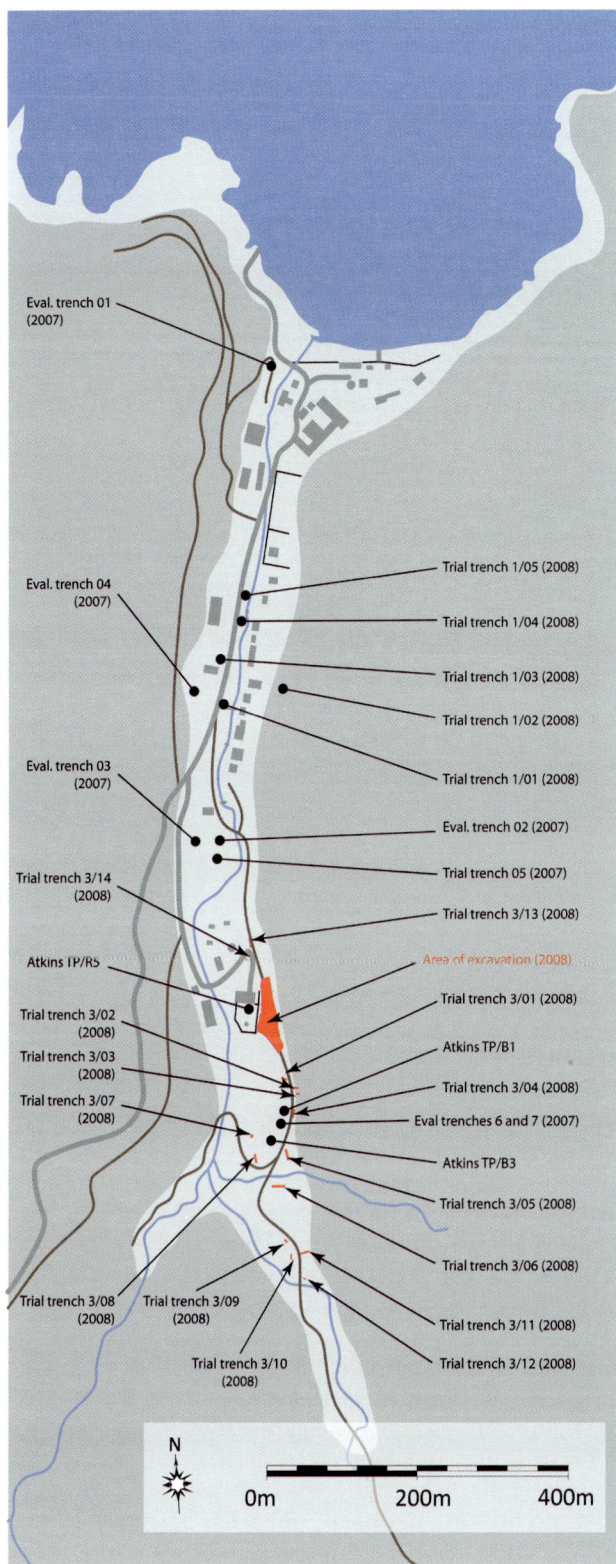

Figure 3.4 Trial pit and evaluation trench locations

At the request of St Helena Government all of the skeletal remains uncovered by these trial pits were exhumed. The bones were placed in wooden coffins and reinterred at the Church of St Paul. No detailed recording or osteological examination of these skeletons was undertaken.

3.3.2 Evaluation Trench 4 (2007)

This trench was located in the lower part of Rupert's Valley, within what is now understood to be the lower graveyard shown on Melliss' 1861 map. Disarticulated human bone was found at a depth of 450mm, whilst at 900mm two skeletons were present (Fig 3.5). The bodies were immediately next to one another, lying parallel and orientated north–south (ie at right angles to the slope and parallel to the line of the valley).

The upslope (westerly) skeleton was partially overlain by the second. Both bodies had been placed in the grave in a supine position, but neither was lying completely flat, their heads being slightly raised and tucked onto the chest. The downslope skeleton was slightly flexed. The arms seem to have been positioned straight at the sides, though only the left arm of the upslope skeleton was fully exposed. Both individuals were approximately 1.40–1.50m tall and the skeletal data indicate that they were in their late teens or early 20s. The skulls were very poorly preserved, but the mandible of one individual suggests that it was female.

The requirement not to leave the trench open overnight precluded further investigation. The skeletons were cleaned, recorded and photographed, then reburied in situ.

3.4 The excavation site

3.4.1 Site location and topography

At 100m long and 28m at its widest point, the main excavation area encompassed 1800 square metres (Fig 3.7).

The topography of this part of the valley is stepped. A series of alluvial deposits cut by water action forms two natural terraces, each approximately 6m high and extending out from the eastern valley wall. The power station occupies the alluvial plain to the west of the stream that runs through the valley, which at this point is uncanalised. To the east of the stream and slightly elevated above the power station, the Mid Valley Fuel Farm and the remnants of the 19th-century gaol sit at the base of the lower terrace. The area of the 2008 excavation lies on the easternmost (highest) natural terrace, just above the fuel farm (see Fig 3.1).

The eastern edge of the excavation area is defined by a marked steepening of the valley side, whilst to the west, north and south its limits are formed by a near-vertical eroded face. This face has been created by a combination of natural and artificial processes: erosion by the stream, and by the cutting of a terrace – first for the gaol in the 1850s and more recently for the Mid Valley Fuel Farm.

The area of excavation occupied the majority of this natural terrace, which is now bisected by the unmetalled track leading to the quarantine station and medical incinerator in the upper valley.

Figure 3.5   Burials in Evaluation Trench 4

3.4.2   *Geology and soils*

The geology of St Helena is primarily volcanic, being formed from two shield volcanoes active between 14 and 7 million years ago (Baker 1969). Rupert's Valley lies within the north-eastern volcanic centre, in basaltic lava flows laid down between 14 and 11 million years ago during the sub-aerial phase of the north-eastern centre. The western edge of the valley forms the boundary between the north and south shields.

Within Rupert's Valley the geology is entirely volcanic, or derived from the erosion products of basalts that make up the valley walls. The valley itself has been cut by water from a catchment that stretches 5km inland, along Sane Valley to the Devil's Punch Bowl at a height of 600m. The catchment is bounded by Munden's Hill and Bunker's Ridge to the west, and Banks Ridge and Deadwood Plain to the east, covering an area of approximately 12km^2. The erosion processes that formed the valley continue; the valley floor has caught large quantities of fluvial and eroded material, forming a wide valley bottom.

The excavated area exhibits no primary volcanic geology. Sitting on or just below the shoulder of the valley, the site is made up of a shallow promontory of alluvium and colluvium over talus and fluvial deposits. The soil is very thin: never more than 100mm and only existing in small patches of a few square metres.

The eastern wall of the valley has a number of eroded gullies and proto-gullies. Material eroded from the valley side is generally channelled into these gullies, creating alluvial fans at their base: the largest material is deposited within the direct run off from the gully, with smaller material dispersed on either side. The valley slopes above the excavation site contained a number of these gullies, resulting in dramatic changes in the make-up of the subsoil between immediately adjacent areas.

The alluvial and colluvial deposits on the site were generally slightly acidic silt clay-loams or silt-clays with no organic material, but with between 10 and 50% inclusions of angular and sub-angular stone from 5mm to 150mm in diameter. The rocky inclusions varied according to their position relative to the erosion gullies on the hillside: fine material was washed from the direct path of the water and large material deposited within the flow.

The main subsoils ranged from a light yellowish-brown through to a dark reddish-brown, darkening significantly when wet. Generally the soils retained more organic material towards the western edge of the promontory and contained a lower proportion of larger stones. The quantity of sand and stone in their make-up meant that all of the soils and subsoils were very free draining.

3.4.3   *Fauna and flora*

Much of Rupert's Valley falls within the coastal Scrub Zone (Ashmole and Ashmole 2000), though areas of the lower valley are planted with introduced ornamental and crop species. Of particular relevance during the excavation were the Tungy: *Opuntia cochinillifera* (English Tungy) and *Opuntia vulgaris* (Red Tungy). These are common on the valley sides and have deep root structures that seek out soft and damp soil, forming resilient mats. The Creeper *Carpobrotus edulis* and the Wild Berry *Lantana camara* were also present on the site and have somewhat invasive root mats. All of these plants caused localised disturbance of archaeological horizons.

The black rat *Rattus rattus* is common in the valley and several burrows and a single live animal were seen during excavation. Burrows from the introduced European Rabbit *Oryctolagus cuniculus*, and several dead individuals, were encountered in the western edge of the site.

3.5   Methodology

Excavations began on the site of the upper African graveyard on 9 June 2008 and ran continuously until the site was regraded by mechanical excavator, following the removal of the last context on 6 September 2008.

3.5.1   *Standards and guidance*

St Helena has no guidance or legal framework for the protection of its archaeology, nor for the monitoring of archaeological excavations. As far as was practical in these unusual circumstances, work was undertaken to the Institute for Archaeologists' *Standard and Guidance for archaeological excavation* (2008) and English Heritage's *Management of Archaeological Projects Second Edition* (MAP 2; English Heritage 1991).

Site methodology followed Northamptonshire Archaeology's *Fieldwork Manual* and the Museum of London's *Archaeological Site Manual*.

3.5.2   *General approach*

The site was characterised by a considerable variation in the thickness of the overburden, by a minimal differentiation between grave fills and natural deposits, and by marked differences in the depths of the graves (even for adjacent burials). The latter was a consequence of the historic terracing of the site, terracing which is now almost completely disguised by erosion and by the creation of the track to the quarantine station.

An open area excavation technique was therefore adopted, with the objective of identifying the historic terracing and excavating the graves from their contemporary ground surface. Restrictions on site access, imposed by the modern landform and the continued operation of the quarantine station track, dictated that the excavation proceeded from north to south. The track through the centre of the excavation area was removed during the last phases of work.

Machine excavation, under close archaeological supervision, was used to remove the deposits down to the historic ground surface. Movement of vehicles over uncompressed deposits was kept to an absolute minimum.

Following the identification of a terrace, the surface was hand-cleaned, a process which allowed the more obvious grave cuts to be identified. Once these graves had been excavated and the human remains lifted, the gaps were investigated by hand. In some cases this exercise confirmed the absence of burials, but often these gaps proved to contain graves. Once complete, each area of the site was reduced by mechanical excavator to at least 500mm below the lowest burial discovered, in order to confirm that no further human remains were present. Finally, each area was backfilled with spoil from the subsequent excavation of the more southerly parts of the site.

3.5.3   *Weather*

The weather during the period of excavation was extremely variable. For much of June there was heavy rain, which at times rendered the site unworkable despite temperatures being high. The situation improved in July, from which point onwards the weather was predominantly hot and dry, albeit with some days when the sunshine was interspersed with short but heavy rain showers.

The near-constant wind and regular high temperatures in the valley resulted in rapid drying of the bones, even during the periods of the project when there was frequent rain. To prevent any damage to the bones, regular misting of the remains was maintained throughout the heat of the day. Where possible, each individual was exposed and lifted within a single day, in order to avoid prolonged exposure and damage.

3.5.4   *Grave identification*

Grave cuts differed from the natural, in texture and colour, to varying extents. Some graves were immediately obvious after hand-cleaning of an area, but most were not visible. Much of the topsoil or organic material included within the grave, which would normally differentiate it from the natural, was washed away from the upper surface. This arose principally because of the regular, rapid, wetting and drying of the valley sides and the free draining, open subsoil. Often, even adjacent to the human remains, there was no discernable difference between the natural and the grave fill. Most graves were not identified visually, but by their less compacted grave fills.

3.5.5   Human remains: excavation

The fills from each cut were removed by hand until the burial level was reached. Each individual within the grave cut was exposed, recorded and lifted in isolation from other remains in the grave cut. Sufficient material was removed from around the skeleton to allow recording, but with enough left to ensure the stability of the human remains. Charnel material was cleaned and lifted in layers, and recorded by photograph and context at each layer. All visible human remains were recovered from the excavation area.

An osteologist (Annsofie Witkin) was present on the island throughout the period of the excavation. Whilst much of the osteological analysis was laboratory-based, this situation nevertheless allowed on-site recording, lifting and preservation techniques to be monitored and adjusted, so as to meet changing circumstances.

3.5.6   Human remains: handling and transport

Human remains were dry-brushed on site to remove loose material and packaged for transport using polyester wadding. Once transported to the storage location in Jamestown the remains were dry-brushed and, where appropriate, washed with sponges to remove further soil. They were then dried slowly in a controlled environment with limited light and stable humidity and temperature. When the bones were dry, smaller elements of the skeleton were transferred to zip-lock polyethylene bags (punched for ventilation). Each skeleton was packed individually, in polyester wadding within heavy corrugated cardboard boxes appropriate for medium-term storage. The storage environment was matched, as closely as possible, to the burial conditions.

3.5.7   Context record

Single context recording was employed, using a system based upon Northamptonshire Archaeology's context recording proforma sheets. Each individual set of human remains was given a single 'Skeleton' number with the complete grave being numbered as a group context. Cuts and fills making up the grave were given separate context numbers, with coffins also recorded as discrete contexts. Small finds were numbered sequentially.

Articulated human remains were recorded on proforma burial sheets, including a record of completeness as a graphical representation and condition on a four-point scale.

3.5.8   Metric record

All metric survey was undertaken to *Metric Survey Specifications for Cultural Heritage* (English Heritage 2009).

There is no universally accepted coordinate system for local survey on Saint Helena. Much of the island's mapping is based on multiple projections, or is incomplete or inaccurate. A site grid was therefore established for the purposes of the excavation, with an arbitrary origin and north aligned parallel to the valley. True north lies approximately 5° east of this axis. All archaeological survey of the valley in 2008 was undertaken on this grid, with fixed elements of the landscape surveyed to provide reference points for future location.

Once it had been completely exposed, each burial was photographed in plan with four numbered survey tags. Photographs utilised a camera and lens calibrated for distortion across a range of focus distances. The three-dimensional position of the survey tags and the edge of the top of the grave cut (where preserved) was determined using an Electronic Distance Measuring theodolite and mobile prism. Each photograph was corrected for lens distortion and then rectified to the four survey tags to provide a metrically accurate representation of the grave.

The rectified photography was digitised by hand in AutoCAD, to obtain metric vector data suitable for display at scales up to 1:10 for adult burials and 1:5 for infant coffin burials. The same data were used to orient and locate the burials within the graveyard, producing location data adequate for display at 1:20.

All grave cut sections were hand drawn at 1:20 in both east–west and north–south planes as well as being measured by hand tape and recorded as part of the context record.

3.5.9   Photographic record

A photographic record was maintained throughout the excavation, including the photography of all contexts, small finds and burials, in plan, before and after excavation. All photography was undertaken using both 35mm black and white negative and high-resolution digital colour.

3.5.10   Archive

A site archive based on standards from *MAP2* (English Heritage 1991) and the Institute for Archaeologists' *Standard and guidance for the compilation,*

Figure 3.6   The excavation site: view south, taken on the public open day. By this point site work was well advanced, and the unmetalled track leading to the quarantine station – which had previously bisected the excavation area – had been removed. This action, and the removal of the modern overburden, revealed the mid-19th-century profile of the graveyard at this location

transfer and deposition of archaeological archives (2009) has been compiled. The physical archive has been deposited with the St Helena Government Archives in Jamestown, whilst an electronic archive containing the core material has been deposited with the Archaeology Data Service (ADS; http://archae-ologydataservice.ac.uk/). The ADS Digital Object Identifier for the project is doi:10.5284/1011174. The content of the archive is set out in Appendix 2.

3.5.11   Terminology

Within this monograph, the term 'Skeleton' is used to describe each articulated set of human remains recovered during the excavation (eg Skeleton 201). This term also includes organic survivals, such as hair and fingernails, that were originally a part of the body and which remained attached to the bones. The word 'burial' is used to denote both the action of interment and the resulting product (ie including all the bodies within each grave and any artefacts present).

The term 'Group' is used to denote all elements of a grave or other archaeological feature. In the case

of a grave it encompasses the cut, fill and all human remains, artefacts and ecofacts present. Thus, Group 2007 incorporates cut [2005], fill (2006), two inhumations (SK208 and SK209), and the metal tag from the neck of SK209 recorded as Small Find 01.

Small Find is abbreviated as SF.

Within this report, the numbers assigned to groups, contexts and skeletons are all prefixed by the number 2 (ie Group 2001; SK201). This denotes the fact that, for the purposes of the archaeological investigation, the excavation site fell within 'Area 2' of Rupert's Valley. This comprised the central part, around the power station and Mid Valley Fuel Farm; Area 1 took in the lower part of the valley, whilst Area 3 comprised the most southerly ground leading to the head of the valley.

3.6   Description of the archaeological findings

Within the area of the main excavation a total of 595 contexts were allocated. A total of 325 distinct articulated skeletons were excavated, together with ten charnel pits of disarticulated human remains. A feature plan labelled by group is shown on Figure 3.7.

The purpose of this section is to offer a narrative of the general character of the archaeology discovered within the excavation area. It is intended to provide a context for subsequent chapters, which describe the skeletal remains and the artefacts, and analyse the site as a whole. The full structural catalogue, supported by group plans, is included within the digital volume as Appendix D1.

3.6.1   Natural deposits

The uppermost context (2000) overlay the whole site, covering the grave cuts. This deposit comprised a loose and friable layer of mid- to dark grey-brown sandy clay-loam. The inclusions were variable, ranging from 10 to 40% angular to sub-angular stone from 10mm to 200mm, with occasional weathered boulders present, up to 1m in diameter. In places a very fine humic layer existed above deposit 2000, though this was limited in depth to 0.1m and in extent to a few square metres. The depth of deposit 2000 varied across the site from 0.1m to 2.5m. This deposit comprises material that post-dates the graveyard.

The lowest deposit excavated (2001) comprised a moderately compact to loose and friable mid-grey-brown sandy clay-loam. This underlay deposit 2000 with a very diffuse, broken and ridged boundary. The inclusions were variable, ranging from 10 to 30% angular and sub-angular stone from 10mm to 300mm. The deposit extended to the deepest excavated sections at 3m below the boundary with 2000. This deposit represents the eroded 19th-century ground surface, and all graves were cut from its upper surface.

The excavation area was bounded to the west by cut [2071]. This cut extends for 110m, forming the edge of the upper terrace and truncating a number of grave groups. The slope profile of this cut varies from vertical to 45°.

3.6.2   The graves

The excavation area was occupied by a dense arrangement of 178 graves. Other feature-types were rare, the exception being ten pits containing disarticulated human bone, a grave-shaped cut containing carefully stacked bottles, and a small extent of cobbling. The graves were distributed fairly evenly across the site, although their spacing was somewhat denser in the northern part. They were only absent from one area, an expanse of particularly rocky ground in the centre of the site. Here, just two pits were found, both containing disarticulated human bone (Groups 2422 and 2494).

Preservation of the human remains was good, with the majority of the skeletons being complete in situ; the condition of the bones themselves was more variable (see section 4.3.1) and many fragmented during excavation and lifting. Hair was found associated with most of the individuals, though fragmentary and often only preserved under the skull. No preserved soft tissue was found.

The archaeological features themselves were largely undisturbed. There were very few intercutting features and only a few instances of truncation, these arising from both human agency (the construction of the fuel farm and quarantine station track) and from the natural erosion of the terrace on its western side. However, it is almost certainly the case that, between the formation of the graveyard in the mid-19th century and the excavation in 2008, graves on the western side of the terrace have been entirely eroded or dug away.

The graves were, broadly speaking, the dimensions that would be expected for a standard burial, typically measuring 1.8 x 0.6m (ie roughly 6ft x 2ft). There was a degree of variation, much of it undoubtedly due to the difficulty of digging graves in such rocky ground. For the same reason, few of the bodies lay at any great depth below the 19th-century land surface. The deepest cut was 1m, with 0.6–0.7m being more common and very shallow scrapes were occasionally used. Many of the uppermost skeletons were only covered by a few hundred milimetres of soil and stone, and sometimes less than 100mm. Large rocks often remained in situ within the grave cuts, simply because they had been too difficult to remove.

Fewer than half of the graves contained just a single body. Of the rest, most contained two or three skeletons, but a few contained between four and seven individuals. Many of those buried were quite evidently children or adolescents, and the osteological analysis has established that even those who had reached full stature were for the most part young adults.

Only a minority of burials exhibited an orthodox, prone, arrangement. Nevertheless, there were a few graves offering evidence for the deliberate laying out of a corpse. Skeleton 393, for example, had been positioned in a well-proportioned grave, lying on its back with the hands crossed neatly over the pelvis (Fig 3.8).

Careful arrangements within the multiple interments were not common. Group 2273 (Skeletons 336 and 337) is one such instance (Fig 3.9), whilst another probably deliberate layout offered one of the site's most poignant finds: Group 2449, in which a young child was buried at the breast an adult woman, plausibly its mother (see Fig 8.1).

More commonly, bodies appear to have been deposited with a view to maximising the available space within each grave. This resulted in a wide variety of 'arrangements': bodies were found lying on their back, side and (less commonly) their front, with their limbs in a multitude of positions. Most graves exhibited some logic in terms of the order and style of deposition, whether multiple head-to-toe or

Figure 3.8 Skeleton 393 (Group 2386)

Figure 3.9 Skeletons 336 and 337 (Group 2273)

'crouched' burials. Some used vertical stacking, the most extreme example being Group 2533 which contained seven bodies (Fig 3.10). In other graves the bodies were worked around each other at the same level, as shown in Figures 3.11 and 3.12.

Other bodies had to be fitted into graves that contained large rocks or which were simply too short, both situations leading to unorthodox positioning of the corpse (Fig 3.13), whilst the rationale behind others is entirely unclear, for example Group 2047 (Fig 3.14). It can be suggested that a minority of bodies had simply been thrown into the grave, perhaps in a state of severe decay, and covered up as they lay. There was certainly evidence for some of the corpses having been in a poor state:

fly pupae (ie maggots) were found in ten graves, either close to the skeletons or actually within the body cavities.

All of the preceding discussion pertains to graves in which the bodies had been placed directly into the ground, without coffins. Historical sources for the depot mention the use of winding sheets, but no archaeological evidence for these was identified within the graves; some textile fragments were recovered from a few of the skeletons, but most have been interpreted as the remnants of clothing (see section 5.9).

Five skeletons in coffins were present: four belonged to still- or newborn infants (one foetus and three neonates), with the fifth belonging to an

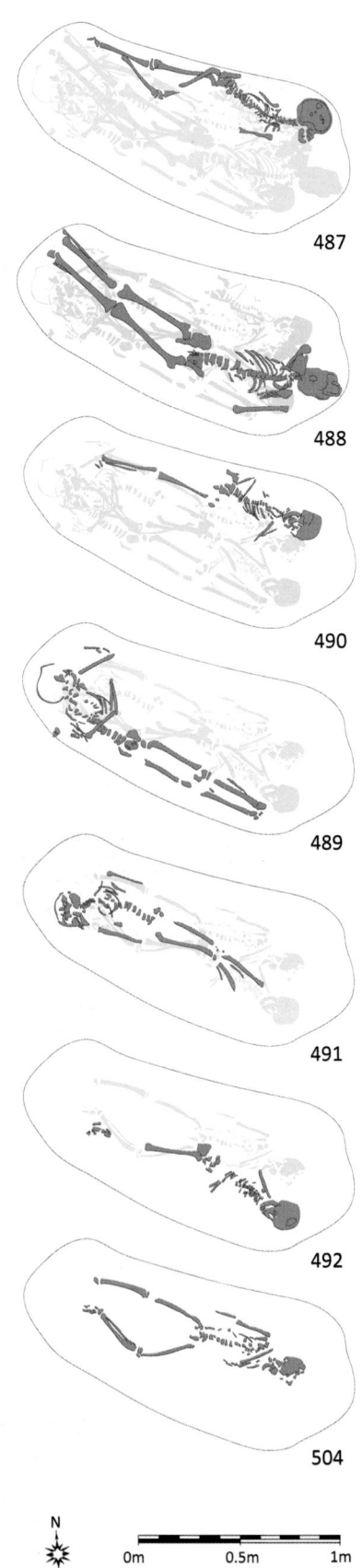

487

488

490

489

491

492

504

N

0m   0.5m   1m

Figure 3.10   Group 2533

adolescent. Three of the foetus/neonate coffins were found in a cluster in the northern part of the site, amidst the general layout of other graves; the fourth was buried 20m to the south, in an area where other cut features were quite sparse. The adolescent coffin burial was found near the southern end of the site, having survived in remarkably good condition given that it lay directly beneath the quarantine station track (Fig 3.15). These few individuals were clearly singled out for special treatment by comparison to those buried around them, and one of the neonate burials was quite elaborate (Fig 3.16). Moreover, they have additional interest because a dispro-portionate number of the artefacts recovered from the site were found within the coffins, specifically those belonging to the foetus and neonates. All are discussed in detail in subsequent chapters of this report.

Finds were, unsurprisingly for a site of this character, generally sparse, and, as noted above, a large percentage was recovered from the four foetus/neonate coffins. They varied in character: many were utilitarian objects relating to the operation of the Liberated African Establish-ment, such as metal 'tin tickets' (comparable to dog tags) and medical ampoules; others were more decorative or personal in character, notably some items of metal jewellery and many thousands of glass beads. Only thirteen individuals were found with items that can be interpreted as objects of adornment: the remaining 312 skeletons (96% of the total) were found without any such objects. As noted above, remnants of clothing also survived on a few skeletons.

3.6.3   Charnel pits

Ten charnel pits were present within the excavated area. The disarticulated human bone that they contained was of two distinct types. Eight pits, dispersed across the site without any discernable pattern, held well-preserved bone, almost exclu-sively long bones and skulls (Fig 3.17). In contrast, two pits, adjacent to each other in the southern part of the site, were of a quite different character: they were markedly larger in size, and the bone that they contained was highly comminuted (Fig 3.18).

3.6.4   Features not relating to burial

There were virtually no features present within the excavated area other than those directly relating to the burials and little stratigraphy was apparent outside of the grave cuts.

A small area of cobbled surfacing was found to the north-west of the excavation area, which is thought likely to be a path that was contemporary with the graveyard (Group 2380; Fig 3.19).

A grave-like cut containing glass bottles was present at the southern end of the site (Group 2189;

Figure 3.11   Skeletons 319 and 321 (Group 2245)

Figure 3.12   Skeletons 275 and 276 (Group 2157)

Figure 3.13   Skeletons 443 and 444 (Group 2482)

Figure 3.14   Skeletons 389 and 390 (Group 2047)

Figure 3.15   Adolescent coffin burial (Group 2298)

Fig 3.20; see also Fig 6.5). Located on the edge of the area of burials, this feature comprised a roughly grave-shaped cut, into which a number of glass bottles had been carefully laid and then covered over with earth. All had contained port or wine, and all had been drunk, some of the corks having been pushed down inside the bottle. This find represented the only cut feature from the site that did not contain human bone. No satisfactory explanation of this discovery has yet been offered: whether it had great symbolism for the graveyard, or none, has yet to be established.

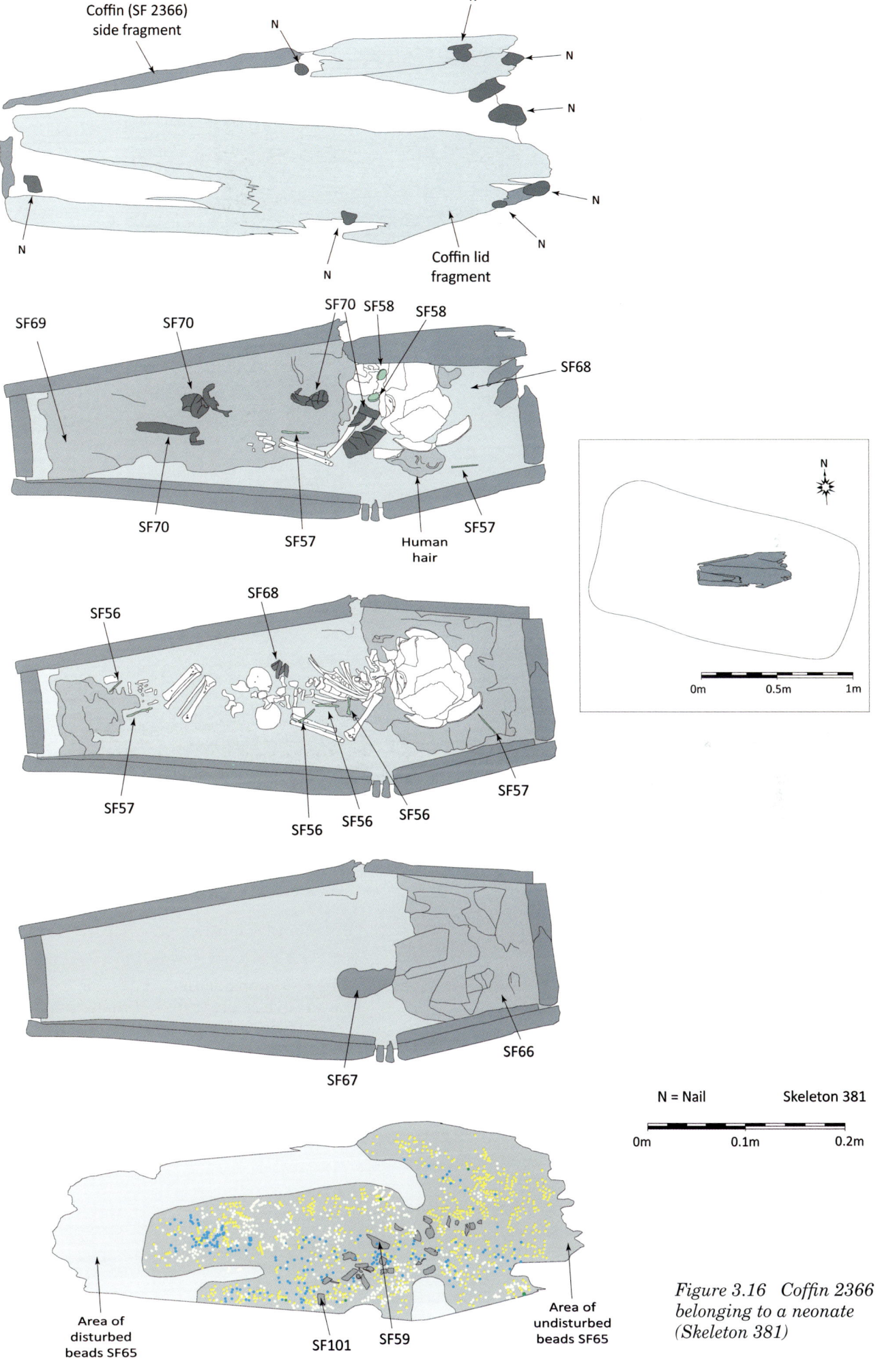

Coffin (SF 2366) side fragment

N

N

N

N

N

N

N

Coffin lid fragment

N

SF69

SF70   SF70   SF58   SF58

SF68

SF70   SF57   Human hair   SF57

N

SF56   SF68

SF57   SF56   SF56   SF56   SF57

SF67   SF66

N = Nail   Skeleton 381

0m   0.1m   0.2m

Area of disturbed beads SF65   SF101   SF59   Area of undisturbed beads SF65

Figure 3.16   Coffin 2366 belonging to a neonate (Skeleton 381)

0m   0.5m   1m

Figure 3.17   Charnel pit (Group 2111)

Figure 3.18   Charnel pit (Group 2494)

Figure 3.19 (above)   Cobbled surface (Group 2380)

Figure 3.20 (left)   The 'bottle pit' (Group 2189)

4   The human skeletal remains   *by Annsofie Witkin*

4.1   Introduction

The analysis of the human skeletal remains was carried out on the island of St Helena by Annsofie Witkin and Diana Mahoney Swales. A total of 325 articulated skeletons were analysed. The results of the analysis are presented here, and are drawn together to determine what may be said of this population of recaptive Africans, in terms of demographic data, metrical and non-metrical traits, and palaeopathology. This makes it possible to gain an impression of the health and cultural environment of these individuals during their early lives, and to comment on the implications of their enslavement immediately prior to death.

Where possible the information is contrasted with available comparative data. However, this skeletal assemblage is unique, with no other directly comparable population group. The majority of the results are therefore presented with minimal discussion. The osteological catalogue is contained in the digital volume, Appendix D4.

In addition to the articulated human skeletal remains, the excavation also recovered a considerable volume of disarticulated human bone. This material was subject to a preliminary assessment at the time of the excavation but has not been analysed in further detail. A summary of this disarticulated material is contained in the digital volume, Appendix D5.

4.2   Methodology

4.2.1   Completeness and preservation

The taphonomic processes that affect the preservation and completeness of human skeletal remains can be divided into extrinsic and intrinsic factors (Roberts 2009, 56–71). In broad terms, these include human, plant and animal actions as well as soil conditions. These may either aid preservation or have an adverse effect upon both the surface preservation and the overall completeness of the skeleton. Some of the factors that have a negative impact include acidic soil conditions, degree of compression, and a shallow burial and subsequent intercutting of graves (Brothwell 1981, 7–9). The size and shape of the bones themselves may also account for differential preservation of individual bones within one skeleton or between subadult and adult remains. The treatment of the bone during the excavation and the processing stage can also be an important variable.

The preservation of the remains was recorded using the grades for recording of erosion/abrasion caused by root/fungal action (McKinley 2004, 16). The surface appearance of the remains analysed did not directly correlate with the specific description of grade. However, the general broader descriptions of each grade were applicable and the method was therefore adapted.

The general changes seen on the cortical surface were crystal formation, surface erosion, fine fissuring, cracking, and flaking. The severity of these detrimental changes to the surface of the bone provided the preservation score given as a sliding scale from 0 to 5. As such, grade 0 translates to no alteration to the cortical surface; by grade 3 most of the surface is affected by some degree of degradation but the general morphology of the bone is maintained; grade 5 correlates with considerable destruction of the cortical surface which has completely masked the normal surface appearance of the bone.

The skeleton was subdivided into ten areas: cranium, torso, right and left arms, legs, hands and feet. Each area was scored individually for the assessment of any major differences of preservation. The mean of these individual scores provided the preservation grade for the whole of the skeleton. The completeness of the skeleton was scored using four broad categories, from <25% complete to >75% complete.

4.2.2   Age and sex

The assessment of age provides the biological age of the skeleton and not the chronological age of the individual. Variables such as general lifestyle, diet and the impact of diseases has an impact on growth and subsequent degeneration of the skeleton (Schwartz 1995, 185). The growth and maturation sequence of children is fairly predictable, uniform and well documented and therefore they can be aged more accurately than adults (White and Folkens 2005, 360). Ageing of adults aged over 25 years is reliant upon the degeneration of various sites of the skeleton which is more variable. When possible, multiple methods were therefore used in conjunction with broad age groups to increase the accuracy of the obtained estimate.

A relatively recent study evaluated the most commonly used ageing methods for their accuracy when applied to black and white adult individuals of known age at death. It was established that apart from inherent problems with the methods that had already been identified, there were no significant differences in the application to either population group (Martrille *et al* 2007). Moreover, a separate study had also previously proven that cranial suture closure had an overall low accuracy amongst white and black individuals (Galera *et al* 1998). The relatively high proportion of young adults amongst the remains from Rupert's Valley also made this method unsuitable.

Adult age was established by using three of the methods evaluated for their accuracy for application to black individuals. These involved the macroscopic assessment of the pubic symphysis (Todd 1920; 1921; Brooks and Suchey 1990), the auricular surface (Lovejoy *et al* 1985) and the sterna rib end (Iscan *et al* 1984; 1985).

For younger adults and adolescents, epiphyseal fusion (Krogman and Işcan 1986; Schwartz 1995) was also used. Subadults were aged by dental development (Morrees *et al* 1963a and b; Anderson *et al* 1976). The age estimates obtained omitted the age provided by the third molar: studies from black population groups in East Africa have shown that the third molar erupts between the ages of 13 and 17 years, which is earlier than amongst Caucasian groups (Chagula 1960; Hassanali 1995). More recent detailed studies looked at the mineralisation of the crown and root. The results indicated that the stages of full crown development to completion of half of the root occur up to two years earlier amongst black individuals (Blankenship *et al* 2007). The neonates were aged using diaphyseal lengths (Fazekas and Kosa 1978; Scheuer *et al* 1980).

Age estimates from diaphyseal lengths using the methods of Hoffman (1979) and Scheuer and Black (2000a) were obtained for individuals younger than 12 years of age, but were not used because it was found that these estimates were consistently providing a lower age than that obtained from the dental development. This may be due to skeletal growth being more sensitive to environmental influences than the development and eruption of both deciduous and permanent dentition (Scheuer and Black 2000b, 12–13). Alternatively, the data used for the development of the methods may not be comparable to this population group.

The determination of the sex of the adults was carried out through the visual assessment of sexually dimorphic traits on the cranium and pelvis (Buikstra and Ubelaker 1994; White and Folkens 2005). The composite score from the pelvis and cranium placed the individual in one of five categories: possible male; male; possible female; female; or indeterminable. For the purpose of this report, the individuals who were scored as possible male/female have been pooled with those scored as definite male/female.

4.2.3   Metric and non-metric traits

Stature estimates were calculated for the sexed adults using the regression formulae for black individuals devised by Trotter (1970). Whenever possible the estimate was obtained from the left femur and tibia since it carries the least error. If this combination was not available from either side,

the leg bones with least error were favoured over the arm bones. Only when there was no other alternative was the upper limb used for the calculation of stature. Various measurements, both cranial and post-cranial, were also taken. The majority of these pertain to the calculation of indices which is a metric way of describing bone morphology.

Non-metric traits are normal variations within the skeleton that are not measured but recorded as present, absent or not observable. These variations have commonly been used to establish relationships links within population groups (Brothwell and Zakrzewski 2004, 28). However, the formation of many cranial and non-cranial non-metric traits is poorly understood and many are subject to both genetic and environmental influences. The use of these traits for establishing family links between individuals within a cemetery may therefore have been overambitious (Tyrrell 2000, 302). Many of the cranial traits such as the suture variations appear to have a strong genetic connection, whilst many of the post-cranial traits, for example tibia squatting facets, are influenced by function (Roberts 2009, 48). Though the issues surrounding the formation of non-metric traits are complex, there is a role for non-metric traits when the data are combined with biomolecular methods or when studying activity-related changes (Roberts 2009, 148). A total of 29 cranial and 28 post-cranial non-metric traits were recorded (Berry and Berry 1967; Finnegan 1978; Brothwell 1981). The traits were recorded on all adolescent and adult remains. It is recognised that some traits appear with advancement of age and the figures presented here will therefore be for the adult individuals only.

4.2.4   Dental pathology

The dentition was recorded using the Zsigmond system with dental annotations as devised by Brothwell (1981). Caries and dental abscesses were recorded according to the standards set out by Lukacs (1989). The size of the calculus deposits was recorded using the guide devised by Brothwell (1981). The locations of the deposits were also recorded in detail. Enamel hypoplasia was recorded according to the standards set out in the Global History of Health Project (Steckel *et al* 2006). Periodontal disease was recording using the relatively recently published scoring system by Ogden (2008). This method removes the uncertainty of recording continuous eruption which may occur if the standards by Brothwell (1981) were used. Moreover, it is also favoured over the more complex and time-consuming method by Kerr (1988).

4.2.5   Skeletal pathology

The pathological lesions present were recorded using the standards laid out by Roberts and Connell

(2004). In addition, certain lesions were also graded according to pre-existing scoring systems. These were spinal joint disease (Brothwell 1981), cribra orbitalia (Stuart-Macadam 1991), maxillary sinusitis (Boocock *et al* 1995), and endocranial lesions (Lewis 2004).

The prevalence of diseases was calculated to provide, where appropriate, both the gross prevalence and the true prevalence. The gross prevalence is the number of individuals present with a specific pathological lesion divided by the total number of individuals within that population. The prevalence is expressed as a percentage. This gross prevalence was also refined to show the prevalence within the age categories and also sex. The true prevalence is the number of bones present with the pathological lesion; these were also subdivided into right and left sides. The result was expressed as a percentage as well as a number.

4.2.6 Dental modifications

The dental modifications were recorded using a system devised by the author. A publication of dental modifications on 19th-century crania from Cameroon used an earlier classification system devised by De Almeida in 1957 (see Reichart *et al* 2008). However, this system did not consider the method used for creating the modifications, and the designs which had clearly been carried out by chipping were in the same category as the designs that had been created by filing (Reichart *et al* 2008). Another system is that developed by Romero (cited in Vukovik *et al* 2009, 11), although this appears to be an updated version based on the system comprising 24 different types originally devised by Borbolla (1940). However, the classification system of the various types was developed for pre-Columbian Mesoamerica.

A new typology was therefore created based on the variations of the modifications present within the population group. The modifications were divided into two basic categories: simple and complex. The simple forms comprised a shaped modification of two teeth from the maxilla. The complex form involved modifications carried out on more than two teeth on either the mandible or the maxilla or a combination of both. The various shapes within each category were numbered with a basic description of the pattern, the teeth affected and the method used to carry out the modification. The method used was determined by using x4 magnification. Certain modifications would have been chipped, then subsequently filed, in order to achieve the final shape. The method suggested per modification is therefore not definitive but rather what was discernable to the naked eye or under low magnification. The resulting typology comprised seven simple forms and twelve complex forms.

Another form of cultural dental modification is that achieved by ablation (extraction). Identification of this practice was more problematic, because teeth lost ante-mortem may not have been deliberately removed. The criterion used for the identification of this type was that the absence had to be bilateral and involve the canines or the incisors. The socket had to be obliterated and no evidence of disease such as an abscess be present that could otherwise account for the loss of the tooth. The individuals with multiple ante-mortem teeth lost in both jaws were excluded because the loss of the anterior dentition may be part of a disease process.

4.3 Results

4.3.1 Preservation and completeness

A high proportion of the excavated skeletons still retained both head hair and body hair in significant quantities. In two instances the hair was of sufficient length to have been braided: Skeleton 379 (an adolescent of unknown sex) and Skeleton 435 (an adult female). In addition, there were a very few instances of the survival of fingernails. A number of samples of hair were taken, and at the time of writing these are in storage with the skeleton to which they related. To date, no analysis of this material has been undertaken.

Close to half (44.61%) of the skeletons were given the preservation Grade 3 and the vast majority (91.69%) were given a score between 2 and 4 (Table 4.1). A slightly greater proportion (by *c* 10%) had a preservation grade of between 0 and 2 compared to the more poorly preserved skeletons that were graded with the score 4 and 5. The more detailed examination of preservation in the ten body areas showed that in the population as a whole the preservation average was between 2.5 and 3.2 (Table 4.2). Although there was little difference in preservation, the hands were the area of the body that was best preserved, and the arms the worst area.

The degradation pattern observed on the bones arose out of a combination of environmental factors and the circumstances of the excavation. The most commonly observed degradation was crystal formation, where minerals had crystallised on the surface of the bones. Where the crystals had been removed the resulting pits were reminiscent of punched-out lesions, especially on elements with a high trabecular content such as ribs and vertebrae. Another feature that mimicked pathological lesions was surface erosion that had a similar appearance to fine porosity or pitting. Many bones also had evidence of fine fissuring of the cortical surface which on occasions had developed into considerable cracks through the whole of the cortex. These were observed on the long bones and especially the femoral shafts. These changes relate to the soil conditions and possibly microbial attacks which have been proven to increase porosity in bones (Jans *et al* 2004). There was also evidence of prolonged sun exposure which had occurred during the excava-

Table 4.1   Preservation of the articulated human skeletal remains

Grade	0	1	2	3	4	5	Total
No.	2	24	80	145	73	1	325
%	0.62%	7.38%	24.62%	44.61%	22.46%	0.31%	100%

Table 4.2   Average preservation by skeleton area

Skeleton area	Average preservation
Cranium	2.7
Torso (including hips)	2.7
Left Arm	3.2
Right Arm	3.1
Left Hand	2.5
Right Hand	2.5
Left Leg	2.8
Right Leg	2.8
Left Foot	2.7
Right Foot	2.7

Table 4.3   Completeness of skeletons

Completeness	No.	%
<25%	8	2.46%
25-50%	15	4.62%
50-75%	63	19.38%
>75%	239	73.54%
Total	325	100%

tion itself, some bones having been completely or partially bleached by the sun. This caused increased fissuring and introduced flaking on the parts of the bones exposed. The fragmentation rate of the remains was generally low and post-mortem breaks of the long bones were infrequent. Fragmentation was commonly confined to the ends of the long bones and the more fragile bones of the torso. However, the high rate of large stones within the grave fills had caused significant fragmentation of the cranial elements, and occasional crania had warped.

A total of 73.54% of the individuals were more than 75% complete (Table 4.3). Overall the completeness was good with only 7.08% being less than 50% complete. Completeness is linked to preservation and may be adversely affected by a high degree of degradation. This was not a factor affecting this assemblage. The high level of completeness was primarily due to the lack of intercutting of graves. Moreover, there was a high recovery rate of small bones of the hands and feet, which had also survived well.

4.3.2   Demography

The skeletons analysed from Rupert's Valley comprised 325 individuals of which 148 (45.54%) were adults aged over 18 years and the remaining 177 (54.46%) were subadults (Table 4.4; Fig 4.1). There were very few foetal and neonatal remains

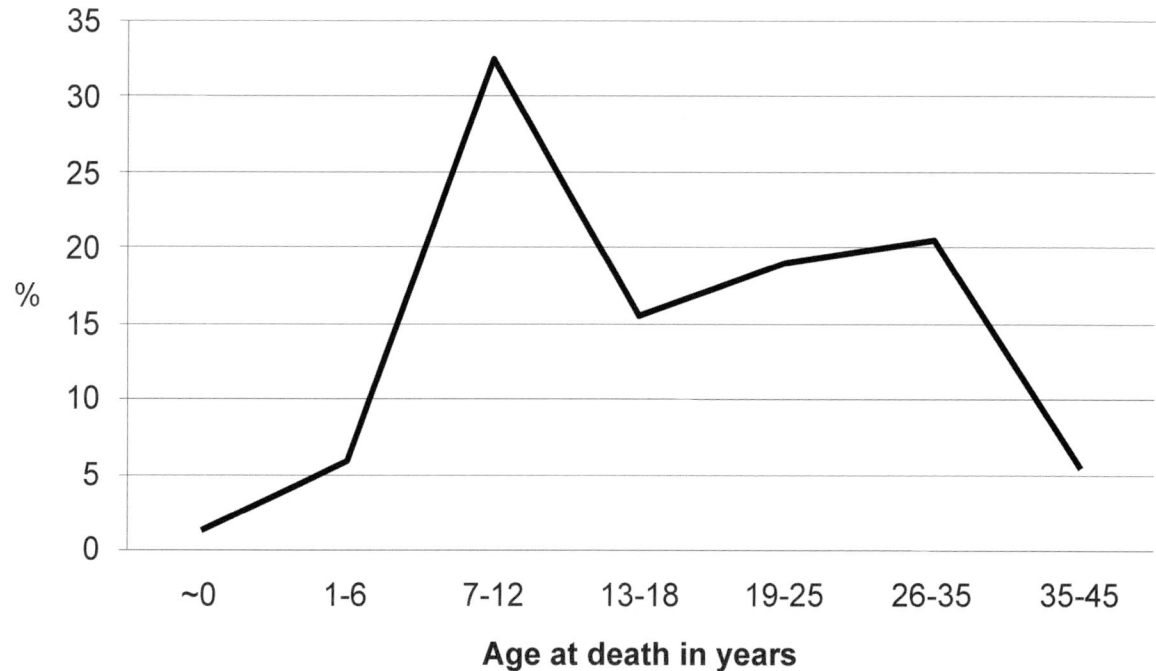

Figure 4.1 Age at death, whole population

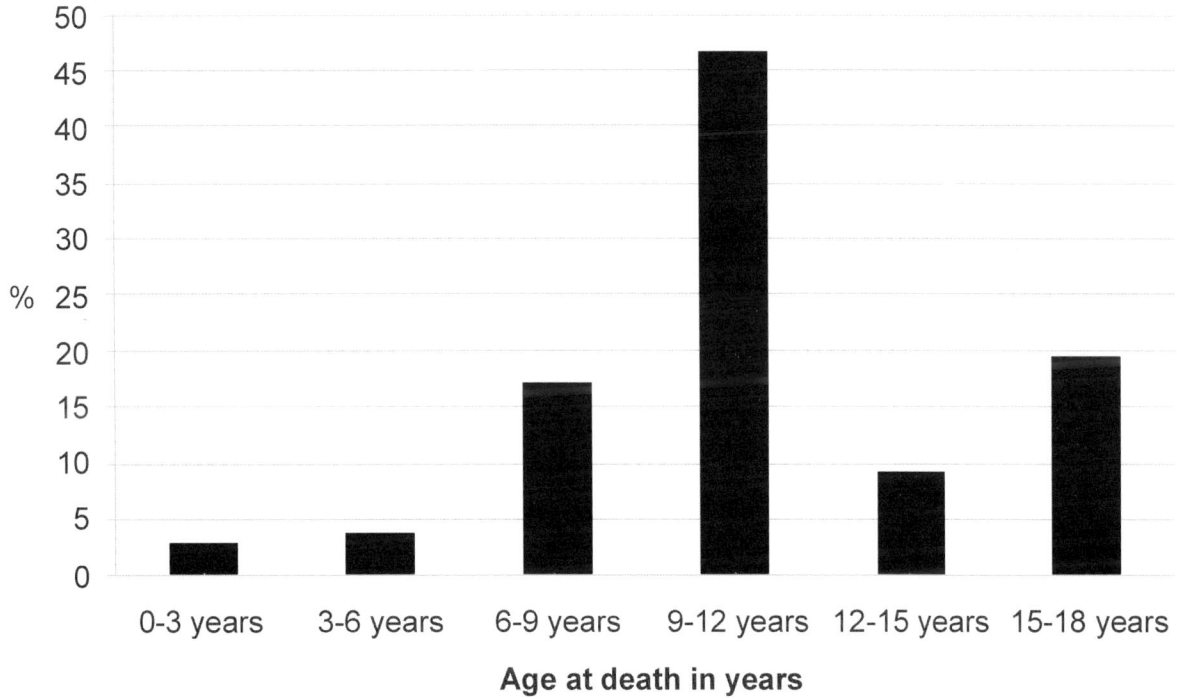

Figure 4.2 Age at death, subadults

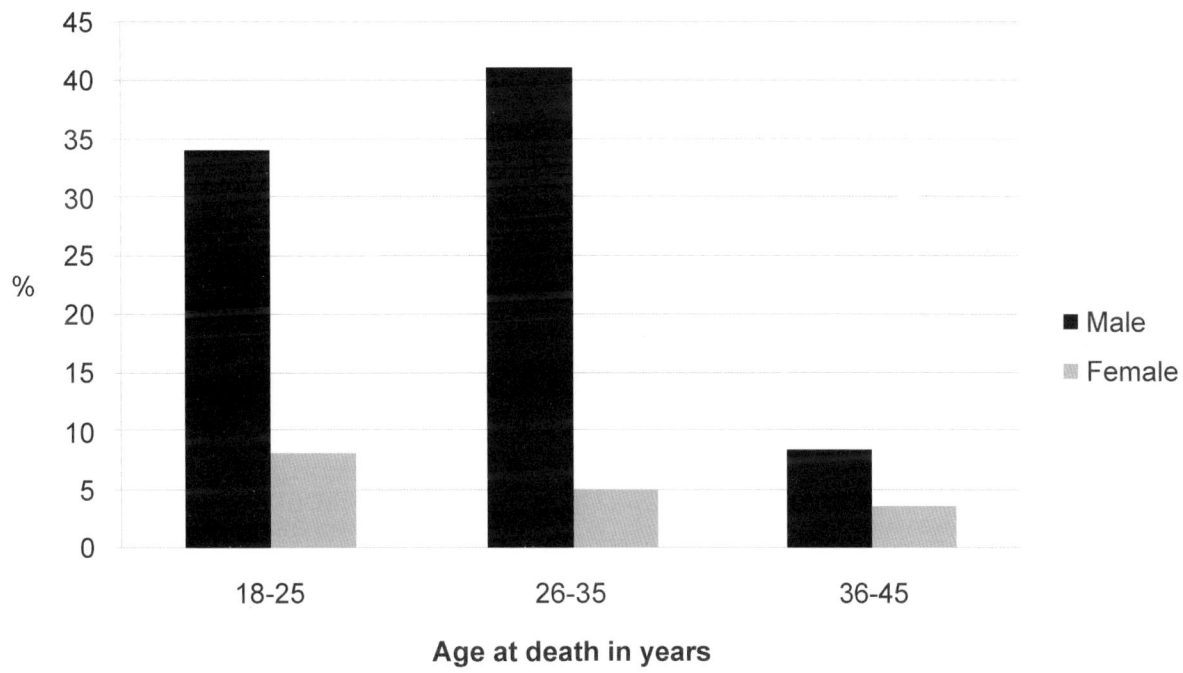

Figure 4.3 Adult age at death with male and female subdivisions (unaged and/or unsexed adults omitted)

(1.24%) and no individuals were aged between 0 and 1 year. There was a high proportion of individuals aged between 7 and 12 years. Due to the more narrow age ranges that can be achieved from the ageing of children, the sample was further subdivided into three-year age ranges (Fig 4.2). The overlap of the actual age ranges of some individuals admittedly makes these three-year brackets somewhat subjective, but it may nevertheless provide a more detailed indication of the population structure of the children. It appears that the majority (46.82%) were aged between 9 and 12 years and that a total of 74.84% were aged between 6 and 15 years. Of the 145 adults that were aged (three adults could not be aged), a total of 45.52% were classified as Prime Adults and 42.76% were Young Adults. Only 11.72% were aged over 36 years, and no individual was aged over 46 years. Subdividing the adults into even decades using the same criterion as for the subadults indicates that most of the adults were aged between 18 and 30 (92/63.45%) with 34.48% (50 individuals) aged between 30 and 40 years. Only

Table 4.4   Age and sex

	Male/Male?		Female/Female?		Undetermined		Total	
	No.	*%*	**No.**	*%*	**No.**	*%*	**No.**	*%*
Foetal <0 months					1	0.31%	1	0.31%
Neonate ~0 months					3	0.93%	3	0.93%
Young Child 1–6 yrs					18	5.53%	18	5.53%
Old Child 7–12 yrs					105	32.31%	105	32.31%
Adolescent 13–18 yrs	8	2.46%	5	1.54%	37	11.38%	50	15.38%
Young Adult 19–25 yrs	49	15.08%	12	3.69%	1	0.31%	62	19.08%
Prime Adult 26–35 yrs	59	18.15%	7	2.15%			66	20.30%
Mature Adult 36–45 yrs	12	3.69%	5	1.54%			17	5.23%
Adult >18 yrs	3	0.93%					3	0.93%
Total	131	40.31%	29	8.92%	165	50.77%	325	100%

three individuals (2.07%) were aged between 40 and 45 years.

A total of 147 adults and 13 adolescents were sexed. Of these, 81.88% (131 individuals) were male and 18.12% (29 individuals) were female. When the unaged and/or unsexed individuals are omitted from the adults it shows that the greatest percentage of males is within the Prime Adult age group, whereas there the greatest proportion of females is within the Young Adult category (Table 4.4; Fig 4.3).

Demographic data from the period of the trans-atlantic slave trade have shown that there were fluctuations in age and sex ratios though time, as well as regional variations (Geggus 1989; Eltis and Engerman 1992; 1993; Eltis 1986). Contributing factors included the slave ship's country of origin, its destination, and the part of the African coast from which the slaves had been purchased (Eltis and Engerman 1993, 311). The general overall trend shows that the ratio of females fell markedly from relatively high levels in the 17th century, and that the proportion of children aged below 15 rose markedly in the 19th century, with the greatest increase being girls (Eltis and Engerman 1992, 241; Lovejoy 2006).

These analyses therefore indicate that adult males and children were very strongly represented in the 19th-century Atlantic slave trade. Figures for slaves shipped to Cuba between 1811 and 1867 show a ratio of 229 males per 100 females, and a total of 39% children younger than 15 years. Similar ratios have been observed within cargoes shipped to Brazil during the same time period, but with a slightly higher percentage of children (42%; Geggus 1989, 24). The increase in the export of men and children in the 19th century may be due to the trade becoming more concentrated on the regions in Africa that were already associated with this high proportion of males. The widening gap between slave prices on the African coast and in the American markets may also have contributed to the high prevalence of children (Geggus 1989, 43).

The analysed sample from Rupert's Valley is characterised by a high proportion of children aged under 18 years (54%) and, amongst the adults who could be sexed, a high proportion of males (84%). Although both percentages are greater than those suggested by historical analyses of 19th-century data, they illustrate a similar trend and the demographic profile is therefore consistent with these studies.

4.3.3   Metric data

A total of 24 females and 106 males had at least one complete long bone present for the calculation of stature. The female stature range was 145–167cm with an average stature of 154.25cm. The male stature range was 150–176cm with an average of 163cm (Fig 4.4).

A study of the achieved height of an Afro-Caribbean slave population, based on slave registrations, offers a comparable data set for stature (Higman 1979). The mean stature of males in Trinidad in 1813 was 163.3cm, whilst for females it was 153.9cm. Similar mean values, 164.3cm for males and 154.6cm for females, had also been calculated from the 1819 slave registry of Guiana (Higman 1979, 376). These values are virtually identical to the averages from the Rupert's Valley population group.

4.3.4   Non-metric traits

The cranial and post-cranial non-metric traits recorded within the Rupert's Valley assemblage are summarised in Tables 4.5 and 4.6.

The cranial non-metric traits which had the highest prevalence were the parietal foramina, of which there were 61.40% lefts and 62.28% rights recorded. There was also a high prevalence of condylar canal presence: 50.55% on the left side and a slightly higher prevalence of 59.5% on the right side.

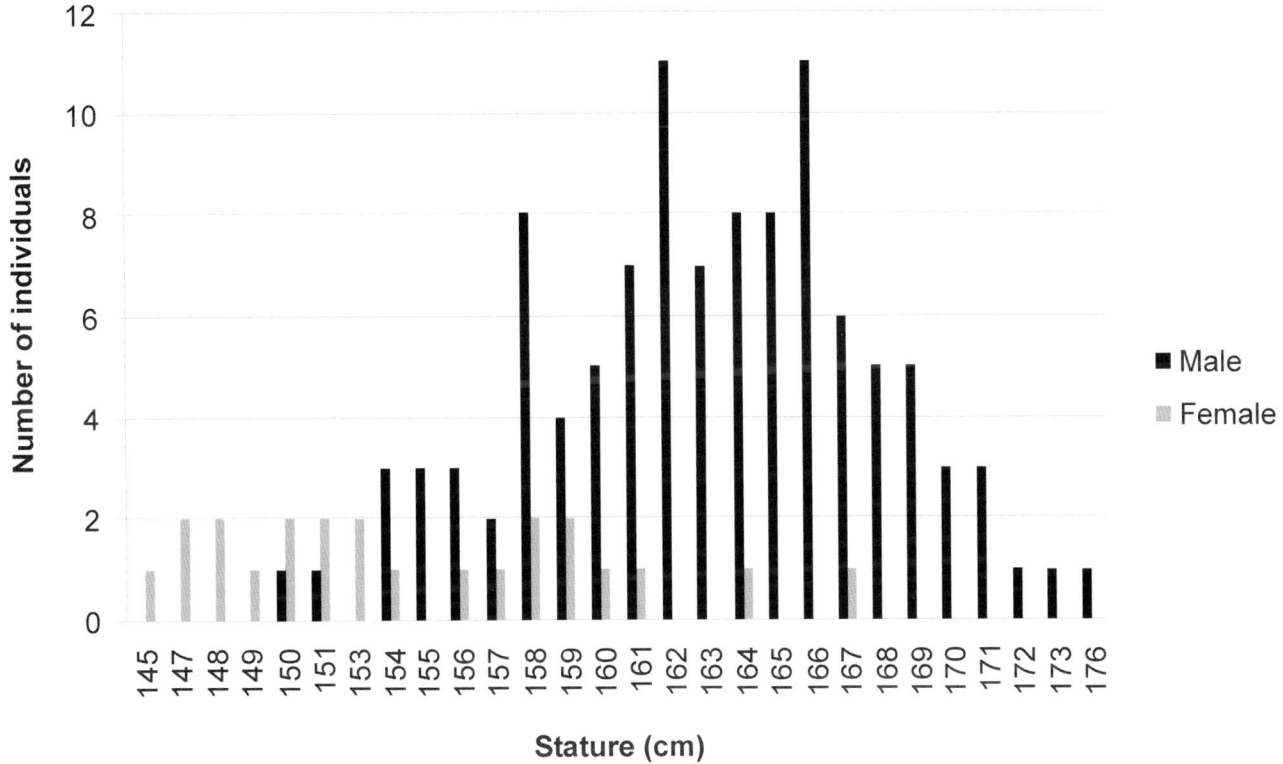

Figure 4.4 Male and female stature

There were few maxillary tori and no mandibular tori recorded. These are associated with high levels of attrition (Roberts and Manchester 1995, 54). The paucity of these features in this population is likely to be a reflection of the overall youthfulness of the adults, which is also reflected in the low levels of attrition present.

There were also no auditory exostoses recorded. These bony nodules situated in the external auditory canal are associated with cold water aquatic activities. A modern study of surfers found a prevalence of 73% of those that surfed in cold waters (Kroon *et al* 2002, 503). A comparative study of coastal and inland skeletal remains from Brazil found that the lesions did not develop in tropical and subtropical regions (Okumura *et al* 2007, 564). It is therefore unsurprising that none of the individuals from Rupert's Valley had auditory exostoses.

Of the post-cranial non-metric traits recorded, the lower limb had some of high prevalence. The trait with the highest prevalence was lateral squatting facets: 51.65% on the left side and 55.56% on the right side. There was also high prevalence of the peroneal tubercle, with 55.17% present on the left side and 49.23% on the right side, followed by a present hypotrochanteric fossa in 43.65% and 41.46% of cases respectively. The latter squatting facets are caused by hyper-dorsiflexion of the ankle. The position is usually adopted by human groups that do not use furniture to sit on (Mays 1998, 118–19) and the high prevalence of the facets in this group of individuals

is, quite literally, likely to be indicative of habitual squatting.

There was also quite a high prevalence of septal aperture present amongst the adults. The septal aperture is the perforation of the thin bone of the olecranon fossa on the distal end of the humerus. It is still unclear whether its presence is due to mechanical stresses or genetics (Mays 2008, 433). However, a high prevalence of 47% has been reported from a medieval black population from North-West Africa (Glanville 1967). This is much higher than the reported prevalence of 5–10% in European populations (Mays 2008, 432).

A sternal foramina is a perforation of the distal part of the breastplate, and this was present in 21.57% of the adults from Rupert's Valley (Fig 4.5). A modern study found an overall prevalence of 7.7% and these were twice as common in males (McCormick 1981). There was also a high prevalence in black individuals (52%), although the sample number of 25 individuals was very low (McCormick 1981, 252). An earlier study found a prevalence of 4% in European populations compared to 13% in East Africans (Ashley 1956, 96).

4.3.5 Cultural modifications

The cultural modification of teeth is represented in the archaeological record across many parts of the world, and is a practice that is known in the prehistoric era and persists to the modern day.

Table 4.5 Cranial non-metric traits

Trait	Present			
	No.		%	
Metopic suture	3/123		2.44%	
Bregmatic bone	0/104		0%	
Saggital ossicle	2/90		2.22%	
Apical bone	13/114		11.40%	
Inca bone	7/114		6.14%	
Palatine torus	11/68		16.18%	
	Left		**Right**	
	No.	**%**	**No.**	**%**
Coronal ossicle	3/95	3.16%	2/94	2.13%
Lambdoid ossicle	29/104	27.88%	31/101	30.69%
Asterionic bone	22/118	18.64%	14/91	15.38%
Occipito-mastoid ossicle	18/90	20%	14/87	16.09%
Epipteric bone	9/78	11.54%	7/79	8.86%
Parietal foramen	70/114	61.40%	71/114	62.28%
Supra-orbital foramen	16/90	17.78%	17/99	17.17%
Frontal foramen	26/89	29.21%	26/99	26.26%
Anterior ethmoid foramen extrasutural	8/45	17.78%	9/47	19.15%
Posterior ethmoid foramen absent	2/45	4.44%	3/45	6.67%
Infra-orbital suture incomplete	15/82	18.29%	20/91	21.98%
Multiple infra-orbital foramina present	6/86	6.98%	3/88	3/41%
Mastoid foramen extrasutural	38/114	33.33%	37/113	32.74%
Foramen spinosum open	16/71	22.53%	19/73	26.03%
Foramen ovale incomplete	3/75	4%	4/75	5.33%
Condylar canal present	46/91	50.55%	53/89	59.55%
Divided hypoglossal canal	12/103	11.65%	4/101	3.96%
Mylohyoid bridge present	5/86	5.81%	6/94	6.38%
Mental foramen	6/87	6.90%	6/91	6.59%
Double condylar facet	0/102	0%	3/101	2.97%
Auditory exostosis	0/133	0%	0/134	0%
Maxillary torus	2/102	1.96%	2/103	1.94%
Mandibular torus	0/99	0%	3/102	2.94%

Modifications comprise inlays, incised grooves, chipped and filed teeth and ablations (extracted teeth) (Vukovic *et al* 2009). The practice of dental modification is known in Africa from the prehistoric period, with examples from Mali, West Africa, dating to the middle of the third millennium BC (Finucane *et al* 2008). A further reported case from Niger dates to AD 1300–1600: it is argued that this was created by occupational activities rather than cultural modification (Haour and Pearson 2005) but its location and appearance is consistent with what is here described as Type 1 simple. It is therefore arguably a modification caused by cultural, as opposed to occupational, practices.

The largest volume of data regarding African modifications date to the historical period when the practice was widespread in the sub-Saharan regions and includes West, West-Central, Central, South-West and East Africa (Handler 1994, 113). The practice is not exclusively found in these regions and indigenous population groups in South and East Africa also practise the art (Goose 1963; Ortner 1966).

Published archaeological evidence of culturally modified teeth from this time period is relatively scant, and mainly comprises data from the Caribbean and America. This includes isolated skeletons from Grenada and St Croix (Stewart and Groome 1968) and Florida (Ortner 1966). Smaller groups of individuals of African descent with modified teeth have

Table 4.6 Post-cranial non-metric traits

Trait	Present			
	No.		%	
Sternal foramen	22/102		21.57%	

	Left		Right	
	No.	%	No.	%
Allen's fossa	26/93	27.96%	21/89	23.59%
Poirer's facet	6/91	6.59%	6/90	6/67%
Plaque	2/90	2.22%	2/87	2.30%
Hypotrochanteric fossa	55/126	43.65%	51/123	41.46%
Third trochanter	8/124	6.45%	7/119	5.88%
Medial tibial squatting facet	3/86	3.49%	7/85	8.23%
Lateral tibial squatting facet	47/91	51.65%	50/90	55.56%
Supracondyloid process	0/131	0%	0/130	0%
Septal aperture	30/108	27.78%	28/115	24.35%
Acetabular crease	5/99	5.05%	7/92	7.61%
Accessory sacral facet(s)	8/88	9.09%	10/92	10.87%
Acromial articular facet	15/60	25%	16/54	29.63%
Bridging of suprascapular notch	4/78	5.13%	3/78	3.85%
Circumflex sulcus	11/75	14.67%	16/73	21.92%
Vastus notch	8/99	8.08%	9/92	9.78%
Vastus fossa	0/99	0%	0/90	0%
Emarginate patella	0/102	0%	0/96	0%
Os trigonum	2/108	1.85%	3/108	2.78%
Medial talar facet	8/99	8.08%	7/100	7%
Lateral talar extension	13/98	13.26%	13/114	11.40%
Double inferior anterior talar facet	12/111	10.81%	11/111	9.91%
Double anterior calcaneal facet	35/114	30.70%	25/112	22.32%
Absent anterior calcaneal facet	2/114	1.75%	5/115	4.35%
Peroneal tubercle	32/58	55.17%	32/65	49.23%
Double atlas facet	9/122	7.38%	11/113	9.73%
Lateral atlas bridging	5/100	5%	3/108	2.78%
Transverse foramen bipartite	14/89	15.73%	20/84	23.81%

been excavated from Campeche, Mexico (Tiesler 2002), and from a slave burial ground in Barbados (Handler *et al* 1982). The cemetery from Campeche contained at least 180 individuals of various population affinities; four individuals that were determined to be of African descent had modified teeth (Tiesler 2002, 278).

The Barbados skeletal population from the Newton sugar plantation slave cemetery dated from the late 17th to the early 19th century. Of the 55 individuals with dentition present, five (9%) had modified teeth (Handler *et al* 1982, 300). The most substantial volume of modification previously reported upon comes from the African Burial Ground, New York. A total of 26 individuals were reported to have modified teeth (Goodman *et al*

2006, 245). This represents 15% of the total number of adults.

The modifications were created by chipping or filing. Some designs were made by initial chipping, with the final design shaped by filing (Van Rippen 1918, 462). The tools varied depending on the tribe but included hammers, chisels, stones and knives for chipping, and stones used as files (Goose 1963, 91). The procedure itself was carried out by a 'special member of the tribe' (Van Rippen 1918, 462).

The cultural context of these modifications is somewhat opaque and several explanations for the practice have been put forward. In some societies the modifications were performed around puberty and may therefore have been part of an initiation ceremony associated with coming of age, but the procedure was not universally performed within the groups that practised it as a rite of passage (Handler *et al* 1982, 308). The reasons may also differ depending on the sex of the individual. The women of the Ibo, Nigeria, had to have their teeth filed in order to be allowed to bear children, whereas the men had the modifications carried out for purely aesthetic reasons (Goose 1963, 12; Finucane *et al* 2008, 638). The latter seems to have been the prevailing reason for dental modifications amongst Tiv men, Yoruba and Mhuila women, and the young women of the Efe pygmy (Finucane *et al* 2008, 638). Hunter magic may also have played a part in certain designs, since both the men and women of modern day Chowke in Angola file their maxillary anterior dentition to points in order to 'impart the courage of their prey' (Jones 1992, 117). The modifications may occasionally also be a marker of belonging for a particular group such as a clan or tribe, or of specific lineage within a tribe (Handler *et al* 1982, 309). Both sexes were subjected to dental modifications and in some groups the practice was equally common for men and women; however, in other groups it was applied only to males (Handler 1994, 113).

Modification involving ablation (deliberate extraction) of anterior teeth is less common in West and Central Africa but has been found on 19th-century remains from Cameroon where all of the anterior incisors had been removed from some individuals (Reichart *et al* 2008, 51). It appears to have been more common in the East-Central Africa where modern studies have shown that ablation is still carried out in Kenya by the Masai, Turkana, Kipsigis, Luhya, Luo Kikuyu and Nubi (Hassanali and Amwayi 1993; Inoue *et al* 1995). This phenomenon was also observed in 1960s Uganda amongst the members of the Bakiga tribe (Pindborg 1969, 385). Ablation is also practised in South Africa where the members of the Damara assert that extraction of the central incisors is necessary for pronunciation to be correct (Goose 1963, 91). The ablation amongst the East-Central groups generally involves the mandibular central incisors and occasionally also the lateral incisors. Generally it is bilateral but may involve only one tooth. The rationale behind the procedure is practical, because it leaves a permanent gap in the dental arcade through which liquid can be adminis-

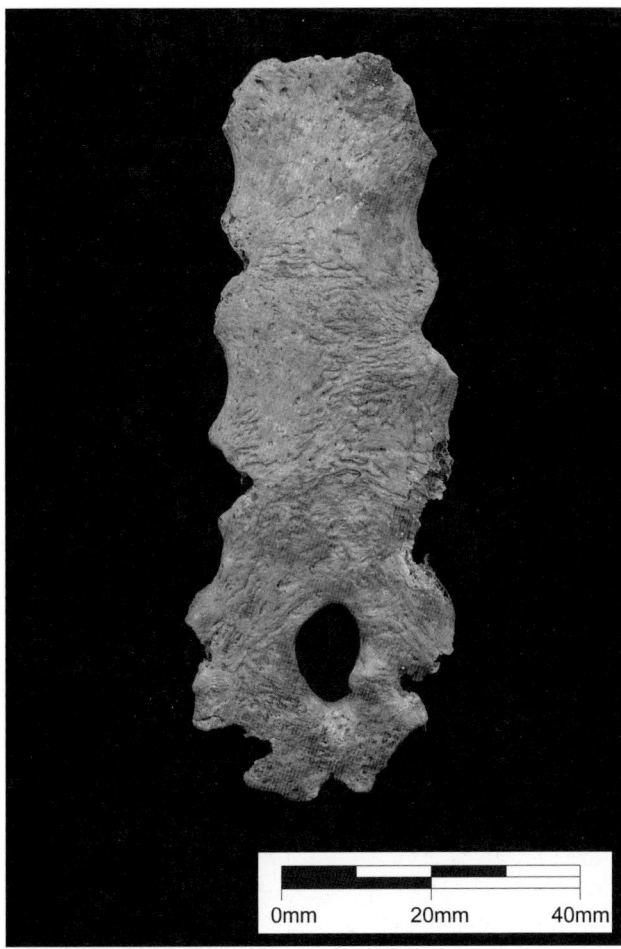

Figure 4.5 Skeleton 220. Sternal foramen

tered in the case of tetanus or other febrile illnesses (Hassanali and Amwayi 1993, 513).

A total of 115 individuals from the Rupert's Valley assemblage had their teeth modified by either chipping or filing (Table 4.7; Fig 4.6). Of the adolescents and adults that could be sexed, 58.01% (76/131) of the males and 37.93% (11/29) females had modified teeth. Only 10.48% of the older children had their teeth modified, the youngest individual being Skeleton 409 who was aged between 8 and 10 years. The percentage of individuals with modifications substantially increases with age and nearly 60% of the Young Adults have modified teeth.

Table 4.7 Age and sex distribution of individuals with culturally modified teeth

	Male/Male?		Female/Female?		Undetermined		Total	
	No.	%	No.	%	No.	%	No.	%
Old Child					11/105	10.48%	11/105	10.48%
Adolescent	5/8	62.5%	2/5	40%	15/37	40.54%	22/50	44%
Young Adult	31/49	62.26%	5/12	41.67%	1/1	100%	37/62	59.68%
Prime Adult	33/59	57.63%	1/7	14.28%			34/66	51.51%
Mature Adult	6/12	50%	3/5	60%			9/17	52.94%
Adult	1/3	3.33%					1/3	33.33%
Total	76/131	58.01%	11/29	37.93%	27/165	16.36%	115/303	37.95%

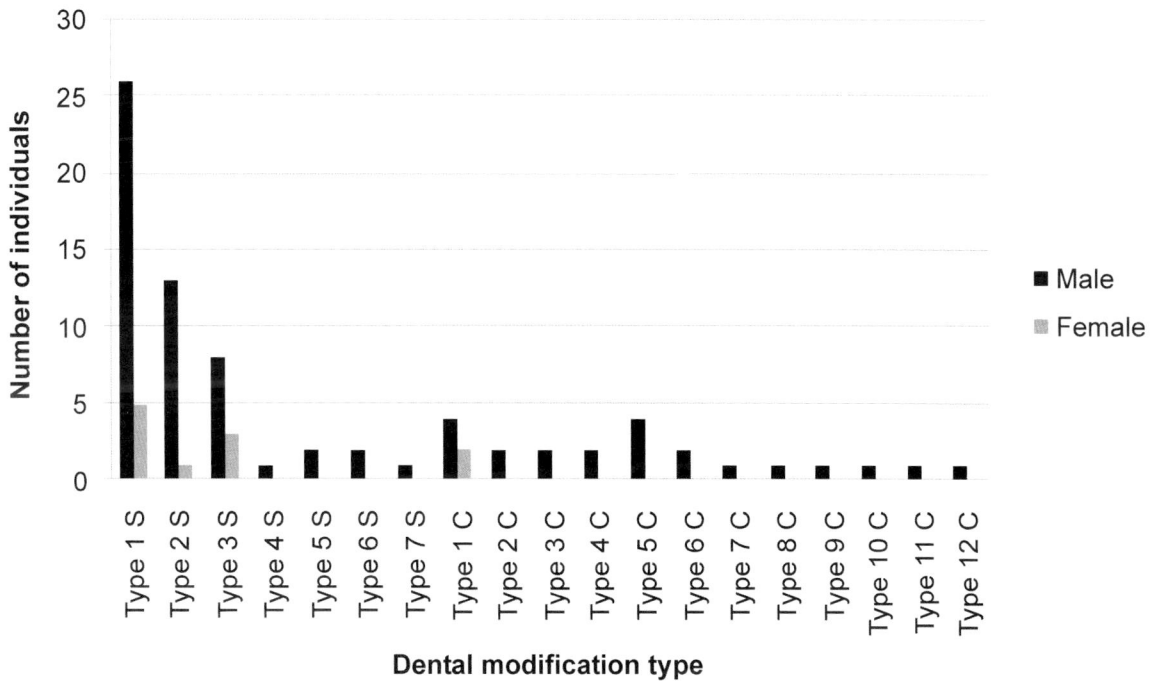

Figure 4.6   Cultural dental modification type and sex distribution

A total of nineteen different modification designs were identified on 113 individuals (Table 4.8). Two individuals had modified central mandibular incisors but the maxillary central incisors had been lost ante-mortem: the original design is therefore unknown and these two individuals have been omitted. The modifications comprise seven simple forms involving only the central maxillary incisors, and twelve complex forms where more than two teeth are modified. The modifications may also be present on just anterior dentition of the maxilla or also the mandibular dentition. The catalogue of dental modifications, accompanied by photographs of each type, can be found at the end of this section.

The most commonly seen design was the inverted V (Type 1 simple form): 47 (41.59%) of all the modifications took this form. Most individuals had designs that only involved the central maxillary incisors and 75.22% were of these types. The more complex forms were often only seen on one individual, but the most common design was the Type 5 complex form, with 5.31% of the modifications being of this type.

Only four designs were present amongst the females, whereas all designs were present amongst the males. Only one of the modification types amongst the females was of the complex form, this being the WW pattern (Type 1 complex form). The most common design amongst both sexes was the inverted V (Type 1 simple form), followed by the inverted U (Type 2 simple form).

A total of seven individuals were identified as having culturally ablated teeth (Table 4.9). Two of these individuals also had filed or chipped maxillary dentition, so it may be that the absent mandibular dentition also contributed to the overall design. In all but a single instance the missing teeth were

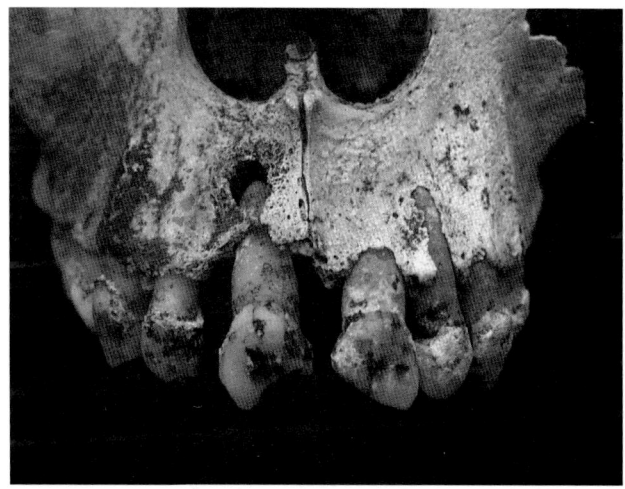

Figure 4.7   Skeleton 237 with modified central maxillary incisors and an associated periapical abscess of the right central incisor

either the central maxillary or mandibular incisors: only one individual, Skeleton 276, had a different pattern in which all the lateral incisors had been removed.

The exposure of the dentine would undoubtedly have made the teeth more sensitive. However, for the majority of the individuals the modifications do not appear to have caused dental problems. A total of 96 individuals with modifications also had the anterior part of the jaw bones present. Of these, 32 (33.33%) individuals had modifications that were so deeply cut that the pulp cavity had been exposed (Fig 4.7). Periapical abscesses were present on 23 individuals (23.96%) that also had teeth with the

Table 4.8 Modification type and sex distribution

	Male/Male?		Female/Female?		Undetermined	
	No.	%	No.	%	No.	%
Type 1 S	26/47	55.32%	5/47	10.64%	16/47	34.04%
Type 2 S	13/17	76.47%	1/17	5.88%	3/17	17.64%
Type 3 S	8/14	57.14%	3/14	21.43%	3/14	21.43%
Type 4 S	1/1	100%				
Type 5 S	2/2	100%				
Type 6 S	2/2	100%				
Type 7 S	1/2	50%			1/2	50%
Type 1 C	4/7	57.14%	2/7	28.57%	1/7	14.29%
Type 2 C	2/2	100%				
Type 3 C	2/3	66.67%			1/3	33.33%
Type 4 C	2/2	100%				
Type 5 C	4/6	66.67%			2/6	33.33%
Type 6 C	2/2	100%				
Type 7 C	1/1	100%				
Type 8 C	1/1	100%				
Type 9 C	1/1	100%				
Type 10 C	1/1	100%				
Type 11 C	1/1	100%				
Type 12 C	1/1	100%				
Total	75/113	66.37%	11/113	9.74%	27/113	23.89%

Table 4.9 Individuals with probable ablated teeth

Skeleton No.	Age	Sex	Teeth
276	Young Adult	Male	All lateral incisors
332	Prime Adult	Male	Mandibular central incisors (Also Type 1 simple modification)
350	Adolescent	Unknown	Mandibular central incisors
353	Prime Adult	Male	Maxillary central incisors
395	Young Adult	Female	Mandibular central incisors (Also Type 1 complex modification)
396	Adolescent	Unknown	Central maxillary incisors
478	Prime Adult	Male	Central maxillary incisors

pulp cavity exposed and three teeth were of a darker colour, signifying tooth death. It is possible that a further five individuals had originally had modified teeth, because both central incisors had been lost ante-mortem due to the presence of abscesses. The maximum number of individuals with modified and/or ablated teeth is therefore 125 individuals.

The Rupert's Valley assemblage contains the largest number of individuals with culturally modified teeth yet to be recovered by archaeological excavation; as such it provides a unique dataset. As discussed above, there are many culturally specific reasons for the modifications to be carried out and these may differ depending on the society. Given that it is not known where these individuals originated

from, it is impossible to draw any specific conclusions regarding the reasons behind or meaning of the modifications that are present within the assemblage. However, the fact that no individuals were younger than 8–10 years chimes with ethno-historical and modern data regarding the time of life at which the procedure was carried out. Some (indeed many) of the individuals may well have had the modifications carried out as part of a coming of age ritual. However, the majority of the adolescents did not have dental modifications, which indicates that there was more than one reason for the tooth alterations.

The data suggest that more males than females had the modifications, but this may simply reflect the paucity of women in the population group rather than a differential cultural practice. It is, however, interesting that there is a wider variety of modifications present amongst the males. Some of the more elaborate styles may have been male-specific and may have carried a deeper meaning beyond that of beautification. For example, the fang-like appearance of Type 4 simple form may have been related to hunter magic, or perhaps was created to make the individual appear more fearsome to the enemy.

Cultural ablated modifications are rare within this population group and only one individual, Skeleton 350, had ablated mandibular central incisors unassociated with modified maxillary incisors. This is a form more commonly seen in Eastern Africa, but such a link between this individual and that part of Africa can only be tentatively suggested.

Scholars have attempted to associate certain designs with specific clans or tribes, but it is clear that some designs are associated with more than one tribe. For example, the Type 3 complex type is present amongst the Bantus (South Africa) and the Mayombe (Congo). Moreover, there may also be more than one design present within a particular tribe. A recent study of 19th-century cranial material from Cameroon of known tribal origin showed that there were three different designs associated with the Dschang; even within this small sample of eleven crania there was variation of design rather than uniformity. One design seen within the Rupert's Valley population, the V-shape (Type 7 simple form), was present amongst the Bali, Bamenda, Batscham, Ossidinge and the Wute (Reichart *et al* 2008, 51).

The modifications on their own, therefore, cannot be used to suggest points of origins for the individuals from Rupert's Valley. However, used in conjunction with biochemical methods it may provide a useful strand of evidence.

Catalogue of dental modifications

Type 1 Simple form
Location: Central maxillary incisors
Description: Inverted V
Method: Chipping

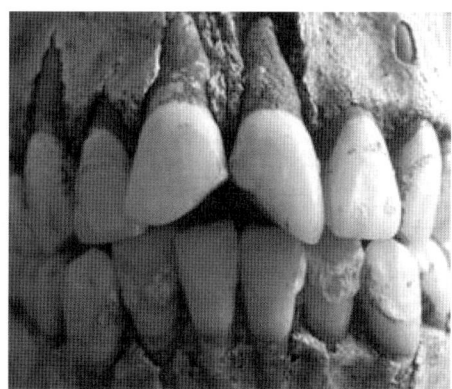

Figure 4.8   Dental modification Type 1 Simple form

Type 2 Simple form
Location: Central maxillary incisors
Description: Inverted U
Method: Filing

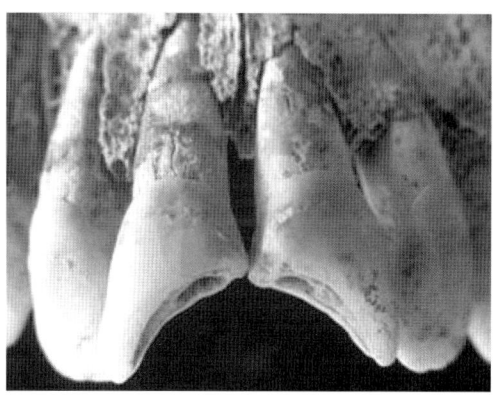

Figure 4.9   Dental modification Type 2 Simple form

Type 3 Simple form
Location: Central maxillary incisors
Description: M shape or squared
Method: Chipping and filing

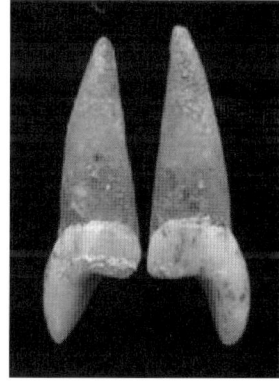

Figure 4.10   Dental modification Type 3 Simple form

Type 4 Simple form
Location: Central maxillary incisors
Description: M shape
Method: Filing

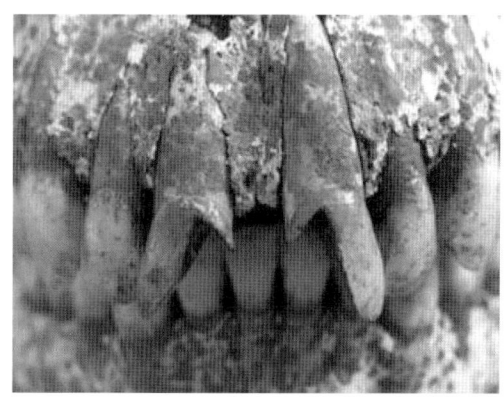

Figure 4.11   Dental modification Type 4 Simple form

Type 5 Simple form
Location: Central maxillary incisors
Description: Central notches
Method: Filing

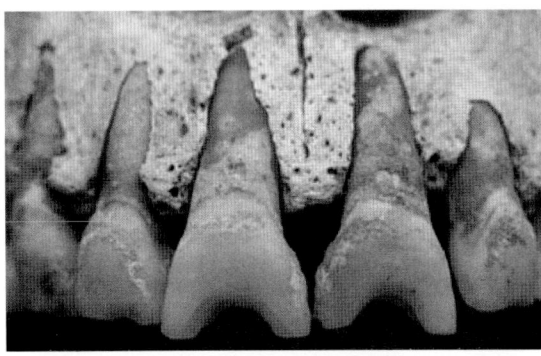

Figure 4.12   Dental modification Type 5 Simple form

Type 6 Simple form
Location: Central maxillary incisors
Description: Inverted V with an incised decorative groove across the labial surface of the crown
Method: Chipping and filing

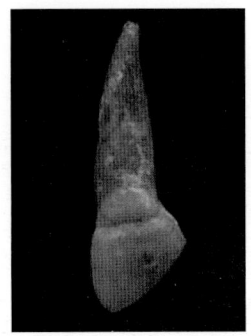

Figure 4.13   Dental modification Type 6 Simple form

Type 7 Simple form
Location: Central maxillary incisors
Description: W shape with the removal of both mesial and distal sides to form a central point
Method: Chipping

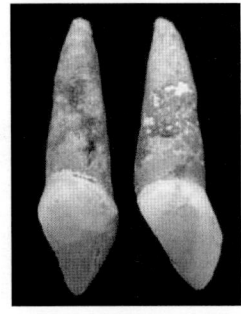

Figure 4.14   Dental modification Type 7 Simple form

Type 1 Complex form
Location: Maxillary central and lateral incisors
Description: WW shape formed by the removal of both mesial and distal sides to form a central point
Method: Chipping

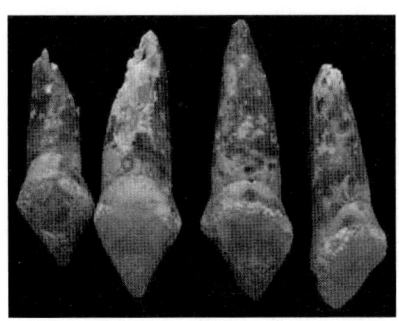

Figure 4.15   Dental modification Type 1 Complex form

Type 2 Complex form
Location: Maxillary central and lateral incisors
Description: Lateral incisors – reduced crown height shaped in a semi-arch with a mesial peak. Central incisors – central notches
Method: Filing

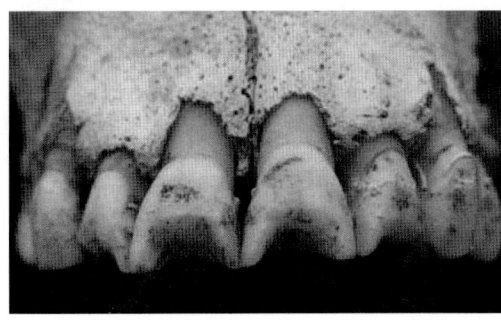

Figure 4.16   Dental modification Type 2 Complex form

Type 3 Complex form
Location: Maxillary central and lateral incisors
Description: Lateral incisors – semi-circular notch that has left the mesial edge intact. Central incisors M shape
Method: Chipping

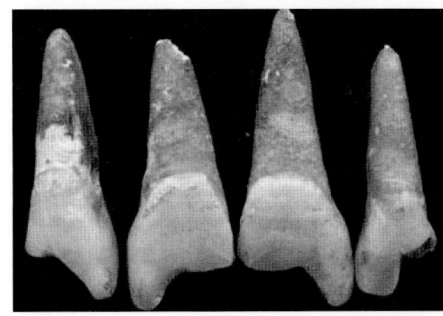

Figure 4.17   Dental modification Type 3 Complex form

Type 4 Complex form
Location: Maxillary central and lateral incisors
Description: Peg shapes where all sides and the height of the crown have been reduced to form rounded pegs at the centre of each crown
Method: Chipping

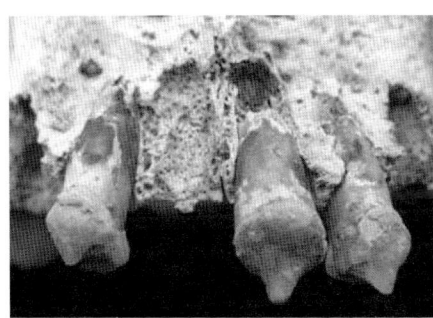

Figure 4.18 Dental modification Type 4 Complex form

Type 5 Complex form
Location: Maxillary and mandibular central incisors
Description: Diamond shape. The mesial corners of the teeth have been removed at an angle
Method: Chipping

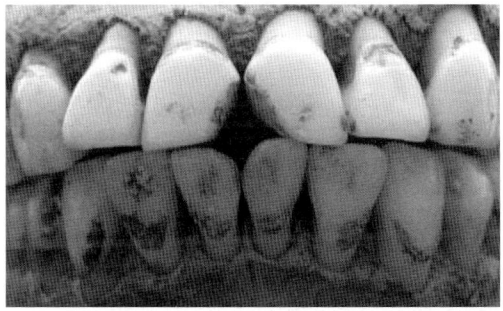

Figure 4.19 Dental modification Type 5 Complex form

Type 6 Complex form
Location: Maxillary central incisors and mandibular central incisors
Description: Inverted U shape of the central maxillary incisors and V shape of the mandibular central incisors
Method: Filing

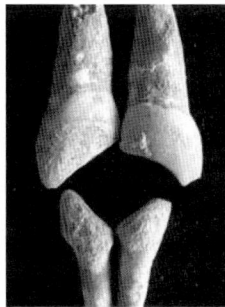

Figure 4.20 Dental modification Type 6 Complex form

Type 7 Complex form
Location: Maxillary central incisors and mandibular central and lateral incisors
Description: Inverted V shape of the central maxillary incisors and WW shape of the mandibular central and lateral incisors
Method: Chipping

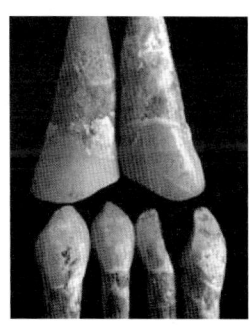

Figure 4.21 Dental modification Type 7 Complex form

Type 8 Complex form
Location: Maxillary central incisors and mandibular central incisors
Description: M shape of the central maxillary incisors and V shape of the mandibular central incisors
Method: Filing

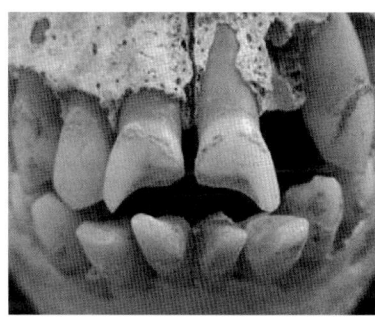

Figure 4.22 Dental modification Type 8 Complex form

Type 9 Complex form
Location: Maxillary central and lateral incisors
Description: Central notches on the maxillary incisors. The lateral incisors are angled to medial points
Method: Filing

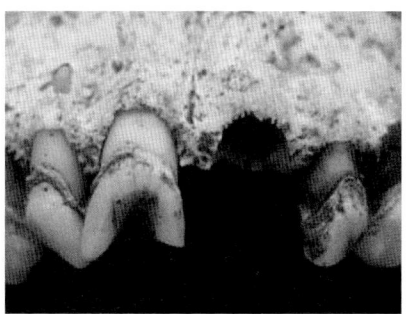

Figure 4.23 Dental modification Type 9 Complex form

Type 10 Complex form
Location: Maxillary central and lateral incisors.
Description: Inverted U shape of the central maxillary incisors. The lateral incisors are modified on both distal and mesial sides to form a V shape.
Method: Filing

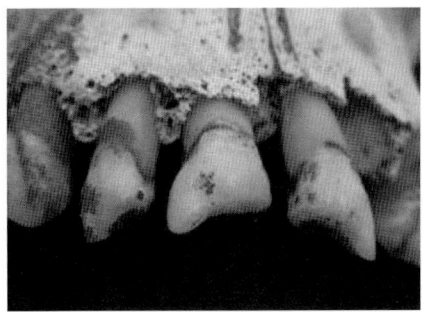

Figure 4.24   Dental modification Type 10 Complex form

Type 11 Complex form
Location: Maxillary central incisors and mandibular central incisors
Description: W shaped central maxillary incisors formed by the removal of both distal and mesial sides to form a central point. V shape of the mandibular central incisors
Method: Filing and chipping

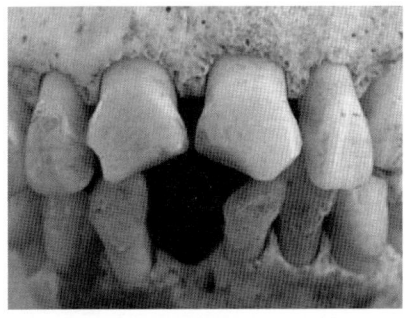

Figure 4.25   Dental modification Type 11 Complex form

Type 12 Complex form
Location: Maxillary central and lateral incisors
Description: Inverted U shape of the central maxillary

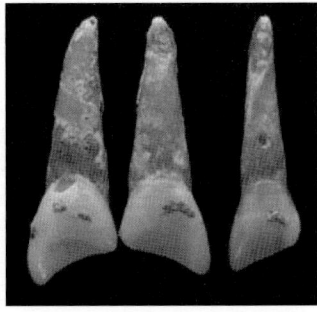

Figure 4.26   Dental modification Type 12 Complex form

incisors. The lateral incisors have been shaped into a semi-arch with the mesial height of the crown intact
Method: Filing

4.3.6   Dental disease

Teeth may provide information regarding aspects of health and lifestyle of the population represented by the sample. For example, caries and calculus may provide insights into oral hygiene and diet. Enamel hypoplasia is an indicator of childhood stress and other practices may also provide information regarding cultural behaviour.

Of the 325 individuals present, 310 had some dentition. A total of 8552 permanent teeth (includes loose, unerupted, partially erupted, impacted, super-numary and broken teeth, and roots only) and 485 deciduous teeth (includes erupting and unerupted/developing crowns) were recorded. There were also 226 sockets recorded where the tooth had been lost post-mortem.

4.3.6.1   Dental caries

Dental caries is defined as a destruction of the enamel, dentine and the cement. It is caused by the fermentation of sugar, especially sucrose, by bacteria in dental plaque (Roberts and Manchester 1995, 46). It is classified as an infectious disease that is also transmissible and is ultimately progressive (Hillson 1996, 269). The formation of a cavity is dependent upon poor oral hygiene, the presence of acid-producing bacteria, and to a certain extent the shape of the tooth (Roberts and Manchester 1995, 46). For example, cavities are often formed in pits and fissures on the occlusal surface of the molars where food debris can be trapped.

A total of 142 carious lesions (121 on permanent and 21 on deciduous dentition) were recorded on 59 individuals. A total of 42 individuals had multiple cavities and the highest incidence of caries was recorded on Skeleton 422 who had 12 cavities. The majority of these were classified as large (more than half the crown destroyed). The prevalence shows that 19.47% of the individuals (omitting the unaged adults and neonatal remains) had one or more cavity (Table 4.10). The highest rate was amongst the mature adults. The caries rate was much higher amongst the adult females, at 50% (11/22), than the adult males, at 20% (24/120).

The overall prevalence of caries per tooth was 1.77% (142/8020). There was a prevalence of 1.59% (121/7584) cavities amongst the permanent dentition and a slightly higher rate of 4.82% (21/436) amongst the deciduous dentition. Of the permanent dentition, a total of 48 teeth had one or more cavity. On the mandibular teeth, all but one was situated on the molars. The location of the caries on the maxillary dentition was very similar and 18 of the 21 teeth with cavities were molars.

Table 4.10 The prevalence of caries per age group

Age Group	Number of individuals	% of individuals
Young Child	5/16	31.25%
Old Child	12/101	11.88%
Adolescent	7/47	14.89%
Young Adult	16/60	26.67%
Prime Adult	12/63	19.05%
Mature Adult	7/16	43.75%
Total	59/303	19.47%

Table 4.11 The prevalence of abscesses per age group

Age Group	Number of individuals	% of individuals
Adolescent	3/47	6.38%
Young Adult	16/60	26.67%
Prime Adult	22/63	34.92%
Mature Adult	4/16	25%
Total	45/186	24.19%

The higher caries rate in females may possibly reflect a higher intake of dietary sugar. However, clinical studies have shown that females have a higher caries rate than males (Hillson 2000, 261). The higher rate here may also be due to the small sample size of females. The overall prevalence of caries is very low; this is likely to be indicative of a diet low in sucrose, and the youthfulness of the population group (since the rate of caries is known to increase with age).

4.3.6.2 Dental abscesses

A dental abscess can occur when the pulp cavity of a tooth is exposed by caries, attrition or trauma. The ensuing inflammation allows pus to form which may track to the apex of the root. This accumulation of pus causes a build up of pressure and eventually a hole may form through the bone that allows the pus to escape (Hillson 1996, 284–5).

There were a total of 81 abscesses present on 45 individuals. The majority of the abscesses were found in the young and prime adult age categories, together with three adolescents (Table 4.11). Of the adults that were sexed and had dentition present, 38.09% (8/21) of the females and 28.33% (34/120) of the males had abscesses.

The vast majority of abscesses, 72.83% (59/81), were situated on the maxilla and the majority of all abscesses, 53.09% (43/81), were located on the central maxillary incisors. Most, if not all of these, were associated with the dental cultural modifications.

4.3.6.3 Calculus

Dental plaque consists of a build up of micro-organisms on the enamel surface. The plaque bacteria mainly derive their nutrients from saliva, but starches and sugars also increase the rate of accumulation (Hillson 1996, 254). Calculus is mineralised plaque that builds up at the base of living plaque deposits and these deposits are most prevalent at the sites of the saliva ducts which are the lingual surface of the anterior dentition and the buccal surface of the molars (Hillson 1996, 255). There are two types of calculus, supragingival (above the gum) and subgingival (below the gum), the former being the most common (Roberts and Manchester 1995, 55). Accumulation of calculus is generally related to poor oral hygiene.

A total of 293 individuals of the 303 individuals aged over 1 year with dentition present had calculus deposits (Table 4.12). When the individuals are sub-divided into their age categories and the unaged adults are omitted, nearly 97% have calculus present. Just over half of all the young children (56.25%) have calculus present and all individuals older than 12 years of age have calculus.

A total of 46.79% (204/436) deciduous teeth (includes in situ and loose teeth) had calculus deposits present (Fig 4.27). Slightly more maxillary teeth had calculus deposits, 48.70% (112/230), compared to the mandibular teeth where 44.66% (92/206) had calculus present. Almost all the calculus deposits were present on the molars and the majority of the deposits on both jaws were small. There was also a higher prevalence of medium to

Table 4.12   The prevalence of calculus per age group

Age Group	Number of individuals	% of individuals
Young Child	9/16	56.25%
Old Child	98/101	97.03%
Adolescent	47/47	100%
Young Adult	60/60	100%
Prime Adult	63/63	100%
Mature Adult	16/16	100%
Total	293/303	96.69%

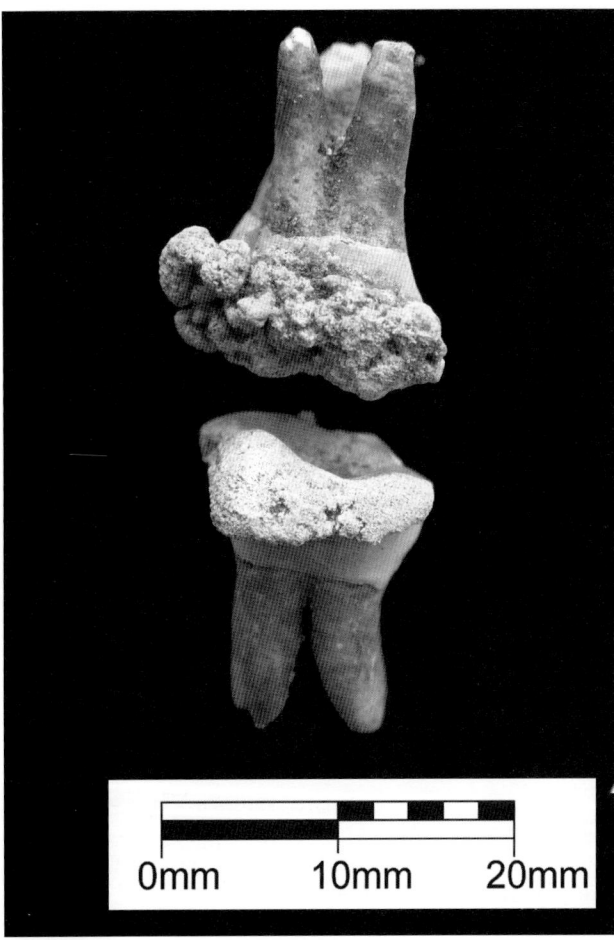

Figure 4.27   Skeleton 417. Right maxillary and mandibular first molars with considerable calculus deposits

considerable deposits on the maxillary dentition (Table 4.13).

Most of the permanent teeth present (includes in situ, loose, broken supernumerary and those classified as roots-only teeth), 78.09% (5984/7663), had calculus deposits present. There was a slightly higher prevalence of calculus on the mandibular dentition, 79.47% (3065/3857), than on the maxillary dentition which had a rate of 76.69% (2919/3806). There was also a higher prevalence of larger deposits on the mandibular dentition where 41.76% had been recorded as medium or considerable and most of these were located on the anterior dentition (Table 4.14).

4.3.6.4   Periodontal disease

Periodontitis is the last stage of an inflammation that involves the gingivae and the alveolar bone. This causes morphological changes to the alveolar margin which initially becomes flattened with a slightly raised rim and, as the disease progresses, the margin becomes rounded and finally ragged and porous. The sockets are widened which loosens the teeth and may ultimately progress to their loss (Ogden 2008, 293). Modern studies have shown that children before puberty are rarely affected and that there is a gradual increase in the proportion of the population affected with the increase of age. Most studies have also shown that the disease is more common in males (Hillson 1996, 266–7). The aetiology is multi-factorial and inheritance, environment, diet and hygiene all play a part in the development of the disease (Hillson 1996, 269).

A total of 39 individuals had evidence of periodontal disease and when subdivided by the number of individuals with dentition present this provides a prevalence of 13.59%. The disease was recorded on both jaws on 22 individuals, on the mandible only on 13 individuals, and on the maxilla only on 5 individuals. Table 4.15 shows that the prevalence of the disease increases with age, with nearly half of the mature adults having periodontitis. Unusually, however, two individuals aged between 7 and 12 years also had periodontitis. The aetiology for these two individuals (Skeleton 230 and Skeleton 390) and also the adolescent Skeleton 350 is metabolic disease. All three individuals had skeletal changes associated with scurvy. This affected both jaws on Skeleton 230 and Skeleton 350, but was only observed on the mandible of Skeleton 390. The most severe lesions, grade 3, were also present on Skeleton 250.

4.3.6.5   Ante-mortem tooth loss

Ante-mortem tooth loss may be the end result of various disease processes such as abscesses and periodontitis. The loss of a tooth may also be caused by trauma or it may have been deliberately removed due to a disease such as caries. Teeth may also be

Table 4.13 Calculus deposit size per tooth, deciduous dentition

Jaw	Mandible (92 teeth)						Maxilla (112 teeth)					
Size	Small		Medium		Large		Small		Medium		Large	
Tooth	No.	%	No.	%	No.	%	No.	%	No.	%	No.	%
a	0	0%	0	0%	0	0%	1	0.89%	0	0%	2	1.79%
b	0	0%	0	0%	0	0%	1	0.89%	0	0%	0	0%
c	9	9.78%	1	1.09%	0	0%	20	17.86%	3	2.68%	2	1.79%
d	25	27.17%	5	5.43%	1	1.09%	20	17.86%	2	1.79%	1	0.89%
e	41	44.57%	4	4.35%	6	6.52%	34	30.36%	19	16.96%	7	6.25%
Total	75	81.52%	10	10.87%	7	7.61%	76	67.86%	24	21.43%	12	10.71%

Table 4.14 Calculus deposit size per tooth, permanent dentition

Jaw	Mandible (3065 teeth)						Maxilla (2919 teeth)					
Size	Small		Medium		Large		Small		Medium		Large	
Tooth	No.	%	No.	%	No.	%	No.	%	No.	%	No.	%
1	183	5.97%	128	4.18%	140	4.57%	277	9.49%	85	2.91%	28	0.96%
2	204	6.66%	121	3.95%	130	4.24%	277	9.49%	87	2.98%	29	0.99%
3	249	8.12%	118	3.85%	73	2.38%	260	8.91%	94	3.22%	25	0.86%
4	264	8.61%	107	3.49%	30	0.98%	294	10.07%	87	2.98%	20	0.69%
5	242	7.90%	87	2.83%	25	0.82%	269	9.22%	79	2.71%	29	0.99%
6	287	9.36%	113	3.69%	52	1.70%	266	9.11%	143	4.90%	57	1.95%
7	229	7.48%	62	2.02%	39	1.27%	240	8.22%	71	2.43%	23	0.79%
8	127	4.14%	35	1.14%	20	0.65%	125	4.28%	40	1.37%	14	0.48%
Total	1785	58.24%	771	25.15%	509	16.61%	2008	68.79%	686	23.50%	225	7.71%

Table 4.15 The prevalence of periodontitis per age group

Age Group	Number of individuals	% of individuals
Old Child	2/101	1.98%
Adolescent	1/47	2.13%
Young Adult	10/60	16.67%
Prime Adult	19/63	30.16%
Mature Adult	7/16	43.75%
Total	39/287	13.59%

deliberately removed for cultural reasons and this would generally involve the canines and incisors (Pindborg 1969, 383). Ante-mortem tooth loss is usually associated with advancing age but a diet rich in sugar and poor oral hygiene may also play an important part in the loss of dentition (Manchester 1983, 51).

A total of 36 individuals had ante-mortem loss of at least one tooth with the highest prevalence in the Mature Adult age group (Table 4.16). More females (29.19%) had suffered from tooth loss than males (18.70%). This difference in sexes may, however, be due to the comparatively low number of females present.

There was no difference in the loss of teeth between the jaws: 1.49% (47/3146) of the maxillary dentition compared to 1.46% (44/3020) of the mandibular dentition had been lost ante-mortem. The most frequently lost teeth were the maxillary central incisors followed by the mandibular central incisors and the first molars (Table 4.17). The most likely cause for the loss of the molars was caries since the irregular shape of the occlusal surface can easily trap food particles that may lead to cavities. Moreover, most of the caries were also located on the molars. The underlying cause of the ante-mortem loss of the anterior dentition is most likely to have been abscesses, especially when consider-

Table 4.16 The prevalence of ante-mortem tooth loss per age group

Age Group	Number of individuals	% of individuals
Old Child	1/101	0.99%
Adolescent	5/47	10.64%
Young Adult	8/60	13.33%
Prime Adult	16/63	25.40%
Mature Adult	6/16	37.50%
Total	36/287	12.54%

Table 4.17 Prevalence of ante-mortem tooth loss per tooth

Tooth	Maxilla		Mandible		Maxilla and Mandible	
	No.	%	No.	%	No.	%
1 (central incisor)	20	42.55%	12	27.27%	32	35.16%
2 (lateral incisor)	4	8.51%	9	20.46%	13	14.29%
3 (canine)	0	0%	1	2.27%	1	1.10%
4 (first premolar)	2	4.25%	1	2.27%	3	3.30%
5 (second premolar)	4	8.51%	3	6.82%	7	7.69%
6 (first molar)	9	19.16%	10	22.73%	19	20.88%
7 (second molar)	5	10.64%	4	9.09%	9	9.89%
8 (third molar)	3	6.38%	4	9.09%	7	7.69%
Total	47	100%	44	100%	91%	100%

ing the high prevalence of abscesses on the anterior maxillary dentition. However, some teeth may also have been deliberately extracted to form part of a designed dental modification.

4.3.6.6 Dental anomalies

There are several anomalies that are either developmental or genetically based variations that can permanently affect the dentition. The number of teeth present may be too great (hyperdontia); these may be situated, and erupt, in a relatively normal position (normotopic). The overall prevalence of supernumerary teeth in a modern population is 1.9% (Suzuki *et al* 1995, 174). Supernumerary teeth may also be formed by the retention of deciduous dentition. Fewer than the normal 32 teeth may also occur (hypodontia) and the most common tooth to be affected is the third molar (Ortner 2003, 597). The shape of the tooth is also susceptible to variation and may affect supernumerary teeth or those normally present in the dental arcade: for example, third molars or the lateral incisors may be peg-shaped. Overcrowding of the dentition may also occur where the jaw bone, typically the mandible, is not large enough to give adequate space for each tooth, causing them to overlap. This is typically seen in the anterior dentition and may also cause teeth

to become impacted. The most commonly impacted tooth is the third molar, followed by the canine (Hillson 1996, 113). One other irregularity of the dental arcade is rotation, which may be caused by overcrowding and can affect more than one tooth, commonly the single-rooted teeth.

A total of seven individuals (7/310, 2.26%) had twelve supernumerary teeth between them. Seven of these were present on the maxilla and most of the supernumerary teeth comprised the molars: two individuals had four extra molars between them and these were all maxillary. The second most common supernumerary tooth was the canine and one individual, Skeleton 359, had bilateral supernumerary premolars (Fig 4.28). There was also a retained deciduous canine present on Skeleton 367.

Hypodontia was present on two individuals, who had three teeth missing between them. A further ten individuals were recorded as having twelve impacted teeth. The third molar was most commonly impacted (9/12) followed by the second premolar and the canine. A total of 21 teeth on eleven individuals were recorded as 'not present'. All but one of these involved the third molar. The teeth that were recorded as not present may have been congenitally missing, impacted or lost ante-mortem. The latter is unlikely considering the low rate of ante-mortem tooth loss within this population. Without radiographic evidence it is not possible to differentiate

Figure 4.28   Skeleton 359. Bilateral supernumary premolars

between the teeth that may be impacted or missing due to hypodontia within this category.

A total of ten teeth in eight individuals were recorded as peg-shaped. The majority of the malformed teeth were present on the maxilla (8/10) and seven of the teeth involved the lateral maxillary incisors. The remainder were third molars. Teeth that were rotated more than 45° were recorded. These amounted to eleven teeth on seven individuals with just over half present on the mandible. The second premolar was most commonly rotated (6/10), followed by the canine and the central incisor.

4.3.6.7   Enamel hypoplasia

Enamel hypoplasia is a defect that arises from periods of non-specific stress which cause the growth of the tooth to arrest temporarily. Upon resumption of growth, a line is left as a permanent record and each period of stress produces a new line. The lines therefore reflect disturbances to the growth of the tooth that happened before the age of 12. The defect is most commonly linear but may also appear as furrows or pits. The development of hypoplastic defects has been linked to periods of childhood diseases such as rubella, chickenpox and rickets.

Nutritional stress has also been linked to the development of these defects (Hillson 1996, 166). The number of enamel hypoplasias recorded amongst these individuals is likely to be an under-representation of the actual number of teeth with the defect because the lines may have been obscured by heavy calculus deposits. Ante-mortem tooth loss may also have somewhat reduced the prevalence.

Enamel hypoplasia was seen in 67 (22.11%) individuals, with the highest prevalence amongst the adolescents (Table 4.18). The number of individuals in Table 4.18 is based on the number of individuals with fully erupted dentition present, excluding the unaged adults. There was little difference in the prevalence between the sexes with 20.83% of the females and 22.76% of the males having hypoplasia. All the defects recorded were linear and were present on 5.02% (381/7592) of the number of permanent teeth which excluded roots, broken, unerupted, and developing teeth. The majority of the teeth had fewer than two lines (92.9%) and the remainder had more than three lines. The lines were most commonly observed on the canine (39.63%), followed by the central incisors (17.32%).

4.3.7   Palaeopathology

4.3.7.1   Congenital anomalies

Congenital anomalies are the result of developmental defects in the soft tissue and/or the skeleton during gestation. These defects may become apparent at birth or years later, and some 40% of these affect the skeleton (Roberts and Manchester 1995, 31). There are a great number of skeletal malformations and these vary from mild defects that would have caused no problem to the individual to the very severe that would be incompatible with life, such as anencephaly (failure of brain and skull vault development). The more severe forms of abnormalities are rarely seen in past populations, possibly due to the child dying in infancy because of the defect, as well as the comparatively poor survival rate of neonatal bones (Aufderheide and Rodríguez-Martín 1998, 52). The defects present amongst the individuals buried at Rupert's Valley were all mild, and most were situated in the spine.

Table 4.18   The prevalence of enamel hypoplasia per age group

Age Group	Number of individuals	% of individuals
Young Child	4/16	25.00%
Old Child	20/101	19.80%
Adolescent	15/47	31.91%
Young Adult	16/60	26.67%
Prime Adult	9/63	14.29%
Mature Adult	3/16	18.75%
Total	67/303	22.11%

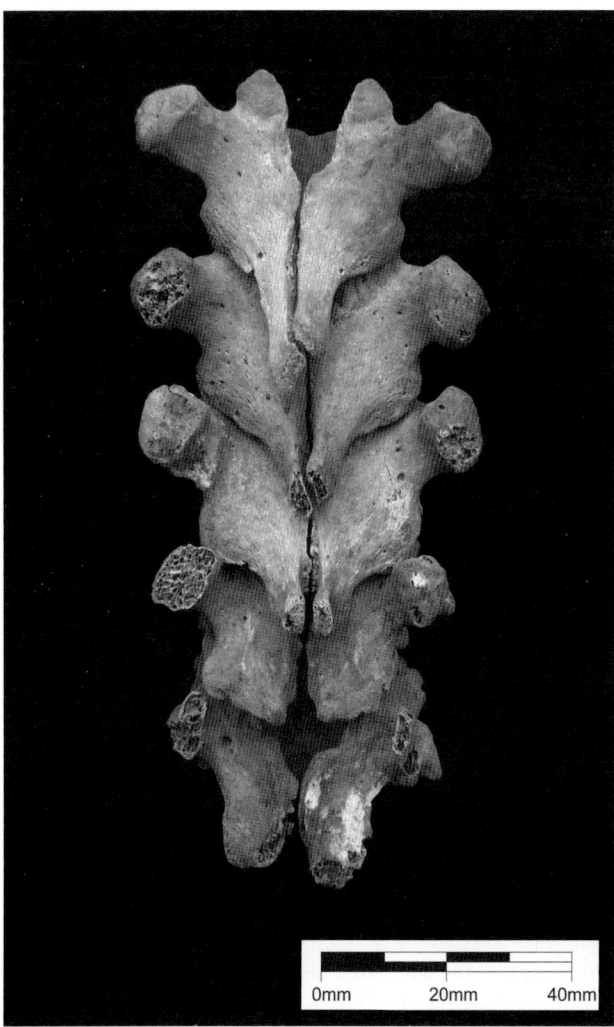

Figure 4.29   Skeleton 520. Cleft vertebral arches of T8 to T12

Figure 4.30   Skeleton 279. Sacrum with partial sacralisation

Spinal anomalies

Defects of the spine are relatively common and comprise the largest group of defects seen within this population group. Cleft vertebral arches is a minor defect that would have been asymptomatic since the two halves would have been joined by fibrous tissue (Barnes 2008, 346). This defect was present on sixteen individuals aged over 6 years (5.28%) and a total of 29 (0.61%) vertebral segments were affected. All of the individuals with this anomaly that could be sexed were male (10/131, 7.6%), comprising two adolescents and eight adults. Multiple vertebrae were involved on two individuals, Skeletons 350 and 520 (Fig 4.29), and ten cleft neural arches were present on Skeleton 350. Most of the anomalies were present in thoracic vertebrae (17/2331, 0.73%) but the most commonly affected vertebral element was the atlas and five were recorded with a cleft posterior arch.

Spina bifida occulta, a cleft defect on the sacrum, was present on two individuals which provides a prevalence of 1.54% (2/130) based on the number of adults with a sacrum present. Both were adult males and the prevalence based on the total number of adult males with a sacrum present was 1.85% (2/108). This is a mild defect that does not produce any pathological symptoms.

The normal number of vertebral segments is seven cervical, twelve thoracic and five lumbar vertebrae. Variation of the normal number of vertebral segments was present in two individuals, 1.01% (2/198). The prevalence is based on the total number of adults and adolescents present. The individuals comprised an adult male and an unsexed adolescent, both of whom had an extra thoracic segment. This condition would not have caused any health problems.

Fusion of two vertebral bodies, a block vertebra, was recorded on one adult male (1/123, 0.81%). The elements involved were the seventh cervical and the first thoracic vertebrae.

A relatively common anomaly is shifting of the lumbosacral border. This takes the form of sacralisation, where the fifth lumbar segment has become part of the sacrum and the sacrum consists of six segments instead of five, or lumbardisation, where the first sacral element has taken on the appearance of a lumbar vertebra and the sacrum now comprises four segments. Either condition can be bilateral or unilateral (Barnes 2008, 342). Of the total number of adults and adolescents, sacralisation was present on three individuals (3/198, 1.51%) (Fig 4.30). All were adult, of whom two were male (2/123, 1.62%)

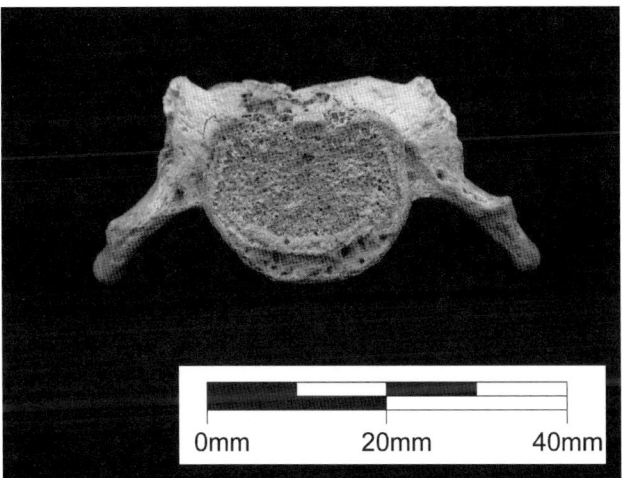

Figure 4.31 Skeleton 342. C7 with bilateral cervical ribs

and one was female (1/24, 4.17%). Four individuals (4/198, 2.02%), two unsexed adolescents and two adult males, had lumbardisation.

Cervical ribs are more commonly found than lumbar ribs and are usually present on C7 but may also occur on C5 and C6. These are more common on females and there is some evidence of a genetic predisposition (Black and Scheuer 1997, 3). The size of the ribs can vary from small rudimentary forms to fully formed ribs; today about one-third of individuals with cervical ribs also present symptoms. These symptoms are caused by the rib compressing the lower trunk of the brachial plexus, which may cause vascular or neurological problems such as pain and paralysis of the hand (Black and Scheuer 1997, 3–4). Cervical ribs were recorded on three C7 (3/187, 1.60%); all were male (3/123, 2.44%). The presence of the ribs was identified by small articular facets or by the presence of the rib itself (Fig 4.31). All appear to have been very small and are therefore unlikely to have caused any symptoms.

One bifid sternal end of the first rib was recorded on one individual (1/303, 0.33%).

Extra-spinal anomalies

Fusion of the lunate and the triquetrum was present on two adult individuals (2/148, 1.35%), both of whom were male (2/123, 1.62%). These were present in the right wrist of both individuals.

Os acromiale is a minor developmental defect. This occurs when the acromion fails to unite to the scapular spine during the late teens and a fibrous joint develops between the two bones instead (Barnes 2008, 353). The anomaly can be either bilateral or unilateral. However, there is some ambiguity associated with this condition and the presence of *os acromiale* can be recorded as a non-metric trait. It may also be related to occupational behaviour. A higher than normal frequency has been recorded in

two medieval population groups with identifiable occupations (Knüsel 2000, 115; Stirland 2000, 121). Knüsel (2000) suggests that the joint formed is an osseous adaptation in the shoulder during growth and development, arising from strenuous movement, and that it can be associated with archery and the use of projectiles in general. Stirland (2000) also associates the high prevalence with archery. *Os acromiale* was present on ten adult individuals (10/148, 6.76%) and all were male (10/123, 8.13%). The condition was bilateral on two individuals and present on seven left (7/139, 5.03%) and five (5/143, 3.50%) right scapulae. Since the prevalence is comparable to that recorded by Knüsel and Stirland it is tempting to associate the *os acromiale* with the habitual practice of projectile weaponry. It is possible some of these individuals may have been warriors or hunters, but this suggestion must be regarded as speculative.

Symphalangism, the congenital absence of the distal interphalangeal joint, is a hereditary trait that is more common in the foot than in the hand (Case and Heilman 2005, 254). It is most frequently observed on the digit of the fifth metatarsal, followed by the fourth and the third. The prevalence based on the number of individuals with the condition present amongst modern skeletal material of Afro-American ancestry was 44% for the fifth digit, 7.9% for the fourth digit and 2.1% for the third digit (Case and Heilman 2005, 257).

There were 34 fused distal and proximal pedal phalanges recorded amongst the skeletons from Rupert's Valley. In the majority of the cases the pedal digit was unknown: only four were known to be of the fifth digit and two from the fourth. The condition was present on nineteen adult individuals (19/148) which provided a prevalence of 12.84%. However, distal pedal digits were recorded on 85 left and 79 right feet and symphalangism was present on 11 left and 17 right feet. This provides a prevalence of 12.95% and 21.52% respectively, of which the mean is 17.24%. The prevalence of the number of digits affected is 7.07% (14/198) for the left foot and 9.84% (19/193) for the right foot. This is based on the number of distal phalanges present. The figures are not comparable to the modern data since the precise digit is not known and not all pedal digits were recovered. Moreover, an unspecified small number of what was recorded as symphalangism may have been caused by trauma. The figures presented here are therefore tentative.

One unsided manual digit was also recorded as having symphalangism, this belonging to an adolescent. The area of the distal joint shows no sign of a fracture nor is there a callous present. However, although trauma is unlikely, it cannot be completely ruled out as an alternative explanation for this lesion.

One young child, Skeleton 438, had bilateral retarded growth of the humeri. The proximal epiphyses were fused prematurely and the shafts are slightly bowed and thickened. The overall

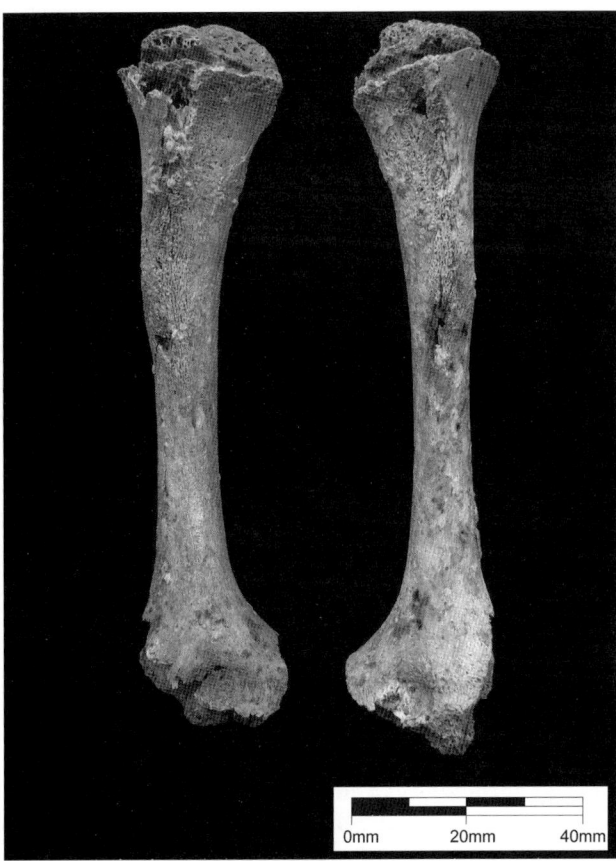

Figure 4.32   Skeleton 438. Anterior view of stunted humeri with premature fusion of the heads

growth of the skeleton was retarded and the lengths of the long bones are much shorter than expected for this age group. However, this individual also had scurvy and rickets which may account for the overall retarded growth. The morphological changes of the humeri may not be related to these conditions and the premature fusion of the humeral heads could be due to a developmental condition (Fig 4.32).

A further malformed humerus belonged to an adolescent male (Skeleton 200). The right proximal metaphysic was flattened anterio-posteriorly and the medial side had slipped inferiorly, thus making the metaphysic elongated and flared. The surviving epiphysis was also elongated and flattened and was fusing prematurely. The glenoid fossa was not present and no morphological changes could be ascertained. The true aetiology of the lesion is not known, partly due to extensive post-mortem damage to the area. The underlying aetiology may be a developmental condition or possibly trauma.

4.3.7.2 Trauma

Trauma may be defined as an injury to the body caused by an outside force or mechanism (Roberts and Manchester 1995, 65; Lovell 1997, 139). The causes may be deliberate or accidental violence, or cultural cosmetic practices, while fractures can also be caused by an underlying pathological condition (Ortner 2003, 119).

Soft tissue trauma

Soft tissue trauma can be identified when the soft tissues such as muscles, tendons and ligaments have ossified in response to an injury. This often happens in association with a haematoma, and the condition myositis ossificans traumatica is more common in the young (Ortner 2003, 133–4).

Two adult male individuals (2/123, 1.62%) had slight enthesophyte formations at the muscle attachment points. These were present on the soleus line, the attachment for the soleus muscle on a right tibia (1/130, 0.77%) and on the medial edge of the linea aspera, the attachment point for the vastus medialis, on the left femur (1/143, 0.70%). Both lesions were slight and probably represent damage caused by muscle strain.

Fractures

Fractures were present on a total of 21 individuals which provided a crude prevalence of 6.93% (Table 4.19). The prevalence amongst the subadults was 3.22% (5/155) and 10.81% (16/148) amongst the adults. The highest rate of fractures was present amongst the prime adults, 16.67%. The highest prevalence of fractures was seen amongst the males in the adolescent age group and in the prime females at 25% and 28.58% respectively. However, this high figure is likely to be due to the small number of individuals within these categories. There was really no difference of the crude fracture rate between the sexes, where there were 10.69% males and 10.34% females with fractures present.

Out of the total of 28 fractures recorded, four were cranial fractures (Table 4.20). Three of these comprised depressed fractures on the parietals (3/600, 0.5%): these fractures were caused by a blunt force, either accidental or deliberate. The remaining cranial trauma was a fractured right zygomatic arch of a male (1/305, 0.33%). The depressed cranial vault fractures were present on an adult male and two subadults: all were healed.

The fractures of the spine were due to compression in all but one vertebra, and the majority were situated in the lumbar region (0.48%). The compression fractures were all present in the lower half of the spine with the most common element being the second lumbar. The underlying aetiology of three of the fractures present on two individuals was metabolic disease. Osteomalacia had caused buckling of L2 and L4 in an adult female, Skeleton 365, and Skeleton 375, an older child, had scurvy, a condition which can cause osteopenia and the subsequent collapse of vertebral bodies (Brickley and Ives 2008, 103). One of the vertebral fractures involved

Table 4.19 Crude prevalence of number of fractures per age group and sex

Age group	% of individuals	% of males	% of females
Older Child	2.8% (3/105)	–	–
Adolescent	4% (2/50)	25% (2/8)	0.00% (0/5)
Young Adult	4.84% (3/62)	4.08% (2/49)	0.00% (0/12)
Prime Adult	16.67% (11/66)	15.25% (9/59)	28.57% (2/7)
Mature Adult	11.76% (2/17)	8.33% (1/12)	20% (1/5)
Adult	0.00% (0/3)	0.00% (0/3)	0.00% (0/0)
Total	6.93% (21/303)	10.69% (14/131)	10.34% (3/29)

Note: The % of individuals column includes unsexed skeletons; this accounts for the seeming discrepancy in the Young Adult row

Table 4.20 Fracture prevalence per skeletal element

Fracture site	Side	Number of bones	Prevalence
Parietal	Left	1/301	0.33%
Parietal	Right	2/299	0.67%
Temporal	Right	1/305	0.33%
Thoracic	–	4/2331	0.17%
Lumbar	–	5/1030	0.48%
Rib	Left	4/2853	0.14%
Rib	Right	3/2773	0.11%
Femur	Left	2/312	0.64%
Tibia	Left	1/303	0.33%
Metacarpal 4	Right	1/225	0.44%
Proximal pedal phalanx	Right	3/745	0.40%
Intermediate pedal phalanx	Left	1/320	0.31%

the lamina and a fracture line was situated inferior to the left superior articular surface.

A total of seven ribs were fractured (7/5626, 0.12%). The fractures were present on three male adults and the prevalence for adult ribs only was 0.24% (7/2943). There were multiple fractures on two individuals and these were healed on Skeleton 249. Four of the fractures were healing at the time of death: three of these were on the long bones.

Three fractures were present on the long bones which comprised two left femora (0.64%) and one intra-articular fracture of the lateral condyle on proximal left tibia (0.33%) (Table 4.20). The two femoral shaft fractures included a possible fracture of an older child. Both fractures were healed and longstanding with minimal callous formation.

Only one fracture was present on the hands and this was situated on the shaft of a right fourth metacarpal on an adult male. This fracture was not united though the presence of a callus indicated that this fracture was healing. There were more fractures of the toes and these were all intra-articular. Three of these were on the proximal pedal phalanges and one on the intermediate.

The distal end of the distal phalanx of the right first pedal digit was largely missing and only the proximal end of the bone was present on Skeleton 423. There is evidence of new bone formation on the distal phalanx and increased porosity at the joint area. The bone may be absent due to traumatic accidental amputation with secondary infection (Fig 4.33).

Sharp force trauma

A possible sharp force trauma lesion was present on a right scapula blade (1/143, 0.70%) of an adult male (1/123, 0.81%) (Skeleton 292). The lesion was situated inferior to the spine and the area had suffered from extensive post-mortem damage. However, a small area where the edges had survived suggested that the lesion had been produced by a narrow blade. The edges of the lesions bevelled anteriorly and new bone formation was present on both the anterior and posterior surfaces around the lesion itself.

Possible evidence of violence: unhealed lesions

Four individuals had traumatic lesions that were healing and these are listed in Table 4.21. The mac-

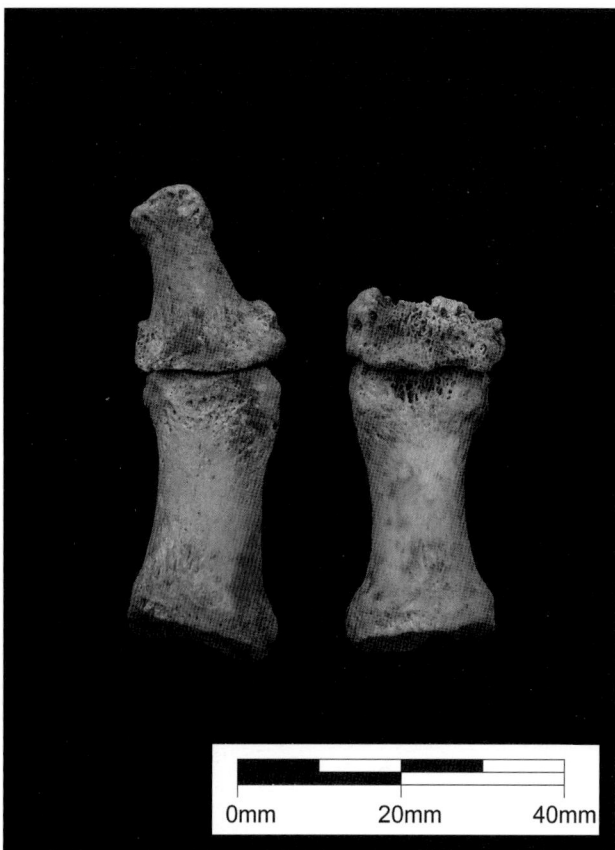

Figure 4.33   Skeleton 423. Left and right phalanges for the first pedal digit. Possible traumatic amputation and secondary infection of the distal right phalanx

Figure 4.34   Skeleton 234. Visceral surface of three left ribs, with healing rib fractures

roscopic evidence of healing is first visible after about two weeks. However, rates of healing vary depending on the location of the fracture, the age of the individual and also the general health of the individual. Fractures in young children heal faster than in adults and certain pathological conditions such as metabolic disorders may also delay healing (Ortner 2003, 126–8) It is therefore not possible to ascertain exactly when the trauma occurred but it is likely to have been in the last few weeks prior to the death of the individual.

Most rib fractures are caused by direct blows or a fall (Lovell 1997, 259). The exact locations of the fractured ribs could not be determined since they were fragmented. However, it was clear these were from the mid-chest region. This is consistent with the evidence that most rib fractures occur between the fifth and the ninth rib (Lovell 1997, 159). The

rib fracture on Skeleton 220 was situated on the anterior part of the shaft, near the sternal end. This indicates that the blow was received on the left side of the body (Lovell 1997, 159). The three right rib fractures of Skeleton 234 were present on body fragments and it was therefore not possible to ascertain where the force was applied (Fig 4.34). A fracture located in the mid-chest region may cause serious complications such as pneumothorax and haemothorax (Brickley 2006, 71).

The fracture of the right fourth metacarpal of Skeleton 235 appeared to be transverse, which is indicative of a direct trauma (Fig 4.35). A transverse fracture such as this can be produced by a relatively small force delivered to a small area (Lovell 1997, 141).

Any of the healing fractures and the sharp force trauma lesion may have been produced accidentally; this cannot be discounted. However, one needs

Table 4.21   Individuals with healing traumatic lesions

Skeleton Number	Age	Sex	Trauma
220	Prime Adult	Male	Rib fracture
234	Prime Adult	Male	Rib fractures (3)
235	Prime Adult	Male	Fractured fourth metacarpal
292	Prime Adult	Male	Sharp force trauma to the scapula

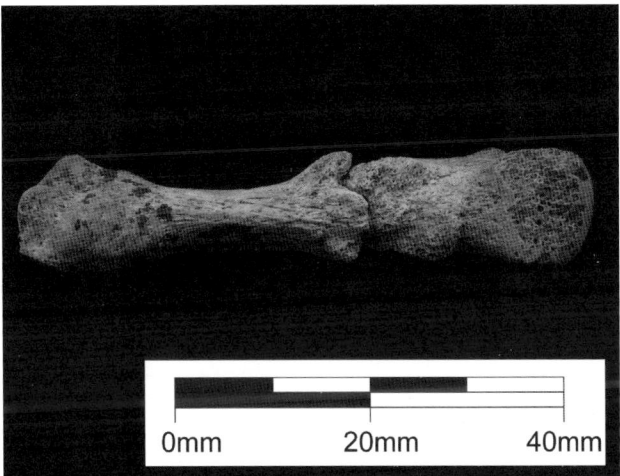

Figure 4.35 Skeleton 235. Palmar view of right fourth metacarpal with healing fracture at mid-shaft

to consider the additional evidence, that these individuals had spent a certain amount of time on board a slave ship where violence was used as a means of control. Also, these were all men and those most likely to cause insurrection on board. As such, the rib fractures were likely to have been sustained by direct blows to the torso. The location of the injury of the hand is consistent with a defensive manoeuvre where the hand and arm is raised to head height in order to provide protection to the head from blows from above. The sharp force trauma may indicate that the individual was stabbed in the back or may have been pushed against a sharp object. These injuries, therefore, probably provide first-hand evidence of the violence that pervaded life on board a slave ship.

4.3.7.3 Circulatory disorders

Osteochondritis dissecans involves the fragmentation of the cartilage and the underlying bone and is caused by a disruption of the blood supply. The underlying aetiology is usually trauma and it is more common in males than in females, with the lesion occurring primarily in adolescence (Ortner 2003, 126–8). The necrotic bone fragment may remain loose in the joint: it can be absorbed or heal

back onto the defect (Roberts and Manchester 1995, 87).

A total of five individuals (5/198, 2.5%), all male (5/131, 3.8%) and adults, apart from one adolescent, had lesions that were consistent with osteochondritis dissecans. The lesions were present on six bones and the most common location was on the patella (2/252, 0.79%) (Table 4.22).

4.3.7.4 Neoplastic disease

A tumour arises from uncontrolled cellular growth (Aufderheide and Rodríguez-Martin 1998, 371). A benign tumour comprises a lesion that is well defined and also remains localised (Ortner 2003, 503).

A button osteoma was present on one adult female individual (1/148, 0.68%). This benign neoplasm was located on the occipital bone (1/142, 0.70%).

A further three possible neoplastic lesions will be mentioned here (Figs 4.36 to 4.38). The lesions were all situated on the anterior border, at mid-shaft, on two left and one right tibia (3/268, 1.12%). All individuals were adults, and consisted of two females and one male. The lesions comprise a build up of cortical bone and they may be consistent with osteoid osteoma. This type of benign tumour is most commonly located in the long bones, specifically the femur and tibia (Ortner 2003, 506). Alternatively, the hyperostosis may have been caused by an exogenous stimulus such as trauma. The bone of the anterior tibia is only protected by the skin and would therefore be highly susceptible to such damage. The left tibia of Skeleton 278 (adult female) also had an intra-articular fracture of the lateral condyle which was healed. It may be that the two lesions are related and the lesions may therefore be secondary to trauma.

4.3.7.5 Joint disease

The most commonly recorded type of joint disease is caused by degenerative change. This is the gradual deterioration of synovial joints with the advancement of age. Osteoarthritis is the most common skeletal pathology recorded on human skeletal remains (Waldron 2009, 26). This disease involves the formation of new bone around the edges of the

Table 4.22 Osteochondritis dissecans prevalence per skeletal element (adults and adolescents)

Fracture site	Side	Number of bones	Prevalence
Femur	Right	1/181	0.55%
Patella	Left	1/114	0.88%
Patella	Right	1/138	0.72%
Talus	Left	1/174	0.57%
First metatarsal	Left	1/154	0.65%
Proximal pedal phalanx	Right	1/519	0.19%

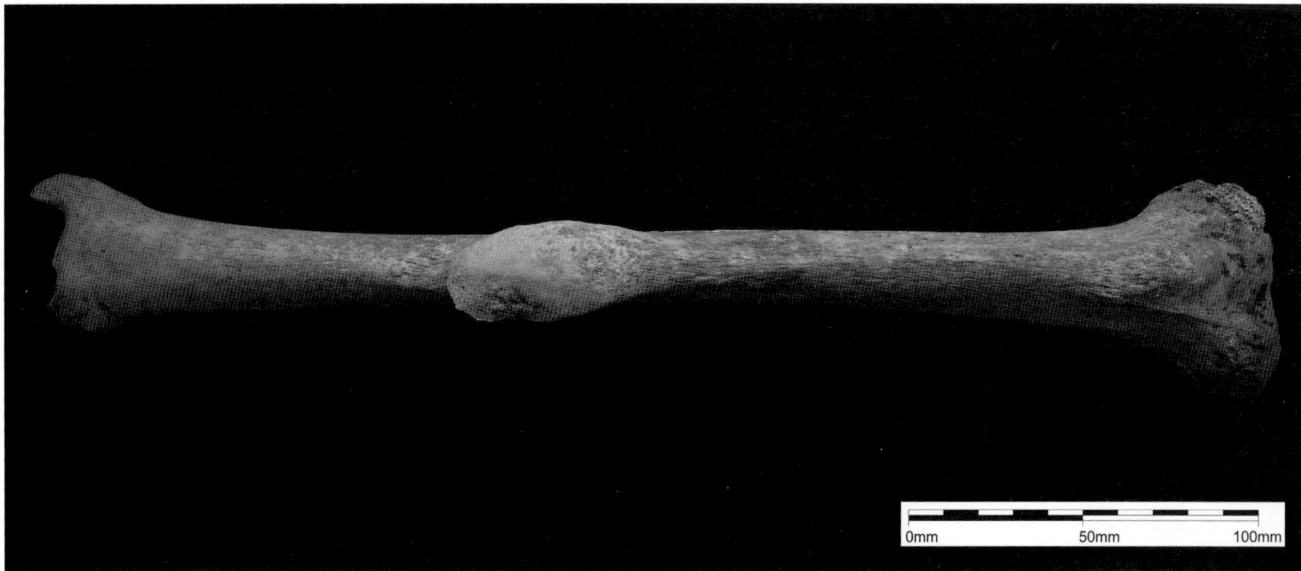

Figure 4.36   Skeleton 211. Possible osteoid osteoma at mid-shaft of left tibia

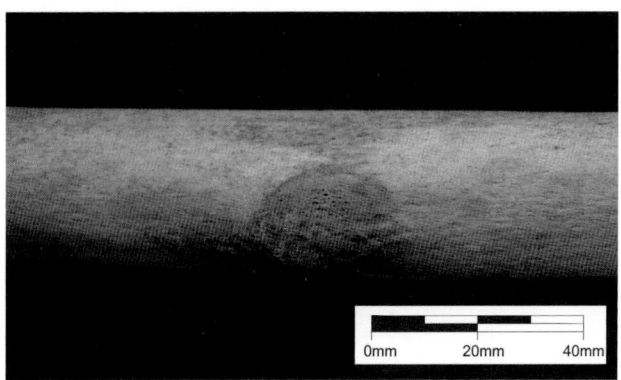

Figure 4.37   Skeleton 278. Possible osteoid osteoma at mid-shaft of left tibia

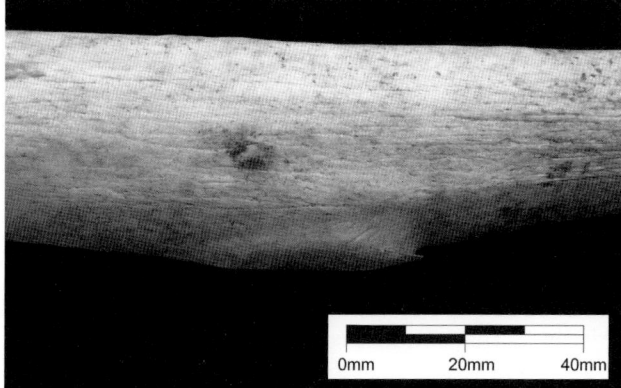

Figure 4.38   Skeleton 347. Possible osteoid osteoma at mid-shaft of right tibia

joint, pitting of the joint surface, changes in the normal joint morphology, and eburnation (Roberts and Manchester 1995, 101–3). Eburnation is a highly polished surface which signifies bone-to-bone contact after the cartilage has been destroyed. The condition is non-inflammatory and is more common in females than in males; the prevalence of the condition increases with age.

Extra-spinal joint disease

Only ten adults (10/148, 6.76%) had osteoarthritis (OA). These comprised six males (6/123, 4.87%) and four females (4/24, 16.67%) (Table 4.23). The gross prevalence is about the same amongst the young and prime adults (4.91% and 4.54%), but as expected more individuals in the mature adult age category (17.65%) had the condition. Again as would be expected, the prevalence of osteoarthritis in males shows a steady increase through the age categories. However, this trend is not apparent

amongst the females, probably on account of the low sample number.

The true prevalence presented in Table 4.24 shows that the degenerative condition was more common in the upper limb than the lower, with the elbow and wrist joints being the most affected. Only one joint was affected in the lower limb – the knee.

Spinal joint disease

Intervertebral disc disease is characterised by pitting of the surfaces of the body and marginal osteophyte formations (Rogers and Waldron 1995, 27). The prevalence increases with age and is rarely seen in individuals below the age of 40 (Waldron 2009, 43).

A total of 16.33%% (24/147) of sexed adults had intervertebral disc disease (Table 4.25). The prevalence increased by age and 29.41% of the mature adults had the condition. There were more females than males with this disease, although this may just

Table 4.23 Crude prevalence of osteoarthritis

| | Young Adult | | Prime Adult | | Mature Adult | | Total | |
	No.	%	No.	%	No.	%	No.	%
Male	1/49	2.04%	3/59	5.08%	1/12	8.3%	6/123	4.87%
Female	2/12	16.67%	0/7	0%	2/5	40%	4/24	19.67%
Total	3/61	4.91%	3/66	4.54%	3/17	17.65%	10/147	6.80%

Table 4.24 Prevalence of osteoarthritis per joint

Bone	Side	No. of bones with OA	No. of bones observed	Prevalence
Scapula	R	1	143	0.70%
Humerus (distal)	L	2	129	1.55%
Radius (distal)	L	1	125	0.80%
Ulna (Proximal)	L	2	118	1.69%
Ulna (distal)	L	1	96	1.04%
Ulna (Proximal)	R	1	116	0.86%
Scaphoid	R	1	106	0.94%
Trapezium	L	1	103	0.97%
Trapezium	R	1	91	1.10%
Triquetrum	L	1	90	1.11%
Metacarpal 1	L	1	122	0.82%
Metacarpal 1	R	2	126	1.59%
Metacarpal 5	R	1	123	0.81%
Femur (distal)	L	1	128	0.78%
Patella	L	1	112	0.89%

Table 4.25 Crude prevalence of intervertebral disc disease

| | Young Adult | | Prime Adult | | Mature Adult | | Adult | | Total | |
	No.	%	No.	%	No.	%	No.	%	No.	%
Male	2/49	4.08%	13/59	22.03%	1/12	8.3%	3/3	100%	19/123	15.45%
Female	0/12	0%	4/7	57.14%	4/5	80%	0/0	0%	8/24	33.33%
Total	2/61	3.28%	17/66	25.75%	5/17	29.41%	3/3	100%	27/147	18.37%

be a reflection on the low number of females present in this population group.

A total of 113 vertebral segments were recorded with pitting of the surface and marginal osteophyte formations. This is a small percentage of 3.43% (113/3292) which is likely to reflect the youthful demographic profile. The condition was recorded at all spinal levels apart from T1. The highest prevalence was in the lower thoracic and the lumbar region (Fig 4.39). The majority (90/113, 79.65%) of the osteophytes were recorded as small and only three (2.65%) were considerable in size. The remaining 20 (17.70%) were moderate in size.

Spinal osteoarthritis was recorded on three individuals (3/148, 2.03%), all being prime adult males

(3/59, 5.08%). Diagnostic eburnation was located on the joint surfaces of one T4 (1/137, 0.73%) and two L5 (2/136, 1.47%) vertebrae.

Schmorl's nodes

Schmorl's nodes are indentations on the vertebral bodies that are formed by the herniation of the intervertebral disc through the end plate. These have been found to be particularly common on individuals who exert considerable stress on their lower spine (Waldron 2009, 43).

Schmorl's nodes were found on eighteen adult males (18/123, 14.63%); none of the females had the

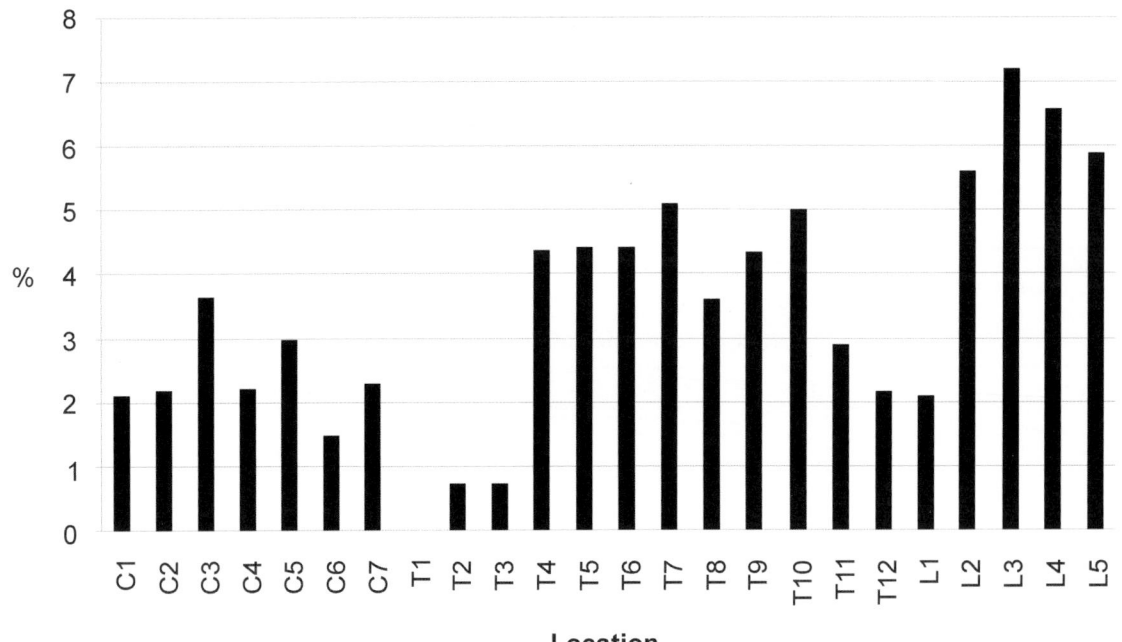

Figure 4.39   Prevalence of intervertebral disc disease per vertebra

Table 4.26   Crude prevalence of Schmorl's nodes

	Young Adult		Prime Adult		Mature Adult		Adult		Total	
	No.	**%**	**No.**	**%**	**No.**	**%**	**No.**	**%**	**No.**	**%**
Male	7/49	14.28%	9/59	15.25%	2/12	16.67%	0/3	0.00%	18/123	14.63%

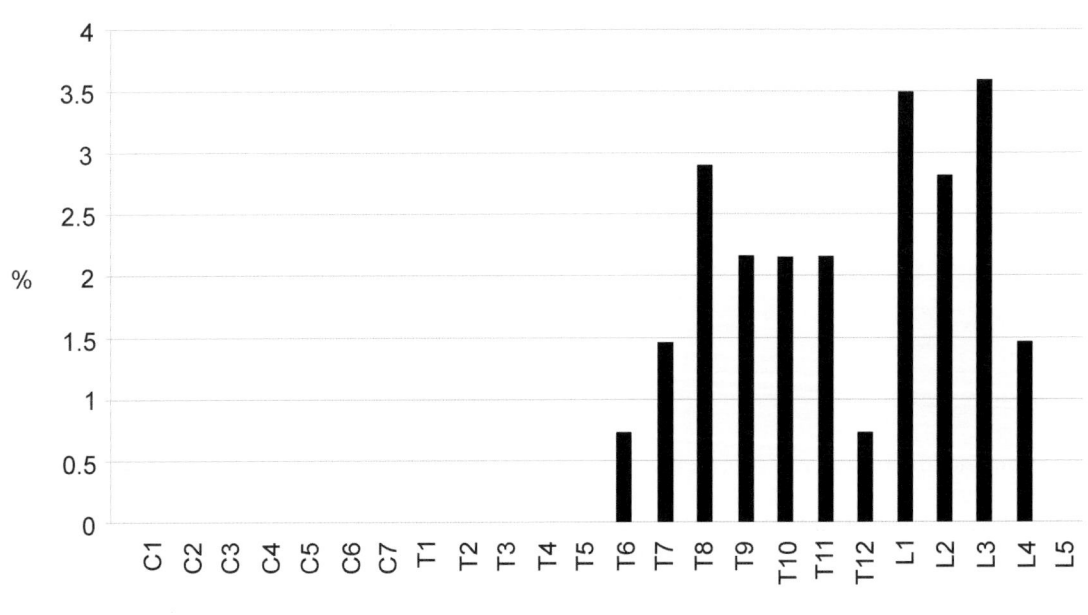

Figure 4.40   Prevalence of Schmorl's nodes

condition. There was no marked difference of the gross prevalence when comparing the different age groups, with a rate of between 14.28% and 16.67% (Table 4.26).

The prevalence per vertebral segment was greatest amongst the lumbars and specifically L1 and L3. There was also a relatively high prevalence of Schmorl's nodes present on T8 (Fig 4.40).

Table 4.27 Crude prevalence of periostitis per age group and sex

Age group	% of individuals	% of adult males	% of adult females
Young Child	5.56% (1/18)	–	–
Old Child	11.43% (12/105)	–	–
Adolescent	12% (6/50)	0% (0/8)	0% (0/5)
Young Adult	37.10% (23/62)	34.69% (17/49)	41.67% (5/12)
Prime Adult	36.36% (24/66)	40.67% (24/59)	0% (0/7)
Mature Adult	52.94% (9/17)	50% (6/12)	60% (3/5)
Adult	100% (3/3)	100% (3/3)	–
Total	24.29% (78/321)	38.17% (50/131)	27.59% (8/29)

Table 4.28 Prevalence of periostitis per bone type

Bone	Side	No. of bones with periostitis	No. of bones observed	Prevalence
Mandible	–	1	144	0.69%
Clavicle	L	1	274	0.36%
Clavicle	R	1	273	0.37%
Scapula	L	1	275	0.36%
Humerus	R	1	308	0.32%
Radius	L	2	291	0.69%
Radius	R	1	286	0.35%
Ulna	L	2	281	0.71%
Ulna	R	1	290	0.34%
Ilium	R	1	140	0.71%
Sacrum	R	1	265	0.38%
Femur	L	18	312	5.79%
Femur	R	17	293	5.80%
Tibia	L	48	303	15.84%
Tibia	R	54	287	18.81%
Fibula	L	7	282	2.48%
Fibula	R	10	287	3.48%

4.3.7.6 Infectious disease

Non-specific infection

Periostitis is the term used for a non-specific inflammation of the bone surface caused by infection. This involves the formation of a layer of new bone on the cortical surface, which as new bone appears woven, and over time remodels into striated lamellar bone. The presence of the lesions has been used for studies of non-specific infections in past populations, but there is overwhelming evidence that periostitis may also be caused by other conditions and new bone formation may be stimulated by anything that breaks, stretches or even touches the periosteum (Weston 2008, 49). Periostitis may be part of metabolic conditions such as rickets and specific infections such as syphilis, but is also a specific condition in itself (Ortner 2003, 208).

Periostitis was present on 24.29% (78/321) of the individuals aged over 1 year (Table 4.27). The greatest prevalence was amongst the adults, and specifically in the mature adult category. There was little difference in the prevalence between the sexes, where there was a 10.58% greater rate amongst the males compared to the females. The prevalence was comparatively low amongst the children aged below 12 years where 10.56% (13/123) had periostitis.

A total of 167 individual bones had periostitis and the true prevalence per bone is presented in Table 4.28. The majority of the lesions were situated in the long bones of the upper and lower limbs, and specifically in the lower limbs. The most common bone that was involved was the tibia with a combined left

Table 4.29   Crude prevalence of rib lesions per age group and sex

Age group	% of individuals	% of males	% of females
Young Child	0% (0/18)	–	–
Old Child	2.86% (3/105)	–	–
Adolescent	2% (1/50)	12.5% (1/8)	0% (0/5)
Young Adult	8.06% (5/62)	8.16% (4/49)	8.33% (1/12)
Prime Adult	3.03% (2/66)	0% (0/59)	28.57% (2/7)
Mature Adult	0% (0/17)	0% (0/12)	0% (0/5)
Adult	33.33% (1/3)	33.33% (1/3)	–
Total	3.74% (12/321)	4.58% (6/131)	10.34% (3/29)

Table 4.30   Crude prevalence of maxillary sinusitis per age group and sex

Age group	% of individuals	% of males	% of females
Young Child	50% (3/6)	–	–
Old Child	19.48% (15/77)	–	–
Adolescent	28.21% (11/39)	57.14% (4/7)	25% (1/4)
Young Adult	16.67% (9/54)	18.18% (8/44)	11.11% (1/9)
Prime Adult	21.05% (12/57)	23.53% (12/51)	0% (0/6)
Mature Adult	31.25% (5/16)	36.36% (4/11)	20% (1/5)
Adult	0% (0/2)	0% (0/2)	–
Total	21.91% (55/251)	24.35% (28/115)	12.50% (3/24)

Note: The totals are based on the number of individuals that had one or more maxillary sinus cavity present, including those that could not be examined. Unsexed adults are included within the totals in the percentage of individuals column

and right prevalence of 17.29% (102/590). The vast majority of the lesions were recorded as striated lamellar bone and 6.59% (11/167) were either active new woven bone or mixed active and healed.

New bone formation on the visceral surface denotes a pulmonary infection and has been associated with tuberculosis; it is also found in other pulmonary diseases such as bronchiectasis and pneumonia (Roberts *et al* 1994, 180–1). A total of twelve individuals (12/321, 3.74%) had new bone formation on the visceral surfaces of at least one rib and the lesions were active on eleven of these individuals. The infection was more prevalent amongst the younger individuals and nine were younger than 26 years; three of these were in the old child category (Table 4.29). The sexed individuals comprised six males (4.58%) and three females (10.34%). A slightly higher number of left ribs (33/2853, 1.16%) than right ribs (25/2773, 0.90%) were affected.

Osteitis is a term often used to denote an infection which also involves the cortex of the bone. Three individuals (3/321, 0.93%) had osteitis: these comprised one prime adult (1/66, 1.52%) who was male (1/131, 0.76%) and two children aged between 7 and 12 years (2/105, 1.90%). The bones affected comprised a left tibia (1/303, 0.33%), a right fifth metacarpal (1/215, 0.46%) and one left fifth metatarsal (1/210, 0.48%).

A non-specific infection that also involves the medullary cavity of the bone is known as osteomyelitis. This infection may be caused by a direct wound that affects either just the soft tissues or also the bone itself. The infection may also have been spread via the blood stream from a distant septic wound (Ortner 2003, 181). Only one individual (1/321, 0.31%) had osteomyelitis, a child aged between 7 and 12 years (1/105, 0.95%). The infection was present in a left tibia (1/303, 0.33%).

Maxillary sinusitis may be caused by respiratory disease and is related to numerous factors that can be subdivided into outdoor conditions (eg pollen allergy, smoke from fires, cold and wet weather) and indoor conditions (eg damp housing, dust mites, animals and open fires) (Roberts 2007, 792). The detection of maxillary sinusitis in human skeletal remains requires fragmented crania that allow the sinus cavities to be examined (Fig 4.41). The gross prevalence is provided for the population as a whole and includes the individuals with at least one sinus cavity present. However, the figure also includes the complete crania where the sinus cavity could not be observed. The prevalence is therefore likely to be somewhat deflated. A total of 55 individuals (55/251, 21.91%) had lesions consistent with maxillary sinusitis and the condition affected 24.35% of the males and 12.50% of the females (Table 4.30).

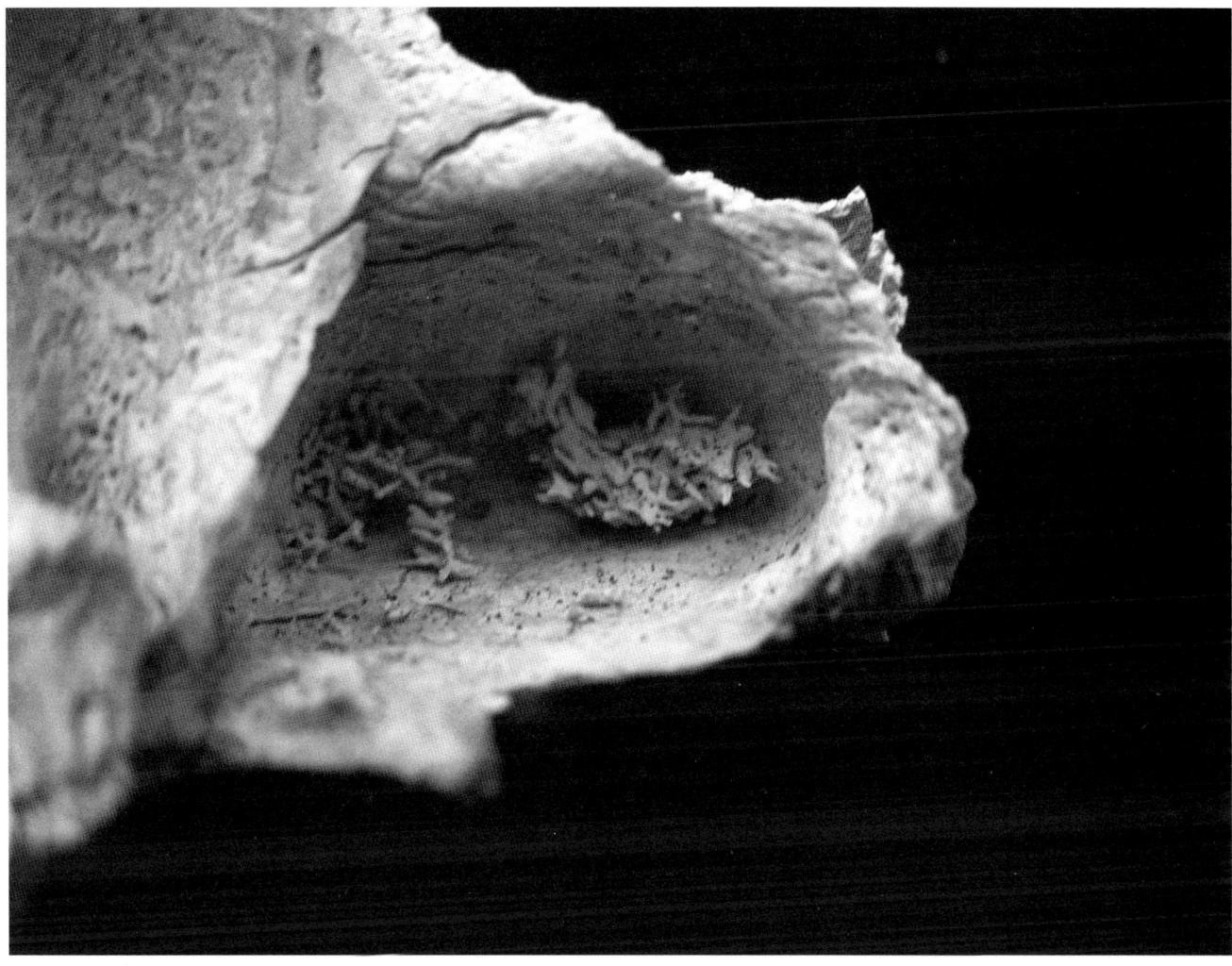

Figure 4.41   Skeleton 223. Bone deposits at the base of the left maxillary sinus cavity

Specific infection

Treponemal infections are global and comprise four types: venereal (acquired) syphilis; bejel (endemic syphilis); yaws; and pinta.

The first three types produce pathological skeletal changes. However, the manifestations and the skeletal distribution of these lesions are near identical, which makes it virtually impossible to differentiate osteologically between these diseases (Ortner 2003, 274). Venereal syphilis is sexually transmitted and is not limited to a specific geographical zone. The infection primarily affects young individuals between the ages of 15 and 30 years (Aufderheide and Rodríguez-Martín 1998, 158). The non-venereal types of treponemal infections are limited to specific climatic zones: bejel is mostly found in subtropical northern Africa, the Near East and temperate Asia, whereas yaws is found in the tropical regions of western and equatorial Africa, Latin America, the Caribbean, south-east Asia and northern Australia (Aufderheide and Rodríguez-Martín 1998, 155–7). Both diseases occur in childhood, with the peak incidence between 2 and 10 years of age (Aufderheide and

Rodríguez-Martín 1998, 155–7). Around 5–15% of individuals who contract yaws develop bone lesions and the bone most frequently affected is the tibia, which is also often bowed (Ortner 2003, 275). Other bones that may display thickening of the cortex are, in descending order of frequency: fibula, femur, ulna, humerus, spine, clavicle, hand, foot, ribs and pelvis (Ortner 2003, 275). The skeletal distribution of the pathological lesions seen in bejel is the same as in yaws.

There were nine (9/321, 2.80%) individuals who displayed lesions consistent with treponemal disease (Table 4.31). These comprised 1.90% (2/105) of the children aged between 7 and 12 years, 6% (3/50) of the adolescents, 4.84% (3/62) of the young adults and 1.51% (1/66) of the prime adults. The lesions were observed only on adult males and 3.25% (4/123) were affected All individuals had tibial involvement. The tibiae were generally primarily thickened on the medial side of the shaft but cortical expansion could be evident on all sides, whilst bowing was also present in some individuals (Fig 4.42). Concentric cortical expansion was present on all other long bones, including clavicles and ribs.

The lesions and their distribution are consist-

Table 4.31   Age, sex and the bones affected by treponemal infection

Skeleton No.	Age	Sex	Skeletal involvement
208	Young Adult	Male	Tibiae, femora, humeri, ulnae, radii, clavicles, scapulae, ilium, ribs
264	Old Child	–	Tibiae, fibulae, femora, humeri, radii, ulnae, illia, ribs and right metacarpals 2–4
349	Old Child	–	Tibiae
351	Adolescent		Tibiae, fibulae and ulnae
371	Adolescent	–	Tibiae and distal third of femoral shafts
389	Young Adult	Male	Tibiae
492	Young Adult	Male	Tibiae
502	Prime Adult	Male	Tibiae and fibulae
507	Adolescent		Tibia, fibula, distal half of femora, humeri, ulnae and clavicles

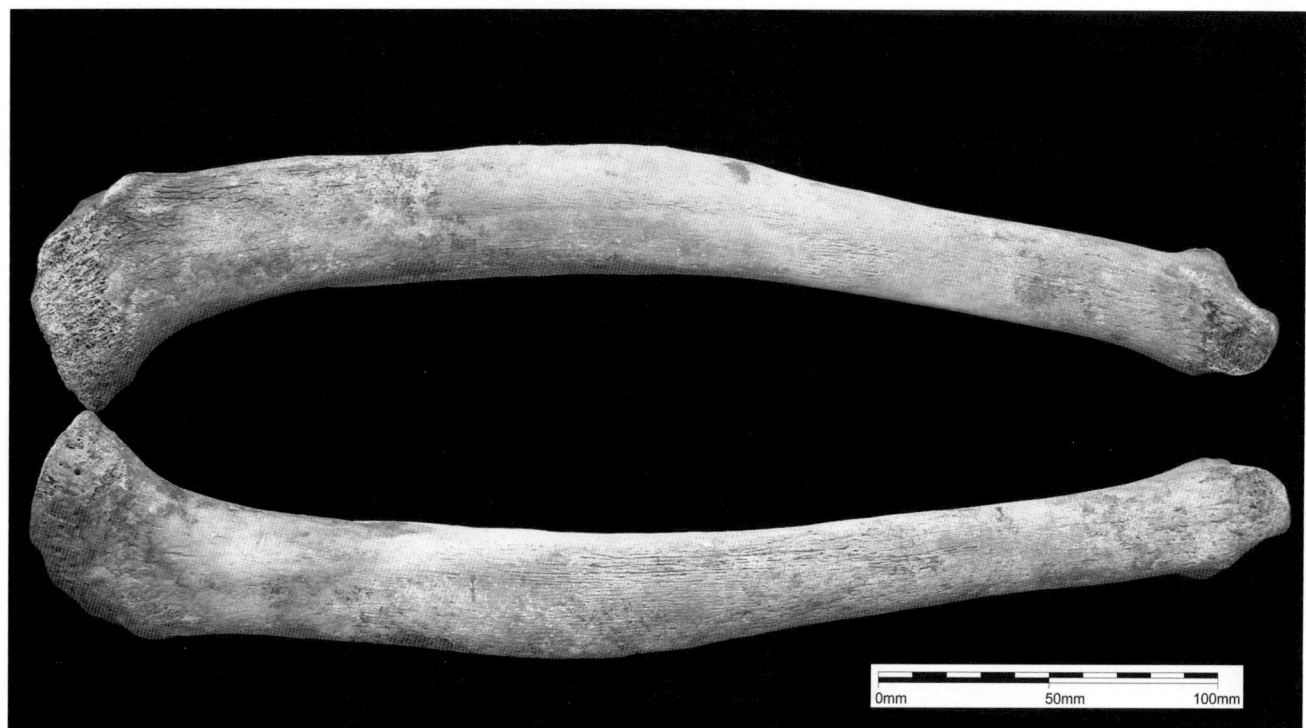

Figure 4.42   Skeleton 502. Bowing of the tibiae associated with treponemal disease

ent with a treponemal infection. Their presence in individuals from the age of 7 years exclude venereal syphilis as the cause. The diagnosis of yaws is the most plausible, given its occurrence in tropical western and equatorial Africa. However, bejel cannot be completely discounted and must therefore remain as an alternative diagnosis.

4.3.7.7   Metabolic disorders

Cribra orbitalia

In the past, the porous lesions seen on the orbital roofs have been linked to anaemia caused by an iron-deficient diet (Roberts and Manchester 1995, 166)

(Fig 4.43). However, it is now recognised that other factors may cause these lesions. These include acute blood loss caused by an injury, chronic disease such as cancer, and parasitic infection of the gut. It has also been suggested that anaemia may be a bodily response to infections since the pathogens require iron for survival and reproduction (Roberts and Manchester 1995, 167). However, there are other causes for the presence of cribra orbitalia, such as scurvy, rickets, and subperiosteal haematomas (Walker *et al* 2009, 115). It is also believed that individuals with these lesions are likely to have suffered from other nutritional deficiencies and cribra orbitalia therefore cannot be ascribed to a single cause (Walker *et al* 2009, 116). Cribra orbitalia is perhaps best viewed as a non-specific stress indicator.

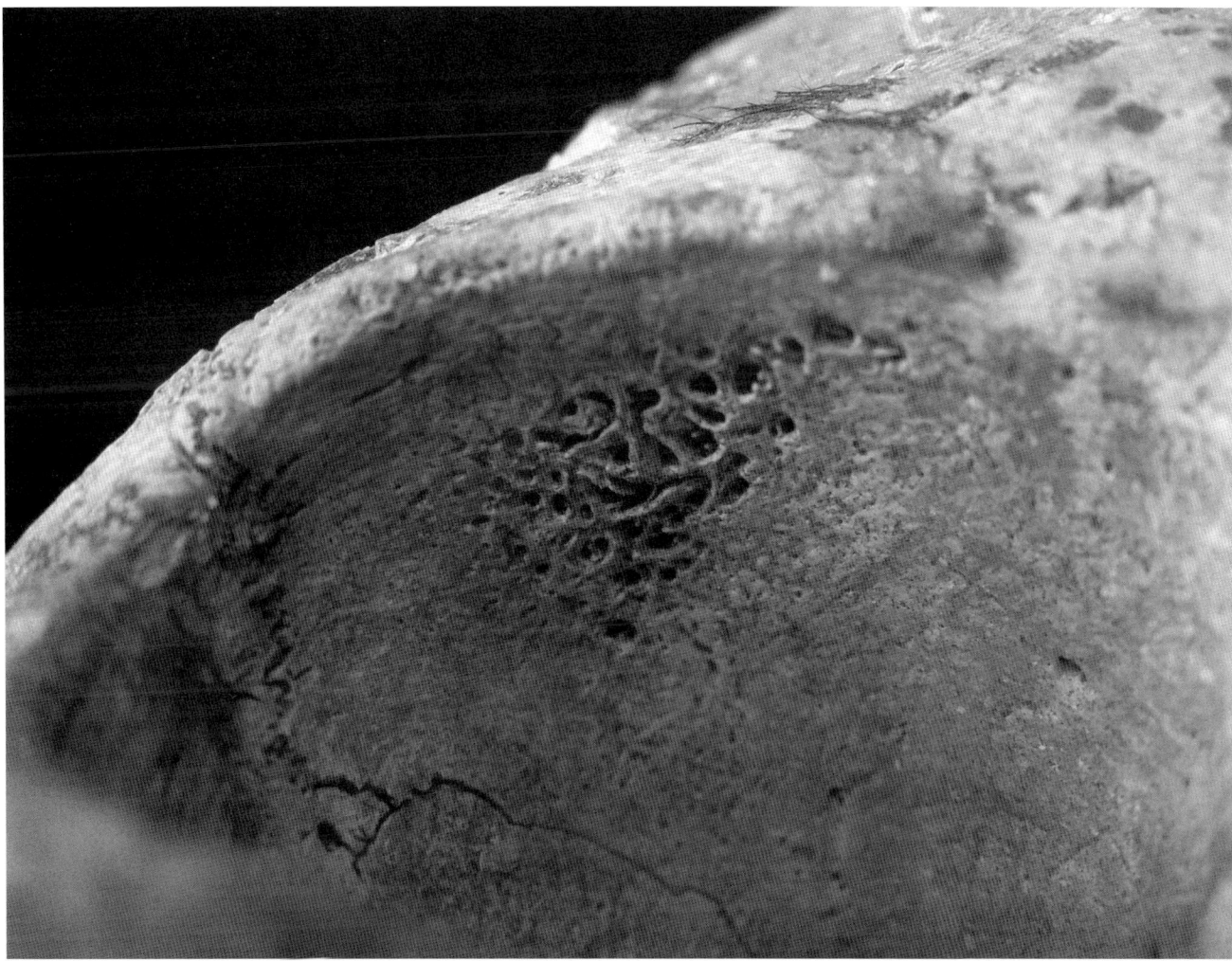

Figure 4.43 Skeleton 478. Cribra orbitalia on the right orbital roof

Table 4.32 Crude prevalence of cribra orbitalia per age group and sex

Age group	% of individuals	% of males	% of females
Young Child	27.78% (5/18)	–	–
Old Child	51.43% (54/105)	–	–
Adolescent	42% (21/50)	75% (6/8)	60% (3/5)
Young Adult	51.61% (32/62)	57.14% (28/49)	33.33% (4/12)
Prime Adult	45.45% (30/66)	44.07% (26/59)	57.14% (4/7)
Mature Adult	23.53% (4/17)	25% (3/12)	20% (1/5)
Adult	0% (0/3)	0% (0/3)	–
Total	45.48% (146/321)	48.09% (63/131)	41.38% (12/29)

Nearly half (45.48%) of all individuals over the age of one year had cribra orbitalia (Table 4.32). This prevalence was highest amongst the individuals aged under 18 years with 51.43% being in the older child category. Of the adults, the greatest prevalence was in the young adults (51.61%). There was nearly a 10% greater prevalence of cribra orbitalia in males than females, with the greatest prevalence seen amongst the younger males.

The most common severity of the lesion recorded was type 4 (which is defined as trabecular structure), followed by type 3 (which is defined as large and small isolated foramina) (Stuart-Macadam 1991) (see Fig 4.44). There was little difference in the prevalence of right and left orbits.

The severity of the lesions per orbit, subdivided into the age categories, is summarised in Figures 4.45 and 4.46. Both orbits exhibit the same general

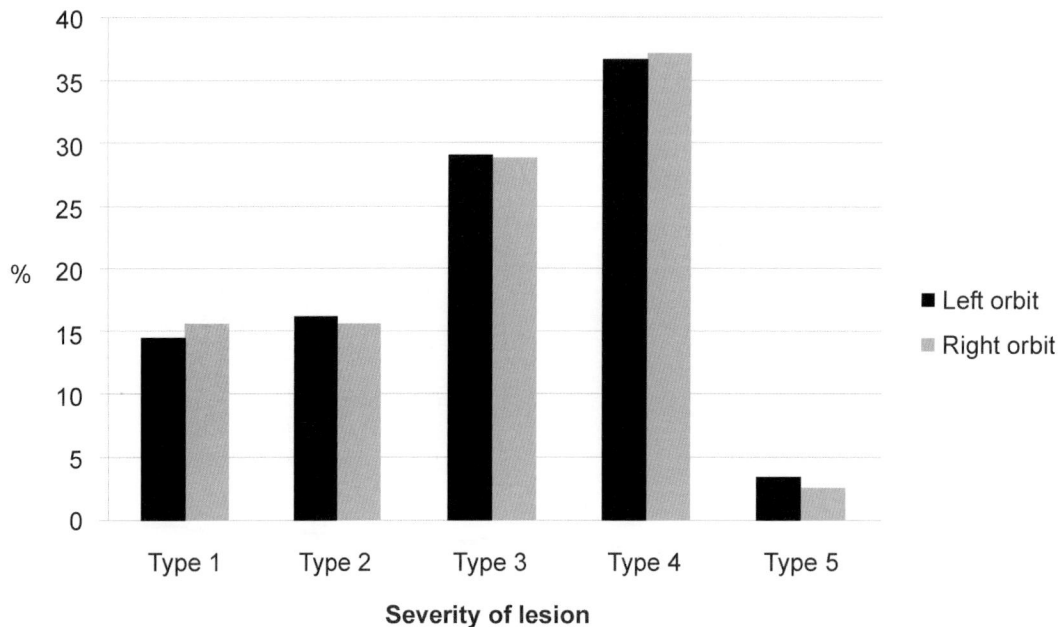

Figure 4.44   Prevalence of cribra orbitalia according to severity and subdivided into left and right orbits

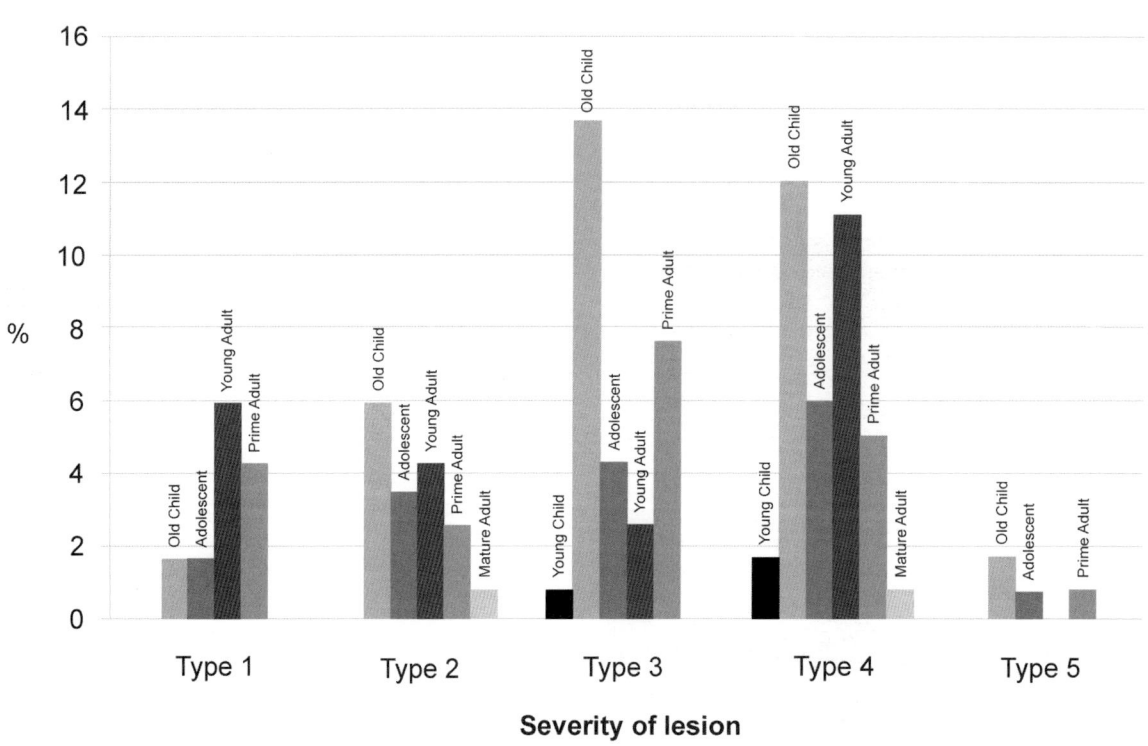

Figure 4.45   Left orbit prevalence of lesion types per age category

pattern in all but the mature adult age group. The majority of the lesions in young children, adolescents, young and mature adults were of type 4 severity, whilst the severity amongst the older children and prime adults was type 3.

Porotic hyperostosis

Porotic hyperostosis is defined as symmetrically distributed areas of porous bone on the ectocranial surface of the vault (Fig 4.47). The lesions involve the outer table and are most commonly situated at the bossing on the parietals and occipital bone (Aufderheide and Rodríguez-Martín 1998, 348). The aetiology of porotic hyperostosis follows closely that of cribra orbitalia and has been linked to the various forms of anaemia, vitamin deficiencies and infection.

There were many fewer individuals with porotic

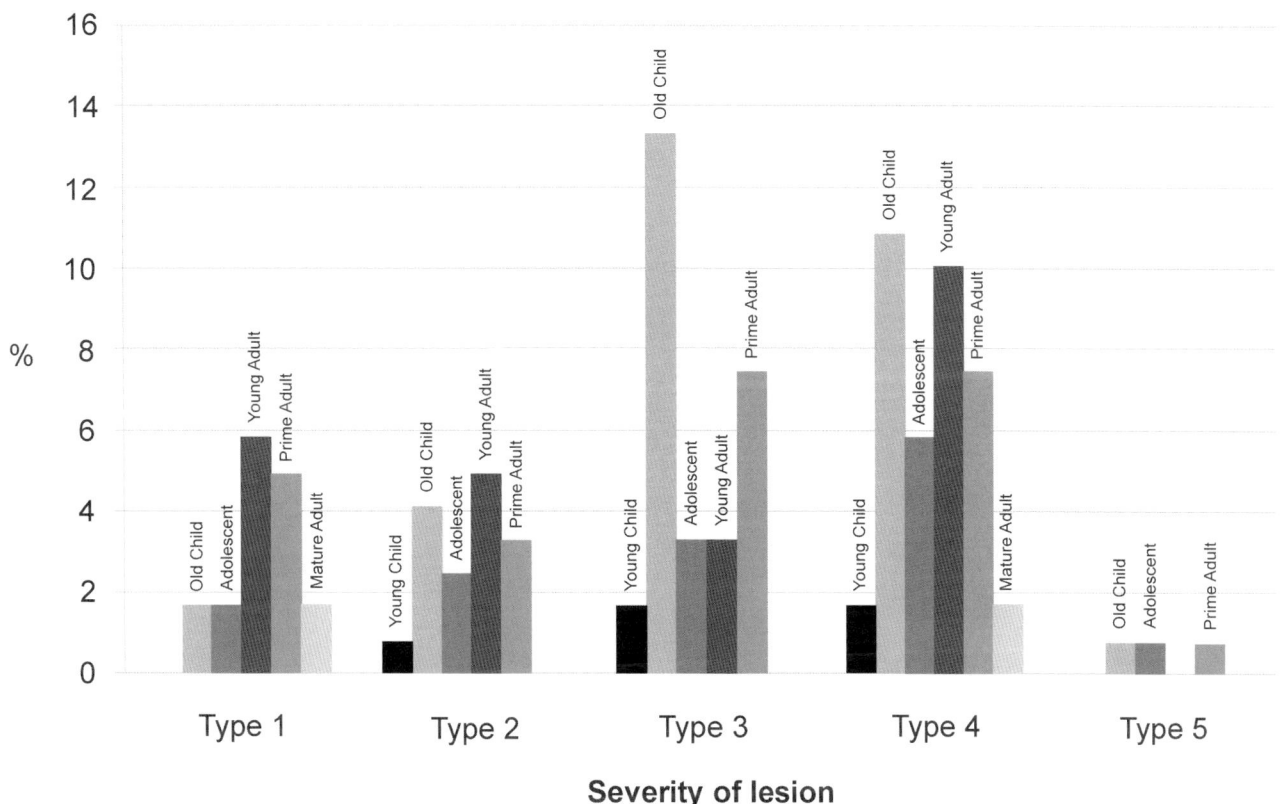

Figure 4.46 Right orbit prevalence of lesion types per age category

Figure 4.47 Skeleton 425. Superior view of the parietals with bilateral porotic hyperostosis

hyperostosis compared to those with cribra orbitalia: the lesions were found on 34 individuals (34/321, 10.59%) (Table 4.33). The prevalence was roughly the same in all age groups with little difference between the subadults and the adults. The overall rate of the lesions amongst the males and females was also quite equal with only a slightly higher percentage of females with the lesions present.

Lesions were observed on 30 left and 30 right parietals. This provides a true prevalence of 10.10% for left parietals and 10.17% for the right parietals.

Scurvy

Scurvy is caused by a deficiency in vitamin C. Vitamin C is present in fruit and vegetables, while smaller amounts are available from fish, meat and milk. The disease was particularly prevalent amongst sailors, both merchant and naval, prior to the use of anti-scorbutics, a practice that had become common on British ships by the end of the 18th century (Maat 2004, 78; Harvie 2002). Seasonal scurvy is also known from the post-medieval period. For example, when potato crops in Ireland were destroyed by blight between 1845 and 1848, this resulted in famine and widespread outbreaks of scurvy. Vitamin C is important for the maintenance of collagen formation and in immune function where

Table 4.33 Crude prevalence of porotic hyperostosis per age group and sex

Age group	% of individuals	% of males	% of females
Young Child	11.11% (2/18)	–	–
Old Child	11.43% (12/105)	–	–
Adolescent	10% (5/50)	12.5% (1/8)	40% (2/5)
Young Adult	11.29% (7/62)	12.24% (6/49)	8.33% (1/12)
Prime Adult	9.09% (6/66)	8.47% (5/59)	14.28% (1/7)
Mature Adult	5.88% (1/17)	8.33% (1/12)	0% (0/5)
Adult	33.33% (1/3)	33.33% (1/3)	–
Total	10.59% (34/321)	10.69% (14/131)	13.79% (4/29)

Table 4.34 Crude prevalence of scurvy per age group and sex

Age group	% of individuals	% of males	% of females
Young Child	22.22% (4/18)	–	–
Old Child	25.71% (27/105)	–	–
Adolescent	22% (11/50)	37.50% (3/8)	40% (2/5)
Young Adult	24.19% (15/62)	28.57% (14/49)	8.33% (1/12)
Prime Adult	15.15% (10/66)	15.25% (9/59)	14.28% (1/7)
Mature Adult	0% (0/17)	0% (0/12)	0% (0/5)
Adult	0% (0/3)	0% (0/3)	–
Total	20.87% (67/321)	19.84% (26/131)	13.79% (4/29)

it helps to destroy pathogens as well as producing antioxidants (Brickley and Ives 2008, 47).

The physical symptoms of scurvy include tiredness, lethargy and pain in the limbs. The condition may also lead to bleeding into the joints, particularly the major joints of the leg which can become swollen and painful. Adults also have swelling of the gums and as the illness progresses the teeth become loose in their sockets, leading to ante-mortem tooth loss (Brickley and Ives 2008, 49).

Detailed descriptions of the skeletal manifestations of scurvy in juveniles have been carried out in the past, specifically by Ortner and Eriksen (1997) and Ortner *et al* (1999 and 2001). It is argued in the current literature that the skeletal expression of scurvy is markedly different in children and adults (Ortner 2003, 387; Brickley and Ives 2008, 61). The lesions in adults are regarded as more subtle, as demonstrated by the analysis of the remains of Dutch Whalers from Spitsbergen (Maat 2004) and the 19th-century mineworkers from Kimberley, South Africa (Van Der Merwe *et al* 2010). Skeletal lesions were rare amongst the Dutch whalers and scurvy was identified by black staining at the joints that had been caused by bleeding (Maat 2004, 79). Symptoms seen on the mineworkers often comprised bilateral ossified haematomas on the tibiae, widespread subperiosteal bone formation and periodontal disease (Van Der Merwe *et al* 2010, 309).

The lesions described in children are very different from those attributed to adult scurvy. The main feature is porosity, which Ortner *et al* (1999, 322) describe as a vascular response to chronic bleeding at the site of porosity. The sites where scorbutic lesions may be present include the greater wing of the sphenoid, internal surface of the zygomatic bone, palate, medial side of the coronoid process and the alveolar margin of the jaw bones, as well as the supraspinatus fossa of the scapula (Ortner *et al* 2001, 346–8). An older adult male excavated from the Spitalfields Market, London, exhibited the same pattern of lesions seen in children: the porosity was attributed to scurvy (Bekvalac 2005).

The same increased porosity and distribution of the lesions observed on the children from Rupert's Valley was also observed on adolescent and adult skeletal remains, albeit at a reduced frequency. The lesions present on the adults are considered to be of the same aetiology as those on the children and were recorded as evidence of scurvy (Figs 4.48–4.51).

The overall prevalence of scurvy was high, at 20.87% (67/321) (Table 4.34). Scurvy was present in all but the mature adult age categories and the greatest prevalence was amongst the children aged between 7 and 12 years (25.71%). The lowest prevalence was in the Prime Adult category (15.15%). Of the sexed adolescents and adults, the greatest prevalence was in the adolescents, with males showing a steady decrease in prevalence with increasing age. This is not the case with the females, although this may be due to the relatively small sample group.

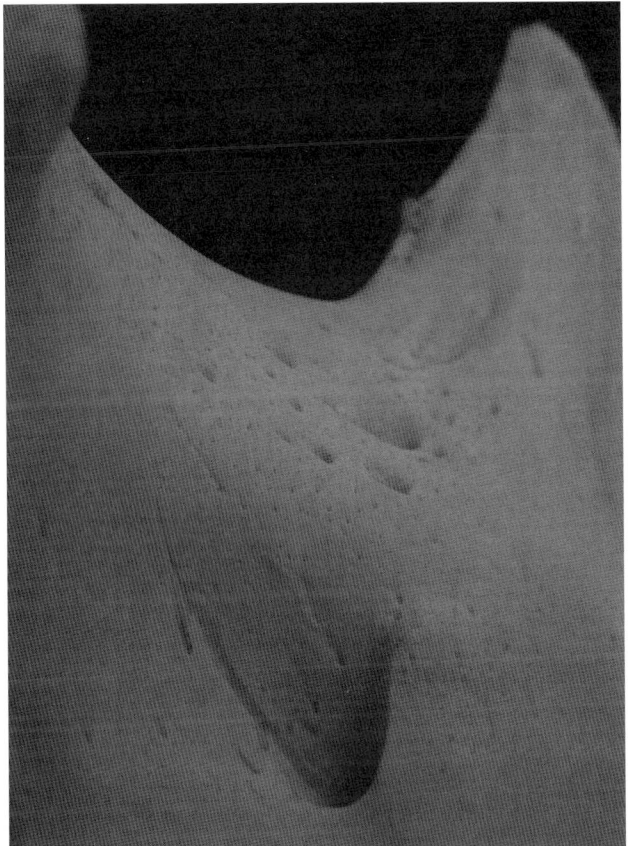

Figure 4.48   Skeleton 460. Medial side of the left mandibular ramus, porosity associated with scurvy. Young Adult male

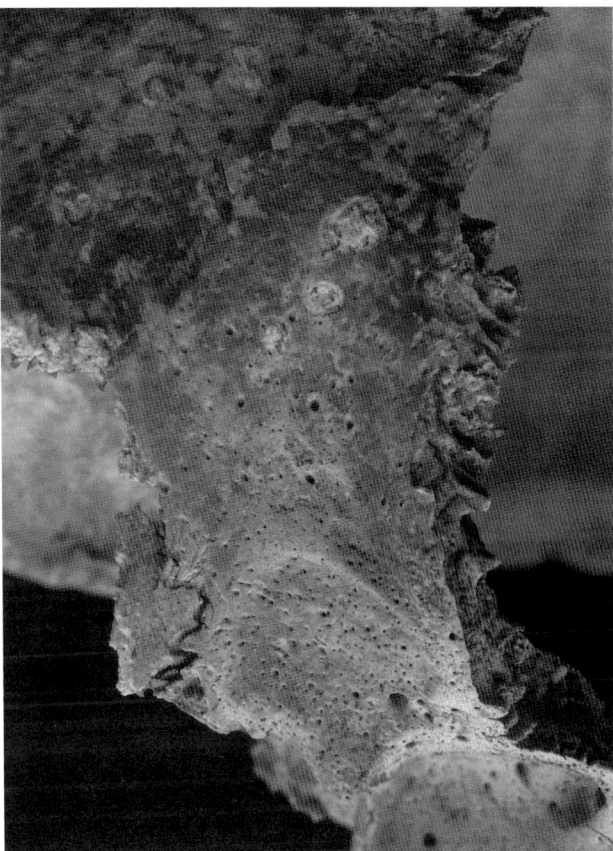

Figure 4.50   Skeleton 389. Increased porosity on the left greater wing of sphenoid, associated with scurvy. Young Adult male

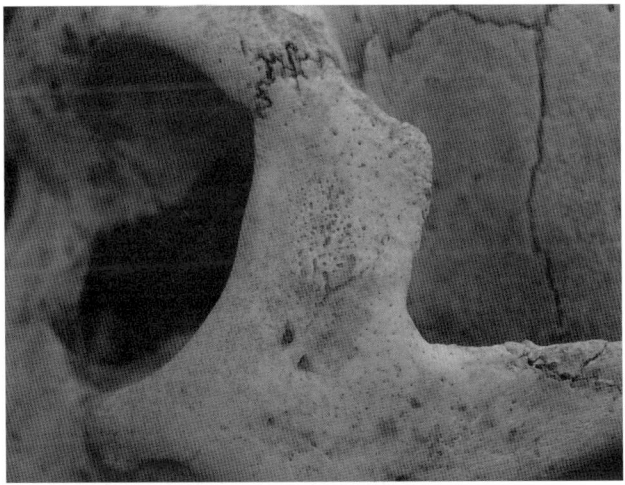

Figure 4.49   Skeleton 460. Deposits of new bone on the body of the mandible at the alveolar margin, associated with scurvy. Young Adult male

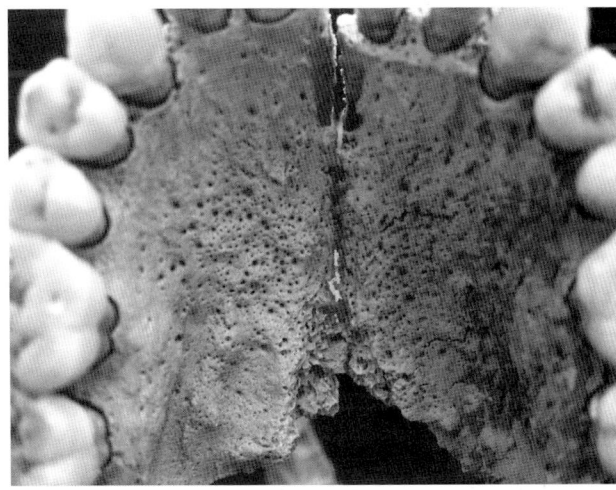

Figure 4.51   Skeleton 389. Increased porosity on the palatine process, associated with scurvy. Young Adult male

The clinical manifestation of scurvy can appear in adults after about 90 days of insufficient vitamin C intake (Hodges *et al* 1971, 432). This time span may be reduced in children due to the rapid turnover of bone (Brickley 2000, 185). The deficiency is associated with malnutrition and it appears that many of these individuals had suffered from poor nutrition for a substantial length of time.

Rickets and osteomalacia

Vitamin D deficiency may produce the skeletal changes that are known as rickets in children and osteomalacia in adults. Up to 100% of vitamin D synthesised by the skin is obtained from sunlight (Holick 2003, 299). The limiting factor in the production of vitamin D is the intensity of the ultraviolet

Table 4.35   Crude prevalence of rickets per age group and sex

Age group	% of individuals	% of males	% of females
Young Child	27.78% (5/18)	–	–
Old Child	5.71% (6/105)	–	–
Adolescent	4% (2/50)	25% (2/8)	0% (0/5)
Young Adult	14.51% (9/62)	16.32% (8/49)	0% (0/12)
Prime Adult	15.15% (10/66)	15.25% (9/59)	14.28% (1/7)
Mature Adult	5.88% (1/17)	8.33% (1/12)	0% (0/5)
Adult	33.33% (1/3)	33.33% (1/3)	–
Total	10.59% (34/321)	22.14% (26/131)	3.45% (1/29)

radiation which depends on the zenith angle of the sun (Neer 1975, 412). It has been established that the tropics provide an ample supply of UV radiation throughout the year for the production of vitamin D (Parra 2007, 92). Fair-skinned individuals in the northern hemisphere require 5–10 minutes of sun exposure to the arms and legs per day in order to prevent rickets (Robins 2009, 449). However, the melanin that provides dark skin with its colour provides protection against sun damage and therefore acts as a natural UV filter. Dark-skinned individuals require at least ten times more exposure to the sun compared to fair-skinned individuals, regardless of latitude (Stearns 1977, 286; Parra 2007, 99).

The lack of vitamin D prevents efficient absorption of calcium, which causes bone to become demineralised. In children, the areas most affected are those that undergo rapid bone growth such as the growth plates in long bones and the costocartilage junction (Holick 2006, 2063). Skeletal deformities usually occur in longstanding cases where the weight-bearing bones develop bending deformities. The condition can also produce other morphological changes such as fraying and cup deformities of the distal growth plates and flaring of the costocartilage junction of the ribs (Brickley and Ives 2008, 104–5). The bowing deformities are also present on adult bones although some remodelling may have occurred.

The adult form of rickets, osteomalacia, produces a different set of lesions, where the softening of the bones produces buckling deformities of the scapula, vertebral bodies and the pelvic bones. Pseudofractures may also be present on the scapula and pelvis (Brickley and Ives 2008, 127–9). The extra-skeletal manifestations of the deficiency include tetany (muscle spasms) and seizures. The altered rib cage morphology that is associated with rickets can also impair breathing and general lung function, sometimes leading to infection. Older children and adults would experience bone pain fatigue and muscle weakness (Holick 2006, 2065).

Rickets or osteomalacia was observed on 37 (11.53%) individuals. Of these, 34 (10.59%) had either active or healed rickets (Table 4.35). The prevalence of rickets was greatest amongst the young children

(27.78%) followed by young and prime adults at 14.51% and 15.15% respectively. The residual rickets present on the adults were mainly on the males and only one female had bowing deformities of the long bones consistent with rickets. The vast majority of the rachitic lesions were healed but six (6/34, 17.65%) were active at the time of death. These comprised three young children and three old children.

Three individuals had lesions consistent with osteomalacia and these consisted of one adolescent and two adults (one female and one male). The adolescent displayed lesions consistent with rickets and osteomalacia, a feature known to occur on juveniles (Brickley and Ives 2008, 91) (Figs 4.52 and 4.53).

The presence of rickets in the populations of tropical regions of African is not unheard of. This may be caused by maternal malnutrition during pregnancy and whilst lactating, or food deficient in vitamin D may have been used for weaning (Brickley and Ives 2008, 93). Cultural practices, for example swaddling, and being constantly carried on their mothers back, as is the practice in Ibadan, West Nigeria, has also produced infantile rickets (*ibid*, 93). Environmental factors such as a dense canopy of trees may also block out a significant amount of sunlight and may promote the development of rickets; this has been observed along the Ivory Coast and Congo (*ibid*, 93). The premise that darker skin requires longer exposure to sunlight in order to produce the same amount of vitamin D as light skin would also make dark-skinned individuals more susceptible to developing vitamin D deficiency. These cultural and environmental factors cannot be discounted for the majority of these individuals. However, the nine individuals (9/321, 2.80%) with active rickets may have developed the condition under more harrowing circumstances: confinement prior to the departure may well have been long enough to cause the condition.

4.3.7.8   Post-mortem intervention

Many of the excavated post-medieval cemeteries in Britain have yielded a small number of individu-

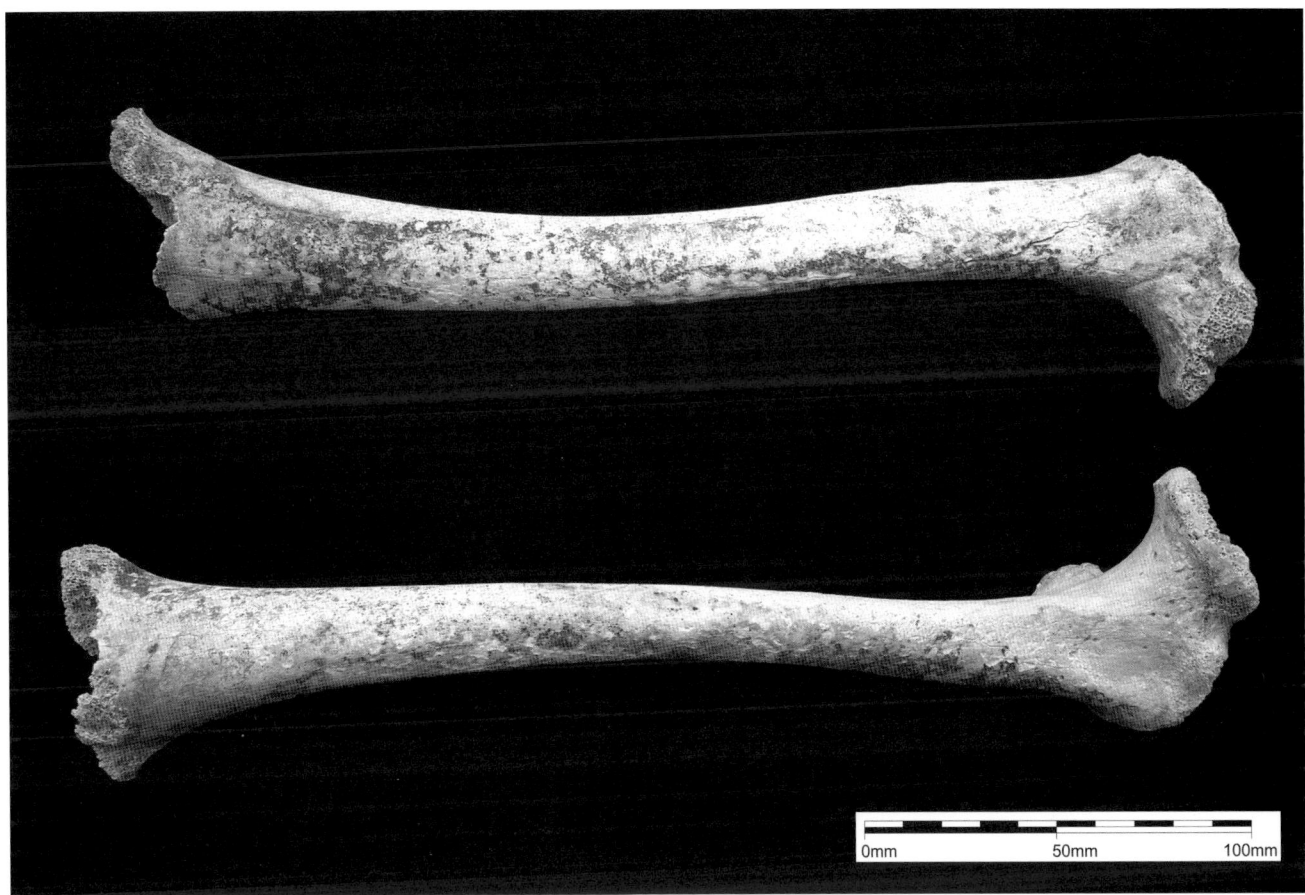

Figure 4.52   Skeleton 501. Right and left femora, bowing of the shafts due to rickets

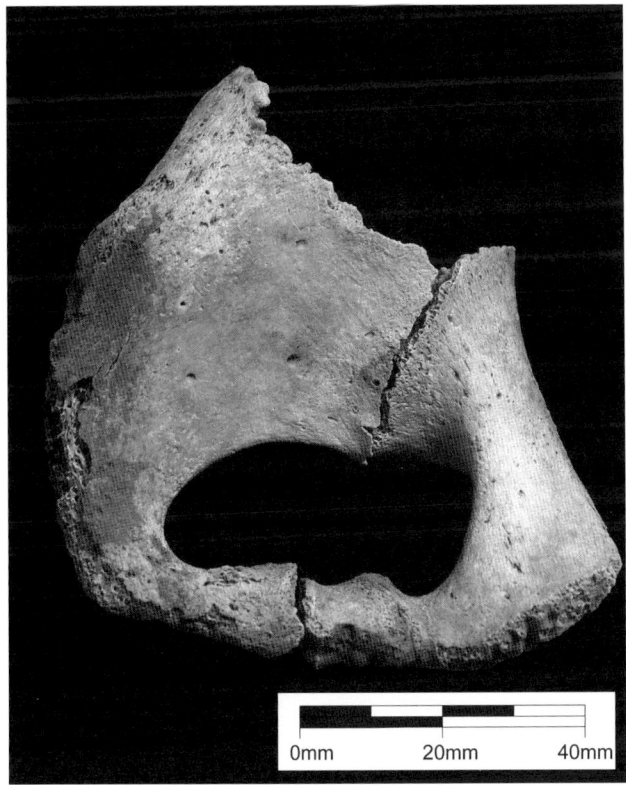

Figure 4.53   Skeleton 501. Left ischium and pubis, buckled obturator foramen, a feature of osteomalacia

Figure 4.54   Skeleton 341. Calvarium with craniotomy and endocranial lesion

als with craniotomies, for example at St Martin's, Birmingham (Brickley *et al* 2006), and St Marylebone Church, London (Miles *et al* 2008). These are also present in greater numbers from post-medieval hospital cemeteries such as Newcastle Infirmary (Boulter *et al* 1998) and the Bristol Royal Infirmary (Witkin 2011). This is a post-mortem procedure where the skullcap is removed in order to enable an examination of the underlying membranes and the brain itself. The procedure is carried out either as part of dissection or during an autopsy and the boundaries may at times be obscured in a hospital. There are differences between the two procedures: dissection is carried out in order to teach anatomy and pathology, and can result in the complete dismemberment of a body; an autopsy is performed to establish the cause of death, and usually involves minimal intrusion. Considering that no other bones had evidence of being cut, these post-mortem procedures are regarded as autopsies.

Craniotomies had been performed on three individuals (3/321, 0.93%). These comprised two older children (2/105, 1.9%) and one adolescent (1/50, 2%). All three individuals had lesions consistent with scurvy. One of these individuals also had endocranial lesions and it has been suggested that lesions similar to these may represent a slow haemorrhage that had stimulated bone formation (Lewis 2004, 88) (Fig 4.54). This haemorrhaging may have led to symptoms that the surgeon in Rupert's Valley thought worthy of investigation, as discussed further in section 7.4.2.

5 The finds *by Helen MacQuarrie (with contributions by Natasha Ferguson, Penelope Walton Rogers, Isabella von Holstein, Josie Sheppard and Quita Mould)*

5.1 Introduction

Over one hundred individual or group-registered finds were recovered from the 2008 excavation, principally comprising coins, iron and copper alloy objects, lead projectiles, glass ampoules and bottles, clay pipes, beads and textile fragments. Five wooden coffins with associated coffin furniture were also found. These finds are catalogued and illustrated in the digital volume, Appendix D2.

All of the finds were cleaned and stabilised during the immediate post-excavation phase on St Helena. The small finds were then brought to the UK, where conservation work was undertaken by Cardiff Conservation Services (Cardiff University). The coffin timbers were recorded in detail on St Helena and remain on the island. All of the finds will be returned to St Helena in due course.

5.2 Coins
Helen MacQuarrie

Eight silver Victorian coins were recovered during the excavation (SF43, SF51, SF52, SF58 [2 coins], SF93, SF94, and SF95). The coins were recovered from three coffin inhumations of neonates (Groups 2363, 2367 and 2579). All of the coins were recovered from the eye sockets or the vicinity of the skull

(Fig 5.1). The coins, dated between 1838 and 1870, correlate with the known date of the graveyard.

Foreign coins had dominated currency circulation in St Helena prior to 1843. However, at this date the British Government demonetised all non-sterling coins on St Helena and all foreign coins in circulation were exchanged for British silver (Vice 1983, 124). The coins found within the excavation are typical of those utilised across the British Empire and all are recorded in circulation in West Africa during the 19th century (Vice 1983, 78). Some issues were specific to the colonies: for example, the silver three-halfpence (SF58) is of a type issued for circulation in the colonies, principally Ceylon and the West Indies (Lobel *et al* 1995, 529).

The placing of coins over the eyes of the deceased has a long tradition in European societies and is often associated with Christian burial practices. In 19th-century Britain the practice of placing coins over the eyes of the deceased is rare but not unknown. Examples are cited at St Marylebone Church and burial ground (Miles *et al* 2008, 53) and Christ Church Spitalfields (Reeve and Adams 1993, 105).

SF43: Silver Britannia groat/four pence
Group 2363; Context 2362; Skeleton 380; 1846; Great Britain[1]
Obverse: left-facing portrait Queen (young), inscription 'VICTORIA D G BRITANNIAR REGINA F D'

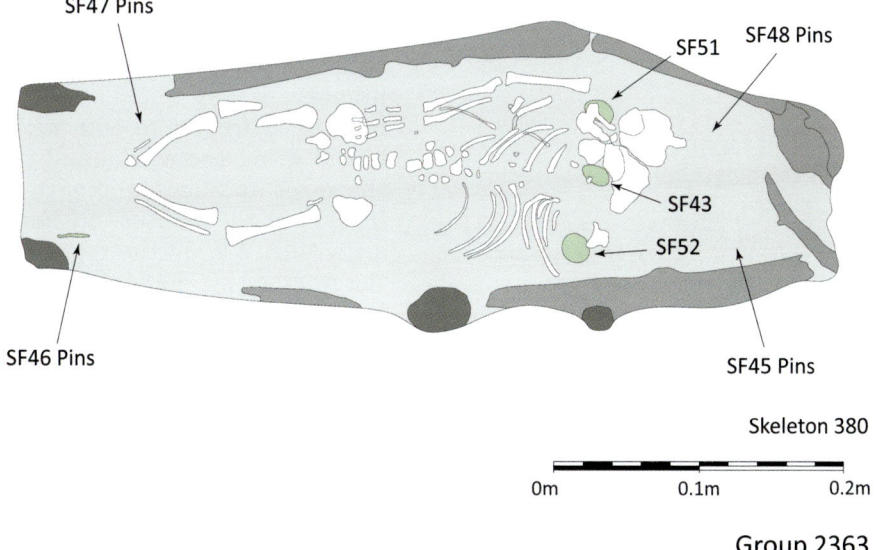

Figure 5.1 Coffin 2362 (Skeleton 380) showing the position of the coins (SF43, SF51, SF52)

99

Reverse: Britannia, seated with shield; 'FOUR PENCE'; date in exergue
Edge: milled
The coin is heavily corroded on the obverse. Weight: 1.96g, diameter: 16.77mm, thickness: 1.26mm

SF51: Silver six pence
Group 2363; Context 2362; Skeleton 380; 1838–66; Great Britain
Obverse: left-facing portrait Queen (young), inscription, 'VICTORIA DEI GRATIA BRITANNIAR REG F D'
Reverse: 'SIX PENCE' within wreath, crown above, date below
The coin is heavily corroded and no design is visible on the surface. The young Victoria's head was identified by x-ray. An exact date for the coin was not ascertained. Weight: 3.19g, diameter: 20.29mm, thickness: 1.85mm

SF52: Silver six pence
Group 2363; Context 2362; Skeleton 380; 1838–66; Great Britain
Obverse: left-facing portrait Queen (young), inscription, 'VICTORIA DEI GRATIA BRITANNIAR REG F D'
Reverse: 'SIX PENCE' within wreath, crown above, date below
The coin is heavily corroded and no design is visible on the surface. The young Victoria's head was identified by x-ray. Fragments of netting are preserved on both sides of the coin, which indicates that it was originally wrapped within the burial shroud. Weight: 3.03g, diameter: 20.21mm, thickness: 2.50mm

SF58: Silver three halfpence (2)
Group 2367; Context 2366; Skeleton 381; 1838–70; Great Britain
Obverse: left-facing portrait Queen (young), inscription, 'VICTORIA D G BRITANNIAR REGINA F D'
Reverse: '1 ½', date below, crown above, all within wreath
Edge: plain
Both coins are very worn and no design is visible on the surface or exposed by x-ray. Identification has been achieved based on weight and dimension of the coins. The coins were recovered from above the eyes of the inhumed neonate. Fragments of textiles are mineralised on one side of each coin which indicates that a cloth or shroud covered the face of the neonate. Coin 1: weight: 0.78g, diameter: 12.85g, thickness: 1.18mm. Coin 2: weight: 0.85g, diameter: 13.25g, thickness: 1.22mm

SF93: Silver three pence
Group 2579; Context 2578; Skeleton 519; 1843; Great Britain[2]
Obverse: left-facing portrait Queen (young), inscription, 'VICTORIA D G BRITANNIAR REGINA F D'
Reverse: crowned '3' and divided date, all within wreath
Edge: plain
The date and design of the coin were exposed by x-ray. Mineralised fragments of textiles on one side of the coin. Weight: 1.62g, diameter: 16.88mm, thickness: 1.42mm

SF94: Silver three pence
Group 2579; Context 2578; Skeleton 519; 1843; Great Britain
Obverse: left-facing portrait Queen (young), inscription, 'VICTORIA D G BRITANNIAR REGINA F D'.
Reverse: crowned '3' and divided date, all within wreath
Edge: plain
The coin is worn and slightly corroded. The date and design of the coin were exposed by x-ray. Fragments of netting are preserved on one side of the coin. Weight: 1.44g, diameter: 16.51mm, thickness: 1.26mm

SF95: Silver three pence
Group 2579; Context 2578; Skeleton 519; 1844; Great Britain
Obverse: left-facing portrait Queen (young), inscription, 'VICTORIA D G BRITANNIAR REGINA F D'
Reverse: crowned '3' and divided date, all within wreath
Edge: plain
The coin is worn and slightly corroded. The date and design were exposed by x-ray. Mineralised fragments of textiles are preserved on one side of the coin. Weight: 1.53g, diameter: 16.80mm, thickness: 1.24mm

5.3 Objects of iron
Helen MacQuarrie

5.3.1 Metal tags

Nine metal tags were recovered from grave fills adjacent to skeletons (Fig 5.2). Complete examples form three distinct shapes: lozenge (80mm height, 65mm width, 3mm thickness, 3mm hole diameter, 9mm from top of tag) (SF01); circular (55–57mm diameter, 3–4mm thickness, 4mm hole diameter, 8–11mm from top of tag) (SF19, SF28, SF84, SF85); and square (49–54mm width, 48–54mm height, 3mm thickness, 5mm diameter hole, 8–10mm from top of tag) (SF63, SF103). Two fragmentary tags were also recovered (SF04, SF34). X-ray reveals folded edges around the side of the objects with notched corners, indicative of cheap industrialised manufacture. A fine white line on the x-ray may indicate evidence of an original metal coating, possibly tin, which no longer survives.

The tags were, apart from one example, associated with children and recovered from multiple graves. The exception is SF34 which was associated with a young adult female (Skeleton 364) who was buried in a single inhumation.

Documentary evidence provides an insight into the use of such tags. They are first mentioned by George McHenry, who describes their use in Lemon Valley as 'tallies':

> He [Stephen Pritchard, senior clerk of the depot] enlisted the services of a tinsmith, and got a number of flat circular bits of tin struck off, numbered from 1 to 500, with the letters m, w, b and g, on them in small text, to distinguish the sexes and ages, and with the addition of the initials of the cruisers in Roman capitals. Thus a tin with WW on the top, and an m below, with the number 20, denoted that the ticket belonged to a man whose number was 20, and who had been captured by the Waterwitch. In like manner a large B stood for 'Brisk', an F for 'Fantome'; and so on for the rest of the cruisers. These tallies, as they were called, were elegantly suspended from the neck by a hempen cord ...

(McHenry 1845–46, chapter 5, 439)

Similar objects, though with a slightly different purpose, feature in 1849 correspondence between

Figure 5.2   Metal tags. From left to right: lozenge-shaped tag (SF01); round tag (SF28); and square tag (SF103)

David McKenzie, Master of the emigration vessel *Euphrates*, Dr Rawlins of the Liberated African Depot, and Governor Patrick Ross. Here, these 'tin tickets' were associated with a number of sick children (House of Commons Parliamentary Papers 1850 [No. 643], 100–1). The use of the tags is a point of contention between McKenzie and Rawlins, as there is an implication that children were embarked for the West Indies in an unfit and sick state. Dr Rawlins states that the tags are a 'distinguishing mark of the different batches', rather than an indication of sickness. Despite the disagreement about their precise use, this evidence indicates that these tags or 'tickets' were still associated with the activities of the hospital and the depot.

Illustrations within newspapers that are con-temporary with the graveyard also show such tags. In 1857 a number of drawings were made to demonstrate the condition of slaves disembarked from the slaver *Zeldina* at Kingston, Jamaica (Fig 5.3). The *Zeldina* had taken on slaves at Cabinda (modern day Angola) and was bound for Cuba when captured by the Royal Navy. Many of the recaptives illustrated have round tokens strung around their necks, similar in form and size to the circular tags recovered from Rupert's Valley. Other pictorial sources illustrating captured slaves at sea do not show such artefacts around the necks of the Africans: this tends to suggest that they were used by the British within the context of administering the recaptives once landed, rather than on the slave ships themselves.

GROUP OF SLAVES ON THE PARADE, FORT AUGUSTA.

Figure 5.3   African recaptives from the slave ship Zeldina. *From* The Illustrated London News *(20 June 1857, Volume 30, 595)*

As far as is currently known, no other tags of this kind have been recovered from an archaeological context. Only one comparable artefact has been located within British museum collections, this being a 'servant tag' from South Carolina, on display at the International Slavery Museum, Liverpool. This object and other similar examples are recorded from 19th-century South Carolina in the *Standard Catalog of Hard Times Tokens 1832–1844* (Rulau 2001). As with the St Helena assemblage, these tags comprise circular, lozenge-shaped, and square discs with a punched hole to attach the tag around the neck. These have been stamped with the year, occupation (ie servant, mechanic, porter) and often an individual number.

SF01: Iron tag: lozenge
Group 2007; Context 2006; Skeleton 209; 19th century
Lozenge-shaped tag in two pieces with a circular hole at the top for attachment. Heavily corroded. No surface decoration apparent but x-ray reveals a possible stamped digit '0' in the centre of the disc. Weight: 12.97g, height: 79.25mm, width: 65mm, thickness: 2.79mm (at edge)

SF04: Fragmented iron tag: lozenge
Group 2013; Context 2012; Skeleton 223/224; 19th century
Seven fragments of incomplete lozenge-shaped tag. Heavily corroded. X-ray reveals folded edges of three corner fragments. No surface decoration apparent. Weight: 14.69g

SF19: Iron tag: circular
Group 2251; Context 2250; Skeleton 322; 19th century
Complete circular tag. Very heavily corroded with a bubbly surface in patches. No surface decoration apparent. The circular hole for attaching the disc, which is not visible, is revealed by x-ray. A number of imprints of fly pupae are visible within the corrosion patterns on one face of the tag. Weight: 14.9g, height: 55.72mm, width: 55.7mm, thickness: 3.92mm (at edge)

SF28: Iron tag: circular
Group 2314; Context 2313; Skeleton 363; 19th century
Complete circular tag. A circular hole is located at the top of the disc, where fragments of mineralised textiles are also preserved. Very heavily corroded with patches of a powdery yellow corrosion product on one side. No surface decoration apparent. Weight: 15.24g, height 56.37mm, width: 54.5mm, thickness: 2.3mm (at edge)

SF34: Fragmented iron tag
Group 2329; Context 2328; Skeleton 364; 19th century
Very fragmented, original shape not determined. Corroded with powdery yellow corrosion product visible. Weight: 6.48g

SF63: Iron tag: square
Group 2401; Context 2400; Skeleton 400; 19th century
Complete square tag with circular perforation at the top for attachment. The object is heavily corroded and with a shiny bubbly surface on one side. The other side has a build up of corrosion and mineralised fabric is preserved across part of this face. No surface decoration apparent. Weight: 14.91g, height: 52.87mm, width: 51.89mm, thickness: 2.8mm (at edge)

SF84: Fragmented iron tag: circular
Group 2416; Context 2415; Skeleton 410; 19th century
Near-complete circular (to sub-oval) tag, fragmented into twelve pieces. Very corroded. No surface decoration apparent. Weight: 10.95g

SF85: Iron tag: circular
Group 2509; Context 2508; Skeleton 458; 19th century
Near-complete circular tag. Corroded. No surface decoration apparent. Weight: 14.62g, height: 56.8mm, width: 55.19mm, 2.7mm thickness (at edge)

SF103: Iron tag: square
Group 2082; Context 2081; Skeleton 305; 19th century
Complete square-shaped tag with a circular hole at the top for attachment. Very heavily corroded with substantial corrosion blisters on one side. Patches of a powdery yellow corrosion product are visible on the other side. No surface decoration apparent. Fragments of textiles are mineralised on one side of the object, around the edge of the hole and down the centre. Weight: 12.26g, height: 48.20mm, width: 49.70mm, thickness: 2.32mm (at edge)

5.3.2   Iron fixings

Four iron objects (SF03, SF14, SF76, SF87) were recovered from grave fills (Groups 2044, 2218, 2455 and 2563). Three lay on or near to the base of the grave cut, in close proximity to the human remains. SF03 was found adjacent to the left femur of Skeleton 230 (see Fig 7.14); SF14 was found above the left arm of Skeleton 302; SF87 was found between the lower legs of Skeleton 507. The fourth object, SF76, was from the grave fill 2457, but its position in relation to the bodies in the grave (Skeletons 427 and 428) is not known.

These objects are structural fixings which are not diagnostic (Fig 5.4). However, given the context of ship-breaking in Rupert's Valley, an interpretation as ship's fasteners is plausible (see section 2.4.8).

SF03: Iron nail
Group 2044; Context 2043; Skeleton 230; Post-medieval
Heavily corroded with layering and fractures throughout the object. Weight: 117.06g, length: 155mm, shaft diameter: 20mm

Figure 5.4   Iron fixings. Top left: iron nut or rivet (SF14); top right: iron fastener (SF76); bottom: iron fastener (SF03)

SF14: Iron nail or bolt
Group 2218; Context 2217; Skeleton 302; Post-medieval
Heavily corroded with layering and fractured throughout the object. Weight: 55.3g, length: 76mm, shaft diameter: 22.35mm

SF76: Pierced iron plate (nut or washer)
Group 2455; Context 2454; Skeleton 427/428; Post-medieval
Heavily corroded with layering and fractures throughout the object. Weight: 57.25g, width: 38.5 x 30mm, thickness: 20.1mm (with 10mm bore)

SF87: Iron bolt
Group 2563; Context 2562; Skeleton 507; Post-medieval
Heavily corroded with layering and fractures throughout the object. Weight: 190.63g, length: 84mm, shaft diameter: 30.6mm

5.3.3   Other iron objects

Two iron hoops were recovered during the excavation (SF20 and SF21). Both were from virtually the same location within grave 2233, but it is thought that SF20 was associated with child Skeleton 311 (neck area) while SF21 was associated with the remains of young child Skeleton 326 (right wrist). However, it is possible that they derive from a single object belonging to either of these individuals.

The form of these objects, and their position within the grave, implies that these made up some form of wrist (bracelet) or neck ornament. Their origin, and whether acquired in Africa, on the slave ship, or on

Figure 5.5   Iron hoop (SF21) in situ at the wrist of Skeleton 326

Figure 5.6   Fragments of iron hoop (SF21) associated with Skeleton 326

St Helena, is unclear. One distinct possibility is that they were made by the Liberated Africans whilst in the depot in Rupert's Valley. Those received into Lemon Valley in 1841 were described by McHenry as being extremely industrious, making numerous items from scrap copper and iron – everything from jewellery to fishing hooks and musical instruments (McHenry 1845–46, chapter 1, 182). Similarly, and of particular interest in respect of these iron objects, it was proposed that the Africans in Rupert's Valley should be kept occupied by the manufacture of small everyday items from raw materials provided by the Establishment. One suggestion was for parcels of iron hoops to be distributed, to be made into knives (House of Commons Parliamentary Papers 1850 [No. 643], 79).

Two other fragments of iron were also recovered (SF33 and SF59). Their original form and purpose is not known.

SF20: Iron hoop
Group 2233; Context 2232; Skeleton 311
Three fragments. Very corroded. Weight: 4.55g, approximate diameter (when placed together) 40mm, thickness: 2.55mm

SF21: Iron hoop
Group 2233; Context 2232; Skeleton 326
Three fragments. Very corroded. Weight: 2.57g, approximate diameter (when placed together): 37mm, thickness: 4.5mm

SF33: Metal fragments
Group 2338; Context 2337; Skeleton 367
One small triangular fragment of iron and six fragments of non-ferrous metal. Original form of the object unknown. Weight: 0.39g

SF59: Metal fragments
Group 2367; Context 2366; Skeleton 381
Two small linear fragments of iron, fused together by corrosion products. Beads, fabric and wood fragments adhere to the object. Length: 50mm, weight: 6.25g

5.4   Objects of copper alloy
Helen MacQuarrie

5.4.1   Pins

Eleven individual or group-recorded finds were identified as copper alloy pins (Table 5.1). All were found within the four coffin inhumations of the foetus and neonates (Skeletons 265, 380, 381 and 519).

Two types of pin were recorded, distinguished by the shape of the head; however, sizes varied within each type. Type 1 comprises a mass-produced copper alloy pin with soldered flat head (28–33.5mm in length). Type 2 comprises a mass-produced copper alloy pin with soldered round head (25–26mm in length).

A number of the pins had textile fragments preserved around them indicating that they were used to secure shrouds around the foetus and neonate burials (see section 5.9).

It is probable that the pins were manufactured

Figure 5.7   Copper alloy pins (SF46) associated with Skeleton 380

in the United Kingdom. The technology to facilitate the mass production of pins had been developed in Birmingham in the 1820s by D F Taylor and Co, and the city rapidly became the centre of British pin production. In 1878 it was estimated that 50,000,000 pins were produced annually in England, of which 37,000,000 were produced in Birmingham; most others were produced in London, Warrington, Stroud and Dublin (Bevan 1878).

SF08: Pins (6)
Group 2142; Context 2141; Skeleton 265; 19th century
Six round-headed pins (fragments), 22 stem fragments. Weight: 0.34g

SF45: Pin
Group 2363; Context 2362; Skeleton 380; 19th century
Flat-headed pin (complete) with mineralised textiles preserved. Weight: 0.11g, length: 29mm, thickness: 1mm

SF46: Pins (2)
Group 2363; Context 2362; Skeleton 380; 19th century

One flat-headed pin (complete) with mineralised textiles preserved. Weight: 0.35g, length: 33.5mm, thickness: 1.2mm. One round-headed pin (complete). Length: 25mm, thickness: 0.8mm. Total weight: 0.4g

SF47: Pin
Group 2363; Context 2362; Skeleton 380; 19th century
Flat-headed pin (complete) with mineralised textiles preserved. Weight: 0.23g, length: 28mm, thickness: 0.8mm

SF48: Pin fragments
Group 2363; Context 2362; Skeleton 380; 19th century
Three undiagnostic pin stem fragments. Weight: 0.07g

SF56: Pins (11)
Group 2367; Context 2366; Skeleton 381; 19th century
Four round-headed pins (one complete: 25mm length, 0.8mm diameter). Seven flat-headed pins (two complete: 28.5mm length, 1mm diameter), and sixteen stem fragments. Total weight: 1.33g

SF57: Pins (4)
Group 2367; Context 2366; Skeleton 381; 19th century
Four flat-headed fragments, plus three stem fragments. Weight: 0.13g

SF97: Pin
Group 2579; Context 2578; Skeleton 519; 19th century
Round-headed pin (complete) with mineralised textiles preserved. Weight 0.13g, length: 26mm

SF98: Pin
Group 2579; Context 2578; Skeleton 519; 19th century
Flat-headed pin (complete) with mineralised textiles preserved. Weight: 0.18g, length: 33mm, thickness: 1mm

SF99: Pin
Group 2579; Context 2578; Skeleton 519; 19th century
Flat-headed pin (complete). Weight: 0.12g, length: 30mm, thickness: 1mm

Figure 5.8   Coffin 2139 (Skeleton 265) showing the copper alloy pins in situ

Table 5.1   Copper alloy pins

Skeleton	Group	Type 1	Type 2	Total
265	2142		SF08 (6)	6
380	2363	SF45 (1), SF46 (1), SF47 (1)	SF46 (1)	4 (plus 3 undiagnostic stem fragments – SF48)
381	2367	SF56 (7), SF57 (4)	SF56 (4)	15
519	2579	SF98 (1), SF99 (1), SF100 (3)	SF97 (1)	6

* The totals are based on the number of pin heads recovered and should not be considered an absolute calculation

Figure 5.9 Copper alloy bracelet (SF54) in situ on the wrist of an older child (Skeleton 399)

Figure 5.10 Copper alloy bracelet (SF54)

SF100: Pins (3)
Group 2579; Context 2578; Skeleton 519; 19th century
Three flat-headed pins (complete) in good condition, with mineralised textiles preserved. Weight: 0.3g, length: 30–32mm, thickness: 1mm

5.4.2 Other copper alloy objects

SF54 is a small copper alloy bracelet (Figs 5.9 and 5.10) which was found around the wrist of an older child (Skeleton 399). It is an open bracelet formed from a single bar of metal, with a *c* 4mm gap.

It is possible that the metal itself originated in Britain, as there was a strong trade with the west coast of Africa in rods of brass (known as Guinea rods) which were predominately produced in Birmingham (DeCorse 2001, 134). Copper alloy bracelets have been well documented in ethnographic and artefactual studies and have also been recovered from archaeological investigations at Elmina, Ghana (DeCorse 2001), and Barbados (Handler and Lange 1999). There exists a tradition amongst West African societies in which children are given copper alloy bracelets for protection (Claude Ardouin, pers comm).

SF86 is an undiagnostic small copper alloy object, recovered from grave 2536 and associated with Skeleton 481. It is not possible to ascertain its original function, although it may have been a small rivet for clothing.

SF71 is an undiagnostic small curved fragment of metal, recovered from grave 2419. The original form and function of the object to which it belonged is not known. It is possibly a fragment of a hoop, similar to SF20 and SF21.

SF54: Hoop or bracelet
Group 2401; Context 2400; Skeleton 399; Provenance uncertain (possibly non-European). Copper alloy object formed from a single metal bar with a 7mm circular cross section. It is an open circle with a 4mm gap. The diameter of the object is 63mm (to the outer limit). Heavily covered with verdigris. Weight: 45.90g

SF71: Fragment of hoop
Group 2419; Context 2418; Skeleton 412; 19th century; Provenance uncertain
Small fragment of non-ferrous metal in a slightly curved form. Possibly part of a hoop. Weight: 0.06g, length: 17.24mm, diameter 2.2mm

SF86: Undiagnostic: function unknown
Group 2536; Context 2535; Skeleton 481
Fragmented (upon excavation) copper alloy object (nine pieces). When put together it forms a solid circular base with four vertical side sections with adjoined flat rim sections. Not possible to ascertain original function. Weight: 0.91g, diameter of inner base: *c* 7mm, diameter of rim: *c* 15mm

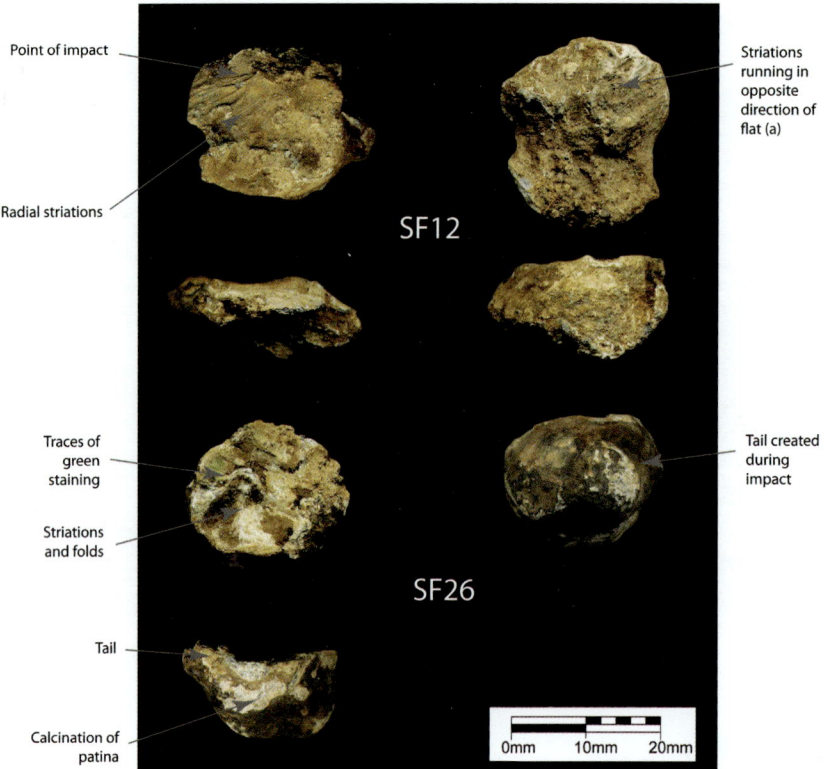

Figure 5.11   Lead projectiles (SF12 and SF26). SF12: top left, flat (a), showing point of impact and radial striations; top right, flat (b) showing rough surface and opposing striations; bottom left, sharp edge; bottom right, sharp edges and folding lips. SF26: top left, flat impact surface showing striations, folds, gouges, and green staining; top right, spherical half of ball showing tail, calcified and darker deposits forming on surface; bottom left, profile of musket ball showing flat surface and tail formed during impact at angle

5.5   Lead projectiles
Natasha Ferguson

Two lead projectiles were recovered during the excavation: SF12 and SF26. They were associated with Skeletons 285 and 348 respectively, each an older child of unknown sex. Both came from the grave fill below the skeletons.

SF12: Lead projectile
Group 2145; Context 2144; Skeleton 285; undiagnostic
Weight: 24.08g. Dimensions: 23.55mm x 9.81mm
  The lead is severely corroded, rough and deeply pitted across its surface. Thick calcified deposits have formed across the patina. Poor surface condition limits identification of the surface morphology. There are no visible casting elements.
  There is severe deformation of the original shape, with flattening on both sides and only traces of spherical form apparent. Flat (a) has prominent radial striations originating from one point; this flat is rough with lips and folds. Flat (b) is very rough with nodules, deep pitting and a trace of striations running in a different direction to the striations on the opposite side. The edges are sharp and defined with a large folding lip at edge of flat (b).
  Diagnostic features indicate impact, or multiple impacts (ricochet), with a solid object, as suggested by the striations running in opposite directions. Radial lines on flat (a) show a point of impact followed by spreading of the lead, which suggests impact at an angle. Similar deformations have been seen on bullets which have hit features such as logs or trees, leaving striations and sharp edges as the ball passed through, although lead

corrosion may have accentuated the level of roughness across the surface.
  The ball has a relatively small estimated bore of 19 (0.626in/15.9mm; 23.9g). A musket ball fired from a Brown Bess musket would have a bore of 14–16 (0.662in–0.693in/16.8mm–17.6mm). It may therefore have been fired from a carbine (a shortened version of a musket designed for use on horseback) or a rifle. The latter would usually leave diagnostic markings on the surface, but deep corrosion will have made any such markings unidentifiable.

SF26: Lead projectile
Group 2291; Context 2290; Skeleton 348; undiagnostic
Weight: 22.08g. Dimensions: 18.62mm x 12.03mm
  The lead is severely corroded, with a thick calcified patina and darker deposits across the surface. There is some loss of surface area due to corrosion. A small patch of green staining is present on the flat surface, possibly due to post-depositional contact with a copper alloy object, or impurities within the lead itself. Poor surface condition limits identification of the surface morphology. There are no visible casting elements.
  The ball is half-flat with a slight tail at one end. There are traces of striations on the flat surface, as well as secondary gouges and folds that make the surface irregular. There is deformation of the spherical half, with a gouge creating a narrow ridge, although this could be due to some surface loss.
  The ball has impacted on a hard, rough surface at an angle, so as to create a tail and the striations on the flat surface. It is not possible to infer what the musket ball has hit. There is also the possibility of ricochet having caused the multiple deformations on the surface. Bore size is difficult to determine due to deformation and possible loss of mass due

to corrosion, but a bore size of 20 (0.615in) is likely. It may therefore have been fired from a carbine or a rifle.

5.6 Glass ampoules and bottles
Helen MacQuarrie

5.6.1 Medical ampoules

Three yellow-brown glass, single-use medical ampoules (SF16) were recovered from the fill of grave 2251. They were recovered from the upper levels of the backfill and are unlikely to be associated with those inhumed within the grave.

The ampoules have been moulded, which indicates a mid-19th-century date (Bennon 1979, 254). They are probably of British manufacture: numerous items of correspondence from St Helena refer to the supply of medicines from England, relating to both the Liberated African Establishment and the civil hospital. Precisely comparable items have not been located within museum collections or published records.

Tests were undertaken at the Chemistry Department of the University of Bristol to establish the composition of the residues within the ampoules.

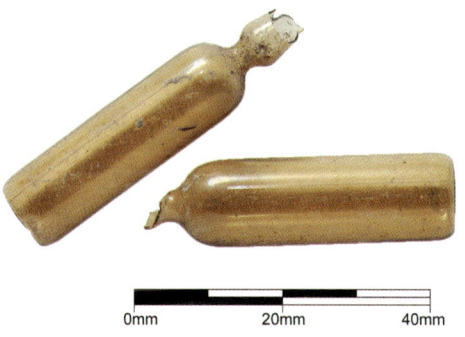

Figure 5.12   Glass ampoules (SF16) from the fill of Group 2251

The residues from one ampoule were dissolved, but the resultant mass spectra were inconclusive when compared with the expected values for opium or heroin (P Gates, pers comm).

SF16: Medical ampoules (3)
Group 2251; Context 2250; mid-19th century; British?
Three yellow-brown glass single-use ampoules: flat base with vertical sides that taper at the neck to a head which has been broken off. Each ampoule weighs 1.4–1.8g and is 35mm in height (from the base to the neck) and 10.5mm in diameter

5.6.2 Bottles

Thirty-six glass bottles were recovered as a bulk find from a rectangular pit (Group 2189; Figs 3.20 and 5.13). The bottles were neatly stacked. Ten of the bottles were complete and the remainder were broken. Although they vary slightly in shape and design they are all characteristic of mid–late 19th-century glass production (Dumbrell 1983, 115).

Two of the bottles have diagnostic lettering embossed on the base, 'J K Pow' and 'Jersey', and the word 'Patent' on the side. Documentary sources indicate that J K Pow was a glass manufacturer based in Jersey until 1832 and Newcastle thereafter and that the bottles were for wine or claret (Anon 1832, 130).

Primary documentary sources indicate that port wine and brandy was shipped to St Helena and prescribed to those suffering from ill health in the hospital at Rupert's Valley (House of Commons Parliamentary Papers 1850 [No. 643], 81). Medicinal alcohol also features in the inventories and order-lists produced by the Establishment and surviving within the CO 247 series of the UK National Archives.

Context 2188: 36 glass bottles (bulk finds); mid-19th century; British

Figure 5.13   Bottles from Group 2189

5.7   Clay pipes
Helen MacQuarrie

Three fragments of clay pipe were recovered (SF32, SF72 and SF73) from two grave contexts (Groups 2326 and 2431). The pipe bowl fragment recovered from Group 2431 (SF73) was complete enough to be dated to the 19th century (Oswald 1975). The bore diameter of all three objects is also in keeping with a 19th-century date (Moore 1980, 6).

During the 18th and 19th centuries tobacco pipe production was dominated by the United Kingdom, Holland and France. The white clay pigment of the pipe fragments indicates a British origin for these objects; Dutch clay pipes utilised grey or yellow clay, whilst red clay was utilised in French clay pipe production (Oswald 1975).

Clay pipes recovered from grave contexts in Barbados (Handler and Lange 1999) and the New York African Burial Ground (Perry *et al* 2006) have been interpreted as grave goods. However, unlike those recovered from Barbados and New York, the pipes from Rupert's Valley had been used. Moreover, the pipe fragments from Rupert's Valley were recovered from backfill deposits, indicating that they were not deliberately deposited within the graves.

Within a British context the retrieval of clay pipes from grave contexts is often interpreted as evidence for grave diggers having smoked whilst they worked (Cowie *et al* 2008, 38). The identity of the grave diggers in Rupert's Valley is unknown: they may have been native St Helenians, or working parties of freed slaves. The latter group are certainly known to have used tobacco: documentary and archaeological evidence indicates that it was distributed to slaves during the Middle Passage (eg Handler 2008) and they continued this habit after emancipation. McHenry (1845–46, chapter 2, 437) commented that 'quite as enthusiastic amateurs as the Europeans, they [the Africans] will make great sacrifices to obtain tobacco; will exchange it for any article of dress, or even give a part of their allowances. All are fond of smoking – men, women and young children – all indulge in the luxury'.

SF32: White clay pipe stem
Group 2326; Context 2325; 19th century
57mm in length, 7mm in diameter with a 2mm bore. No maker's mark or decoration

SF72: White clay pipe stem and neck
Group 2431; Context 2430; mid–late 19th century
Broken spur, bowl broken off but appears to rise sharply from the neck. 55mm of stem survives, 6–9mm in diameter (ellipsoid) with a 2mm diameter bore. No maker's marks or decoration recorded. Pipe has been used

SF73: White clay pipe bowl
Group 2431; Context 2430; mid–late 19th century
Bowl squat and narrow with an upright angle from the neck of the stem. Diameter of bowl is 22mm and it is 35mm tall. Diameter of stem is 6–9mm (ellipsoid) with a 2mm diameter bore. Bowl has no spur or heel and there are no maker's marks or decoration. Pipe has been used

5.8   Beads
Helen MacQuarrie

A total of 12,845 complete glass beads weighing 617.09g were recovered from the excavation, comprising fourteen individual or group finds from eleven graves. The number of beads per group ranged from a single object to over 9400 items. In addition to the beads, a perforated horn, shell button and two cowrie shells were utilised for adornment and are included within this discussion.

Of the 325 interred individuals, eleven had beads associated with them: 3.4% of the total population. Of these, one was a neonate (Skeleton 381), five were children (Skeletons 305, 326, 413, 424, 438) and four were adults (Skeletons 279, 324, 353, 365). It is unclear to which person SF64 belonged: two adolescents and an older child were inhumed within the grave.

Forty varieties of beads have been identified, a figure that includes the three non-glass varieties. Each variety is described in full in the inventory in the digital volume, Appendix D3 and illustrated in Figure 5.16. Non-glass beads are described in section 5.8.3.

5.8.1   Methodology

The methodology utilised within this report is based on the Systematic Bead Description System (SBDS) (DeCorse *et al* 2003) which incorporates methodologies developed by Kidd and Kidd (1970) and Karklins (1985). The SBDS is based on the presentation of the bead attributes and the formation of manageable varieties based on shared attributes. The glass bead type attributes defined are as follows:

- **Material of composition**: only glass beads are included within this section. The horn and shell beads are described separately
- **Manufacturing method**: the methods of glass bead manufacture represented within this assemblage are either *wound* or *drawn*. For a full description of the variety of techniques and the identifying features associated see Kidd and Kidd (1970)
- **Bead structure**: varieties of bead structure represented within the assemblage include *simple* beads made from a single layer of glass; *compound* beads made from one or two layers of undecorated glass; and *complex* beads, which are simple beads to which secondary ('advantageous') decoration has been added
- **Secondary modification**: this includes intentional modification of the bead after initial manufacture, either undertaken by the manufacturer or locally. Secondary modification identified within the assemblage comprises *reheating* and *grinding*
- **Shape**: as defined by Beck (1928), the shape of the bead is based on the longitudinal and trans-

verse section. Principal shape types identified during this study comprise: *cylinder* (round transverse section; rectangular longitudinal section); *barrel* (round transverse section; square/short longitudinal section); *annular* (round transverse section; short longitudinal section with rounded profile); *ellipsoid* (elliptical transverse and longitudinal section); and *spherical* (round transverse and longitudinal section). It should be noted that shape attributes should be considered with secondary modification, ie a heat-rounded cylinder has bevelled ends, whereas a cylinder with no secondary modification has not

- **Measurement**: maximum length, diameter and weight are given for each bead variety. For each bead variety batches of 50 were examined and the largest and smallest examples were weighed and measured. The largest and smallest were identified from these calculations and included as the range for each type. All measurements are given in millimetres
- **Lustre**: lustre is described as *dull* or *shiny*
- **Diaphaneity**: refers to the ability of the bead to transmit light and is defined as *opaque, translucent* or *transparent*
- **Colour**: each bead was cross-referenced with the *Munsell Colour Chart* (1966 Glossy Edition) in natural light when wet. The Munsell colour reference was also cross-referenced with the (United States) National Bureau of Standards (1976) for the appropriate colour name
- **Description of bead decoration**
- **Origin and age of the beads**: where possible to ascertain
- **Remarks**: this includes specific idiosyncratic information such as weathering, patination, pitting, or breakage

A systematic and scoped approach was adopted in order to record the attributes of all the beads within the assemblage, and combine these attributes to create manageable varieties. This involved visual inspection, followed by the inspection of every bead under a magnification of x10 with strong light to check the attributes as defined above. Every 50 (or fewer) beads were weighed and attributes recorded, including the dimensions and weight of the largest and smallest bead. The attributes of the 87 initial varieties were added to a database which was then interrogated in order to group varieties from different contexts. In this way the final list of varieties was established, of which there are 40 (including the non-glass beads).

In the following inventory and catalogue, 'type' refers to the typology series produced by Kidd and Kidd (1970), as modified by Karklins (1985), but without the colour number, as this is given in the colour attributes. 'Variety' is used for every number assigned by the author for the purpose of this report.

Comparative material used in conjunction with this analysis comprised: the Victoria and Albert Museum (including the National Art Library);

the British Museum (including the Anthropology Library); and the Pitt Rivers Museum, Oxford. Marilee Wood provided additional advice regarding the identification of some bead varieties. Advice on the identification of the non-glass beads was provided by the Natural History Museum, London.

Some manufacturing techniques provide an indication of the date of production. For example, in 1817 a technique developed by the Italian Luigi Pusinich revolutionised the way that drawn beads were heat-rounded, replacing the '*a speo*' process of heat-rounding (Karklins 1993). Similarly, the Prosser-moulding technique, patented in the 1840s, results in a distinctive product (DeCorse *et al* 2003). Within the catalogue (digital volume, Appendix D3) a date for each bead variety is given only when it is clearly inferred by the manufacturing technique.

5.8.2 Results

Of the 37 glass beads varieties identified, twelve registered within the comparative bead data (see the digital volume, Appendix D3). Five wound beads (Varieties 1–5) and four drawn beads (Varieties 11–14) are associated with Venetian glass production. These are predominately associated with 19th-century production, although the large red on translucent green bead (Variety 13) is associated with 17th-century production. A Dutch wound bead was identified which is associated with 18th-century trade and two drawn, faceted varieties (29 and 30) are associated with 19th-century Bohemian production. Variety 11, the Venetian 'galet rouge', also pre-dated the graveyard, as production is dated to the 17th to early 19th century.

The majority of the seed beads have no diagnostic features to aid dating or provenance. The lack of diagnostic features, however, for example the '*a speo*' process of heat-rounding (Karklins 1993) are not represented within this assemblage, suggesting a post-1817 date for manufacture.

The glass beads probably all originated in Europe. By the 19th century Europe had developed a prolific glass bead trade which extended across the Atlantic seaboard and to the east. Bead varieties represented in the assemblage reflect the domination of Venice, Bohemia and Holland in 19th-century glass bead production, although Germany, France, Spain and England also developed glass-making industries (Sherr 1987). One of the largest markets for European glass beads was Africa, where they were traded for palm oil, gold, ivory and slaves (Karklins 2004). There is also a strong tradition of bead production in West Africa based on the adaptation of imported glass bottles and beads (Van der Sleer 1967); however, characteristics relating to this tradition of bead manufacture were not detected within the assemblage.

The dominance of European-made beads within this assemblage is unsurprising given the context of the site and Europe's general monopoly of the market. However, the ubiquity of these bead

Figure 5.14   Coffin 2366. Photograph taken after the removal of the body, showing the bead mattress (SF65), leather shoe (SF67) and pillow

Figure 5.15   Bead necklace (SF39; Group 2305) in situ around the neck of Skeleton 353

varieties throughout both Europe and Africa makes it difficult to comment with certainty as to where they may have been obtained by those buried in Rupert's Valley. They may have been objects worn prior to enslavement, given at sea by either the slavers or the naval prize crew, or acquired in the depot in Rupert's Valley.

The original form of the objects made up by the beads is not always clear, although the very large numbers of beads registered as SF65 formed a mat that was placed in the base of the neonate coffin, Group 2366. This single object accounted for 9485 beads, 73.8% of the total assemblage (Fig 5.14).

Outside this coffin, the beads have been interpreted as personal adornment. Some are likely to have been necklaces, the beads having been recovered near the neck area of the individual. Others may have been worn on the wrist or arm: Group 2082 comprised a number of beads recovered by the left upper arm (SF15) and two beads by the left wrist of a young child (Skeleton 305; SF104a), which may have been a bracelet or arm decoration. In several

cases the number of beads recovered from the grave was extremely small. For example, six beads were recovered from Group 2233 and eight from Group 2449. Examples of West African jewellery are known to incorporate small number of beads, though it is also possible that those comprising only a small number of beads might have come from very small items of jewellery such as an ear-ring (as described by McHenry 1845–46, chapter 1, 183) or have been beads worn in the hair.

No evidence was recovered to indicate what material was used to string the beads, although it is presumed that a degradable organic material rather than metal was used.

5.8.3   *Non-glass beads*

The recovery of non-glass beads used as artefacts of personal adornment is very significant, not only because they are a non-European cultural expression, but also the materials are not common on St Helena. Two cowrie shells (Variety 40) were recovered from the neck area of Skeleton 279, a mature female (Group 2163). As well as a historic tradition as currency, cowrie shells were also associated with themes of femininity and fertility (Sherr 1987, 124). Examples of cowries are common within West African art and adornment and cowrie shells were also recorded at the New York African Burial Ground, associated with an adult female (Burial 340: aged 39–64 years in age) (Perry *et al* 2006). Cowrie shells were also recovered in association with an adult male buried in the 17th- to 18th-century Plantation Slave Cemetery, Barbados (Handler *et al* 1982).

Shell buttons were also recovered from the Rupert's Valley site (Variety 39); these were associated with glass beads, indicating that they were incorporated into an item of adornment, as opposed to being part of clothing. Similar buttons have also been recovered associated with textiles (section 5.9.7).

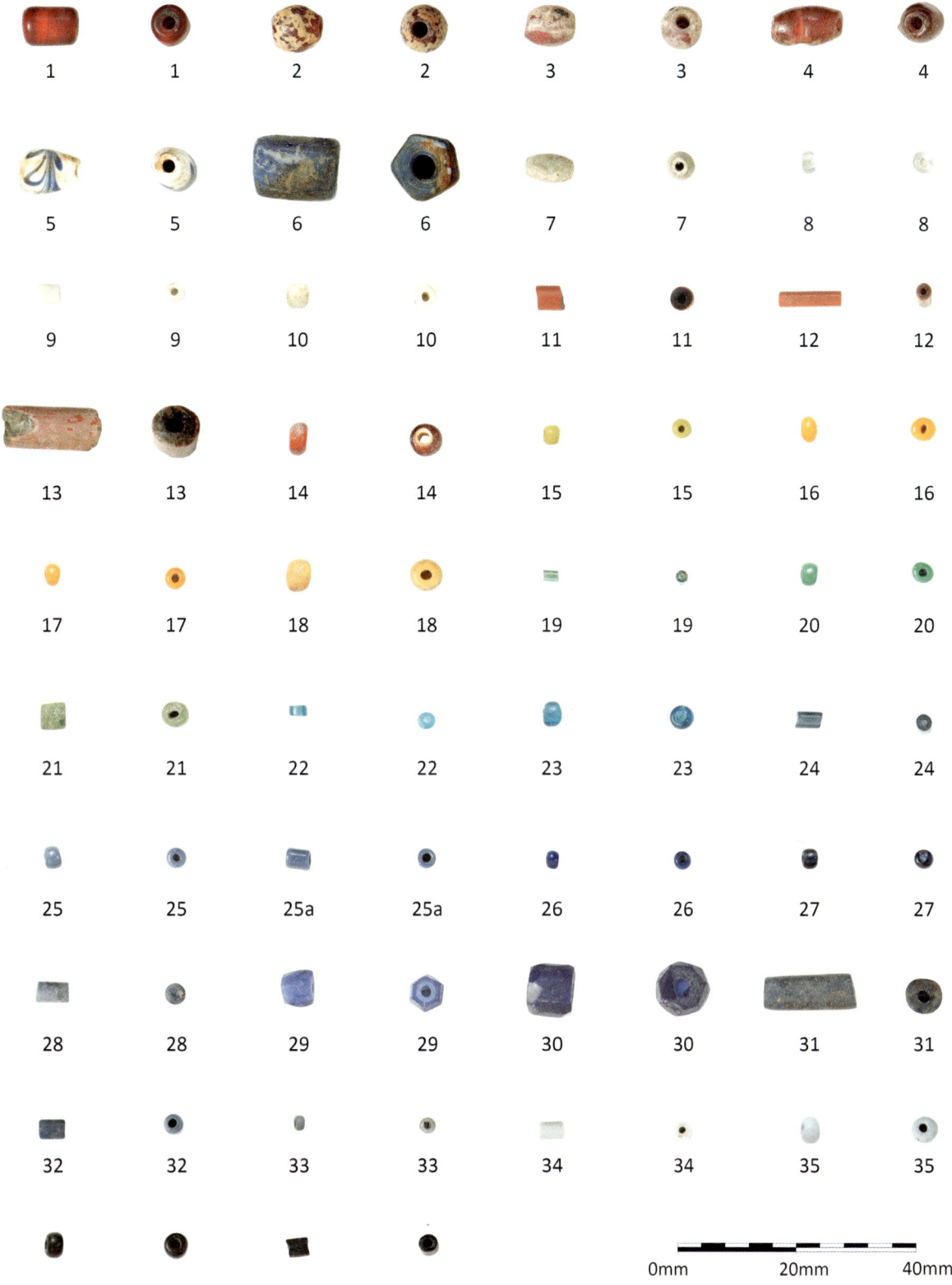

Figure 5.16   Illustrated bead catalogue

A perforated bovid horn was recovered (Variety 38) associated with a young child (Skeleton 326, Group 2233). It was not possible to determine the species from which it may have originated (Roberto Portela Miguez, pers comm). However, the horn is dissimilar to that of a goat, which is the only known horned bovid on St Helena, indicating that this item was imported to the island. Significantly the bovid horn was associated with five beads which greatly pre-date the graveyard. The necklace comprised a Dutch Pentagon bead (Variety 6) of 18th-century date, and an earlier

17th-century red on translucent green Venetian drawn bead (Variety 13). At the very least these beads were 50 years old at the time of burial and must have passed down at least one, if not two, generations. Associated with beads of some age, the poor condition of the horn may be attributed to its antiquity. Examples of horn pendants associated with burials are rare within the archaeological record, although ethnographic examples are known, for example a 19th-century necklace from Barambo in the Democratic Republic of Congo previously exhibited at the Metropolitan Museum of Art, New York (LaGamma 2000, 58–9).

Variety 38: Perforated bovid horn, Africa
This item comprises four parts, which fit together. The largest part is the keratinised sheath, which is pierced at one end (so as to be used as a pendant); it has collapsed in the centre, as the horn core became dislodged from the sheath, forming a ridge. The other three pieces belong to the bony core; they fit together and provide an indication of the diameter of the original horn. The horn compares favourably to those of many African bovid species (notably Antilopinae) but, due to the absence of any distinctive morphological characteristics and its deformed and possibly incomplete condition, it was not possible to determine the species from which it may have originated (Roberto Portela Miguez, pers comm; Bubenik and Bubenik 1990). However, the horn is dissimilar to that of a goat, the only known horned bovid on St Helena, indicating that this item was an import to the island.
Dimensions: diameter 14.47mm x 12.06mm (based on core), length 50.54mm (based on sheath), diameter of perforation 3.92 x 3.48mm. Weight 1.30g

Variety 39: Shell button; undiagnostic
Fragmented shell button with two visible perforations. Similar button recovered as part of group find SF13. The species of shell could not be determined.
Dimensions: diameter 6.88mm, thickness 1.18mm. Weight 0.03g

Variety 40: Cowrie shells (2)
Two very worn cowrie shells (*Cypraeoidea* superfamily). The dorsum on both molluscs has completely worn away leaving very few diagnostic features to aid identification. The shell wall is very thin and the aperture edges are quite wide, indicating that this is a juvenile shell. Due to the poor condition of the shell and its juvenile state it is not possible to determine species beyond that of superfamily. Cowrie shells are found worldwide across the tropical and sub-tropical oceans and seas (Allan 1956). They are found on St Helena but are not common (Rebecca Cairns-Wicks, pers comm).
Dimensions: Shell 1, length 14.81mm, thickness 5.08mm, weight 0.42g; Shell 2, length 13.62mm, thickness 4.24mm, weight 0.35g. Total weight of both shells 0.77g

5.8.4   Catalogue of bead objects

Group 2082; Context 2081; Skeleton 305; SF15, SF104a; 17th–19th century
SF15 comprises 22 (1.08g) beads in five varieties: 09, 11, 28, 34 and 36. SF15 was recovered below the left upper arm of Skeleton 305, a young child of unknown sex (one of two inhumations within the grave). Of these only one is diagnostic: 'galet rouge' (Variety 11) which is associated with 17th- to early 19th-century Venetian bead produc-

tion. SF104a comprises two beads in two varieties: 01 and 04 (1.57g). These beads were recovered by the left wrist of the young child: it is presumed that they all formed part of a single object which broke during or after burial

Group 2163; Context 2162; Skeleton 279; SF07; 17th–19th century
SF07 comprises 153 (7.65g) beads in eight glass bead varieties: 09, 11, 21, 22, 28, 32, 35 and 37. Of these only Variety 11 is diagnostic, being associated with 17th- to 19th-century Venetian bead production (DeCorse *et al* 2003). SF07 also incorporated non-glass bead Variety 40: two undiagnostic cowrie shells (*Cypraeoidea* superfamily) (Allan 1956). The beads were recovered from the neck area of Skeleton 279, a mature adult female (single inhumation)

Group 2233; Context 2232; Skeleton 326; SF22, SF23; 17th–19th century
SF22 comprises five beads (3.92g) in three glass bead varieties: 07, 13 and 31, and a perforated bovid horn (Variety 38). SF23 comprises a single bead (2.18g) in Variety 06. In total the object comprises six beads (6.1g). The necklace comprised a Dutch Pentagon bead (Variety 6) of 18th-century date, and an earlier 17th-century red on translucent green Venetian drawn bead (Variety 13). SF22 was recovered in the vicinity of the neck and SF23 was recovered at the right hip. The beads may have formed part of a single object which broke during or after burial. The object is associated with Skeleton 326, a young child of unknown sex (one of three inhumations within the grave)

Group 2254; Context 2253; Skeleton 324; SF17, SF18; 17th–19th century
SF17 comprises 1732 (56.76g) beads in seven varieties: 09, 11, 15, 20, 22, 24 and 37. SF18 comprises three (0.07g) beads in three varieties: 09, 25 and 33. Of these Variety 11 is diagnostic: the 'galet rouge' a drawn glass bead produced in Venice between the 17th and early 19th century. SF17 was recovered in the vicinity of the neck and SF18 was recovered close to the skull of Skeleton 324, a mature adult male (one of two inhumations within the grave)

Group 2305; Context 2304; Skeleton 353; SF39; 19th century
SF39 comprises 941 beads (40.06g) in ten varieties: 08, 14, 15, 17, 19, 20, 23, 24, 25 and 29. The beads were found in a linear pattern around the neck of Skeleton 353, a prime adult (probably male) (one of two inhumations within the grave). The beads recovered from this grave include two diagnostic Venetian 'white heart' beads (Variety 14) and two Bohemian faceted beads (Variety 29). Both are associated with 19th-century production

Group 2332; Context 2331; Skeleton 365; SF38; 19th century
SF38 comprises eight beads (3.39g) in four varieties: 01, 17, 29 and 30. It was recovered from the lower hip of Skeleton 365, a prime adult female (single inhumation). Five diagnostic 19th-century Bohemian faceted beads were recovered, one slightly larger in size (Variety 30) than the rest (Variety 29)

Group 2367; Context 2366; Skeleton 381; SF65; 19th century
SF65 comprises 9484 beads (467.27g) in ten varieties: 08, 15, 16, 17, 19, 20, 23, 26, 27 and 29. The only diagnostic varieties recovered from the coffin were five Russian blue/faceted beads, Variety 29, which are attributed to 19th-century production. The beads formed a mat within coffin (2366), which contained Skeleton 381, a neonate of unknown sex (single inhumation). The mat was a deliberate deposit within the coffin

Table 5.2 Bead catalogue

Small Find Number	Variety	Total number	Total weight (g)
Group 2082			
SF15	09: Drawn, simple, cylindrical – barrel, dull, opaque, white, 2.47–4.38mm (diameter) × 1.96–4.54mm (length)	15	0.78
	11: Drawn, compound, heat-rounded, annular; barrel; cylindrical, dull, opaque, deep reddish-brown, on transparent light green, 2.2–4.32mm (diameter) × 1.2–3.48mm (length). 'Galet rouge', Venetian, 17th–early 19th century	1	0.04
	28: Drawn, simple, cylindrical, dull, opaque, dark blue, 2.62–4.39mm (diameter) × 1.9–5.00mm (length)	4	0.17
	34: Drawn, simple, heat-rounded, cylinder, dull, opaque, light bluish-grey, 3.12mm (diameter) × 4.03mm (length)	1	0.05
	36: Drawn, simple, heat-rounded, annular, dull, opaque, blackish-blue, 3.05–4.85mm (diameter) × 2.15–4.2mm (length)	1	0.04
SF104a	01: Wound, simple, cylindrical, shiny/dull, translucent, very deep red; moderate reddish-brown, 6.12–7.20mm (diameter) × 8.9–10.07mm (length). Venetian	1	0.84
	04: Wound, simple, ellipsoid, shiny, translucent, very deep red, heat damaged, 6.66mm (diameter) × 11.76mm (length). Venetian	1	0.73
Total	**7**	**24**	**2.65**
Group 2163			
SF07	09: Drawn, simple, cylindrical – barrel, dull, opaque, white, 2.47–4.38mm (diameter) × 1.96–4.54mm (length)	63	3.12
	11: Drawn, compound, heat-rounded, annular; barrel; cylindrical, dull, opaque, deep reddish-brown, on transparent light green, 2.2–4.32mm (diameter) × 1.2–3.48mm (length). 'Galet rouge', Venetian, 17th–early 19th century	53	1.85
	21: Drawn, simple, heat-rounded, annular; barrel, dull, opaque, dark yellowish-green, 4.18–4.43mm (diameter) × 2.91–4.11mm (length)	1	0.14
	22: Drawn, simple, heat-rounded, annular, dull, transparent, dark greenish-blue, 2.99–3.81mm (diameter) × 1.77–2.63 (length)	8	0.4
	28: Drawn, simple, cylindrical, dull, opaque, dark blue, 2.62–4.39mm (diameter) × 1.9–5.00 (length)	6	0.63
	32: Drawn, simple, cylindrical, dull, opaque, moderate blue, 2.95–3.32mm (diameter) × 3.35–4.24mm (length)	6	0.32
	35: Drawn, simple, heat-rounded, annular, shiny, opaque, pale blue, 2.86–4.41mm (diameter) × 2.29–3.03mm (length)	2	0.13
	37: Drawn, simple, cylindrical, shiny, opaque, blackish-blue, black, 2.67–4.21mm (diameter) × 1.41–5.37mm (length)	12	0.29
	40: Cowrie shells	2	0.77
Total	**9**	**153**	**7.65**
Group 2233			
SF22	07: Wound, simple, ellipsoid, dull, opaque, moderate yellowish-green, 7.28–7.83mm (diameter) × 4.61–4.79mm (length)	2	0.5
	13: 16th–20th century, drawn, compound, cylindrical, dull, translucent, dark red on transparent light green, 7.12mm (diameter) × 17.30mm (length). Venetian	1	1.2
	31: Drawn, simple, cylindrical, dull, opaque, dark blue, 15.86mm (diameter) x5.82mm (length)	1	0.92
	38: Perforated bovid horn	1	1.3
SF23	06: Wound, simple, ground facets (5) and heat-rounded, ellipsoid, dull, opaque, strong blue, 14.03mm (diameter) × 9.77mm (length). Dutch pentagon, 16th–19th century	1	2.18
Total	**5**	**6**	**6.1**
Group 2254			
SF17	09: Drawn, simple, cylindrical – barrel, dull, opaque, white, 2.47–4.38mm (diameter) × 1.96–4.54mm (length)	2	0.05
	11: Drawn, compound, heat-rounded, annular; barrel; cylindrical, dull, opaque, deep reddish-brown on transparent light green, 2.2–4.32mm (diameter) × 1.2–3.48mm (length). 'Galet rouge', Venetian, 17th–early 19th century	1685	55.58
	15: Drawn, simple, heat-rounded, annular, shiny – occ. dull, translucent, strong yellow, 2.05–4.89mm (diameter) × 1.16–3.08mm (length)	4	0.08

Table 5.2 (*cont.*)   Bead catalogue

Small Find Number	Variety	Total number	Total weight (g)
SF17 (*cont.*)	20: Drawn, simple, heat-rounded, annular, shiny, opaque, dark yellowish-green; deep yellowish-green, 2.47–3.75mm (diameter) × 1.36–2.61mm (length)	1	0.01
	22: Drawn, simple, heat-rounded, annular, dull, transparent, dark greenish-blue, 2.99–3.81mm (diameter) × 1.77–2.63 (length)	3	0.08
	24: Drawn, simple, cylindrical, shiny, transparent, dark blue, 2.40–3.77mm (diameter) × 1.93–4.81mm (length)	3	0.08
	37: Drawn, simple, cylindrical, shiny, opaque, blackish-blue, black, 2.67–4.21mm (diameter) × 1.41–5.37mm (length)	34	0.88
SF18	09: Drawn, simple, cylindrical – barrel, dull, opaque, white, 2.47–4.54mm (diameter) × 1.96–5.45mm (length)	1	0.03
	25: Drawn, simple, heat-rounded, annular; cylindrical, shiny, opaque, moderate blue; dark blue, patented surface, 2.60–3.94mm (diameter) × 2.03–4.91mm (length)	1	0.03
	33: Drawn, simple, heat-rounded, annular, shiny, opaque, greyish-blue, 2.62mm (diameter) × 1.76mm (length)	1	0.01
Total	**10**	**1735**	**56.83**
Group 2305			
SF39	08: Drawn, simple, heat-rounded, annular, shiny, transparent, clear, 3.29–3.87mm (diameter) × 2.17–2.19mm (length)	1	0.03
	14: Drawn, compound, heat-rounded, annular, dull, translucent dark red (5R 3/8), on opaque white, 3.81–6.03mm (diameter) × 2.60–2.71mm (length)	2	0.13
	15: Drawn, simple, heat-rounded, annular, shiny – occ. dull, translucent, strong yellow, 2.05–4.89mm (diameter) × 1.16–3.08mm (length)	464	17.33
	17: Drawn, simple, heat-rounded, annular, shiny, translucent, strong yellowish-brown, patented surface, 2.63–4.33mm (diameter) × 1.47–2.94mm (length)	451	21.26
	19: Drawn, simple, cylindrical, shiny, transparent, dark yellowish-green, 2.20–2.78mm (diameter) × 2.17–2.60mm (length)	5	0.08
	20: Drawn, simple, heat-rounded, annular, shiny, opaque, dark yellowish-green; deep yellowish-green, patented surface, 2.47–3.75mm (diameter) × 1.36–2.61mm (length)	4	0.21
	23: Drawn, simple, heat-rounded, annular, shiny, transparent, very dark greenish-blue, 3.05–4.02mm (diameter) × 2.23–2.60mm (length)	1	0.02
	24: Drawn, simple, cylindrical, shiny, transparent, dark blue, 2.40–3.77mm (diameter) × 1.93–4.81mm (length)	4	0.2
	25: Drawn, simple, heat-rounded, annular; cylindrical, shiny, opaque, moderate blue; dark blue, patented surface, 2.60–3.94mm (diameter) × 2.03–4.91mm (length)	7	0.4
	29: Drawn, simple, ground facets (15, 17, 18, 20 and 23), hexagonal, shiny, translucent, deep blue, 4.44–6.15mm (diameter) × 4.42–6.89mm (length). 19th century, Bohemian	2	0.4
Total	**10**	**941**	**40.06**
Group 2332			
SF38	01: Wound, simple, cylindrical, shiny/dull, translucent, very deep red, moderate reddish-brown, 6.12–7.20mm (diameter) × 8.90–10.07mm (length). Venetian	2	1.44
	17: Drawn, simple, heat-rounded, annular, shiny, translucent, strong yellowish-brown, patented surface, 2.63–4.33mm (diameter) × 1.47–2.94mm (length)	1	0.04
	29: Drawn, simple, ground facets (15, 17, 18, 20 and 23), hexagonal, shiny, translucent, deep blue, 4.44–6.15mm (diameter) × 4.42–6.89mm (length). 19th century, Bohemian	4	1.12
	30: Drawn, simple, ground facets (21), hexagonal, shiny, transparent, deep blue, 6.95mm (diameter) × 8.80mm (length). 19th century, Bohemian	1	0.79
Total	**4**	**8**	**3.39**
Group 2367			
SF65	08: Drawn, simple, heat-rounded, annular, shiny, transparent, clear, 3.29–3.87mm (diameter) × 2.17–2.19mm (length)	7	0.28
	15: Drawn, simple, heat-rounded, annular, shiny – occ. dull, translucent, strong yellow, 2.05–4.89mm (diameter) × 1.16–3.08mm (length)	3146	170.05
	16: Drawn, simple, heat-rounded, annular, shiny, translucent, dark orange yellow, patented surface, 2.66–4.38mm (diameter) × 1.58–3.25mm (length)	676	39.23
	17: Drawn, simple, heat-rounded, annular, shiny, translucent, strong yellowish-brown, patented surface, 2.63–4.33mm (diameter) × 1.47–2.94mm (length)	4860	237.80

Table 5.2 (*cont.*) Bead catalogue

Small Find Number	Variety	Total number	Total weight (g)
SF65 (*cont.*)	19: Drawn, simple, cylindrical, shiny, transparent, dark yellowish-green, 2.20–2.78mm (diameter) × 2.17–2.60mm (length)	2	0.06
	20: Drawn, simple, heat-rounded, annular, shiny, opaque, dark yellowish-green; deep yellowish-green, patented surface, 2.47–3.75mm (diameter) × 1.36–2.61mm (length)	22	0.98
	23: Drawn, simple, heat-rounded, annular, shiny, transparent, very dark greenish-blue, 3.05–4.02mm (diameter) × 2.23–2.60mm (length)	5	0.20
	26: Drawn, simple, heat-rounded, annular, shiny, opaque, dark blue, 2.38–2.98mm (diameter) × 1.76–2.65mm (length)	756	17.65
	27: Drawn, simple, heat-rounded, annular, shiny, transparent, dark blue, 2.95–3.53mm (diameter) × 2.36–2.96mm (length)	5	0.24
	29: Drawn, simple, ground facets (15, 17, 18, 20 and 23), hexagonal, shiny, translucent, deep blue, 4.44–6.15mm (diameter) × 4.42–6.89mm (length). 19th century, Bohemian	5	0.78
Total	**10**	**9484**	**467.27**
Group 2428			
SF74	24: Drawn, simple, cylindrical, shiny, transparent, dark blue, 2.40–3.77mm (diameter) × 1.93–4.81mm (length)	150	7.96
	35: Drawn, simple, heat-rounded, annular, shiny, opaque, pale blue, 2.86–4.41mm (diameter) × 2.29–3.03mm (length)	1	0.02
	36: Drawn, simple, heat-rounded, annular, dull, opaque, blackish-blue, 3.05–4.85mm (diameter) × 2.15–4.20mm (length)	7	0.46
	37: Drawn, simple, cylindrical, shiny, opaque, blackish-blue, black, 2.67–4.21mm (diameter) × 1.41–5.37mm (length)	259	6.36
	39: Fragmented shell button	1	0.03
Total	**5**	**418**	**14.83**
Group 2449			
SF77	01: Wound, simple, cylindrical, shiny/dull, translucent, very deep red–moderate reddish-brown, 6.12–7.20mm (diameter) × 8.90–10.07mm (length). Venetian	2	1.54
	02: Wound, simple, spherical, dull, translucent, very deep red, 7.20–8.11mm (diameter) × 7.00–7.72mm (length). Venetian	4	5.36
	03: Wound, simple, ellipsoid, dull, opaque, very deep red, 6.45–6.75mm (diameter) × 8.04–8.94 (length). Venetian	2	1.2
Total	**3**	**8**	**8.1**
Group 2404			
SF64	01: Wound, simple, cylindrical, shiny/dull, translucent, very deep red–moderate reddish-brown, 6.12–7.20mm (diameter) × 8.90–10.07mm (length). Venetian	1	0.77
Total	**1**	**1**	**0.77**
Group 2470			
SF78	05: Wound, complex, ellipsoid, shiny, opaque, white, light blue floral leaf design, 8.04mm (diameter) × 10.00mm (length). Venetian	1	1.06
	10: Drawn, simple, heat-rounded, annular, shiny, opaque, white, 2.83–4.58mm (diameter) × 2.66–3.33mm (length)	12	0.7
	12: Drawn, compound, cylindrical, shiny, opaque, moderate reddish-brown on transparent light green, 2.72–3.39mm (diameter) × 9.67–9.90mm (length). Venetian	4	0.52
	14: Drawn, compound, heat-rounded, annular, dull, translucent, dark red, on opaque white, 3.81–6.03mm (diameter), 2.60–2.71mm (length). Venetian	23	3.09
	18: Drawn, simple, heat-rounded, annular, shiny, transparent, strong yellowish-brown, patented surface, 5.26–5.45mm (diameter) × 2.99–3.57mm (length)	28	5.86
	21: Drawn, simple, heat-rounded, annular; barrel, dull, opaque, dark yellowish-green, 4.18–4.43mm (diameter) × 2.91–4.11mm (length)	1	0.24
Total	**6**	**69**	**11.47**

Group 2404; Context 2403; Skeleton 402, 403, 405; SF64; 19th century
SF64 comprises a single bead (0.77g) in Variety 01. The bead is attributed to 19th-century Venetian production. At the time of excavation it was unclear which burial this bead was associated with. Skeleton 402 is an adolescent (probably female); Skeleton 403 is an adolescent of unknown sex; and Skeleton 405 is an older child of unknown sex

Group 2428; Context 2427; Skeleton 413; SF74
SF74 comprises 418 beads (14.83g) in four glass varieties: 24, 35, 36 and 37. No diagnostic beads were identified. One shell button was also utilised as a bead (Variety 39). SF74 was recovered at the base of the grave cut, near the neck of Skeleton 413, an older child of unknown sex (one of two inhumations within the grave)

Group 2449; Context 2448; Skeleton 424, SF77; 19th century
SF77 comprises eight beads (8.1g) in three varieties: 01, 02 and 03. SF77 was recovered near the neck of Skeleton 424, a young child of unknown sex (one of two inhumations within the grave). All of the beads recovered are associated with 19th-century Venetian production.

Group 2470; Context 2469; Skeleton 438; SF78; 19th century
SF78 comprises 69 beads (11.47g) in six varieties: 05, 10, 12, 14, 18 and 21. Diagnostic beads recovered include an elaborate wound Venetian lamp bead with a blue floral pattern (Variety 05), 'galet rouge' beads (Variety 12), and the 'white heart' beads (Variety 14). All these varieties are associated with Venetian production. The beads were recovered at the base of the grave cut near the neck of Skeleton 438, a young child of unknown sex (one of two inhumations within the grave).

5.9   Textiles and clothing

Penelope Walton Rogers (with contributions by Isabella von Holstein, Josie Sheppard and Helen MacQuarrie)

5.9.1   Introduction

Recording the textiles, whether through their visual appearance or through scientific analysis, presented a considerable challenge. They had mostly survived as small clumps of fabric, arranged in dense layers and folds, often by the skull or in the pelvic area of the body. Plant roots had worked their way into the material and held the fragile layers together, so that they could not be easily unfolded. The acidic soils seem to have been especially harmful to plant-fibre textiles, except where corroding metalwork has preserved patches of cotton and linen; they have also attacked the animal fibres in a way that complicates identification by microscopy. Dyes, where detectable, were difficult to analyse. The crumbling nature of the material meant that gloves and face-masks had to be worn, to protect the analysts from dust.

Nevertheless, the results have justified the effort. Remains of garments and other cloths in which the dead were buried have been recorded for 25 individuals, from 23 graves (Table 5.3), and some of the collection has proved to be unique. The striped fabrics made of goat fibre and dyed with Prussian Blue are,

to our knowledge, entirely new in the archaeological record. Some interesting details of clothing have also been recorded, including remains of cotton trousers and a dress or shirt of fine worsted twill that has been cut up and used to stuff a pillow. Most importantly, the silk ribbons, cotton lace and other good-quality textiles associated, not with adults, but with neonates, present an interesting side-light on attitudes towards newborn infants. The study of the textiles therefore extends our knowledge of the graveyard and enhances its interpretation.

5.9.1.1 Data collection

Technical details of the textiles were recorded with a ×10 binocular microscope. Fibres were prepared as whole mounts and cross-sections and examined by incident light up to ×320 and transmitted light up to ×640 magnification. Plant fibres were additionally viewed with a polarising light microscope, which accentuates their structural details. The plant fibre in the cordage has been identified by Dr Allan R Hall, archaeobotanist, University of York.

Identification to species in animal coat fibres is usually based on the morphology of the fibre, especially the cuticular scale pattern (Appleyard 1978), but the scale pattern was only visible in patches in this material. Goat fibre, however, has a characteristic range of diameters which distinguishes it from sheep's wool. Figure 5.17a–d illustrates four samples from two of the Rupert's Valley striped textiles, which have the typical features of the winter coat of goat, namely a fine undercoat, with a mode (most common measurement) of 14 microns, medullas in fibres of intermediate diameter and fibres over 100 microns wide with wide latticed medullas (Wildman 1954, 106–23; Ryder 1987, 8–9; Ryder 1993, 41). Sheep's wool was identified by the absence of medullas in all but the coarsest fibres, oval cross-sections and by patches of scale pattern which were irregular waved mosaic with smooth near margins (Appleyard 1978, 26–7, 107–17). The 'fleece-types' in wool, which are usually identified by the measurement of fibre diameters, could not be fully explored because the fibres were not well enough preserved to allow the extra precision required for these, but yarns from one textile were measured for a rough comparison with the goat fibre (Fig 5.17e–f).

Dyes were analysed by solvent extraction, followed by absorption spectrophotometry and chromatography of the extracts (Walton and Taylor 1991). As the blue colorant in the striped textiles could not be extracted, the following test for the inorganic pigment, ferric ferrocyanide, $Fe_4(Fe(CN)_6)_3$, commonly known as Prussian Blue, was applied. Samples of blue yarn were immersed individually in a 4-molar solution of sodium hydroxide and then rinsed and immersed in 4% aqueous sulphuric acid: the colour changes of the fibre, from blue to brown in alkali and then back to blue in acid were regarded as confirmation of

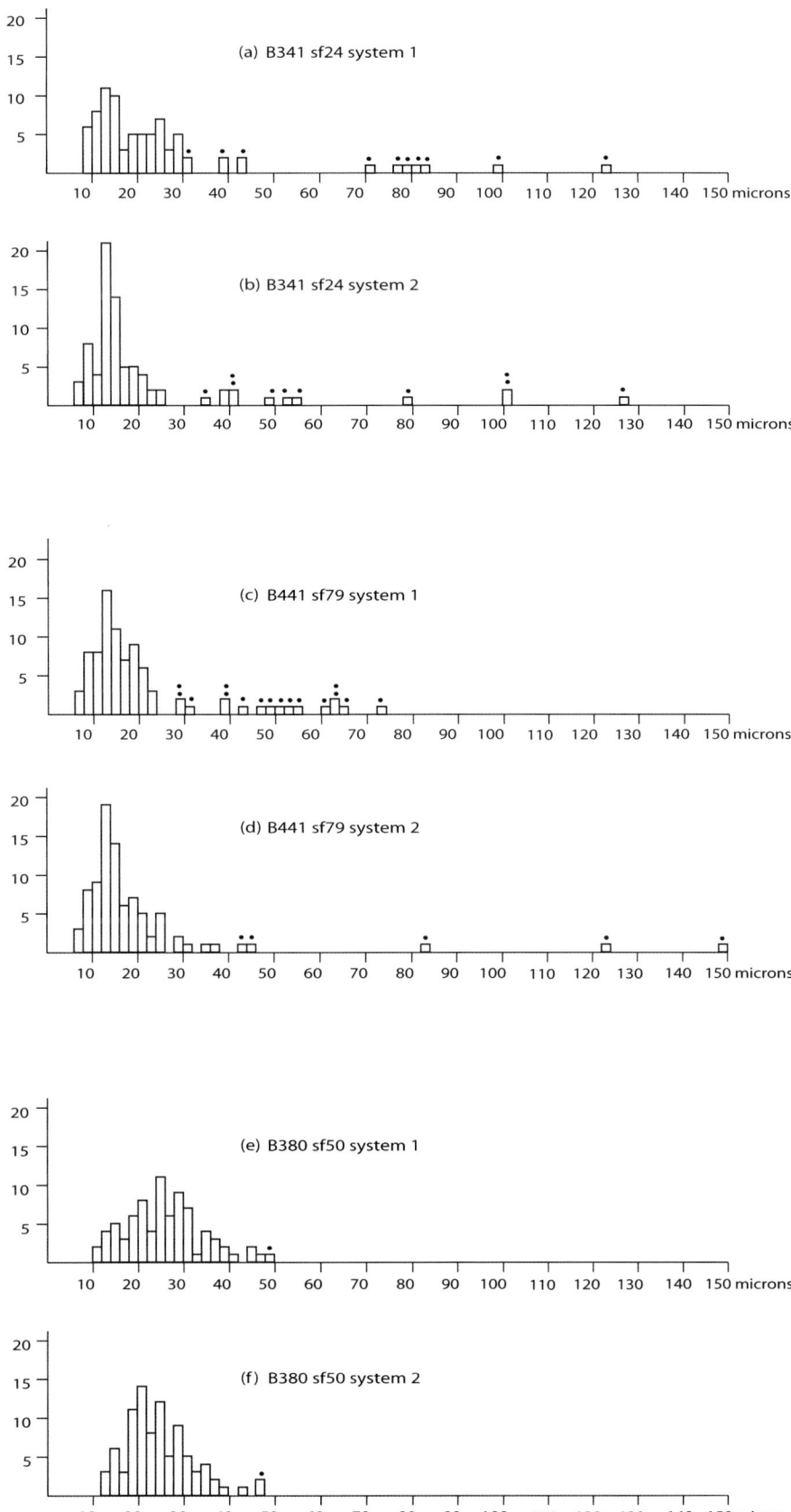

Figure 5.17 Histograms to show the diameters of fibres in warp and weft of three textiles. Histograms a–d represent goat fibre: note the peaks at 14 microns and the medullas in fibres 30–45 microns diameter. Histograms e–f represent wool. Dots indicate the presence of medullas

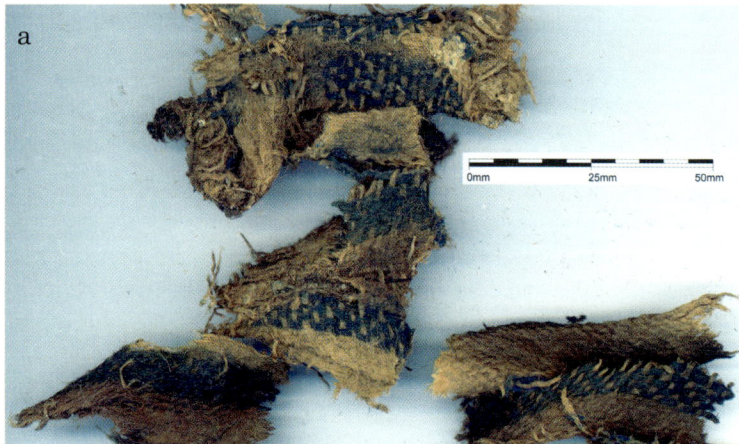 

Figure 5.18   Striped goat-fibre textiles: (a) From pelvic area of Skeleton 441, SF79; (b) from head of Skeleton 341, SF24

Prussian Blue (test procedure courtesy of Jo Kirby Atkinson, The National Gallery).

A detailed catalogue, including analytical results, has been placed in the site archive and a grave-by-grave summary is presented in Table 5.3. Expert comments on 19th-century costume details have been provided by Josie Sheppard of the Castle Museum, York, (identified in the text as 'JS') and the garment fragments used to stuff the pillow in the burial of Skeleton 381 have been the subject of a special study by Isabella von Holstein.

All of the above work was carried out at The Anglo-Saxon Laboratory, York, whilst the examination of the buttons was undertaken separately by Helen MacQuarrie.

5.9.1.2 Bias in the evidence

The 25 skeletons with textiles represent a small proportion of the 325 bodies excavated and it cannot be assumed that these were the only bodies buried with garments or shrouds. The survival of organic materials in the archaeological record depends on many factors, such as climate, the nature of the raw material, soil conditions (especially soil pH and the degree of aeration), and the presence or absence of corroding metalwork. Textiles buried without a coffin and in an exposed part of a site will decay more quickly and comprehensively than those in more protected burials, and the degree of preservation can vary within the grave itself. In particular, the cellulosic plant fibres, flax, hemp and cotton, will be at greater risk in acidic aerated soils than the protein-based fibres, goat-fibre, wool and silk, but they will be better preserved where corroding copper alloys inhibit biological damage (Jakes and Sibley 1983; Sibley and Jakes 1984; Janaway 1985; Janaway 1989). This is especially noticeable in the burial of Skeleton 351, where part of some cotton trousers had been preserved in the area fastened by metal buttons (see Fig 5.24), whereas the fabric of the

garment on the top half of the body, which had buttons of other materials, had not survived.

The textiles were therefore selectively preserved by the burial environment, and do not necessarily represent the full range of textile-types originally present in the graveyard.

5.9.2   The striped goat-fibre textiles

The most common textile-type was a striped fabric recovered from eleven graves (Table 5.3; Fig 5.18a–b). It was found with children and adults of both sexes and was mostly recovered from the head or pelvis, although there is a single example from the torso of a child (Skeleton 431). It was stained from burial, but it can be reconstructed as a natural (white) fabric with bands of stripes which could be dark blue and natural, or dark blue, red/brown and natural. The natural areas dominate in each case and four examples of similar textiles without stripes almost certainly represent burials where, fortuitously, only the natural sections have been preserved. These, too, came from the head and pelvis.

All fifteen examples are very much alike in technical terms. They are woven in a loose, relatively coarse tabby weave, which has S-spun yarn in warp and weft. The natural areas are more densely woven, 8–10 × 5–6 threads per cm, than the stripes, 5–8 × 5–6 threads per cm. The coloured stripes are nearly always made up of five or six yarns, although the areas between them are variable. Three samples of the deep blue yarns were tested and identified as Prussian Blue, but the two red/browns were poorly preserved and could not be identified. As described above, the raw material in two textiles was determined as goat fibre by measuring the fibre diameters (Fig 5.17) and microscopy of the other examples suggested that they were probably the same, although sheep's wool could not always be excluded. All fibres examined lacked pigmentation, which indicates that they came from white animals. In every case, the yarns were dominated by the undercoat fibres (sometimes termed cashmere) and the felting that can be seen in the examples associated with Skeletons 300, 398 and 405 probably represents over-washing of these fine crimpy fibres.

The origins of these textiles are not easily determined. The cashmere goat of Asia produced fibre of this type, which was traded commercially (Cook 1968, 136–8), but the feral goats of Scotland and British dairy goats, for example, yield a similar quality of fibre (Ryder 1987, 8–9; Ryder 1993, 41–3) and there were probably small-scale producers in many locations. The dark blue colorant, Prussian Blue, was a paint pigment developed as a dye in 18th-century France, first for silk and cotton and then for wool (Brunello 1973, 231; Schweppe 1992, 144–5, 548–9). The extent of its use historically is unknown and it has not been previously encountered in our laboratory's 30 years of analytical work on textiles. Neither fibre nor dye, therefore, has given any indication of the geographic source of the textile.

Illustrations and travellers' descriptions reveal that striped fabrics, known as 'country cloths' were made and worn in the West African homelands (Kriger 2006, 19, 34–57 and 117–70; Fellner 2011). They were rectangles of cloth worn by non-Muslim men and women, wrapped around the body and secured at the waist, under the arm or over the shoulder; or sometimes they might be smaller cloths wrapped around the head. They were usually made of cotton, or other plant fibres, and the blue stripes were dyed with local indigo (*ibid*). The technical similarities between all fifteen examples from the Rupert's Valley graveyard, the goat fibre and the absence of indigo, argue that these are not West African products, but more probably a standard issue provided by the British. No comparable textiles have been discovered in British burials of the period, but the fabric is coarse enough to be compared with sackcloth, which sometimes incorporated stripes: textiles of this sort were probably available in navy stores, as an all-purpose cloth used for wrapping goods, covering mattresses and so on (JS). Since the textiles were mostly found in the burials at the head and pelvis, it is possible that they represent clothes adapted by the Africans out of the materials made available to them by the British. Research planned for the future will include analysis of stable isotopes, which may identify the geographic origin of the raw material, and a more extensive study of the relevant historical documents.

5.9.3 *Textiles from the neonate burials*

Textiles were, paradoxically, recovered in their greatest numbers from three small graves of newborn babies. There were at least seven different textile-types associated with Skeleton 381, five with Skeleton 380 and three with Skeleton 519 (Table 5.3). Each of these textiles has close parallels in Britain in intramural graves (that is, in vaults and shafts within the church) accompanying adults and children. Fewer comparisons can be made with textiles from more ordinary burials in churchyards.

The silk satin ribbons, one tied in a bow (Skeleton 380) and the second cut with a swallowtail end (Skeleton 381), are of the same type, a little over 10mm wide and woven in plain 8-end satin with a decorative looped selvedge (Fig 5.19). The selvedge has been worked in tabby weave and the weft alternates two plain returns with two returns where the weft yarn has been extended to form a short loop. Similar ribbons appear in British burials, sometimes as functioning garment ties, but mostly as decorative trims on garments and coffin furnishings. Those in intramural graves at St Martin's-in-the-Bullring, Birmingham, and Christ Church, Spitalfields (London), included several examples in satin weave (5-end and 8-end) with a variety of decorative looped selvedges, although they were broader, 14–58mm wide, and none has exactly the same selvedge construction (Janaway 1993, microfiche catalogue entries, 'RIBB'; Walton Rogers 2006, 171, 177–8, colour plates 129 and 131). Ribbons were also used on garments worn by the living, as bonnet ties and dress ornaments, although these examples represent the cheaper end of what would be available in a haberdasher's shop (JS).

Two layers of fine machine-made lace net were present on a coin beside the head of Skeleton 380. This has been worked in cotton, but visually it is very like the silk lace trims on bonnets worn by women in two 19th-century burials, one at All Saints, Pavement, York, and the other at St Peter's, Barton-on-Humber, Lincolnshire (Walton Rogers unpublished a; 2011, 713). Cotton lace has also been recorded on the sleeves of a linen dress worn by an adult at Spitalfields in a burial of uncertain date (Janaway 1993, 113–14, figure 6.18; burial 2329). Ready-made burial garments of standard types were often supplied by the undertaker, but the two bonnets and the dress, from their styling and fine details, were almost certainly made for the living (*ibid*). It seems likely, therefore, that the lace net from within the coffin of Skeleton 380 came from another made-for-life garment, and its position would suggest the baby's cap. It can be compared with a burial at Spitalfields, where an eleven-month-old male child was buried in 1825 in a made-for-life cotton cap, with a fine cotton frill instead of a lace trim (Janaway 1993, figure 6.14, burial 2373).

Gauze-weave and gauze-like textiles represent a similar category of fabric. In true gauze weave, of which there is a single example in silk from within the coffin of Skeleton 381, well-spaced pairs of warp ends twist clockwise then anti-clockwise so that they grip the weft firmly, the result being an open, net-like fabric (Fig 5.20). In other textiles a gauze-like appearance has been achieved with well-spaced ultra-fine yarns in an ordinary tabby weave (Fig 5.21). In the coffin of Skeleton 381 the gauze weave lay on top of the body, seemingly as part of a quilt or coverlet, but a fine white cotton gauze-like textile in association with head hair, and another example, possibly the same, on a coin over the eyes, are likely to have come

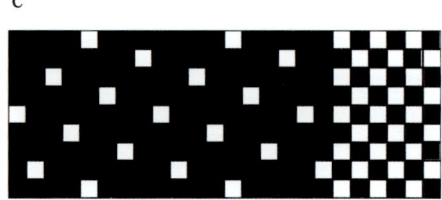

Figure 5.19   A silk satin ribbon, from the chest area of the newborn, Skeleton 381 (SF70). (a) The whole ribbon; (b) close-up of looped selvedge; (c) weave diagram (black square represents warp crossing weft; white square represents weft crossing warp)

from another baby cap. A poorly preserved gauze-like textile on a coin from below the head of Skeleton 519 probably represents something similar. One further example, from the pillow stuffing found with Skeleton 381, lines part of the worsted twill garment (see below), as an interfacing rather than ornament. Silk gauze-like textiles were recovered in association with the two bonnets in burials in Britain previously mentioned and bands of gauze weave were recorded in a silk facing for an adult garment made-for-life from Spitalfields (Janaway 1993, 111, microfiche 6.6–6.9 – burial 2058).

Traces of fine textiles were recorded in association with copper alloy shroud pins from the coffin burials of Skeletons 380 and 519. They were of cotton tabby, possibly brushed cotton in the case of Skeleton 380, but full technical details could not be recorded in the case of Skeleton 519. These may represent funerary

garments, which, from the 1810s onwards were most commonly made of cotton, but it is likely that everyday baby clothes were also made from similar fabrics. Comparable textiles were recorded in church-yard burials at St Mark's Lincoln (Walton Rogers unpublished b) and in numerous intra-mural burials at Spitalfields (Janaway 1993, 118, figure 6.21).

The panels of parallel wool yarn from the burial of Skeleton 381 will originally have had crossways threads in linen or cotton which have decayed during burial (SF69) (Fig 5.22). Fabrics of this general type – termed 'unions' – were used for winding sheets and coffin linings in northern Britain (Walton Rogers 2006, 166–7, 174), but this particularly soft lightweight example is more like the fabrics used to pad garments and quilts (JS). It was found with a napped (teaselled and sheared) wool textile, probably dyed red (Skeleton 381; SF69)

Figure 5.20   The silk gauze found with wool textiles and silk ribbons covering the newborn, Skeleton 381 (SF69)

Figure 5.21 A gauze-like cotton tabby, from above the head of the newborn, Skeleton 381 (SF68)

Figure 5.22 The wool union from the burial of Skeleton 381 (SF69)

(see digital volume, Appendix D2, Fig D2.64) which covered the baby, in association with a satin ribbon and the silk gauze weave. Since it was described by the excavators as a 'quilt', it seems likely that it represents a small coverlet placed over the child. It is possible that a matted pad of wool textiles, covering the body of Skeleton 519 from the neck down, represents another such coverlet (SF96).

A pillow was identified from its position in the coffin of Skeleton 381, although its cover seems to have disintegrated. Its stuffing was a mixture of cut-up pieces of a garment (described below) and feathers (Figs 5.23 and 5.27). This must have been a pillow used in life, as the textiles show wear acquired after they had been reused as wadding. In Britain, most pillows seem to have been supplied by the undertaker and were stuffed with wool, feathers

or hay (Janaway 1993, 103; 1998, 22–3), but there is an example from Spitalfields of a pillow stuffed with rags with a 60-year-old man buried in 1798 (Janaway 1993, 104, 117, burial 2634). Fragments of a wool textile with cut edges and seams, SF49, placed over Skeleton 380, appear to represent another garment, perhaps torn up and used to stuff a quilt.

Taking the evidence together, it seems likely that newborn babies, Skeletons 380 and 381 (and perhaps also Skeleton 519), were buried in caps which had a fine net trim (Skeleton 380) and satin ribbons (Skeletons 380 and 381). One baby, Skeleton 381, was covered with a little quilt of red-dyed woollen cloth, lined with a lightweight wool union, with a silk gauze and ribbon trim; and another baby, Skeleton 380, may also have had a quilt. These all have the characteristics of items intended for a living child.

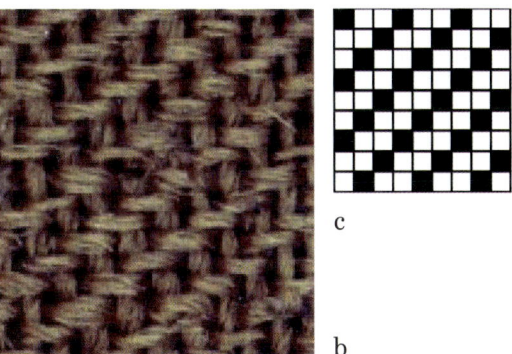

Figure 5.23 One fragment of the combed-wool (worsted) garment cut up and used as wadding in the pillow of the burial of Skeleton 381 (SF66). (a) The whole fragment; (b) close-up of weave; (c) weave diagram, 2/1 twill. See also Fig 5.27

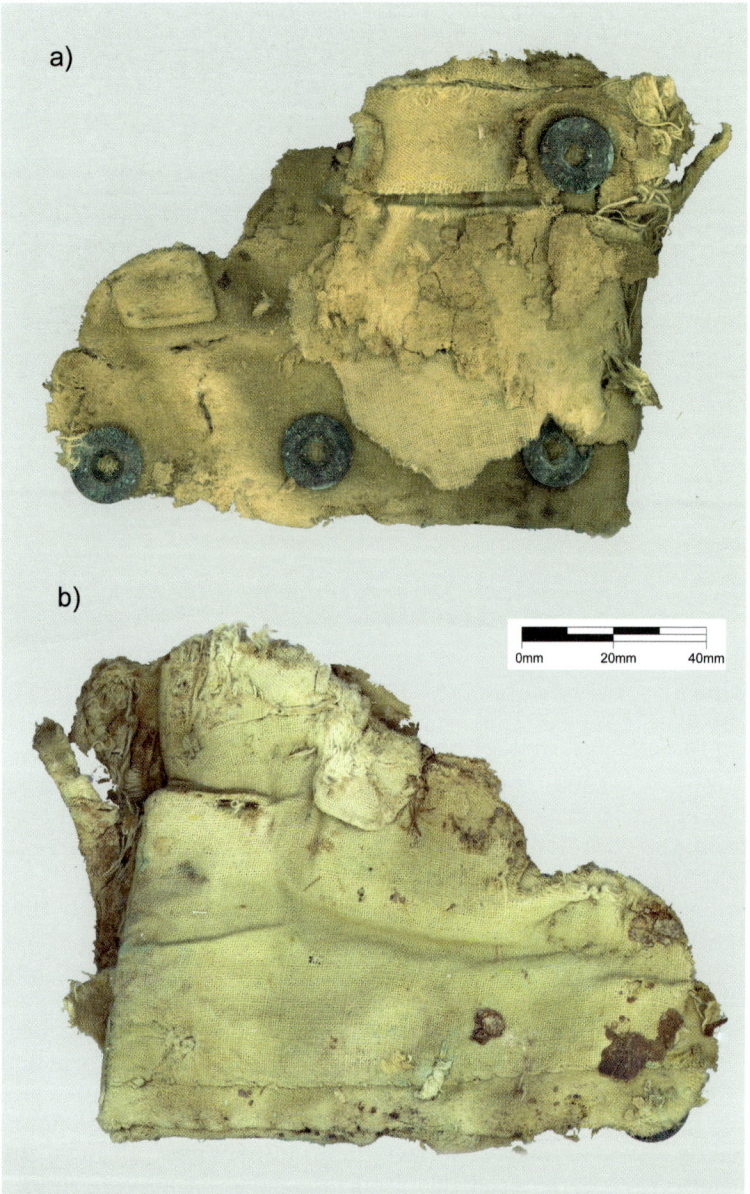

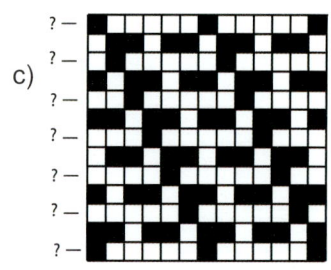

Figure 5.24   A fragment of the buttoned cotton trousers from Skeleton 351 (SF31) made of a double-faced weave and tabby. (a) Front; (b) back; (c) possible weave diagram of double-faced textile. The 2/1 rows are correct, the 1/5 rows less certain (black square represents warp crossing weft; white square represents weft crossing warp)

5.9.4   Costume details

Aside from the baby clothes, a garment worn on the body could be confidently attested in only one case, the britches or trousers of Skeleton 351. However, the textiles associated with Skeletons 227, 522 and 523 appear to be clothing fabrics and, as already noted, fragments of garments were used for pillow wadding in the burial of Skeleton 381. Braids associated with Skeleton 365 and a cord in the burial of Skeleton 442 are likely to represent thin fasteners around the waist.

The fragmentary remains recorded during excavation as 'shorts' (SF31) were recovered from the pelvic area of the adolescent male Skeleton 351 (Fig 5.24a–b; Fig 5.25). It is probable that they continued down the legs into full-length trousers, but they are made of cotton, and, as already described, the upper parts will have been preserved by the biocidal properties of the corroding metal buttons in that area.

The main body of the fabric is a thick brushed cotton double-weave and there is a lining of plain cotton tabby. The garment has a complex construction: in places there are four layers, sometimes two of the double-faced weave over two of the lining and in other fragments the two fabrics are in alternating layers. There are metal, bone and wood buttons, their function uncertain, although it seems likely that some of them fastened the 'fall front' opening seen on men's britches and trousers of the period (JS). There are also two stitched-on straps of fabric, 20mm wide, parallel but offset, which probably represent tabs for tightening the garment. The sewing thread is plied linen throughout. Overcasting has been used to join the layers together and the metal buttons, which have bars instead of perforations, have been very securely fastened with repeated stitching, first across the bar and then across the ends of the stitches. In the absence of any fastening at the knee, it seems likely that these

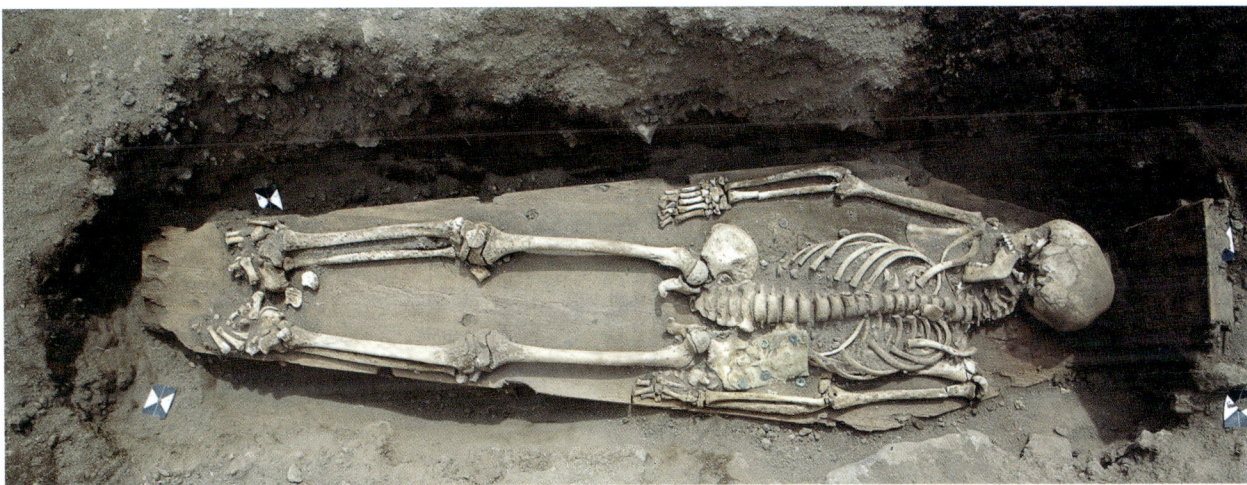

Figure 5.25 Coffin 2297 (Skeleton 351). Photograph taken after the removal of the coffin sides, showing the fragments of trousers in situ (SF31)

Figure 5.26 Flat plaited combed-wool (worsted) braids from pelvic area of Skeleton 365 (SF37)

were trousers worn by working men and seamen, rather than britches worn by, for example, officers in the navy (JS).

A heavy dyed wool textile woven in 2/2 broken twill appeared with two older children (Skeletons 227 and 523) and an adult (Skeleton 522). To the naked eye, these textiles were dark bluish-brown, but microscopy revealed that there were fibres of three different colours present, blue, light brown and dark brown, the blue being derived from woad or indigo. They were around the head of Skeletons 522 and 523, and from the chest of Skeleton 227. Tweed-like textiles in this weave had been used since the 17th century for outer clothing and would probably be employed for jackets and hats in the 19th century. A dark tabby-weave wool textile of similar quality around the head of a young adult (Skeleton 437) belongs in the same category. Where the sex of the bodies could be identified, the wearers were males or probable males. These provide further examples of people likely to have been buried in their clothes.

Four pieces of a flat plaited braid from the burial of Skeleton 365, 1.5mm wide and made of smooth combed-wool yarn (Fig 5.26), represent an accessory used since the medieval period for lacing and tying garments. In this instance the braid's position in the

pelvic area of an adult female suggests that it was a drawstring for a garment such as a petticoat (JS). A hemp multi-ply cord, 2.5mm thick, found at the waist of Skeleton 442 (a young adult male), was described as 'loin cloth string' in the excavation record and there is no reason to dispute this interpretation.

5.9.5 Pillow wadding
Isabella von Holstein

The garment cut up and used to stuff the pillow in the coffin of Skeleton 381 includes a number of significant features (SF66). The wadding consists of approximately 26 fragments of the same fabric, some of which are still folded together as in the original garment, though no stitching remains (Fig 5.23). All sections appear to be the same fabric, a 2/1 worsted twill with occasional weaving faults and a selvedge of seven warp threads of degraded plant fibre. There are very small areas of badly degraded tabby cloth remaining in a few folds. Sections include an upstanding ('mandarin') collar, parts of a sleeve, and part of the front of a garment with a facing (Fig 5.27). All are folded together at random. Wear is present along the folds of the wadding (digital volume, Appendix D2, Fig D2.61), but there are other thin patches of cloth which probably indicate wear during the use of the garment. There are a number of small holes with blackened edges which appear to be burn holes.

The main pattern pieces have been cut on the grain. Cut edges have seam allowances 6–11mm deep and rows of stitch holes are visible on many of these, mostly along the fold. The stitch holes are typically 1–3mm apart. Some such lines appear to consist of two lines of stitching superimposed, which may indicate backstitch. Some seam allowances show a second line of stitch holes closer to the edge of the fabric, which are 5–6mm apart. A small triangular gore with very deep seam allowances may represent a rather crude alteration to the garment.

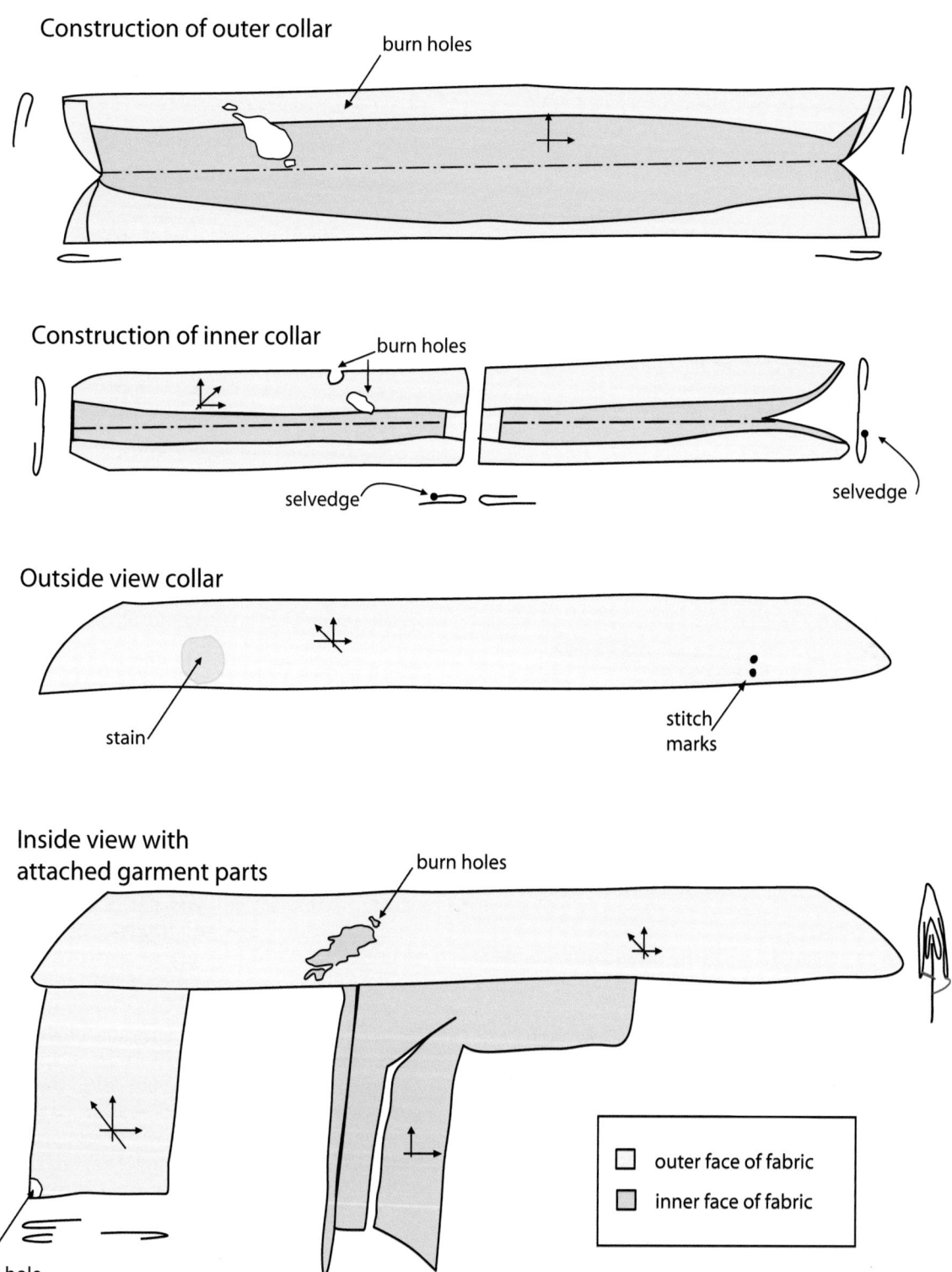

Figure 5.27 The construction of the collar area of the cut-up garment used to stuff a pillow found with Skeleton 381 (SF66). See also Fig 5.23a–c

The collar consists of two layers, the inner functioning as a binding strip round the neck opening of the garment body. The middle of the garment body is indicated by a notch cut into it. The binding strip is in two sections which \lare not of equal length; both incorporate the selvedge, on a transverse edge on one, but a longitudinal edge on the other. The seam allowances on the outer layer of the collar are folded back inexpertly, the collar ends have slightly different shapes and their edges and the inner hem are puckered by the stitching. It is most likely that the collar was constructed by sewing the right side of each layer down using what appears to have been backstitch, and then folding the layer over and catching the inner edge down with overcast stitch.

The collar is 38–42mm high and shows two stitch

holes on the right side, 65mm from one end, which may have been for a fastening hook. The other part of this arrangement is not present, but at this date it may well have consisted of a loop of thread (JS). The collar would therefore have a circumference when fastened of approximately 320mm. The shoulder seam appears to be 90–115mm long. Sections of one sleeve indicate a possible upper arm circumference of 240mm. The facing which appears to have backed the front opening of the garment is 59–66mm wide (tapering towards the bottom) and 234mm long from collar to a seam at right angles, possibly a waist seam.

The largest of the areas of burning is approximately 20 × 30mm. They occur on the inside of the collar, the middle of the front of the garment and on the facing, but not on the sleeves.

This analysis appears to indicate the garment was a shirt or part of a dress, cut and sewn by hand (very solidly) by a non-professional. It may have been the garment of a slightly built adult with little room for breasts – either a man or a young girl – with particularly small arm circumferences, as is typical of this period (JS). The double collar construction is unusual and may represent an alteration (JS), as does the gore. The garment appears to have seen considerable wear before being burnt. The burning cannot have occurred while the garment was being worn. The garment was cut up to be used as pillow wadding without being unpicked: this is particularly clear from the sleeve sections where front and back pieces occur in association with each other. The fabric was subsequently further worn during use as wadding, which implies that the pillow was not made for the burial.

5.9.6   Comment
Penelope Walton Rogers

Historical sources show that in 19th-century Britain the funeral trade supplied ready-made shrouds, caps, sheets, mattresses and pillows, as well as coffins lined and covered with textile (Litten 1991). Archaeological excavations have produced many representatives of these goods, but amongst them there are also occasional examples of garments intended for wear during life. Several of the St Helena textiles appear to belong in this second group. Although the silk ribbons and a few of the undyed wool fabrics are found in both categories, the babies' caps, the trousers and the tweeds are all most likely to represent garments worn in life and the baby's quilt belongs in the same class.

The textiles with the newborn babies are of particular interest, as they find closest parallels in intramural burials in Britain, in the graves of the well-to-do middle classes. Along with coffin burial they suggest a degree of status for the burial that is not seen elsewhere in the graveyard. The striped goat-fibre textiles, on the other hand, have proved to be more difficult to interpret and it has been suggested that these represent West African clothing styles recreated in the nearest available fabric, possibly a form of sacking supplied by the colonial authorities or the navy.

The surviving textiles do not on the whole correspond with the clothing which, according to the written sources, was supplied by the British for the Africans to wear (section 2.4.7). This may be because most of the materials described in the documents – cotton, duck and calico – were made of plant fibres and, if buried, would have decayed. Of the listed goods, only flannel, blanket and other woollens might have survived in the ground. Perhaps the tweed-like fabrics associated with Skeletons 522 and 523 represent 'woollen caps', but there are no identifiable examples of 'men's guernseys' or 'women's flannel petticoats or undergarments'. On the other hand, the Governor noted in 1841 that clothing was not 'procurable in sufficient quantity to meet the demand'. The use of some wrapping fabrics from the stores might have been a response to this problem.

5.9.7   Buttons
Helen MacQuarrie

A total of eighteen buttons were recovered from the excavations, from four individual or group-registered finds (SF02, SF13, SF29 and SF31a). Seven types are represented, made from four materials: copper alloy (brass), glass, worked bone and shell.

The buttons are undiagnostic. However, four holed shell buttons and a small opaque glass button, similar to those found in Rupert's Valley, have been recovered from 19th-century contexts at All Saints, Chelsea Old Church, London (site code OCU00) (Cowie *et al* 2008).

The majority of bone (and horn) buttons made in the 19th century were purely utilitarian and intended for underwear, shirts and trousers or household linen (Peacock 1972, 21). During this period Birmingham was a centre for British production of horn, bone and brass buttons, but they were also produced in the United States, France and Germany (Houart 1977, 62).

For shell buttons it is generally very difficult to ascertain the species used (Luscomb 1967, 117). In this case the problem is compounded by the very poor condition of the objects.

Figure 5.28   Buttons (SF29) associated with Skeleton 351

Table 5.3 Textile catalogue

Group	Skeleton No.	Age Sex Number in grave	Position found	Small Find No.	Description	Fibre	Construction	Thread-count per cm and spin	Additional information
2038	227	Older child Unknown 1 of 3	From the chest	106	Pads of textile, often 3 layers thick. Largest 110 × 80mm	White wool	2/2 broken twill	6/S × 6/S	Yarns are a blend of 3 colours: dark brown, light brown and blue. Indigotin (woad/indigo) detected
2041	219	Prime adult Male 1 of 3	From below pelvis	104b	Small tattered fragments, largest 70 × 30mm	White wool or goat	Tabby, striped	8/S × 6/S	Some blue yarns present
2160	278	Prime adult Female 1 of 2	Around pelvis	10	(i) Textile in curving folds, 120 × 40 × 15mm (ii) crimpy brown-black hair on one face	White goat	Tabby, striped	10/S × 5/S	A single blue yarn runs along one torn edge on several fragments
2213	300	Young adult Male	From pelvis area	25	(i) 'loin cloth': two ends of a textile tied in a reef knot; and further fragments (ii) coarse black crimpy hair in association	White wool or goat	Tabby, striped	8/S × 5/S, felted	Remains of blue stripes visible
2273	337	Older child Unknown 1 of 2	From below the pelvis	27	'Loin cloth': several fragments, largest 100 × 85mm	White wool or goat	Tabby, striped	8/S × 5/S; 5/S × 5/S in stripes	Stripes in blue (B) and natural (N): 5(+)N, 6B, 12N, 6B, 14N, 6B, 38(+) N
2279	341	Older child Unknown	From head area	24	(i) Fragments, largest 50 × 35mm (ii) black crimpy hair	White goat	Tabby, striped	10/S × 4/S; 8/S × 5/S in stripes, felted	Stripes in blue, natural and red (R): (a) 2R(+), 5B, ?10N, 6N, 6B, 2R (b) 2N, 6R, 6B Red could not be extracted or identified
2298	351	Adolescent Unknown 1 of 1	From pelvis area	31	'Shorts': (i) fragment of clothing made up of two different textiles; buttoned; 130 × 105mm (ii) smaller fragments in two and four layers; buttoned	(A) cotton (B) cotton Stitching is linen	(A) tabby (B) double-faced weave	(A) 20/Z × 20/S (B) 20-24/Z × 40/S, brushed	A = lining for B (i) Layered A-B-A-B. Four buttons hold layers together. Remains of two fastening straps made of B (ii) Layered B-B and B-B-A-A
2323	360	Young child Probably male 1 of 4	From pelvis area	41	Fragments, largest 25 × 15mm	White wool or goat	Tabby, striped	8/S × 4-5/S	Band of 6B in predominantly N
2332	365	Prime adult Female 1 of 1	From arm area	35	Poorly preserved, largest fragment 10 × 7mm	Not identified	Tabby	16/?Z × 16/?Z	Coated in powdery brown material. Fibre too decayed to be identified
			From pelvis area	37	Four flat braids, each 30mm long and 1.5mm wide	White wool	Flat multi-strand diagonal plait, probably 9-strand	yarn plied Z2S	Made from smooth combed-wool yarn
2363	380	Neonate Unknown 1 of 1	South-west corner (of coffin)	46	Around shanks of shroud pins	(i) Cotton (ii) ?Wool	? ?	Z × ?, fine ?	

Table 5.3 (*cont.*) **Textile catalogue**

Group	Skeleton No.	Age Sex Number in grave	Position found	Small Find No.	Description	Fibre	Construction	Thread-count per cm and spin	Additional information
2363 (cont.)	380	Neonate Unknown 1 of 1	North-west corner (of coffin)	47	Several fragments in association with shroud pin	Cotton	Tabby	20-25/Z × 20/Z, ?brushed on one side	Yarn, probably from same textile, on pin itself
			Covering the body, from lower chest to feet	49	Several tattered fragments, largest 105 × 55mm	Wool	Tabby repp	18-20/S × 14/S, fulled	Remains of several seams present. Probably the remains of an adult dress or jacket. Tested for dye but none detected
			Laid between skeleton and coffin base	50	Wadding material from coffin	White wool SF × SF Fleece types	Tabby	16/S × 12/S, fulled	Fleece types examined for comparison with goat-fibre textiles
			Left of head	52	On one face of coin, in two layers	Cotton	Fine machine-madeNet	Yarn Z2S, mesh 1.5mm gauge	
			From pelvis area	53	Two ends of ribbon tied in a bow. Overall length 85mm	Silk	8-end warp satin	As elsewhere	Complete width of ribbon 11m. Looped selvedges. Silk degummed cultivated
2367	381	Neonate Unknown 1 of 1	Over eyes	58	On one face of coin	?Flax	Tabby, open, gauzy	24/? × 22/?	
			Beneath head	66	Pillow wadding pad of cut-up fragments, 170 × 120 × 30mm	Wool, Worsted	2/1 twill	Warp 22/Z × weft 28/Z	Remains of a garment, including collar and sleeve. Selvedge with threads of different fibre.Tabby lining/interfacing. Weak trace of red mordant dye detected. Feathers and wood shavings present
						Unident. Plant fibre	Tabby, open, gauzy	c 26/Z × c 24/S	
			From above head	68	White textile, 20 × 15mm, stained with copper alloy	Cotton	Tabby, open, net-like	22/Z × 22/Z	
					Fine dark brown crimpy hair				
					A few loose yarns	Wool, worsted	Yarns	Z	Possibly from 2/1 twill. Feathers in association
			Laid covering the skeleton	69	Many fragments, largest 150 × 60mm	Wool	Tabby	16-18/S × 12-13/S	Dense nap in places. Weak trace of red mordant dye detected

Table 5.3 (*cont.*) **Textile catalogue**

Group	Skeleton No.	Age Sex Number in grave	Position found	Small Find No.	Description	Fibre	Construction	Thread-count per cm and spin	Additional information
2367 (*cont.*)	381		From around the chest	70	Several fragments of ribbon, longest 100mm long	Silk	8-end warp satin	140-160/I or Z x 88/Z	Fully degummed cultivated silk. Complete width 10-11mm. Selvedges in tabby weave. Decorative edge formed by looped weft returns. Cut swallowtail end on one
2398	398	Adolescent Male 1 of 1	At pelvis	62	Fragments, 30 × 15mm and 25 × 10mm	White goat	Tabby	7-9/S × 4-5/S, felted	
2404	405	Older child Unknown 1 of 3	From pelvis area	55	Several interfolded fragments, largest 45 × 45mm	White goat	Tabby	7/S × 4/S, felted	
2416	410	Older child Unknown 1 of 3	From below the pelvis	102	Tattered fragment, 45 × 20mm	White wool or goat	Tabby	8/S × 4/S	
2428	431	Older child Unknown 1 of 3	Above and below the chest	75	Very tattered fragments, largest 100 × 20mm	White goat	Tabby, striped	?/S × ?/S	Too decayed to count threads in stripes, but R and B present. Red could not be extracted or identified
2470	437	Young adult Male 1 of 2	Under skull	80	Several fragments, largest 25 × 20mm	White wool	Tabby	9/Z × 7/S	More closely woven than other tabby weaves and darker
2471	441	Mature adult Male 1 of 2	At pelvis	79	Several matted pads, largest 80 × 40 × 10mm	White goat	Tabby, Striped	6/S × 5/S	Bands of blue (5B and 6B) and some red in natural ground. Blue colorant is Prussian Blue
2477	442	Young adult Male 1 of 1	At the waist	81	'Loin cloth string' Fragments of cord, longest piece 25mm	Bast fibre, probably hemp	Multi-strand cord	Z/S, 2.5mm diameter	
2482	443	Older child Unknown 1 of 2	From pelvis area	83	Tattered fragments, largest 60 × 50mm	White wool or goat	Tabby, striped	7/S × 5/S	Some loose blue threads almost certainly come from stripes
2554	500 502 510	Prime adult male Prime adult male Adolescent Unknown 3 of 4	Within the grave fill	90	Several fragments, largest 55 × 45mm	White wool or goat	Tabby, striped	8/S × 4/S	Bands of 6B in natural; some possible red yarns. Blue colorant is Prussian Blue

Table 5.3 (*cont.*) **Textile catalogue**

Group	Skeleton No.	Age Sex Number in grave	Position found	Small Find No.	Description	Fibre	Construction	Thread-count per cm and spin	Additional information
2566	511	Adolescent Probably male 1 of 2	From around skull	88	(1) Several fragments, largest 200 × 140mm (2) black crimpy hair in patch, 40 × 40mm, on textile	White goat	Tabby	8/S × 5/S	
2566	512	Older child Unknown 1 of 2	From around skull	89	(1) 'head sack' A fold of textile, 100 × 90 × 10mm (2) dark brown crimpy hair folded into textile	(1) white wool or goat	(1) tabby, striped	5-6/S × 5/S	Stripe represented by some blue-green yarns along one torn edge. Blue colorant is Prussian Blue
2579	519	Neonate Unknown 1 of 1	Below the head	93	On one face of coin	?	Tabby, open, gauzy	25/?Z × 20/Z	Fold runs across coin
			Covering the skeleton below the neck	96	Part of a matted pad of textile, 125 × 80 × 20mm	Wool	?Tabby	12/S × 12/S, soft-finished	
						Wool	Tabby repp	16-20/S c 12/S, ?soft-finished	
			Within the coffin	97	Traces of textile, but no technical details could be recorded	?	?	?	
			Within the coffin	98	On shank of pin	?	?	Z × Z, fine	
			Outside the coffin	100	On shank of pin	?	?	fine	
2588	522	Adult Male 1 of 2	Around skull	91	Poorly preserved fragments, largest 65 × 15mm	Wool	2/2 broken twill	6/S × 6-7/S, fulled	Yarns are a blend of blue/green fibres and two shades of brown. Indigotin (woad/indigo) detected; and unidentified brown dye
2588	523	Older child Unknown 1 of 2	Around skull	92	(1) poorly preserved yarns, probably same as SF91 (2) dark brown crimpy hair in association	Wool			

SF02: Button
Group 2038; Context 2037; Skeleton 227; undiagnostic
Shell button, very poor condition/fragmentary. Weight: 0.06g

SF13: Buttons (2)
Group 2207; Context 2206; Skeleton 298
Bone buttons: one complete and one fragmented in moderate condition. Circular with sunken frontal section with four holes for threading. Dimensions of complete button: diameter: 13.34mm, thickness: 2.98mm, weight: 0.31g (total weight of the two objects: 0.41g)

SF29: Buttons (11)
Group 2298; Context 2297; Skeleton 351
Two shell buttons: white flat circular button with four holes (poor condition). Button 1, diameter: 9.01mm, thickness: 1.6mm, weight: 0.16g. Button 2, diameter: 8.8mm, thickness: 1.4mm, weight: 0.10g
Three opaque glass buttons (small): circular with ellipsoid profile, with a sunken section towards the front and four holes (good condition). Button 1, diameter: 8.9mm, thickness: 2.4mm, weight: 0.2g. Button 2, diameter: 8.85mm, thickness: 2.4mm, weight: 0.2g. Button 3, diameter: 8.85mm, thickness: 2.2mm, weight: 0.16g
Two opaque glass buttons (large): circular with ellipsoid profile, with a sunken section towards the front and four holes (good condition). Button 1, diameter: 10.1mm, thickness: 2.8mm, weight: 0.31g. Button 2, diameter: 10.1mm, thickness: 3mm, weight: 0.33g
Four green flat disc bone buttons, circular flat discs with a single perforation for threading, dyed mid-green (fair condition). Button 1, diameter: 9.47mm, thickness: 2.36mm, weight: 0.17g. Button 2, diameter: 9.8mm, thickness: 2.4mm, weight: 0.22g. Button 3, diameter: 9.5mm, thickness: 0.19mm, weight: 0.2g. Button 4, diameter: 9.3mm, thickness: 2.4mm, weight: 0.12g

SF31a: Buttons (4)
Group 2298; Context 2297; Skeleton 351; 19th century
Four buttons recovered with textiles (SF31). Stamped copper alloy with sunken central section towards the front and two rectangular perforations for threading. Two complete buttons, one with central area damaged, one partial rim

5.10   Leather
Quita Mould

5.10.1 Methodology

All measurements are in millimetres. Shoe size has been estimated from measurement of the sole. Shoe sizing has been calculated according to the modern English Shoe-Size Scale; continental sizing is also given. The measurements were rounded up to the nearest equivalent modern English shoe size as appropriate. No allowance has been made for shrinkage, although it is possible that conservation may have resulted in a small amount of shrinkage.

Leather species were identified by hair follicle pattern using low-powered magnification. Where the grain surface of the leather was heavily worn identification was not always possible. The term bovine has been used when the distinction between mature cattle hide and immature calfskin proved difficult to distinguish.

5.10.2 Description

The remains of a small shoe of bovine leather, probably calfskin, were found in the coffin of Skeleton 381, a still-born or a newly born baby. The fact that this leather was within a coffin may be of significance in determining the circumstances of its preservation.[3] The shoe had been placed by the head.

The remains of the shoe comprised a near-complete sole and a fragment thought to be from the insole. The sole had a broad, round toe, as one might expect for a young child, the shape being dictated by practicality rather than fashion. The sole and the associated component had tunnel stitching on the flesh side by which they were joined to the other shoe parts that are now missing. Fragments of the stitching medium (a twisted fibre) survive on the second component. The second component appears to be part of the left side of the insole. However, it is notably larger than the sole and it is possible that the fragment represents the flattened remains of an area of lasting margin broken from the shoe upper. A line of five small impressed dots on the grain side of this second component appears to represent a simple decorative feature.

Though not quite complete, the shoe sole (as conserved), measures 77mm. This is significantly smaller than the smallest shoe size (child's size 1/ continental 16) on the modern English Shoe-Size Scales in use today. It may be that the shoe upper was made of a soft material, such as a textile or a tawed leather, that wrapped around the foot before being sewn to the insole and a disproportionally small sole. The presence of areas of another organic material, now gingery brown in colour, preserved on the underside (flesh side) of the second component, with associated stitching preserved, may support this idea.

The sole appears to have moulded to the shape of a foot through wear, suggesting that the shoe had been worn by another infant before it had been placed in the grave. It is possible, however, that the impression seen, though appearing to have been made by a foot, may be the result of later distortion during burial. The baby's shoe would appear to be of European style and is most unlikely to be of African origin.

The other finds from Skeleton 381 appear to be chiefly associated with the internal furnishing of the coffin and a selection of deliberately placed keepsakes within it. The position and recovery of the remains of a single shoe, apparently for a left foot, suggests that it was also placed as a keepsake in the coffin and had not been part of the burial clothing. In north-west Europe the use of a left-footed shoe as a charm to ward off bad luck has a long history in local folklore and this may go some way to providing a possible explanation for the occurrence of a single shoe in this context. Interestingly, this tradition is noted in 19th-century African-American burial practices. Six of 140 burials at the First African Baptist Church cemetery in Philadelphia had a single shoe placed on the coffin lid (Jamieson 1995, 53).

0mm   20mm   40mm

Figure 5.29 Leather shoe sole (SF67) associated with Skeleton 381

SF67: Shoe sole
Group 2367; Context 2366; Skeleton 381; European
1. Near-complete shoe sole, made virtually straight but appears to have been worn on a left foot. The edges of the sole are broken away for much of the 'waist' and seat area but most of the sole is present. The sole has a broad, round toe and tapers to the round seat; there is no waist. Tunnel stitching, stitch length 5mm, runs parallel to the edge on the flesh side. The sole profile is not flat but is slightly sinuous through moulding to the foot, suggesting that it has been worn. Leather is black and shiny in colour, worn bovine 1.98mm thick. Length 77mm, max width (tread) 39mm, min width (seat) 19mm
2. Part of the left side of shoe insole, but as it is longer than the associated sole, possibly part of the right side of the shoe upper. Remains of an original cut edge present along one side, torn along the other. Part of the grain surface is now missing through delamination/degradation. A line 10mm long of five small impressed dots, each 1mm in diameter, is present on the grain surface. The flesh side has a single tunnel stitch, stitch length 4.5mm, parallel to the edge and three smaller tunnel stitches at an oblique angle to the edge to attach the upper. Areas of an organic material, ginger brown in colour, adhere to the flesh side in places, and original sewing thread of a twisted fibre *c* 1mm thick (max) also survives associated with the largest area. Leather is black and shiny in colour, worn, probably bovine 1.42mm thick. Length 96mm, max width 28mm

5.11 Coffins and coffin furnishings
Helen MacQuarrie

Five coffins were recovered from the excavation (1.5% of the total excavated individuals). All came from earth-cut graves and contained single inhumations.

The coffins were exposed, excavated and recorded in situ and the timbers drawn and recorded at the post-excavation stage. Two timber fragments were brought back to the UK for species analysis. Each coffin was assigned a unique context number, while objects associated with the construction or decoration of a coffin were given a small find number and included in the catalogue. Artefacts not associated with the construction or decoration of the coffins (such as coins, beads and textiles) are discussed separately under their individual small find number.[4]

The preservation of the coffins was variable: although generally moderately well preserved, most had suffered partial deterioration due to the differential ground water drainage on the site. Burial condition also affected the condition of the iron coffin nails: some were preserved within the timber but the position of others was only marked by stains in the wood.

5.11.1 The coffins

Four of the coffins contained a foetus and three neonates. These coffins ranged in size between 0.51 and 0.58m in length, 0.14–0.23m in width and 0.10–0.18m in depth. One coffin containing an adolescent was also recovered, which measured 1.75m in length, 0.31–0.52m in width and 0.35m in depth. Table 5.4 summarises the detail of the coffins.

All of the coffins were built according to typical standards of the period, as indicated by their construction method, shape and furnishings (eg Dottridge Brothers Ltd, *c* 1925; Ingall, Parsons, Clive and Co, *c* 1890). Each conformed to the same standard style: single-break, single-case, and wooden.[5] This style is representative of standards recorded in Britain at the same period (Boston *et al*

Table 5.4 Coffins: summary of construction, furniture and fittings

Coffin (Context No.)	Shape	Coffin furniture	Coffin nails	Lined	Pitched	Wood shavings
2139	Single-break	–	Iron tacks (uncatalogued)		–	–
2297	Single-break	–	Iron tacks (uncatalogued)		Yes	–
2362	Single-break	SF60, SF61	Iron tacks (uncatalogued)	Yes	–	Yes
2366	Single-break	–	SF59, Iron tacks (uncatalogued)			Yes (SF101)
2577	Single-break	–	Iron tacks (uncatalogued)		–	–

2008; Boston *et al* 2009; Brickley *et al* 2006; Cowie *et al* 2008; Miles *et al* 2008).

Kerfing (the sawing of lines to allow the side timber to bend and the shoulder break point) was recorded on one of the coffins (2577). On the other four coffins this area was poorly preserved, but it is likely that they were constructed in the same manner, thus contributing to the weakness in the timber at this point. This method of coffin manufacture is described by Plume (in a document dating to *c* 1900) as 'ordinary' and 'in regular use' across the British Isles in the late 19th and early 20th century.

Two coffins contained wood shavings (2362 and 2366), which were used to absorb the fluids of the decaying body. In the UK sawdust, bran, cotton waste, or any similar material which could be easily and cheaply obtained was used for this purpose. Further evidence of traditional coffin manufacturing techniques is represented by adult coffin (2297) which was painted or blackened. In the United Kingdom turpentine and lampblack was traditionally used to blacken adult coffins. Children's coffins were left natural and there is no evidence of blackening on the neonate coffins.

5.11.2 Coffin timber

Samples were taken from two coffins (2366 and 2297) and sent for species identification at the Jodrell Laboratory, Royal Botanic Gardens, Kew. The findings indicate that both samples were of the subgenus *Pinus* which includes the species *Pinus sylvestris* from Europe, *Pinus resinosa* from eastern North America, and *Pinus densiflora* from China (P Gasson, pers comm). Pine trees were allegedly introduced to St Helena by Governor Pyke in the early 18th century (Gosse 1938, 137); it is therefore not possible to establish if the timber used for coffin manufacture was grown in St Helena or imported.

Traditionally, oak or elm was held to be the best choice of timber for coffin manufacture, and soft woods such as pine, spruce and larch (known collectively as deal) were a cheaper alternative (Brickley and Miles 1999, 26). However, in this instance, there is insufficient information to determine whether less superior or cheaper timber was utilised because it was all that was available.

2139: Coffin
Group 2142; Context 2139; Skeleton 265
Single-break, single-case wooden coffin constructed of *Pinus sylvestris*. Base constructed of a single piece of wood with the sides attached with iron tacks. Lid of coffin was fragmented upon excavation and partially collapsed. No coffin furnishings or additional detail noted. Dimensions: length 0.5m, width 0.14m, depth 0.1m

2297: Coffin
Group 2298; Context 2297; Skeleton 351
Single-break, single-case wooden coffin constructed of tongue and groove pine planks of *Pinus sylvestris*. Base,

lid and sides all constructed from two planks. Coffin in good condition when excavated. Evidence of paint or tar visible on parts of the coffin. Secured with iron tacks. No coffin furnishings or additional detail noted. Dimensions: length 1.75m, width 0.31–0.52m, depth 0.35m

2362: Coffin
Group 2363; Context 2362; Skeleton 380
Single-break, single-case wooden coffin constructed of *Pinus sylvestris*. Coffin constructed of seven planks and in poor condition; very little evidence of lid and sides. Secured with iron tacks, which survived only as stains in some instances. Iron tacks visible in the base of the coffin which may indicate that the coffin was originally lined. Two coffin plates adorned the lid of the coffin (SF60 and SF61). Dimensions: length 0.57m, width 0.1–0.2m. Depth of coffin not preserved

2366: Coffin
Group 2367; Context 2366; Skeleton 381
Single-break, single-case wooden coffin constructed of *Pinus sylvestris*. Coffin constructed with one base plank, four side planks and a lid comprising two pine planks, secured with iron tacks. Condition of coffin upon excavation was good. Wood shavings (SF101) recovered from within the coffin. No adventitious decoration was recorded on the coffin. Dimensions: 0.55m length, 0.22m width, 0.18m depth.

2577: Coffin
Group 2579; Context 2577; Skeleton 519
Single-break, single-case wooden coffin constructed of *Pinus sylvestris*. Coffin constructed of a single piece of wood for the base, sides and lid. Three incisions were recorded on each of the side sections of the coffin, which was a traditional method of bending the sides (ie kerfing). No adventitious decoration was recorded on the coffin. Dimensions: 0.58m length, 0.13–0.23m width, 0.17m depth

5.11.3 Coffin furniture

The two stamped tin coffin plates (SF60 and SF61) recovered from the lid of coffin (2362) are likely to be unregistered coffin furniture (Figure 5.30). Both plates appear to be the same design: a 'winged face' of thin stamped tin attached at the head and feet of the coffin lid. This design was quite popular in the 19th century and a similar example came from a coffin at Christ Church, within the Spitalfields cemetery, which dated to the period 1700–1850 (Escutcheon No. 8). Another example is depicted within a trade catalogue by 'A T', held in the Prints and Drawings room of the Victoria and Albert Museum (No. 60, Acc No. E1019-1978).

The coffin plates were in quite poor condition when excavated and as a result it is not possible to find an exact match for these objects. However, the evidence indicates that they are of 19th-century date and of probable British origin, although not as sophisticated a design as those in the trade catalogues held at the Victoria and Albert Museum. It is possible that these coffin plates were produced in Birmingham, which had begun to mass-produce stamped coffin furnishings in the late 18th century, often utilising fashionable designs from London (Aitken 1866).

Figure 5.30 Stamped coffin plate from coffin 2362 (SF60)

SF60: Stamped tin coffin plate
Group 2363; Context 2362; Skeleton 380; 19th century; probably British
Coffin plate constructed of thin stamped zinc alloy (tin), fragmentary around the edges. Design is of a 'winged face' (revealed by x-ray). Attached in an inverted position, ie with the face at the end of the coffin and wings spread towards the centre of the coffin. Attached to the coffin lid at the feet end with iron tacks (four of which were noted during excavation). Dimensions (as excavated): thickness 0.3mm, height 48mm, width 88mm. Weight: 3.38g

SF61: Stamped tin coffin plate
Group 2363; Context 2362; Skeleton 380; 19th century; probably British
Coffin plate constructed of thin stamped zinc alloy (tin). Incomplete and fragmented. Design is of a 'winged face'. Attached to the coffin lid at the head end with iron tacks (five of which were noted during excavation). Dimensions (as excavated): thickness 0.3mm, height 45mm, width 97mm. Weight: 2.39g

5.11.4 Discussion

The assemblage of coffins from the Rupert's Valley excavation is typical of 'ordinary' coffins of mid-19th-century Britain. The fact that they have been constructed in a standardised and recognisable way implies that they were manufactured by a professional carpenter on St Helena, who possibly served the island as a whole.

Traditionally, higher-status coffins of the period were decorated with one breastplate and either six or eight handles or grip plates around the side. Further decoration could be added, such as lid motifs and escutcheons. 'Registered' coffin furniture comprised a complete set of items, predominately made of brass, for a single coffin. This was the more expensive variety. A less expensive option was to buy cheaper, often mass-produced individual items. The coffin plates recovered represent the less expensive, mass-produced variety.

The study of coffin manufacture and coffin furniture in traditional cemeteries provides potential insights into the status, wealth and religion of the inhumed population. However, in this instance the potential is limited due to the small size of the assemblage and the lack of comparable data from the island. It is also probable that these objects were donated to the depot; the choice of coffin and coffin furniture is likely to have been expressed by the donor rather than those held at the Liberated African Establishment. Nevertheless, the assemblage does provide a very important insight into burial practices within the graveyard. In particular, it begs the question of why only certain individuals were provided with coffins, whilst the vast majority were not. It is notable that all of the still- and newborn children within the excavated area were given a coffin burial, which clearly marks this group out as having been given special treatment. The possible reasons for the single adolescent coffin burial are discussed below (sections 7.5.1 and 7.7.2). The assemblage also raises issues about the level of control that individuals had over the burial rites of those with whom they had familial, ethnic or other close associations.

Notes

1   The Britannia groat was circulated within the British Isles and the colonies and introduced as the equivalent of a quarter guilder in British Guiana. No Britannia groats were struck after 1855, apart from the 1888 issue for British Guiana (Lobel *et al* 1995, 511).

2   The silver three pence was initially struck for colonial use, but in 1845 it entered general use within the British Isles (Lobel *et al* 1995, 516).

3   A second item, believed to be a belt, was found in association with Skeleton 351. However, later analysis proved that this was not leather, but fragments of organic material – perhaps tree bark or root.

4   The funerary traditions of Victorian Britain were used as the basis for comparative analysis of these coffins. The primary comparative data were drawn from excavation archives of two contemporary British cemetery sites held at the London Archaeological Archive and Research Centre (St Marylebone Church and Burial Ground, site code MBH04, and All Saints Chelsea Old Church, site code OCU00) and Trade Catalogues held at the Victoria and Albert Museum, London.

5   Single-break refers to the shape of the coffin; expanding from the head end to the shoulders and then with a single break, tapers down towards the feet. Single-case refers to a single skin of timber.

6 Spatial analysis *by Ben Jeffs*

6.1 Introduction

The purpose of this chapter is to offer a short analysis of the site, combining the structural data presented in Chapter 3 with the osteological and artefactual data presented in Chapters 4 and 5. As such it provides a bridge between these initial chapters, whose purpose is to convey objective information about the excavation, and the discussion in Chapter 7 whose content is more subjective.

Due to the lack of stratigraphy within the site, the analysis is largely of a two-dimensional nature. A number of the patterns investigated are quite standard in terms of a cemetery report, notably those showing the distribution by age and sex. Others are more specific to this project, for instance the plotting of single versus multiple burials, and of the coffin burials. There is also an element of hypothesis-testing, the aim of which has been to comment in more detail about the formation of this part of the graveyard, and about the people within it. For example, was this area the product of a single, brief, episode of burial (derived from a single vessel, or several arriving near-simultaneously) or of a more prolonged period where deaths occurred at a lower but constant rate? These queries have been quite fruitful, in that they show a burial area that divides into two distinct parts. By contrast, other queries have been less successful. Attempts to identify status (through the artefact distribution), and family or tribal groups (through the distribution of dental modifications) were also made, but no patterns were discernable.

This chapter divides into three parts. The first is concerned with structural archaeological data, addressing the historic landform, the overall layout of the graveyard, and the orientation of the graves and the bodies within them. It also examines issues such as the distribution of burials containing lime and fly pupae, and of the charnel pits within the site. In overall terms, this part of the analysis has been the most successful in adding detail to our understanding of the graveyard.

The second part of the chapter addresses the osteological data, beginning with an analysis of distribution by age and sex. It goes on to analyse certain observable traits, notably the dental modifications and the presence of scurvy. As discussed above, the former of these was thought to have potential for comment upon the issue of ethnicity, although in the event this does not appear to be the case. The distribution of scurvy was examined in an attempt to establish whether any clusters were present: since not every slave ship carried victims of this disease,

this analysis offered a possible means of identifying victims from different vessels.

The third part of the chapter presents the analysis of artefact distribution. However, except to show the self-evident concentration of objects within the child coffin-burials, and a paucity of material culture elsewhere, this aspect of the analysis has not yielded any meaningful results.

The interpretation of this analysis, and of the site as a whole, is given in Chapter 7.

6.2 The arrangement of the graveyard

6.2.1 Stratigraphy

Within the graves themselves there was often a clear stratigraphic order, namely that of the deposition of the bodies within the graves. However, on a site-wide scale there were very few stratigraphic relationships between the graves, charnel pits and the few other feature-types present. Indeed, the only significant stratigraphy outside the grave cuts was provided by a pair of charnel pits (see section 6.2.9).

6.2.2 Site terracing

The overall framework of the excavated part of the graveyard was defined by a series of area-wide features, which related to the eroded 19th-century ground surface (deposit 2001). The upper profile of deposit (2001) was broken and ridged which, as discussed below, is the product of artificial terracing. This terracing process had formed distinct, steep sections ranging from 1m to 3m in width and rising up to 1.2m from the net grade of the slope (see section 3.4.1; Fig 6.1). The terraced ridges ran north–south along the valley wall and delineated flatter areas. The exact form of this surface was difficult to discern, due to the indistinct boundary with (2001). However, a partial reconstruction of its profile was possible from the relative vertical position of adjacent burials.

The western edge of the site was defined by the steep slope formed by cut [2071], which truncated deposit (2001) as well as several burials.

6.2.3 Graveyard layout

The graveyard layout followed a sequence of lines running north–south along the valley (see Fig 3.7). There are nine separate, but broken, alignments of

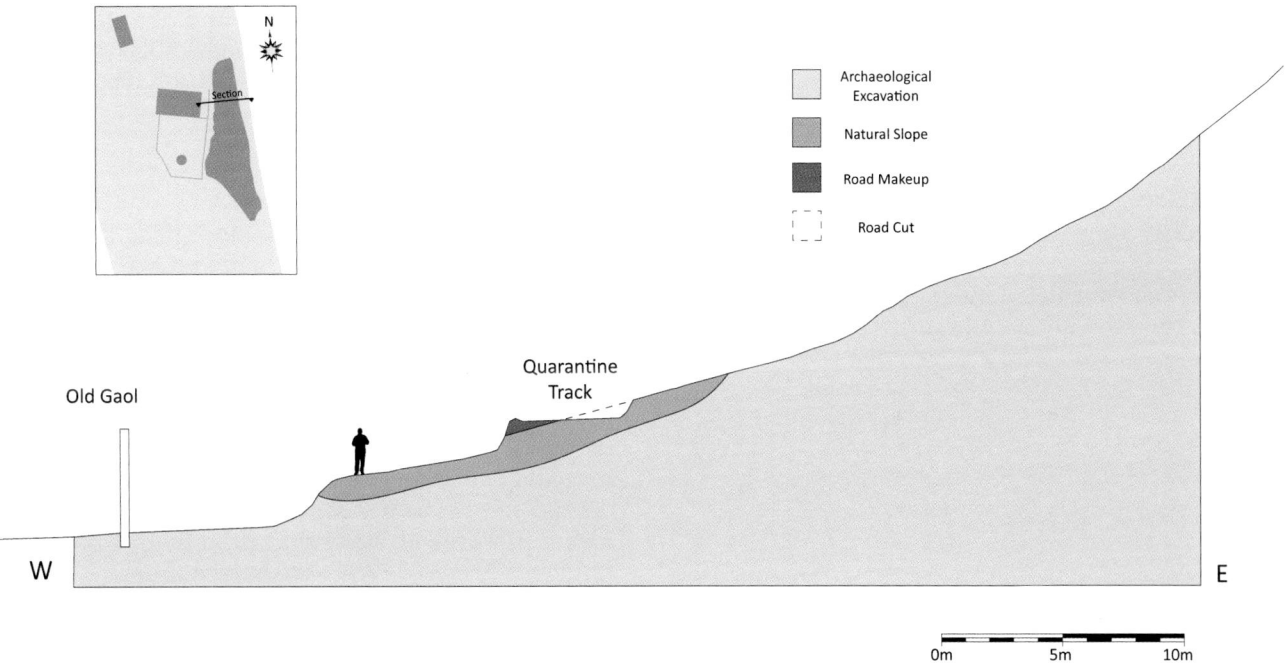

Figure 6.1   Site profile

graves, following the valley topography. The main breaks occur in the centre of the excavation area, where very stony ground is present.

Each grave was allotted a space that was approximately 1.2m in width: the grave cut itself was 0.6m wide, and there was an allowance of approximately 0.6m between each grave. This practice was not always adhered to – indeed it only applied to half of the grave cuts. However, departures from this practice only occurred in areas of stony ground or where grave-digging had to respect the form of the terrace.

The level of each body (which was usually placed on the base of the grave cut) differed considerably across the site. Bodies from adjacent graves were found at heights varying by as much as 1.5m.

6.2.4   Grave fills and inclusions

All grave fills were loams or modified loams that were similar in composition to the natural (2001). All fills included between 5% and 45% angular and sub-angular stones, with the majority containing about 25% stone but with no other inclusions. Almost all fills were loose and friable. The difference in inclusion content within grave fills, particularly in terms of the amount of stone that was present, seems to relate entirely to geological factors. However, nine of the graves included a distinct layer of stones, which appear to have been deliberately placed some distance above the body: these graves are not grouped in one particular area of the site, and their distribution seems to be random.

A small number of graves (15 out of 178) included residual traces of quicklime (chemically altered to calcium carbonate) immediately adjacent to the base of the cut and close to the skeletal remains. These traces often comprised no more than white staining of the grave base, although some concentrations of larger fragments existed in certain places.

Nine of the graves included significant numbers of fly pupae casings, preserved close to the human remains or within body cavities. A single charnel pit (Group 2494) also included fly pupae; these may well have been transferred from the original burial context, rather than the flies having been being introduced into the charnel at the time of its reinterment.

The number of graves containing fly pupae and lime-staining was too small for any significant conclusions to be drawn about their distribution (Fig 6.2). There was a notable concentration in the southwest part of the site, but the observable pattern may result from differences in preservation and recovery, rather than deposition events.

6.2.5   Grave form

Where clear cuts were visible, the graves were typically *c* 1.8m by 0.6m with a sub-rectangular plan and near-vertical sides. Many had a straight western end with sharp corners and tapered out to the east, terminating in a more rounded profile. However, there was a considerable deviation from this basic form, with cuts from 0.5m to 1.8m in width and from 1.2m to 2.5m in length. A very irregular plan was apparent for about a quarter of all the burials.

The deepest cut, from the base of the disturbed overburden (2000), was 1m, although 0.6m–0.7m was more typical and shallow scrapes of 0.1m were not unknown (Fig 6.3). Roughly half of the bases of the cuts were level (86 out of 178), with almost as

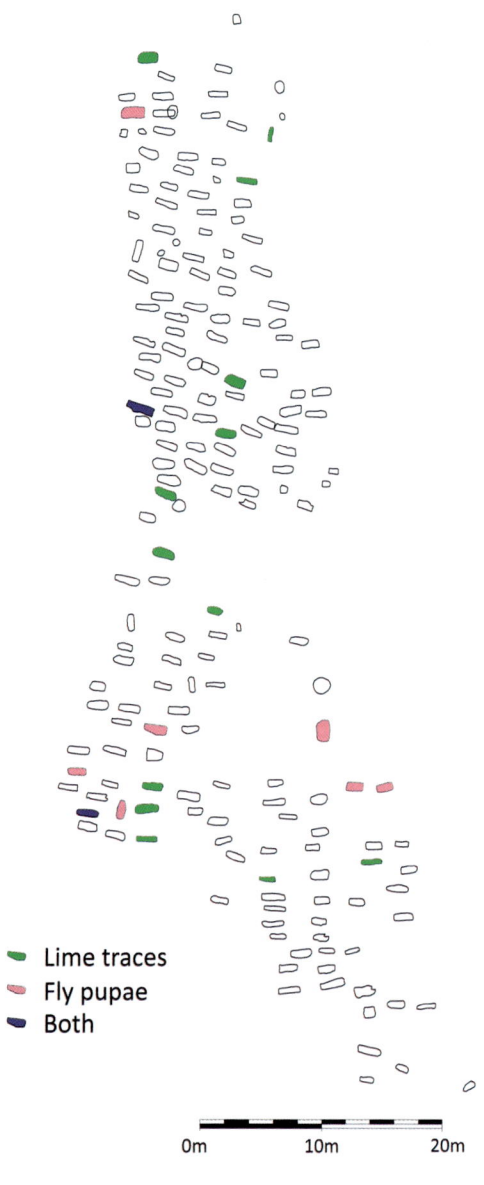

- Lime traces
- Fly pupae
- Both

N

0m　10m　20m

Figure 6.2　Distribution of fly pupae and lime-staining

many sloping down to the west (83 out of 178). Very few sloped down to the east (9 out of 178).

Many of the cuts (62 out of 178) were considerably shorter than the individuals buried within them, resulting in flexed burials.

6.2.6　Grave orientation

Nearly 95% of the grave cuts (171 out of 178) were oriented east–west. The graves divide into two groups (Fig 3.7): a minority of graves, 45 in the southern extreme of the site, and 5 in the very north, shared a similar orientation, which was 10° south of that for the majority of graves across the rest of the site. The orientation of neither group respects the wider topography, being approximately 12° north of perpendicular to the valley wall in both cases.

Considering the stony ground and the large area involved, the orientation is remarkably consistent within each group, the main axis for most graves being within 5° of the mean.

6.2.7　Body orientation

Where the graves were oriented east–west, the majority of skeletons were interred with their head to the east, although a lesser number (29 out of 325) were oriented the opposite way around. Burials with the head to the west were generally part of a multiple interment (ie as part of a head-to-toe arrangement); only one body (Skeleton 436 in Group 2467) was buried alone and with the head to the west.

Most of the bodies were on their back or side, facing upwards or sideways, although a significant number (20 out of 325) were buried prone.

There was a great deal of variation in the position of limbs, the vast majority showing no particular arrangement, or only partial arrangement. Thirty-three individuals out of the 325 excavated showed a more deliberate layout, buried supine with their arms folded across their chest or abdomen.

6.2.8　Multiple burials

Of the 178 graves excavated, 73 contained a single individual. Of the remainder, 74 contained two bodies; 21 contained three; 7 contained four; whilst two cuts were found containing five and seven individuals respectively (Fig 6.4).

The distribution of single and multiple graves was not consistent, the north and south halves of the site having distinctly different characters.

The northern part of the site contained a large number of densely spaced single burials. However, the majority of graves containing more than two individuals, and all the burials of more than three, were also located here – within two loose groupings. The northern part of the site had an average of 1.83 individuals per grave.

The southern part of the site had slightly more double burials than single interments. However, there were only four triple burials, and no graves containing a greater number. The southern part of the site therefore had a lower average density of 1.59 individuals per grave.

6.2.9　Charnel deposits

The majority of charnel deposits occurred in a rough alignment, towards the western edge of the site (Fig 6.5). These pits included well-preserved but disarticulated human remains. Two pits on this alignment cut burials and disturbed the remains within them; this clearly establishes a secondary phase of activity within the burial ground.

Two very large pits were found in the south-east

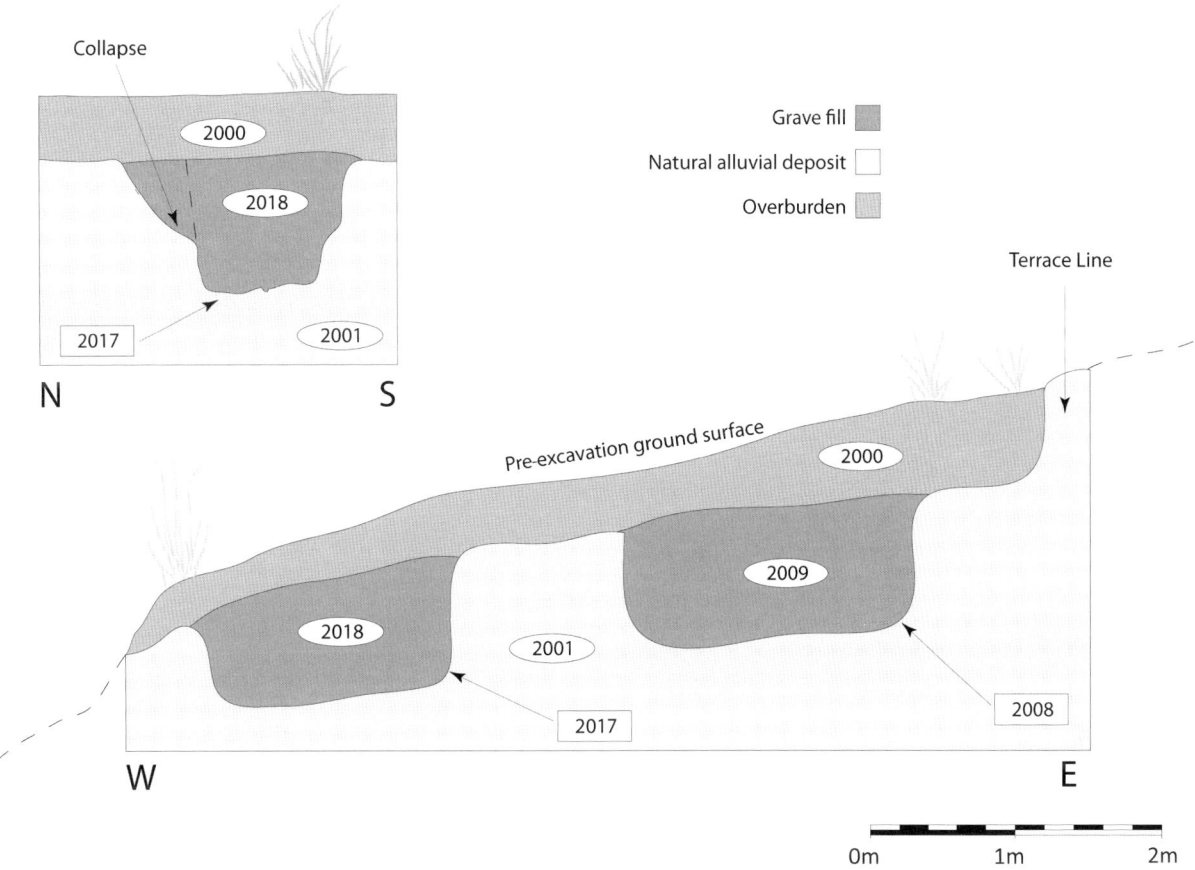

Figure 6.3 Grave profiles

part of the site, within an area where no burials were present. These pits contained a large quantity of heavily comminuted remains, different in character and quantity from the other charnel deposits.

6.2.10 Features not relating to human remains

The vast majority of features within the excavated area related directly to the burial process. However, a small expanse of cobbled surfacing was found to the north-west of the main excavation area (Group 2380) and a grave-like cut containing glass bottles (Group 2189) was present in the most southerly part of the site (Fig 6.5). There was no stratigraphic relationship between these two features and the graves, so they could not be dated in relative terms. However, they related to the same horizon as the burial groups and there was no evidence for them being of a different date. It is thought likely that they are contemporary with the graveyard.

6.3 Distribution by osteological features

Generally, the discernable patterns of distribution are site-wide. There does not appear to be any specific distribution of sex or age within the individual graves, although there is a single grave with an older female and young child (Group 2449; Skeletons 422 and 424; see Fig 8.1). These two bodies appear to have been deliberately laid out as a group, but this is an isolated case and the exclusive association of adult females and children is not otherwise apparent.

6.3.1 Age

The most immediately obvious grouping is that of foetus and neonate burials: all are found within coffins and all occur within the northern half of the site (Fig 6.6). Three of these burials form a tight grouping, with a single burial 20m further to the south.

This pattern is reversed when looking at young children (Fig 6.7): out of the eighteen individuals assessed as young children, six were buried in the northern part of the site – two within the same grave (comprising 3.1% of the burials in this half). Twelve were interred in the southern part (comprising 8.8% of the burials here).

Other age ranges show no significant pattern of distribution.

6.3.2 Sex

Any comments concerning the sex ascertained from the visual examination of human skeletal remains

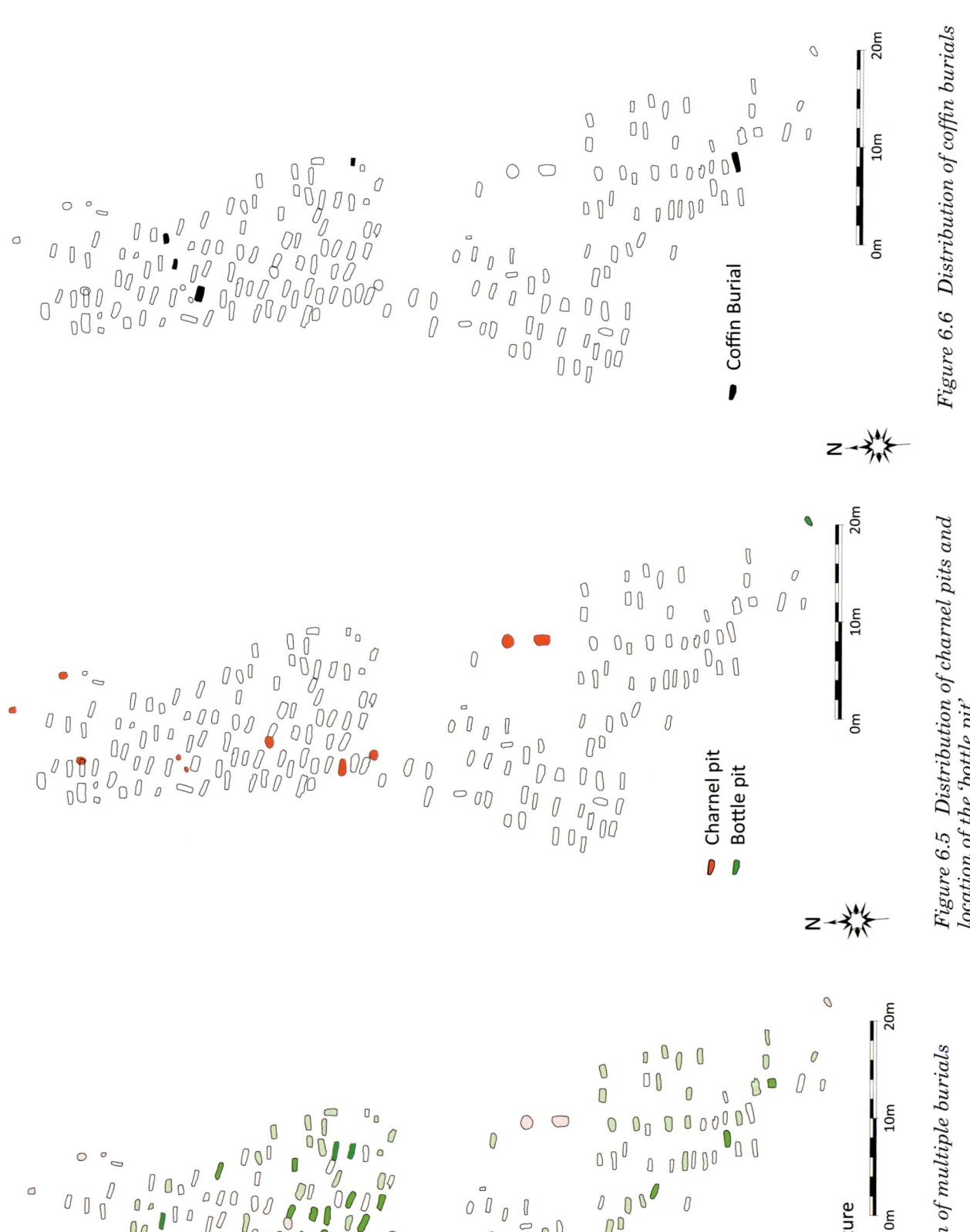

Figure 6.6 Distribution of coffin burials

Figure 6.5 Distribution of charnel pits and location of the 'bottle pit'

Figure 6.4 Distribution of multiple burials

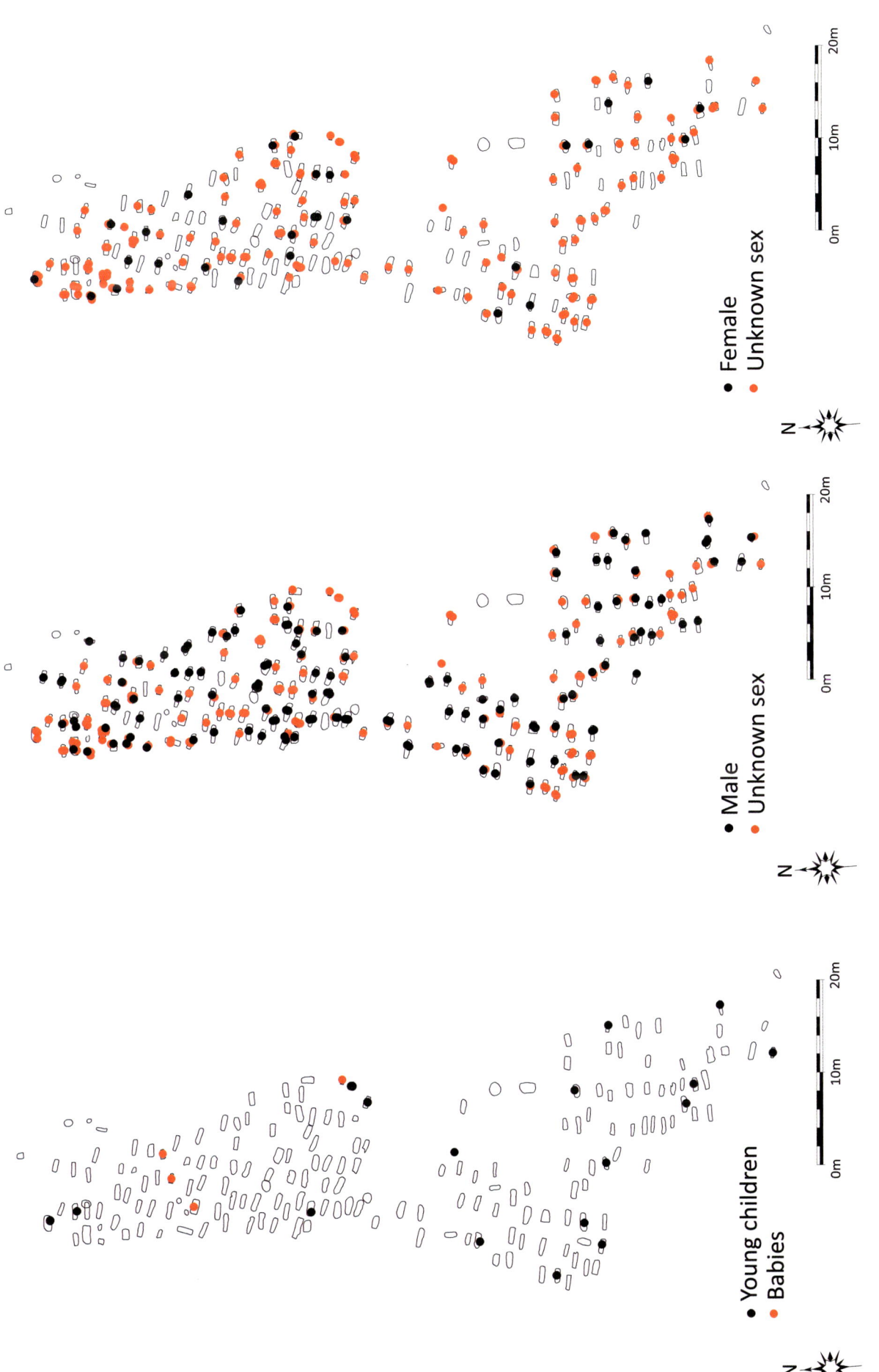

Figure 6.9 Distribution of female burials

● Female
● Unknown sex

Figure 6.8 Distribution of male burials

● Male
● Unknown sex

Figure 6.7 Distribution of child and baby burials

● Young children
● Babies

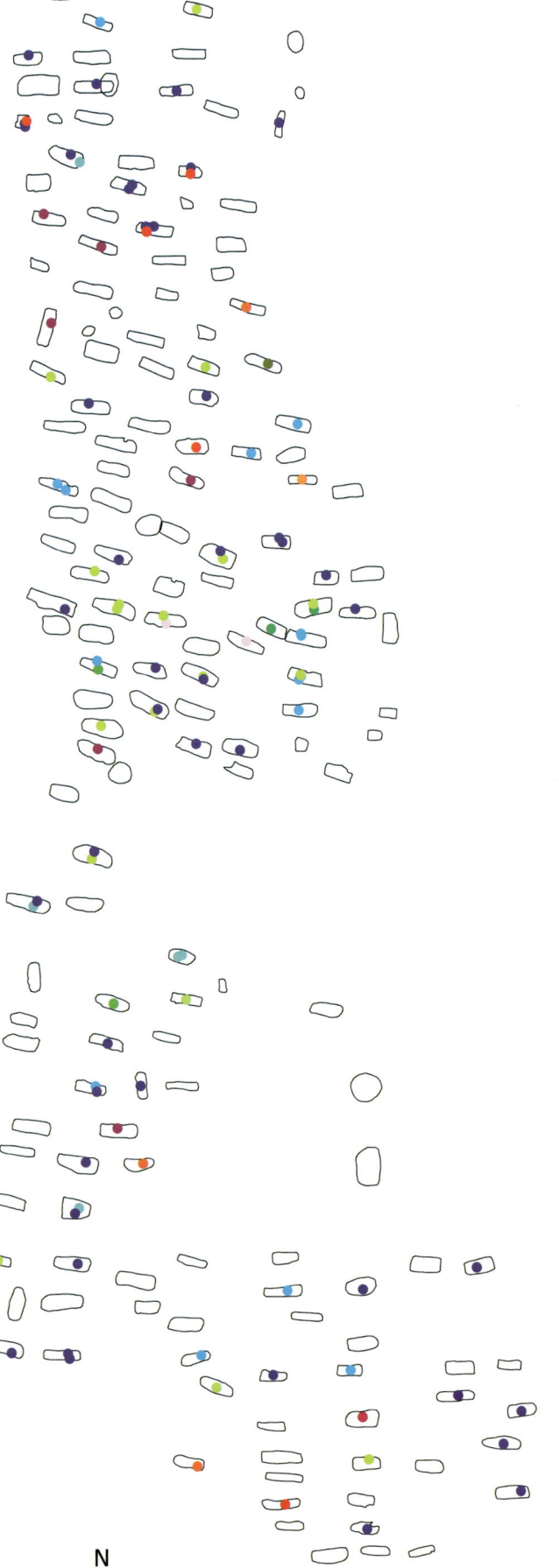

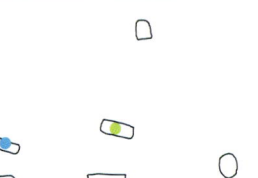

N

Figure 6.10 Distribution of dental modifications

Type 1 C
Type 1 S
Type 10 C
Type 11 C
Type 12 C
Type 2 C
Type 2 S
Type 3 C
Type 3 S
Type 4 C
Type 4 S
Type 5 C
Type 5 S
Type 6 C
Type 6 S
Type 7 C
Type 7 S
Type 8 S
Type 9 C

0m   5m   10m

must always be tempered by the uncertainty inherent in such an analysis. Of the 325 individuals excavated, 21 were considered female, 8 probably female, 115 male, and 16 probably male. The sex of 165 skeletons (50%) was not discernable.

For this spatial analysis the probable and definite males and probable and definite females have been grouped together. The 165 individuals for whom no sex was assigned have been removed from the analysis.

The pattern of sex distribution once again appears to split the excavated area into northern and southern halves. In the northern half of the site 73% of the burials with discernable sex were male, while in the southern half males made up 85% of all burials. However, with so many skeletons for which the sex was not determined, this observation must be regarded as tentative (Figs 6.8 and 6.9).

6.3.3 *Tooth modification*

There is no discernable pattern for the overall distribution of dental modifications, the individuals with modified teeth being widely and evenly dispersed (Fig 6.10). There are a few possible groupings of certain types of modification, but they are not clearcut. Moreover, the sample is too small and the types too numerous for patterns to be distinguished with any certainty.

6.3.4 *Scurvy*

Scurvy is present across the whole of the site, with no apparent clusters or areas in which it is absent. It is found equally within single and multiple graves.

6.4 Distribution of artefacts

There is no apparent pattern to the distribution of beads and metalwork. The only discernable trait is a paucity of finds in the south-eastern quadrant of the site, an area that exhibits an alignment of grave cuts that is distinct from that found elsewhere in the graveyard.

There is, however, a correlation between the age of individuals within a burial group and the presence of beads or metal in the grave, in that most of the artefacts or objects that might be considered as 'decorative' were found within graves containing children.

As observed above, three of the four coffins belonging to foetuses and neonates were grouped together in the north-central part of the site, with the fourth, and that of the adolescent male, located elsewhere. The four foetus and neonate coffins accounted for a large proportion of the individual- and group-numbered finds recovered during the excavation.

7   Discussion   *by Andrew Pearson and Ben Jeffs*

7.1 The location of the graveyards

The archaeological investigations carried out between 2006 and 2008 have established the location of the Liberated African graveyards in Rupert's Valley with reasonable certainty.

Melliss' 1861 map has proved to be a reliable source, at least as far as it could be tested by archaeological evaluation and excavation. However, whilst it depicts the two main graveyards with a good degree of accuracy, the map is unlikely to be comprehensive. Outlying burials are likely to exist which are not marked.

The 1872 revision of Palmer's map is a more problematic source. It does not show the graveyards depicted by Melliss, but instead marks a burial ground high up in the valley. Here, the archaeological evaluations of 2008 failed to find graves, and indeed most of the ground here was so rocky as to preclude burials having been dug. The straightforward explanation is that the map is simply wrong. Alternatively, it may be based on memories of the last burials to have taken place in the valley, perhaps within the two pits described in 1860, located 'about 200 yards above the old well' (discussed below in section 7.2.1.2). Regardless, the map's failure to mark the two main graveyards indicates how quickly the Establishment was forgotten.

In terms of archaeological work, there was relatively little investigation of the lower (northern) graveyard. This was principally because the area fell outside the development footprint of the haul road, but investigation was also hindered by the presence of buried fuel pipes. The one evaluation trench dug within the graveyard (in 2007) encountered a multiple burial, whilst evaluation in the centre of the valley (in 2008), along the line of the existing road, seemed to demonstrate convincingly that no graves were present in the floodplain. This is the key point of difference between the 1861 map and the modern survey: Melliss shows burials extending into the very centre of the valley, up against the uncanalised stream, whereas the evaluation trenches dug in 2008 found no graves and ground so rocky as to preclude burial.

The upper graveyard was more extensively investigated. In addition to the open-area excavation, a large number of trial pits and evaluation trenches were dug in this area between 2006 and 2008. These investigations added to what was already known from the discoveries made in the 1980s, at the time of the construction of the power station and fuel farm. The known extent of burial broadly corresponds to that shown by Melliss, although his map does not

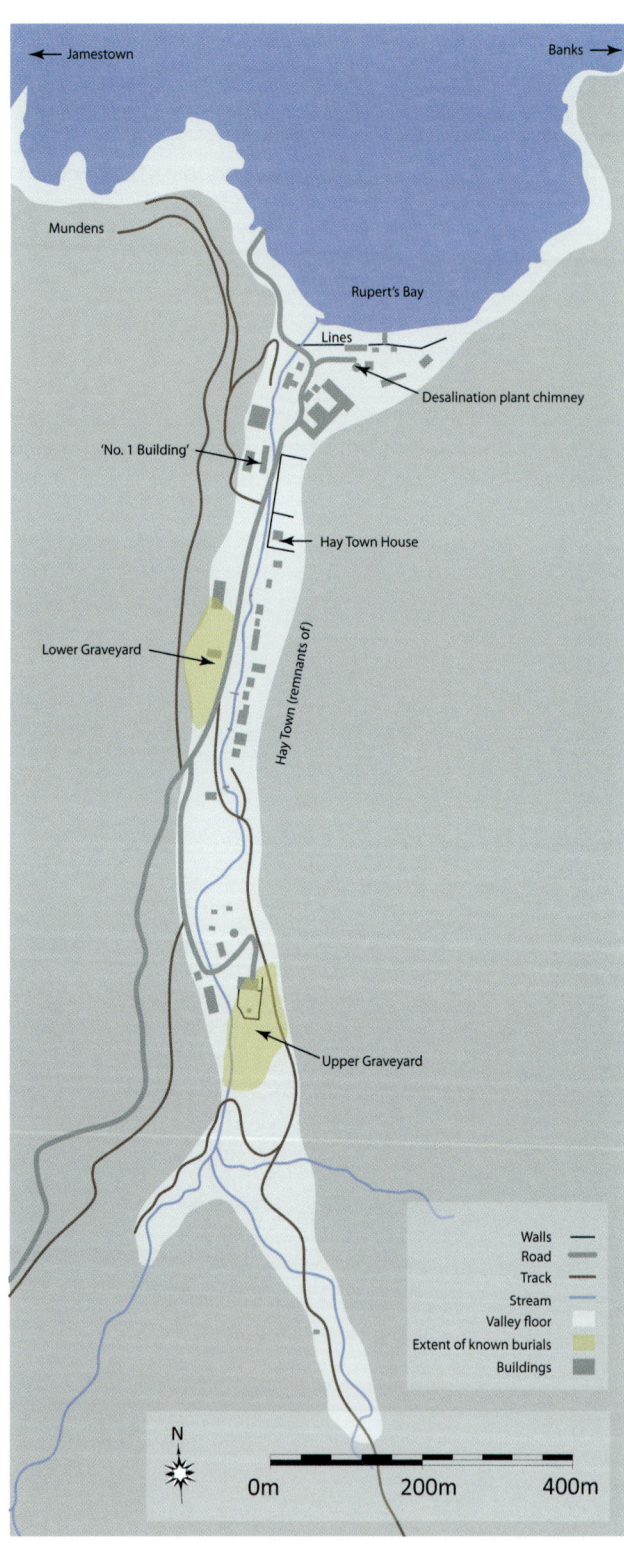

Figure 7.1   The location of the graveyards in Rupert's Valley

142

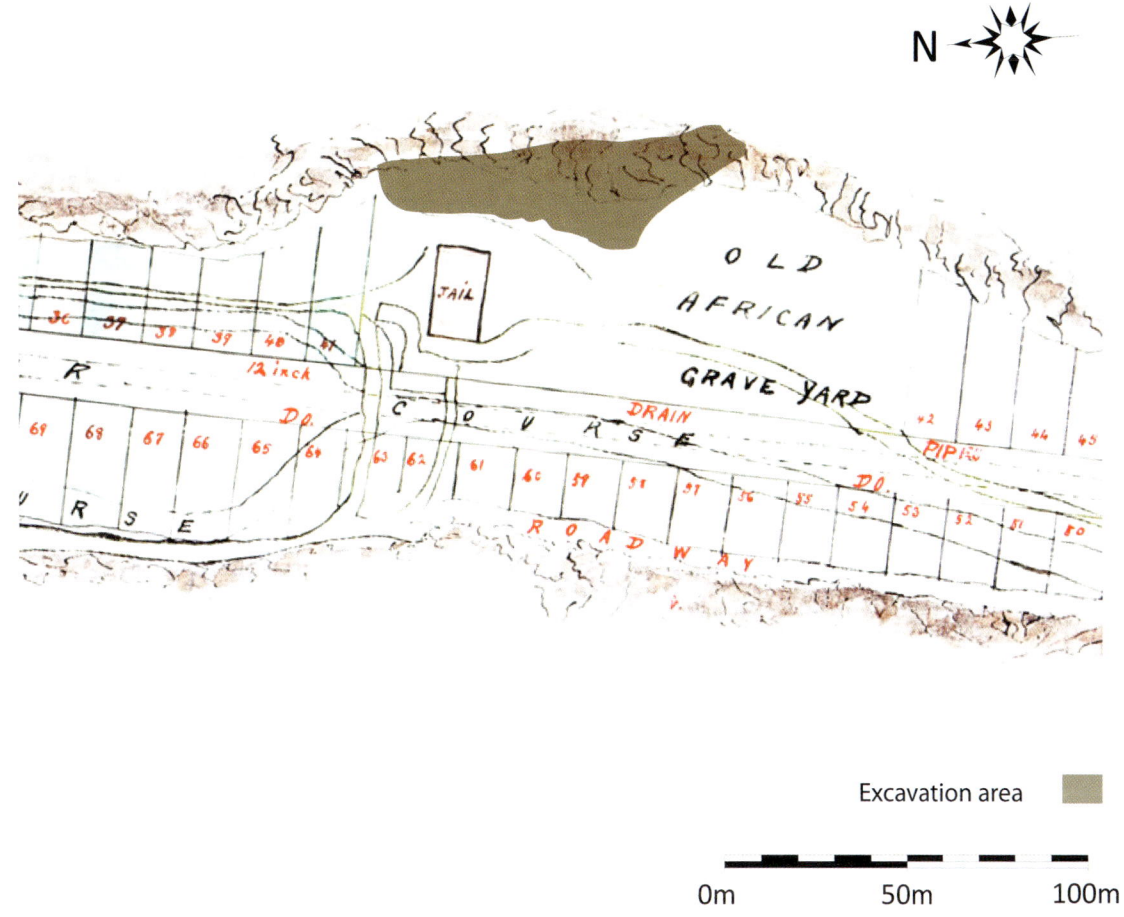

Excavation area

0m   50m   100m

Figure 7.2   The excavation area, overlaid on Melliss' map of 1861

define the boundaries of the upper graveyard particularly precisely (Fig 7.2).

In terms of rationale, large parts of the graveyards were placed on the lower valley sides, on gently sloping ground above the central floodplain. Rocky ground unsuited to grave-digging was avoided, notably the floodplain and land at the base of gullies in the hillside. Areas prone to flash floods were also not utilised. The lower graveyard completely occupied elevated, sloping ground which then (as now) would have been rough scrub. The upper graveyard took in an extensive part of the valley floor, probably where the power station now stands, and certainly the area immediately to the south. More burials were placed on the natural terraces above, on land now beneath the gaol and Mid Valley Fuel Farm, and in the area of the 2008 excavation. It is known that there are some burials away from the main graveyards, but it is not thought that they exist in large numbers.

Knowing the boundaries of the graveyards, it is possible to offer an estimate of the total number of burials within the valley. The excavation took in an area of 1800 square metres and contained 325 bodies. However, when considering this figure, it is important to note that graves were completely absent from the rocky central part of the site, and

that the topsoil strip was deliberately extended beyond the area of burials in order to ensure that all human remains were recovered. The actual density of bodies varied across the site, from 5 square metres per body in the sparsest areas to 1.2 square metres per body in places where multiple graves were most concentrated.

The total area occupied by the burial grounds in Rupert's Valley is approximately 16,000 square metres, which divides more or less evenly between the two known graveyards. Adopting the lowest density, 3200 individuals would be buried in the valley; adopting the highest density, 13,000 would be present. Clearly neither figure is realistic, but the median of just over 8000 is quite plausible. Certainly it chimes with the reported mortality rate for the depot: during the 1840s this averaged 31% (see Table 2.1) and medical reports from the later decades do not suggest that it ever improved to any appreciable extent. Some 26,000 recaptives were brought to St Helena, and an average mortality rate of 30% would have resulted in 7800 deaths. Only a few hundred Africans were buried in Lemon Valley and only a limited number seem to have been buried at sea. The remainder, a vast number by any standard, were interred in Rupert's Valley.

7.2 The date of the excavated area

7.2.1 The graves

The Liberated African Establishment on St Helena was in operation between 1840 and 1867, with Rupert's Valley in use from early 1841 onwards. The graveyards in the valley can therefore be dated with certainty to this 27-year period. However, whilst it cannot be proved beyond doubt, a more refined date range can be offered. The evidence for burials within the valley, and for their location, can be summarised as follows.

7.2.1.1 Cartographic evidence

In terms of cartographic evidence, there are two sources: Melliss' 1861 map, and the 1872 revision of Palmer's map (Figs 2.10 and 3.2 respectively).

Melliss' map shows two areas of burials, one a short distance from Rupert's Bay and the other further up the valley, around and to the south of the gaol. The burial ground nearest to the bay is labelled as 'African Graveyard', with an adjacent sub-area labelled as 'Addition to Graveyard since 1851'. The upper burial ground is labelled as 'Old African Graveyard'. The 1872 revision of Palmer is less useful, showing only a single undated area of burials high up the valley.

7.2.1.2 Historical evidence

The historical evidence is rather slight. There are only a few references to the burial grounds within the primary sources, and nearly all are confined to the late 1840s and early 1850s. Nevertheless they provide a useful insight into the formation of the main graveyards within the valley. An 1849 Parliamentary Report into emigration includes two references to these burial grounds. The first is by the Colonial Surgeon Dr Vowells, in which he states that:

> The distance to the old ground was about a quarter of a mile up the valley, and the effluvia perceptible in its immediate vicinity mark clearly enough the purpose to which it is assigned ... a new one is now selected, rather more distant.

Appended to Vowell's report were remarks by John Young, Collector of Customs, who adds further detail by saying that 'the nearest burial ground is at the distance of 1,020 feet from the habitations of the Africans.' Both comments clearly indicate that the graveyard in use in 1849 was the lower graveyard shown on Melliss' map, the centre of which lies some 400m from the sea.

In September 1850 the new Superintendent in Rupert's Valley, Edward Griffiths, reported that 'the present [burial] ground is fast being filled up, when it is so it will be our duty in opening a new one to carry as far as possible from the encampment'. By 5 April 1851 Griffiths had apparently acted on this matter, informing the Governor that:

> I have removed the burial ground further away from the encampment, the soil of the valley is of a light loamy description and a few days since, I noticed in visiting the burial ground that an effluvia was discernible, but being so distant from the encampment it cannot have any injurious effects upon it, but it might be prejudicial to those employed in the carrying and burying the dead. I have therefore given instructions to the overseers to deepen the graves in future.

The final letter in this sequence comes from Commander Rowlatt, who took charge of the Establishment in June 1851 after Griffiths' brief tenure. His report on the depot contained the comment that amongst other tasks the Africans were employed in 'forming a good wall to the burial ground *at the head of the valley*'.

There is then a gap of nearly a decade before the subject recurs. On 16 January 1860 the Civil Engineer's Office wrote to the Colonial Secretary, informing him that 'two pits to bury dead Africans in have been excavated in Rupert's Valley about 200m above the old well'. This area is well beyond the limits of the graveyard shown by Melliss.

Finally, in 1863, there is a series of letters which address the fact that all suitable land for burial in Rupert's Valley had been taken up. In May of that year there are references to the Governor's instructions to bury the recaptives in Half Tree Hollow.[1] On 11 August the Half Tree Hollow burial ground was described as being 'in execution', whilst attempts to find land for burial that was rather nearer to Rupert's Valley were noted to have failed.[2] A letter dated 20 August 1863 suggests that suitable ground might exist on the ridge connecting Sugar Loaf Hill and the inland valleys (ie at the head of Banks Valley, near the northern tip of the island). Whether this suggestion ever came to anything is not known, as this is the last letter so far found that mentions the subject of burials.

7.2.1.3 Archaeological evidence

The only dateable items recovered from the excavations were the coins, all of which were found within the foetus and neonote coffin burials. An exact date can be discerned for four of these coins, whilst the other four can only be placed within a range of around 30 years. Coffin 2362 (Skeleton 380) contained a coin minted in 1846 (SF43) and two coins minted between 1838 and 1866 (SF51 and SF52). Coffin 2577 (Skeleton 519) contained two coins minted in 1843 (SF93 and SF94) and another minted in 1844 (SF95). Coffin 2366 (Skeleton 381) contained two coins minted between 1838 and 1870 (SF58). All three of these coffins were found in a cluster in the northern part of the site. The fourth of these coffins (2139), which lay in a separate part of the site, did not contain coins.

Several of the coins are worn, including two for which the precise date of minting is known (SF94 and SF95). This wear indicates a period in circulation prior to their placement in the burials. However, all of the coins are low-denomination silver issues, and as such they could easily have reached this state of wear in only a few years, particularly on St Helena where the volume of coinage in circulation was quite small, and coin-wear consequently fairly rapid.

As a group, the coins infer a date for the coffins that falls within the 1840s. Strictly speaking they only provide a *terminus post quem*, but the fact that all four coins for which a precise date could be established belong to the mid-1840s seems significant. That several showed signs of wear implies that the coffins belong to the later part of the decade, but this is beyond proof.[3]

It is possible that some or all of the foetus and neonate coffins were later insertions into an existing graveyard. In favour of this argument is the fact that three of the four were found in a close grouping. However, the holes dug for these coffins respect the alignment of the surrounding graves, and do not intercut them, as was likely to have happened if there had been a long interval between the original burials and the interment of the coffins. Therefore, even if the coffins were later insertions, it seems probable that they were still broadly contemporary with the surrounding graveyard.

7.2.1.4 Discussion of the evidence

On the basis of the evidence outlined above, the following chronology can be postulated.

In 1841 the original burial ground for the recaptives was opened in the upper valley. This is the 'Old African Graveyard' shown on Melliss' map, and is where the 2008 excavation was located. At some point during the mid- or later 1840s this burial ground was closed in favour of a new site closer to the bay: Melliss' 'African Grave Yard'. By 1849 this area had become full, or nearly so, and was also considered a health hazard. It was closed in late 1850 or early 1851, with burials taking place within an area that was contiguous, but nevertheless a little further removed from the depot at the bay: this is the ground marked by Melliss as 'Addition to Graveyard since 1851'. By the time of Melliss' survey in 1861 this new graveyard had itself become disused, and an *ad hoc* approach to burial was being practised, as illustrated by the pits dug in the upper valley in January 1860. By 1863 all ground in Rupert's Valley that was suitable for graves had been used up, and from that point onwards the recaptives were buried elsewhere, most if not all in Half Tree Hollow.

This reading of the evidence is not without its difficulties, and primarily rests on the labelling on Melliss' map, a survey whose purpose was to show the proposed layout of Hay Town, and not the African depot or its graveyards. It also begs some slightly awkward questions of the historical evidence: most notably, if the upper graveyard had been abandoned for several years, why was a wall being built there in 1851? Moreover, the proposed three-phase chronology – of upper graveyard, lower graveyard, and lower graveyard extension – may also be too simplistic. The 1860 pits in the upper valley, and the reports of bone from the ground near Hay Town House (see section 1.4), serve as an indication that a sizeable number of burials, whether individual or multiple, may well exist elsewhere in the valley.

Nevertheless, it seems reasonable to propose that the excavated area falls within a burial ground that as a whole belongs to the 1840s. As described immediately below, the excavated area divides into two halves: if the coffins are not later insertions, then the coins found within them suggest that at least the northern half of the site was formed in the later part of that decade.

7.2.1.5 A graveyard of two halves

As shown in Chapter 6, there is a north–south division of the excavated part of the graveyard. That division can be seen in a number of ways: it is apparent in the alignment and spacing of the graves, and is also reflected in the spatial distribution of osteological traits and the finds. The northern area, on its separate alignment, has fewer young children, a greater density of finds, fewer males and a concentration of foetus/neonate burials in coffins. As such, the northern and southern halves of the site are distinct from one another in a number of important aspects.

The division must reflect two different periods of burial, although these may be separated by only a short period of time. Given the episodic nature of the arrival of prizes (see section 2.4.4) it is possible that the break occurred between the arrivals of two slave vessels, or between two concentrations of vessels. This would explain the demographic differences between north and south, whilst the interlude probably explains the slight change in alignment. As discussed further in section 7.4 below, there may be still finer chronological divisions, primarily detectable in the concentration of multiple interments in certain parts of the northern half of the site.

7.2.2 The charnel pits

In addition to the graves, ten charnel pits containing disarticulated human remains were found within the area of excavation. Eight were located in the northern part and were interspersed amongst the graves; the remaining two pits, which were markedly larger, had been dug in the central-southern part of the site, in an area that was devoid of graves (see section 6.2.9; Fig 6.5). All are round or sub-round in shape, indicating that they have been dug by hand.

Neither the reason for their presence, nor their date, is obvious. Eight of the pits are discrete features that avoid the graves (though whether intentionally or by luck is unknown) whilst the other two (Groups 2359 and 2425) are cut into graves. The latter clearly represent a secondary phase, but whether the other eight are contemporary with the surrounding burials, or are also later, has not been established.

The eight pits in the northern part of the site all contain well-preserved, near-complete long bones and skulls, with little by way of the smaller bones relating to, for example, hands and feet. This material would have originated from burials of articulated remains, but how it came to be reinterred in the pits is unclear. One possibility is that these pits contain bone that had become exposed by soil erosion from earlier parts of the burial ground, perhaps from the shallower graves. Regardless of whether the pits were contemporary with, or later than, the adjacent graves, the bone itself must have been derived from bodies that had been buried several years earlier.

The two pits in the southern part of the site are isolated from the other eight and are of a quite distinct character: they are significantly larger in size, and contain bone that is highly comminuted. Again, an explanation for their presence is not immediately obvious. However, one possibility is that these represent the remains of bodies that were disturbed during the construction of the adjacent gaol. In this case the scenario would be as follows. Burial of recaptive Africans took place on the future site of the gaol in the 1840s. (That graves exist on this lower terrace is quite clear: a large number were disturbed during the building of the fuel farm in the 1980s, whilst a 2006 trial pit encountered a burial less than a metre from the wall of the adjacent ruined stone building; see section 3.3.1.) The site of the gaol was selected in 1852, and the fact that it overlay graves was probably not too great a concern: after all, the slightly later plans for Hay Town also envisaged development over the former African burial grounds (see section 2.4.2). The digging of the foundation trenches, probably in 1854, disturbed bodies that had been buried fairly recently but which were already in a reasonably advanced state of decay. Their exhumation, using tools such as pick-axes and shovels, could well have resulted in a great deal of comminuted bone. The remains were gathered up in sacks, carried a short distance up the slope from the gaol, and buried in pits.

The foundations required for any of the gaol walls would have been substantial, and could easily account for the volume of disarticulated bone found buried on the excavation site. The use of several pits would fit with a scenario in which bodies were exhumed over the course of several days or weeks, during the sequential digging of foundation trenches.[4]

Alternatively, it is quite possible that the comminuted bone could relate to an entirely different episode of construction within the valley. During the post-War period there have been a number of building projects undertaken, both of large and small scale. Any of these could have produced the material present within the two pits.

7.3 The excavated area at the time of the graveyard

In spite of its proximity to the gaol, and to a well house further up the valley, the burial ground would have been, intentionally, a place apart. Few men would have been involved in the task of burial on a daily basis, and the ten-minute walk to the hospital would have separated the graveyard from the life of the Establishment.

The archaeological and historical evidence combine to show that the burial ground would have closely resembled its present-day form. It was not an attractive proposition: the rocky ground, with its sparse vegetation, would have been dusty in dry weather and impassably muddy after even a little rain.

Entrance into the graveyard was via a steep path to the north, cobbled against the mud but still slippery in wet weather. (This path is shown on Melliss' map, and Group 2380 is thought to be a remnant of it; Fig 3.19.) The steep slope of the hillside, being uneven and difficult to work on, was terraced along much of its length, forming a series of irregular platforms retained by crudely constructed loose stone banks. It is likely that access from terrace to terrace was via paths of rammed earth, which would have been particularly unsatisfactory when carrying tools or bodies for burial.

The lower valley slopes, in which the graveyard was situated, would have needed regular maintenance in order to keep the area useable: vegetation does not regenerate quickly after having been cleared, but rockfall from the steep hillsides above would have been a frequent occurrence. Moreover, although grave markers must have existed, not for memorial but to prevent old burials being re-dug, they would have been of an ephemeral nature. Probably just low stone cairns or timber stakes, they would have been disguised by the shifting hillside within months, making the identification of previous burials difficult.[5]

The ground taken in by the excavation area was barely suited to grave digging. Free-draining and full of stone, it would have been difficult to dig and would have had a frustrating tendency to give way while the graves were open. Nevertheless, and despite their propensity to collapse, it seems that a number of holes were dug, then left open in anticipation of bodies. Attempts at a regimented layout were thwarted by the rocky ground, but a constant effort was maintained to enforce order upon what must have been a somewhat chaotic landscape of collapsing terraces, open graves, spoil heaps, and the mounds of previous burials.

Figure 7.3   The excavation site in June 2008. This photograph was taken after heavy rain had transformed the site from its usual arid state to an unworkable condition. The state of the graveyard at the time of its operation may often have been similar to this

Whilst bodies were being interred, and for some months following, the graveyard would best be described, in the words of Edward Griffiths, the Superintendent of the Valley in 1850, as 'prejudicial'. The stench of decay, or 'effluvia', mentioned by Griffiths was accompanied by clouds of flies and plagues of rats and mice. A report in 1849 by Dr Vowells, Colonial Surgeon, commented that:

> The ferocity of the rats in a few instances which I traced, attacking the dying and almost universally the dead, was a subject of frequent communication on my part to the Collector of Customs.

The Collector's response confirmed Vowell's observations and indicated that little could be done to improve the situation. Home-made poison was found to be more effective than prepared chemicals, but it was reported that rats killed during the daytime were being eaten by the Africans, and so the use of poison was discontinued (and all cooked rats confiscated). Cats and traps were also introduced to reduce the rat population. However, attempts to exterminate rats are invariably doomed to failure and their numbers doubtless increased with every slave ship that was broken up in Rupert's Bay. Small quantities of quicklime and deeper burial were both tried as a means of reducing the health risk posed

by the site, but the sheer number of dead, and the close confines of the valley, would have rendered these attempts ineffectual. In such a landscape it is no wonder that many of the bodies show signs of a rapid burial.

7.4   An institutional burial ground

7.4.1   Factors influencing the overall burial practice

Throughout the 19th century the transatlantic slave trade changed in character and practice, responding to a variety of factors. Some arose directly from Britain's pursuit of her abolitionist policy, whilst others were only tangentially connected or entirely unrelated. The size of the West Africa Squadron varied over time, as did the tactics it employed and the political support it received from the British government. The diplomatic situation also formed an essential, albeit highly complex, backcloth. Relations between Britain, the European Powers and the United States were continuously in flux, and the abolitionist agenda assumed a greater or lesser importance at given periods. West African politics, and Britain's willingness to interfere in them, were also a significant factor. In the slave-owning nations, the volume of imports ebbed and flowed according to political, economic and social circumstances.

As a result, neither the flow of slaves across the Atlantic nor the number of vessels captured by the Royal Navy and other preventative squadrons was constant. As Chapter 2 makes very clear, the history of St Helena's Liberated African Establishment was characterised by extreme unpredictability. The Rupert's Valley depot often went for many months without receiving a slave ship, only to be confronted by the arrival of many hundreds of people, usually without any warning. The medical treatment of the Africans, and the burial practices within the valley, therefore need to be viewed within this context.

Chapter 2 outlines the historical sources that describe the running of the depot. Collectively these address many issues in exhaustive detail, including the process of unloading the slave ships, medical care, and the day-to-day running of the Establishment. However, these same sources, so detailed in most other respects, fail to discuss the process of burial. Only a handful of sources mention the graveyard and these are predominantly concerned with its position rather than any procedure for burial. There seems to be a clear division between those subjects thought worthy of discussion, and those which were not: essentially, this division occurs at the point of death. The brief comment by Edward Griffiths (quoted in section 7.2.1) is the most detailed discussion of the graveyards, but even his text is more concerned with the effects of the burials upon the living.

This omission is strange, given the Victorian obsession with cataloguing and their fascination for the details of death, which a modern audience might find morbid. However, much of the correspondence about the Establishment was concerned with expense: if the burials cost nothing then comment may simply not have been deemed necessary.

7.4.2 Practicality and rationale

Any archaeological discussion of a burial is, inevitably, the product of a restricted view of the very end of the process of death. In the case of the Rupert's Valley graveyards, the interments represent the last act of a complex logistical process.

At various points in the Establishment's history the expedient of burying corpses at sea was adopted. It seems to have been the first method of disposal tried in Lemon Valley in 1840, and the practice was apparently revived around 1850 in Rupert's Bay. For various reasons it was a failure: in Lemon Valley it proved impractical, whilst in 1850 the islanders petitioned for this method to be abandoned, because the fishermen working around the coast were catching fish that had been feeding on the corpses. The existence of the land-based burial grounds is, therefore, a corollary of the failure to bury at sea.

There are two places from which a recaptive would

have reached the graveyard: directly from the slave ship; or subsequently from the hospital. As the contemporary sources make clear, a laden slaver would have arrived carrying a number of corpses, whilst other recaptives did not survive the landing process. As discussed in section 2.4.5, unloading a slave ship could be a protracted operation, taking many hours and perhaps, in the worst cases, spanning several days.

Immediately after a slave ship's arrival there would have been constant traffic between the bay and the burial ground, carrying those who had died on board or during disembarkation. This would have continued in the days that followed, as those who only barely survived the landing process also succumbed. Most of the multiple interments probably belong to such a period, as no grave would have been left open for long in such a hot, rat-ridden environment.[6] After the initial crisis, however, the number of deaths per day tended to decrease, although the trend could be broken by sporadic outbreaks of disease. In this subsequent period, burials would have been undertaken singly, or in small group graves.

It can therefore be postulated that most of the northern part of the excavated area derives from periods of high mortality, almost certainly after the arrival of a slave ship. As Figure 6.4 shows, multiple burials are prevalent here, with two sub-areas in which there is a particularly high density of bodies. The north-west corner of the graveyard is one of these sub-areas: measuring 11m x 7m, it contained 45 bodies in 15 graves. By contrast, in the centre of the northern part of the excavated area, and the whole of the southern part, single and double interments were prevalent: in the southern part there are only four triple interments, and no graves holding a greater number of individuals. These areas would appear to reflect times of lesser crisis, when deaths occurred only singly or in very small numbers. The formation of these parts of the graveyard would have been more gradual, and rather more reminiscent of a normal domestic graveyard.

The actual burial process was probably very quick. Slave vessel holds were notoriously hot: McHenry cites figures of up to 120°F or 49°C. Therefore, when bodies came directly off a slaver, they could already be in an advanced state of decomposition. These rotting corpses would have provided one incentive for rapid burial, whilst the graveyard itself was hardly a place in which one would wish to linger. These factors partially explain why most of the bodies were not laid out within the graves: this was a necessary process of disposal, with all other considerations being secondary. Interestingly, however, the method of disposal does not seem to have differed between those who came directly off the slave ship, and those who died later. As far as can be seen from the archaeological evidence, the people interred with 'tin tickets' (who must have died in the hospital and were presumably interred before decay set in) received no more care in their burial than any other.

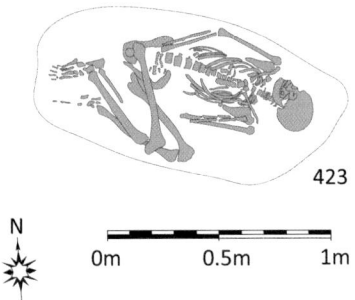

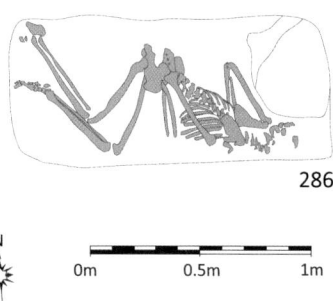

Figure 7.4 Skeleton 423 (Group 2064)

Figure 7.5 Skeleton 286 (Group 2176)

A small number of bodies do display some degree of orthodox layout, that is to say supine and with the arms either straight at the sites or crossed over the pelvis. This is most commonly seen with the single interments, where there was generally greater space within the grave cut and which presumably occurred at times of lesser crisis. A smaller number of double burials also appear to have been deliberately arranged. The majority of burials lack such a layout, however. Generally, the only attempt at a standard convention appears to have been the placement of the head to the east and the body supine, but as discussed below, even this practice was not universally followed.

The disarray of the limbs and the occasional prone burial suggests that many corpses were simply dropped into the grave. Where the grave cut was

small, or where it contained large boulders which could not be removed, this was not possible. In these cases the bodies were packed into the available shape and space of the grave, usually in a flexed position (Figs 7.4 and 7.5).

Placement was also necessary for most of the multiple interments. In these, the majority of corpses were laid in the same direction, although an appreciable number were arranged head-to-toe (Fig 7.6). An effort was clearly being made to pack the bodies efficiently into the grave although some attempts were not particularly logical (see Fig 3.14).

The insanitary condition of bodies taken directly from a slave vessel perhaps led to a requirement for some form of wrapping or binding to facilitate transfer from ship to land. Any such items would have been buried with the bodies rather than risk the spread of contagion through their reuse. However, most of the textiles found within the burials have been interpreted as clothing (see section 5.9.2), and so it is assumed that if shrouds were used then they have not survived in the archaeological record.

It is quite possible that many of the bodies were wrapped prior to burial, even those who died and were buried before decay set in. The same 1863 letter which discusses the opening of a new graveyard at Half Tree Hollow (see section 7.2.1.2 above) also makes a detailed comment on this issue:

> I am informed that it is usual in the case of the Negroes to carry them to the burial ground, not as is the case with White people in coffins, but simply wrapped in a rough description of winding sheet, the body being carried on a pole by a couple of men. I consider that it would be highly dangerous to have their bodies, some of them in a state of partial decomposition, carried through this crowded and unhealthy town [Jamestown].

Despite this description of what appears to have been a common practice, there was no archaeological evidence for winding sheets or shrouds identified from the excavation.

The arrangement of most skeletons within the graves argues against a tight wrapping of the body, but this does not rule out the use of a loose covering in order to make handling easier. The presence of a covering may explain the small number of prone

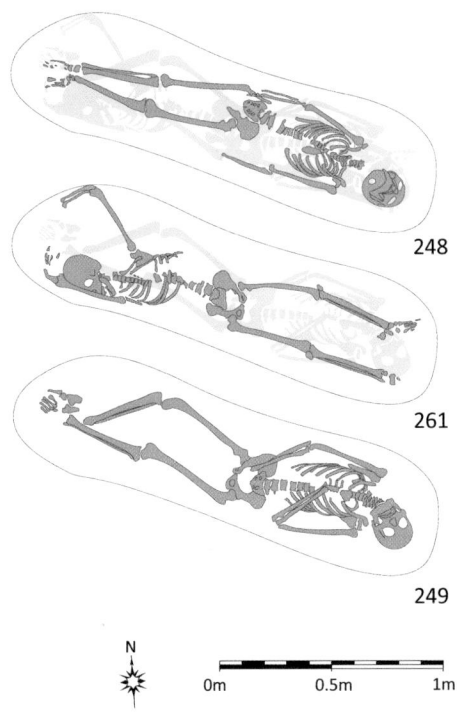

Figure 7.6 Skeletons 248, 261 and 249 (Group 2114)

Figure 7.7 Evidence for post-mortem investigations: Skeleton 502, one of three bodies within burial group 2554. The head of this individual is missing, despite the grave being undisturbed

burials found during the excavation: if the body was obscured, the person burying it may not have been able to assess or lay out the body in a supine position.

In a few instances, there was evidently an interim stage between death and burial. Three skeletons showed evidence for autopsy in the form of craniotomies (341, 511 and 512). In each case the skull had been carefully sawn so as to separate the upper part of the cranium (see Fig 4.54). After examination the head and body were buried together, the parts of the skull being reunited and held in place by some form of wrapping or even a hat or cap. Remnants of goat-fibre textile were recovered from the skull of each of the three autopsy subjects (SF24, SF88 and SF89), and these could have been used for precisely this function. Interestingly, two of the autopsy subjects were buried together (Skeletons 511 and 512), which clearly indicates that the procedure was carried out at the same time. Normally there would be a particular reason for carrying out an autopsy: in the case of the excavated examples the cause is not clear, although all three had suffered from scurvy and one (Skeleton 341) may have had haemorrhaging within the skull.

Several other skeletons were found without skulls, despite the rest of the bones being well preserved and the body lying in an undisturbed grave cut (Fig 7.7). The presumption is that these bodies were also the subject of an autopsy: the skulls must have been buried separately, or retained for study. These discoveries complement historical accounts of such investigations (see sections 2.4.6 and 4.3.7.8).

The small structure marked as a 'dead house' on the later plans of the depot was probably the place where such interventions took place (see section 2.4.1). At this period the term 'dead house' refers to a structure that was separated from a hospital building or situated close to a cemetery, used for the storage of the dead. When associated with hospital buildings, it normally included facilities for dissection or autopsy (Oppert 1867). The example in Rupert's Valley was too small to have accommodated any significant number of bodies but it was large enough to store a few corpses prior to burial, or to serve as a space for autopsies.

7.4.3 The management of the burial ground

Managing burials on such a large scale required significant organisation, and this is manifested in the archaeology of the excavated area. Overall, the site exhibits evidence of an attempt to produce a consistent arrangement. The lack of straight lines within the burial ground is a function of topography: where a regimented layout was possible, within softer open ground, it was adopted. The high consistency in the orientation of the individual grave cuts also indicates a planned layout, maintained throughout the site's use as a graveyard. In order to achieve this, either the burial period had to be quite brief, or durable grave markers would have been needed. In either scenario it would have been possible visually to offset the new graves from previous burials.

The graves themselves, when cut into soft natural, were often a classic shape: wider at the shoulders and square at the feet, 2ft wide and 6ft long (0.61 x 1.83m). Considerable variation of this model was seen in the majority of the graves, due in part to a difficulty digging the rocky soils, and also to the loose nature of the ground and frequent collapses. Even so, there appears to have been a concerted effort to maintain a consistent form to each cut.

Maintaining such an order must have been extremely difficult. The burial site was far from ideal, and the arrival of a slave ship often prompted the need to dispose of a great many corpses very quickly. Consistent organisation must have been required, central to which was a tight control of those digging the graves and burying the dead. This control seems to have rested with the Superintendent. Edward Griffiths, for example, wrote in 1851: '... but it might be prejudicial to those employed in the carrying and burying the dead. I have therefore given instructions to the overseers to deepen the graves in future'.

The use of overseers in the burial ground is noteworthy. They seem to have been employed for a variety of tasks within the Establishment and were discharged when no longer needed. Such men came from the lower classes, as is made clear by various documentary references. Those originally assigned to George McHenry in early 1841 were (according to his account) an extraordinary group, whom he condemned for being drunkards, wastrels or simply too old to be of any use. One allegedly only signed up for the job in the hope that his overbearing wife would accompany him, and then contract some form of fatal disease. Apparently she obliged in both respects. Most startling of all was the employment of the nine Portuguese crew of the slaver *Dous d'Abril*, brought to the island as captives of HMS *Fantome*.

In the longer term the selection of overseers could be made at greater leisure, with a consequent improvement in both the personnel and the standard of care. It remained a lowly job: McHenry refers to them in 1843 as 'half a dozen labouring men', whilst a list of pay from 1846 shows them to have received a wage approximately one-third that of the surgeon, half of that of a clerk, and comparable to that of a matron. Two classes of overseer are listed, 1st and 2nd, both paid three shillings per day for work 'in charge of Africans'. It is probable that such people were drawn from the existing island population: one of the surnames given for the overseers in 1846, Knipe, was – and still is – common amongst the St Helenians.

Despite McHenry's description of the overseers as labouring men, their job title was something of a misnomer. In practice they carried out much of the general work in the Establishment. Amongst other duties, they were responsible for the digging of graves and the transportation of bodies to the burial ground: this is made clear by a letter from the Collector of Customs to the Colonial Secretary in 1842, describing an 'overseer with responsibility for burying the dead'. The Collector went on to comment that this duty 'might possibly be performed by an Overseer of the 1st Class', implying that the task of burial usually fell to the lowest-ranked personnel in the depot. Experience during the 2008 excavation indicated that one person can dig holes suitable for three or four graves per day. At this rate, two or three men could operate the graveyard. When larger numbers of bodies needed to be interred, or terraces constructed, further labour could be pressed into service.

As noted in Chapter 2, the recaptives were set to work in various capacities, and some may have been employed in the burial process. However, when long periods elapsed between the arrival of prizes, the enforced process of emigration could often leave the depot virtually empty. Thus, when a new slaver was finally brought in, there might have been no recaptives to use as a burial work force. It may be that some of those Africans retained as servants on St Helena were employed for this task, or perhaps other local labour was used – doubtless from the bottom of the social spectrum.

7.5 Origins and identity

7.5.1 *A Liberated African graveyard?*

That the vast majority of burials are those of recaptive Africans is beyond doubt. Nevertheless, it is possible that some others were interred within these 'Liberated African' burial grounds. The graveyards were an institutional area for the disposal of corpses; they were not consecrated ground and therefore only specific groups of people, at the lowest end of society, could be expected to be buried there.

One group who meet this criterion are the crews of slave ships. These men were of very mixed ethnicity, of European, American and African descent, and were the scum of the maritime world. The conditions of their service were appalling, and their life expectancy aboard slave ships was no better than that of their African captives (Christopher 2006). Mortality was particularly high during the period spent on the African coast and in the time immediately following departure for the Americas (eg Behrendt 1997, 57; Steckel and Jensen 1986, 61). During a voyage deceased crew and slaves would all be disposed of overboard – food for the sharks that invariably followed slaving vessels. Shared burial also continued on land: Rediker (2007, 352) draws attention to the fact that slave ship crew were interred in African burial grounds in the West Indies. This may also have been the case on St Helena, particularly given that the slavers were being captured close to the coast, when malaria and yellow fever were most likely to be rife.[7]

Skeleton 351, the only non-infant to be buried within a coffin, may fall within this group (Fig 7.8; see also Fig 5.25). There is relatively little that can be said about this person: osteology indicates an age between twelve and fourteen, whilst the preserved clothing, trousers that would have been worn by a working man or seaman, suggests that this was a male. Whether he was of European, African or mixed ethnicity has yet to be investigated, but DNA analysis may be able to establish this fact. He had no dental modifications, and no other traits which might suggest an origin in Africa.

His interment within a coffin was a European trait, and one that singled him out from every other older child, adolescent and adult within the excavation area. Apart from his clothing, there were no other artefacts preserved within the burial. In common with many of the individuals within the graveyard, he suffered from scurvy, a disease which commonly afflicted both the slaves and the crews of

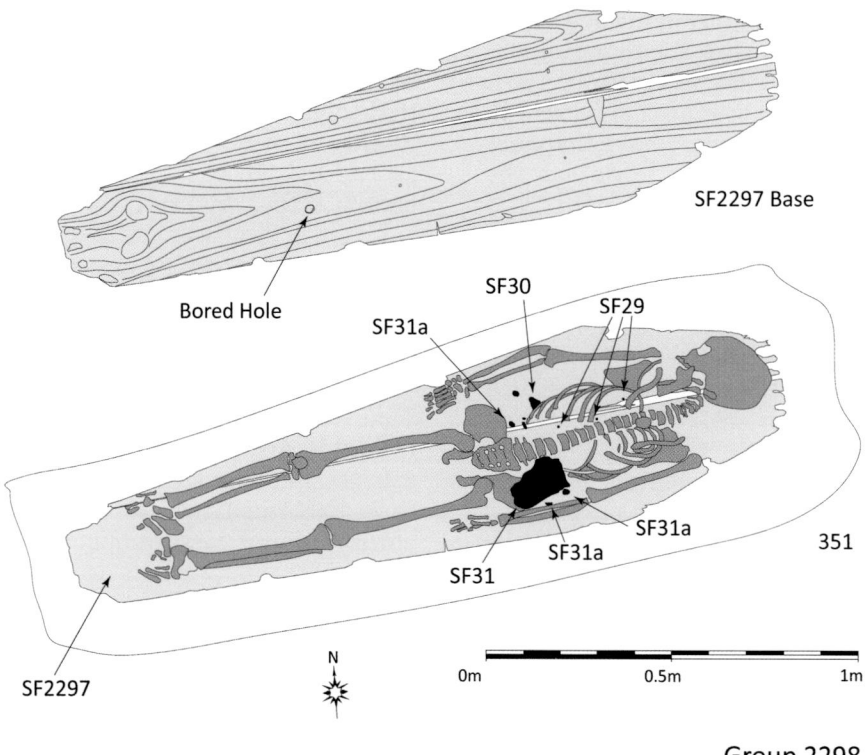

Figure 7.8 Skeleton 351

slave ships. Plausibly, this person belonged to the latter group – someone of sufficiently low status to be buried amidst these hundreds of recaptives, but in some way distinct from them. He may have been a young sailor, or perhaps a cabin-boy.

A second group which could have been buried amongst the recaptives comprised 'Coolie' labourers. Indentured Indians and Chinese were carried in large numbers to the West Indies during the 19th century, essentially as a replacement for the African slaves no longer available after Abolition (Ramdin 1994; Hu-Dehart 2007). Mortality on 'Coolie Ships' could be very high: it averaged over 17% in 1856–57, although this figure is unusual, and in earlier years it had ranged between 2% and 6% (Tinker 1991). Nevertheless, ill-fated vessels such as the *Salsette* (whose 1858 voyage was recorded in the journal of its captain and later published; Carlile 1859) touched at St Helena and there may have been a need to bury a small number of dead in unconsecrated ground. Whether this happened, and whether Rupert's Valley was used for such a purpose, is not known.

7.5.2   Osteological and archaeological evidence

There is no archaeological evidence to suggest that any of the excavated individuals were anything other than recaptive Africans. Artefacts of potentially African origin are not found in many burials; however, those showing evidence for the influence of African cultural practices, for example in the use of beads, are more numerous.

Osteological non-metric traits, including a high prevalence of lateral squatting facets, would be consistent with an African population, as is the widespread occurrence of dental modification (see sections 4.3.4 and 4.3.5).

In excess of two-thirds of the burials show positive evidence for an origin in Africa. Given the consistent burial practices and regular and contiguous nature of the graves, it would seem fair to conclude that the population is, at least largely, homogeneous.

7.5.3   Origins and early life

The locations of prizes taken by the West Africa Squadron and adjudicated by the Vice-Admiralty court at St Helena are shown on Figure 7.9. The majority were captured close to West and Central Africa, from Sierra Leone to the Congo–Angola region. A lesser number were intercepted in the open ocean, whilst a few were taken on the South American coast, including from the harbour of Rio de Janeiro, during Palmerston's assault on the Brazilian slave trade.

These data are of great interest in terms of the relationship between naval operations and the St Helena Vice-Admiralty court. Unfortunately, they shed little light on the origins of the slaves aboard the captured vessels – and therefore the potential homeland of those buried within Rupert's Valley.

As noted in Chapter 4, even the clearest evidence

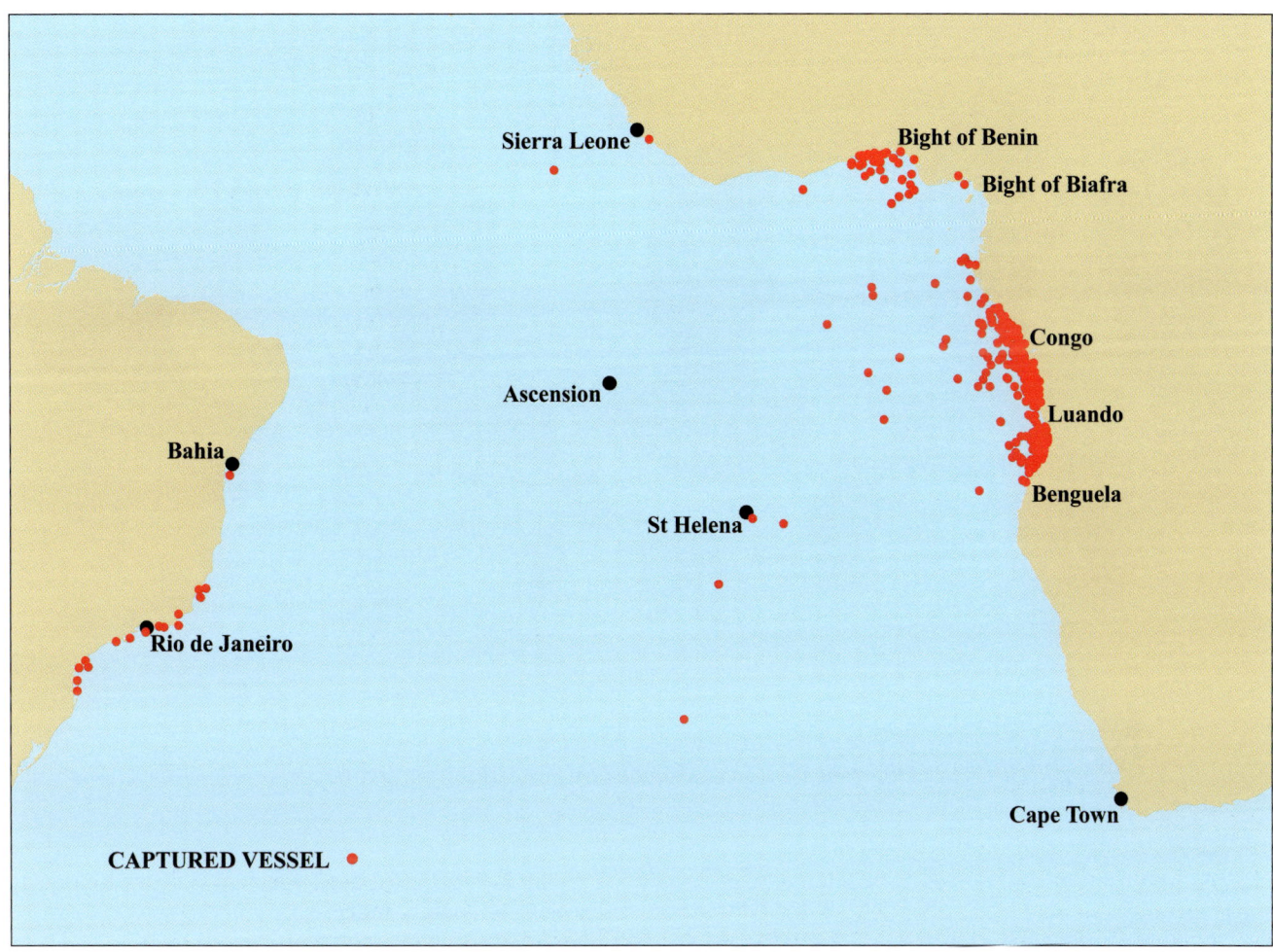

Figure 7.9 Royal Navy prizes adjudicated by the St Helena Vice-Admiralty court

of African culture exhibited by the skeletal remains, the dental modifications, do not allow conclusions to be reached about the ethnic or tribal origin of the individuals to whom they belonged. However, the historical evidence does offer some information on this subject, albeit not particularly precise in character. It is certainly the case that those involved with the Establishment, most notably those working in the depots, understood that their charges did not form a homogeneous group but instead came from a diversity of regions and cultures.[8] For example, writing in early 1842, only a few months after taking up his post in Lemon Valley, Dr McHenry wrote that:

> All the Negroes introduced to St Helena have been brought from the countries bordering on the Congo River, from Angola or Benguela, or the Mozambique coast. The languages spoken by them are of course dialects prevailing at the above-mentioned places. Some few individuals come from the interior of Africa whose language is totally incomprehensible to the rest of the Negroes.

After his departure from St Helena, the doctor went on to write extensively about his experiences in Lemon Valley, in which he paid particular attention to the racial character and the customs of the Africans who had been under his care. McHenry was only one of several senior staff within the depots who took an interest in this subject, and because of the need to communicate with the Africans many of its personnel must have become able to distinguish between the different groups present – or at least believed themselves able to do so.

It is also the case that the slavers were expert in identifying the regional origin of their captives. There is every reason to assume that there was a dialogue between the crews of captured slave traders (who were neither subject to imprisonment nor prosecution) and those working in the Establishment. Indeed, as discussed in section 7.4.3, some of the overseers appointed to Lemon Valley in 1841 were former Portuguese slave ship crew. In later years there is also historical evidence for slavers having given advice on possible treatment regimes for the Africans.

Even the casual visitor to Rupert's Valley was able to recognise the diversity of those present:

> They are of so many different tribes and districts that it would be curious, if one knew the languages,

Figure 7.10 'Female Slaves of Different Nations': sketches by Jean-Baptiste Debret depicting slave women in Brazil in 1830

to trace them out. All talk differently. A boy from Ambriz won't talk to a boy from Cabenda, because the Cabenda people eat dogs! But then the Ambriz people eat one another, and some of them have their teeth cut to sharp points like a shark or an ogre's.

(Lefroy 1895, 54)

When it came to identifying origins, McHenry and his contemporaries had advantages that are unavailable to the modern archaeologist. Some would have been physically intangible, such as language or dialect and customs. Others rested in the physical appearance of an individual and were not confined to dental modifications. Scarification of the face or body was a cultural practice applied to both males and females, as a marker of tribal, familial, social or life-stage status, or simply as a means of beautification (see Diouf 2009). Quite often the scars formed by this process were distinct for a given tribal or regional group, as remains the case in parts of Africa where scarification is still practised. Tattoos also fulfilled similar functions. Less permanent but equally distinctive could be the way that hair was arranged or jewellery was worn, which again could directly reflect native African culture (Debret 1834–39; Fig 7.10). Together, these visual attributes conveyed cultural information that would have been readily understood by many of the recaptives, and also to an extent by their European captors and liberators.[9]

At the present time, the archaeological data gleaned from the skeletal remains cannot identify the homeland or cultural affiliations of any of those excavated from the Rupert's Valley burial grounds. However, it is hoped that that further scientific research, notably stable isotope and DNA analyses, can be combined with the historical evidence to shed more light on this key question.

7.6   Enslavement and the Atlantic crossing

7.6.1   Demographics and social status

The osteological analysis identifies an assemblage that is dominated by young people. Children aged up to 12 years accounted for one-third of the population of this part of the graveyard, whilst young adult and prime adult males were also well represented. Only seventeen people (5%) were in the age bracket of 36–45 years, and this group represented the oldest individuals who were present. The proportion of the sexes was more difficult to determine, largely as a result of the youth of this population (see Table 4.4).

In Chapter 4 it is pointed out, quite correctly, that the age and sex ratios of the skeletal remains from Rupert's Valley conform to what is known about the late slave trade, in which adult males and children were well represented (section 4.3.2). However, any attempt to draw wider conclusions about the demographics of the slave trade from this assemblage would not be valid: the number of skeletons is too small, and indeed it cannot even account for the cargo of a full medium-sized slave vessel. Moreover, the assemblage comprises a group of people who died as a result of their transportation, and it is known that mortality rates were generally higher for infants and young children but lower for women (Klein *et al* 2001). Children and adult males should therefore be over-represented in the graveyard. Other factors, such as genetic or acquired immunity, also played a major role in determining who survived the Middle Passage and who did not (Curtin 1968).

Finally, there is the essential unpredictability of the slave trade, particularly in its final phase. This is borne out by St Helena's Vice-Admiralty court records, which note cargoes that varied wildly in their age and sex profile. In every case men were more numerous than women, but the ratio varied greatly, from nearly 1:1 to over 7:1. The ratio of children to adults is less commonly stated in the records and it is therefore more difficult to discern any trends.

The court records show that there were certainly some extraordinary cargoes: in 1852, for example, it was recorded that a slave ship arrived containing 'chiefly very aged or mere children, and among them is a wife and child of one of the chiefs or kings of a tribe on the African coast who had sold them to the slaver'. Two captures by the United States Navy also illustrate the same point, although neither prize was taken to St Helena: the *Wanderer* carried a cargo of 750 boys and girls under the age of 18, whilst the *Erie* carried 890 slaves, of whom 600 were boys under 14 (Lloyd 1949, 173–5).

There is also relatively little that can be discerned about the social status of those within the graveyard. The paths into slavery were many and varied, but most would be expected to come from the lower elements of society (see Rediker 2007, 100). Nevertheless, the example cited above (whether or not apocryphal) indicates that not all of those brought to St Helena had such humble origins.

Osteological traits which might arguably identify people of low status are fairly rare within the Rupert's Valley assemblage. Perhaps the strongest evidence are the Schmorl's nodes present on eighteen adult males: these are common on those who exert stress on their lower spine, for example during repeated heavy labour. The osteoarthritis identified in a few of the older individuals may also be evidence of a hard working life. Two other traits, enamel hypoplasia and cribra orbitalia, offer evidence that is far less conclusive. Enamel hypoplasia was identified in 22% of all individuals from the excavation, and one cause is nutritional stress; however, it is also associated with childhood diseases that could afflict any member of a pre-industrial society. The same is true of cribra orbitalia, which was found in nearly 50% of all individuals in the assemblage aged over 1 year: it has been linked to a dietary deficiency of iron, but

may also be present because of injury, disease or parasitic infection.

Finally there is the question of the 'quality' of the cargo, as seen from the viewpoint of the slave trader or plantation owner. Whilst demand for age and sex varied over the lifetime of the slave trade, better specimens always fetched a higher price in the slave markets of the New World. Once again, the present analysis cannot shed light on this issue. In part this arises from the fact that this is an assemblage of those who died during the Atlantic crossing: all other factors being equal, the weak or physically flawed should be over-represented. There is also the problem of comparative data: it is not known where these people came from within Africa, nor their occupation (for example agriculturalists or pastoralists). Without an understanding of the attributes of a 'comparable' group of non-enslaved within Africa, it is impossible to determine whether those in Rupert's Valley are a typical physical cross-section, or exhibit some element of selection on the part of the slave traders. It is a subject of great interest, but one which must await further research.

7.6.2   *Pathology and cause of death*

Africans subjected to Atlantic transportation fell victim to numerous injuries and diseases. These were widely described in contemporary sources, although the diagnoses were not always correct and the precise causes were often misunderstood (eg Bryson 1847; Buxton 1838). The subject is also discussed by modern scholars, for example Klein *et al* (2001), Miller (1981), Steckel and Jensen (1986) and Eltis (1984). The diagnoses by medical staff in the St Helena depots generally agree with the modern analyses, describing smallpox, a wide variety of fevers (including yellow fever and malaria), gastro-intestinal diseases such as dysentery and diarrhoea, respiratory diseases, and ailments arising from malnutrition (including but not exclusively confined to scurvy). Dehydration was also identified by 19th-century observers as a cause of suffering, but its lethal effects were not fully recognised (see Kiple and Higgins 1989; 1992). To these may be added physical trauma (arising both from accidents and deliberate violence), suffocation and suicide.

The bodies interred in Rupert's Valley are all (or if not, then virtually all) African victims of the slave trade, but the skeletal remains from the excavation do not, in the main, show evidence for the precise cause of death or for the hardships of enslavement. This is unsurprising, as much pathology leaves no osteological trace, whilst some of the most horrific injuries inflicted upon the slaves, for example those by the *chicotte* whip of twisted hippopotamus hide, also leave no trace on bone.[10]

There were, however, a significant number of bone fractures identified, present on 21 individuals and with just over half being on adult males. Not all need have resulted from assaults during the period

Figure 7.11   'The slave deck of the bark Wildfire' *from* Harper's Weekly, *June 1860*

of enslavement, but the rib fractures on Skeletons 220 and 234, and sharp-force trauma to the scapula of Skeleton 292, resemble injuries resulting from direct blows. The fracture of the hand of Skeleton 235 also has the look of a defensive injury (see section 4.3.7.2.). All four of these individuals were prime adult males, precisely the group on which violence was most likely to be visited.

There was a high prevalence of scurvy (21%) amongst the skeletal assemblage, present across both sexes and all age groups apart from mature adults (see section 4.3.7.7). Although scurvy does not directly cause death, it is a debilitating disease which induces both internal and external haemorrhaging, physical weakness and mental fatigue: the immune system breaks down, leaving the body vulnerable to infection (Harvie 2002). Scurvy arises from long-term vitamin-C deficiency and generally does not develop in less than four to six months (Kiple and Higgins 1989; Postma 1975).

Scurvy was evident in bodies from the entire excavation area, which is interesting in itself: it is argued above that this part of the graveyard is the product of several distinct episodes of burial, but scurvy victims were being buried throughout the whole period of its use. It can therefore be assumed

that it was a very common disease amongst the Rupert's Valley receptives during this time – and these people must have been brought on several vessels, and most probably from different locations on the African coast. It is an open question as to how widespread scurvy had become in the late slave trade as a whole, but these findings indicate that it was common.

Data from the logs of slave ship surgeons in the 1790s show that scurvy occurred at the middle or end of the crossing, particularly on voyages which were unexpectedly long (Steckel and Jensen 1986). However, most of the slave ships brought to St Helena were captured at or near the Central or West African coast, presumably after just a few days at sea. From here, the Vice-Admiralty court records show that the journey to St Helena took a maximum of three weeks, and usually rather less. There were a number of exceptions, notably for vessels coming from the East African coast, and for these the journey was markedly longer. For example, in late 1841 a Portuguese vessel carrying 444 slaves from Mozambique to Rio had been at sea for 61 days at the time of its capture by HMS *Fantome*.

Nevertheless, as Klein *et al* (2001) point out, the

Middle Passage was only one part of the mortality experience of the enslaved. Many scholars now place significant emphasis on the trauma of the initial journey through Africa, and the conditions of captivity on the coast (see Lovejoy 2000, 63–4; Miller 1988, 384–5). There is also recognition of the influence of the victims' pre-slavery environment, where famine or other economic hardship could deliver people into bondage who were already in a poor state of health.

The osteological evidence from Rupert's Valley would seem to support these arguments. Whilst accepting the possibility that some of the bodies in the excavated area could be those of people transported from Mozambique, the analysis seems to indicate that pre-embarkation (ie African) conditions were poor. Whether this reflects an underlying economic crisis prior to enslavement, a long journey to the coast, or a prolonged period in the barracoons, cannot be established with any certainty.[11]

Historical evidence from St Helena's Liberated African Establishment also points to worsening conditions during the last years of the slave trade, notably in terms of the prevalence of smallpox. Klein (1978, 229) observes that smallpox inoculation pervaded the slave trade by the late 18th century (see also Alden and Miller 1987), though smallpox occurred with reasonable regularity amongst the prizes sent to St Helena: McHenry, for example, recorded nine separate outbreaks in Lemon Valley during his two and a half year tenure. Such evidence is clearly an indication that inoculation had ceased to become a standard practice.

In combination, the osteological and historical evidence relating to St Helena imply an inadequate food supply at the African coast and a lack of will, or ability, on the part of slave traders to carry out inoculations. The picture is therefore one of an activity operating under the pressure of blockade, and one working on an increasingly *ad hoc* basis.

Two of the individuals from the excavated part of the graveyard appear to have been shot. In both cases projectiles (ie round lead shot) were recovered from the base of the grave cut, directly underneath the body cavity. The most plausible explanation for the projectiles' presence is that they were lodged in the bodies prior to decomposition. Whilst it is also possible that they had been deliberately placed in the grave, or dropped by accident, this seems far less likely: it is hard to see how such a scenario could have come about.

Both of the bodies belonged, rather surprisingly, to older children. Assuming that they were indeed shot, it seems improbable that these wounds were inflicted prior to embarkation, as no slave trader would have bought anyone in such a condition. Nor is it likely that the shootings occurred in Rupert's Valley: the staff at Rupert's Valley do not appear to have been armed with guns, and in any case such an incident would surely have featured in contemporary correspondence.[12]

Instead, the most logical scenario is an event that occurred aboard the slave ship. Revolts against slave crews are well attested (Richardson 2001), whilst on rare occasions some of the captives were armed by the slavers during attempts to repel naval boarding parties. Attacks by the Africans on Royal Naval prize crews are also documented – after all, they had little means of distinguishing one European from another, and often had no concept that they had been liberated. Additionally, it is known that prize crews resorted to considerable violence on occasions, both as a means of self-defence and as a way of keeping order amongst their volatile charges (Burroughs 2010).

The projectiles are badly deformed and affected by corrosion processes. As such it is impossible to determine the type of weapon from which they were fired (see section 5.5). Nevertheless, the fact that both victims were children suggests that they were not the intended target. It is therefore tempting to envisage the shootings as having taken place during a chaotic mêlée – either during the boarding of the prize crew, or during a subsequent revolt against the naval personnel. Clearly this is beyond proof, but interestingly there is evidence to show that such attacks did take place on ships bound for St Helena. In 1850, the Vice-Admiralty court recorded an uprising on a prize carrying 260 males and 195 females: six slaves were killed, and the Brazilian cook was severely wounded by a musket ball.

7.6.3 *Physical evidence of the slave ship*

The excavations revealed a very small number of items which may relate to the Atlantic crossing and, more precisely, to the slave ships themselves. These comprise the timber from the adult coffin, which is certainly reused, and the iron fixings SF03, SF14, SF76 and SF87. The latter objects are structural fixings which are not diagnostic. However, given the context of ship-breaking in Rupert's Valley an interpretation as ship's fasteners is very plausible. Some could have been scavenged from firewood, in similar manner to the copper bolts which McHenry recorded the Lemon Valley Africans having fashioned into jewellery and fishing hooks.

A few vestiges of slave ships survive in the archaeological record, but they are extremely rare. They include a small number of wrecks, the two which have been investigated being the *Henrietta Marie* and the *Fredensborg* (Burnside 2002; Svaleson 2000). These vessels not only survive on the sea-bed but have also yielded a significant number of artefacts. Other 'souvenir' or commemorative artefacts derived from slave ships are also known, two examples being a wine cooler and base made from the timber of the *El Almirante* and a snuff box made from wood in the *Black Joke*, both in the National Maritime Museum, London.[13]

Figure 7.12   The coffin of adolescent Skeleton 351, prior to removal of its lid (SF2297)

7.7   Material and social culture

7.7.1   The origin of the artefacts

The precise geographic origin of the individuals found in Rupert's Valley is not known. However, as section 7.5.2 makes clear, their status as recaptive Africans is incontrovertible. By comparison, the provenance and cultural significance of the artefacts found buried with them is a more complex question, and one for which the answer is less clear cut. A brief discussion is made below, but this subject has been addressed in more detail by MacQuarrie (2010).

The most striking aspect of the assemblage is that virtually all of the finds are of European origin. Even the items chosen as decorative or symbolic objects, either in life or at the time of burial – the beads, coins, coffins and clothing – are largely European in style, manufacture and materials. The dearth of African artefacts used as part of the burial practice or as personal adornment is unsurprising, however, given the circumstances of the burials and the naked condition that is often assumed for the slaves at the point of disembarkation.

The finds assemblage divides into two distinct categories: utilitarian items that derive from the process of caring for the Africans within the depot; and those that are of a more decorative or symbolic nature, which could be termed possessions. Whilst this distinction is useful, the category into which each object falls is not always obvious. Objects may acquire significances beyond those inherent in their function, through patterns of use or association. This form of assimilated significance is of particular relevance when objects are transferred between cultures, as will be discussed further below.

The utilitarian objects relating to the functioning of the Establishment would not have been out of place in the context of organisations catering for the poorest in England. As Chapter 2 sets out, large stores of workaday items, particularly clothing and medical supplies, were imported to the island by its colonial administration. Their place of manufacture is less certain, and whilst some items probably came directly from government stores, others were procured through private contractors (section 2.4.7).

Despite the lack of evidence for specific origins, it is clear that many items were of cheap mass-produced character, which could have been lost or discarded without consequence. The glass drug ampoules (SF16) are typical of such objects and were almost certainly supplied from Britain, ready filled with medicines. The coarse textiles found buried with the recaptives may also have been a standard institutional issue. The character of the fabric recovered during the excavation was extremely consistent. Fifteen identical examples of a tabby weave striped cloth, thought to represent sackcloth, were found: the material is of a previously unknown manufacture, and uses a dye rarely seen in the archaeological record. Nevertheless, its consistent nature and widespread occurrence suggests that it derived from a central point of supply, and certainly does not represent a relic of the Africans' former clothing.

The metal tags (SF01, SF19, SF28, SF34, SF63, SF84, SF85, SF103 and SF04) found close to the necks of skeletons are comparable to the 'tin tickets' referred to by Dr McHenry in 1841 and Dr Rawlins in 1849, used to distinguish between different 'batches' of recaptive (see section 5.3.1). The term 'tin ticket', and presumably the item itself, was not uncommon in the mid- to late 19th century. It was employed almost exclusively in situations relating to poor or illiterate people: they were used, for example, as a means of allocating food in the cheapest of lodging houses in London (Mayhew 1861).

There are some utilitarian objects which could have been manufactured on St Helena. The island, in common with most mid-19th-century communities, had a large number of craftsmen, including carpenters and blacksmiths, mostly within Jamestown. The economy was geared up to provide for shipping and would have been eager to take advantage of any avenue of income available from the Establishment. The coffins are the most obvious class of object likely to have been locally made – bulky to ship, and requiring only minimal carpentry skills.

Establishing the origins of the more 'personal' artefacts is perhaps a rather more important question, but is one that is far harder to resolve. However, some of them undoubtedly arrived on St Helena in the possession of the recaptives. Dr McHenry's account of the landing of a slave ship – surely a conflation of his experiences rather than of a single event – describes 'ample' bead necklaces, heavy polished brass bracelets and anklets, and items of clothing in the possession of newly arrived Africans (see Appendix 1). He offers no opinion as to how they came to be in possession of these items, but as Handler (2006; 2009) makes clear, despite the physical 'stripping' process that the newly enslaved underwent at the point of embarkation, they often managed to keep hold of a surprising number of their personal possessions.

Even these retained possessions often had a European origin – many formed part of a wider trade structure, linking the ports of Western Europe with Africa. Glass beads, fabrics, firearms and raw materials, particularly copper alloys and iron, were all used to match the European economy to African market demands. The large copper alloy bracelet (SF54) and several metal rings (SF20, SF21 and SF71) may be exceptions to the dominance of European-made goods, but even these may have been reworked from European raw ingots or bars imported in forms specifically for the purpose.

Some of the bead objects may also have accompanied their owners from their pre-slavery lives. The horn and bead object associated with Skeleton 326 (SF22) seems likely to have an African origin: the horn is of a species not present on St Helena, and some of the beads are of types which were at least 50 years old at the time they were deposited in the grave. Similarly, the necklace associated with Skeleton 324 (SF17/SF18) was mainly composed of beads attributed to Venetian production between the 17th and early 19th century. It is reasonable to suppose that they had been in circulation, and probably possession, for some time (MacQuarrie 2010, 38–40).

7.7.2 The coffin burials

The four foetus and neonate coffin burials (Skeletons 265, 380, 381 and 519) provide the strongest evidence for an expression of culture beyond that of the purely practical. This set of burials is completely different from all the others: they contain the greatest density of finds, represent four out of five of the coffins present, and account for all foetus and neonate burials within the excavated area.

Given the very young age of these bodies and their burial in unconsecrated ground, each seems certain to have been unbaptised. Nevertheless, the single most distinguishing feature of each burial is the apparent care and emotion lavished upon it, in marked contrast to the adult burials in adjacent graves. The actual cost may not have been great, but it indicates a wish to express publicly sympathies towards the babies concerned.

The presence of glass beads in the coffins indicates that those involved in the burial had access to a source of such items, whether drawn directly from slave ships or obtained in the depot. It is tempting to explain the burials in terms of children conceived in Africa and born to recaptive mothers – infants who died shortly before reaching the island or soon after in the depot. This is certainly plausible, but other possibilities cannot be discounted. For example, they could be the children of others involved in the process of transportation and liberation, perhaps naval or slave ship crew, or depot staff. They could equally be the offspring of recaptives who settled on St Helena, as these are known to have kept themselves apart from the wider St Helenian population. All such possibilities suggest a mother of African descent.

Whatever the explanation of these coffin burials, their physical form exhibits an unusual mixture of European and African cultural practices. All of the artefacts are European-made and most would not be out of place in an English burial; similarly, the textiles within the coffins were also of European character (see sections 5.9.1 and 5.11.1). On the other hand, the huge numbers of beads recovered from one of the coffins represent something quite atypical of European burial practice; instead, these

Figure 7.13   Close-up view of the coffin burial of neonate Skeleton 381

mass-bead decorations are reminiscent of African traditions (eg Handler 2009).

It is possible that each of the foetus and neonate burials is an entirely European artefact. The laying out of the coffin may have been undertaken by Establishment staff, using European objects that simply happened to have an African context. Perhaps their use was out of sympathy for the origins of the infant, or maybe the artefacts simply offered an expedient aesthetic. It would be satisfying to think that the mothers of these babies were responsible for some of the emotion and cultural expression attached to these burials, but this is far from certain and completely beyond proof.

The adolescent coffin burial (Skeleton 351) is the sole example of what, in another context, would appear to be a completely English burial. As with the foetus/neonate coffin burials, this individual was singled out for particular treatment, whilst having enough in common with the rest of those interred in the graveyard to be buried with them. As discussed above, he was well enough integrated into a European context to be buried in British civilian clothing and within a coffin of standard construction.[14]

7.7.3   *Cultural expression*

The cultural context of the burials is dominated by the institutional character of the Establishment. The depot was (where circumstances permitted) rigidly organised, with all positions of authority occupied by Europeans. This has resulted in a situation where the overbearing cultural expression identified within the graves is that of a British colonial institution. Nevertheless, and in spite of this dominance, it is clear that the recaptives managed to express a culture that was neither European nor institutional. The finds assemblage provides a number of tantalising glimpses of cultural practices in which European objects appear to have assumed a significance uncontrolled by the establishment, and often one that had little to do with their original or intended function.

The precise cultural role or meaning of these artefacts is impossible to discern. Many separate African groups were present within the depot, and any notion of a homogeneous 'African' culture would be false. In-depth interpretation of each object's significance is therefore fraught with difficulty: most derive from a situation where European items were adopted by Africans whose enslavement and subsequent incarceration on St Helena had radically altered their social context and sense of identity.

The beads are an excellent example of this complexity: European in origin but associated with African cultural expression. The difficulty in assigning a meaning to these items arises not simply because of the complex cultural identity of the Establishment community but also because the artefacts are

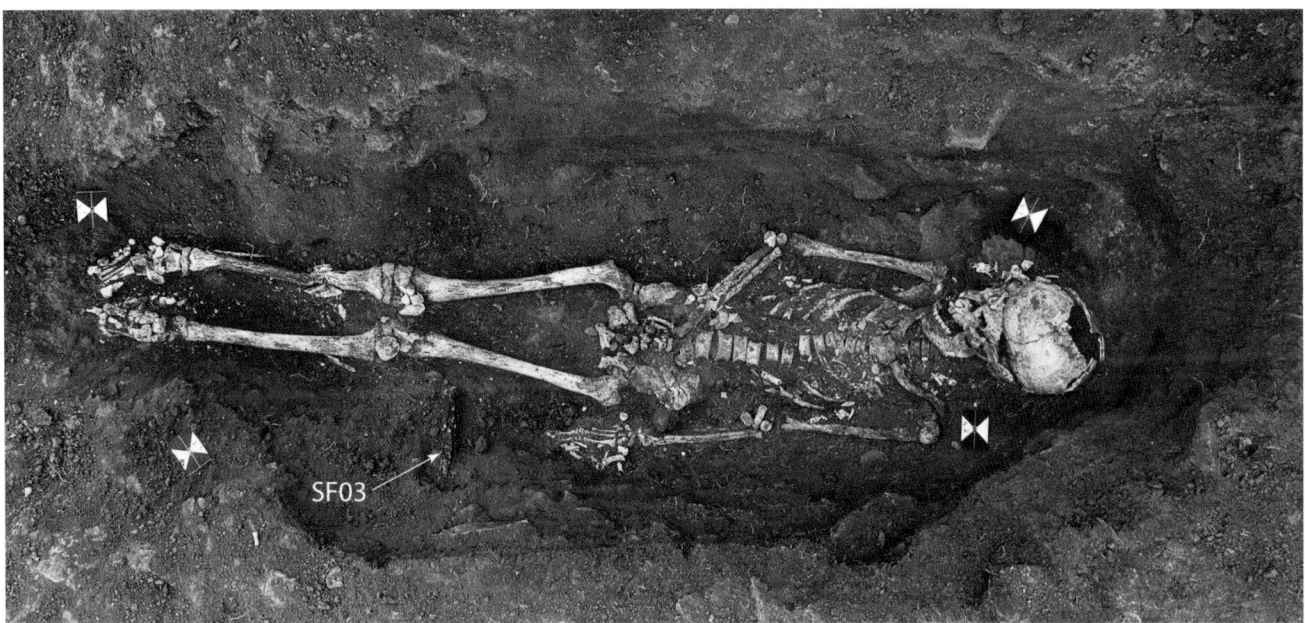

Figure 7.14   Iron fastener (SF03) lying adjacent to the body of an older child (Skeleton 230)

not necessarily artefacts of one cultural location, either spatially or temporally. They could have been acquired at various life stages: in Africa pre- or post-capture; during the Atlantic crossing; or in the Establishment on St Helena. They could even have been given after death. The cultural expression that we might infer for these beads, and other such artefacts, would differ greatly according to the point at which they came into the possession of the wearer. Interpretation is complicated still further by the fact that artefacts could have migrated between individuals within the valley.

Items that were in the possession of the individual prior to enslavement can be attributed a purely African cultural significance. Some of the artefacts recovered from the graveyard, especially those of possible African manufacture, may represent just such remnants of the individuals' lives prior to slavery. Their explanation, at least in terms of the Middle Passage, is therefore relatively straightforward. These items comprise the cowrie shell necklace (SF07), and the horn and bead necklace (SF22 and SF23).

Where an object was acquired post-capture, its significance becomes a more complex issue. It is known that many items were acquired by the Africans during their time aboard the slave ship. On such vessels it was common practice for objects (in particular beads) to be given as a means of preoccupying the female captives, who often had more freedom than their male counterparts (see for example Falconbridge 1788, 210). Similarly, it was also quite common for trinkets to be given to the recaptives by the naval prize crews. An account by W Cope Devereux, paymaster of HMS *Gorgon* (albeit relating to anti-slavery in the Indian Ocean), provides a good illustration of this point. He makes

it clear that sailors plied young girls with beads and clothing:

> … every one of our little slave girls has her sea-daddy, who gives the beads, shows her how to thread them, puts them, in his own peculiar fashion, about her neck, and clothes her little black corpus in gaudy clothes generally from his dhow spoils …

(Devereux 1869, 121)

These and other commentaries tend to suggest that possessions predominantly belonged to women or young girls. They were probably still a minority: McHenry's account only attributes a loin cloth to 'some few' women and the more decorative items to an even smaller 'favoured one or two'. Nevertheless, if the Establishment items are discounted (including the coarse fabrics and tags), then this literary evidence goes some way to explain the demographic distribution of finds within the graveyard. The majority of items were buried with children, and although they could not be attributed a sex they could certainly represent the 'little slave girls' mentioned by Devereux. The three instances of beads found with females could also be explained in this way, although not completely, as one male was also buried with beads. The uneven distribution of these items between males and females implies an underlying pattern – although whether this reflects African culture, or European masculine control of the process of distribution, is difficult to determine.

Finally, it is possible that some items were made by the recaptives whilst in the Rupert's Valley depot: as noted in section 2.4.9, there are several references to the supply of beads or metalwork to occupy the Africans within the Establishment. These present another, different scenario – of objects manufactured by the recaptives themselves, but from European raw materials and within a radically different cultural context than anything that had gone before.

There are a few objects recovered from during the excavation that seem to have a clear line of acquisition, but may have a very complex significance. These are the iron fixings SF03, SF14, SF76 and SF87, all of which were found in close association with bodies in graves (as opposed to coming from within unconnected backfill; Fig 7.14). All began as utilitarian objects, most probably being derived from dismantled slaving vessels. They are large, and would have needed to be deliberately carried up the valley from the bay. They have no obvious use in the grave-digging or burial process, and so it might reasonably be inferred that they had been kept by the recaptives as fetishes or items otherwise perceived to have significance. Once again this suggests a deliberate cultural assimilation of these artefacts, although their precise meaning cannot be known.

7.7.4   Conclusion

There are no direct archaeological parallels for the finds assemblage from Rupert's Valley. The processes that led to its deposition are unique and have crystallised a moment when the material cultures of Africa, the slave trade and Colonial Britain were interacting on several levels. The artefacts themselves are intrinsically important and the information they offer is of great value. Moreover, in the contexts of enslavement and freedom, the presence or absence of personal possessions, and the manner of their deposition, is as significant as the artefacts themselves.

As a whole, these objects offer a potential insight into the Establishment, which was a place where European and myriad African cultures interacted. Some were purely utilitarian and European, but many others, despite difficulties in interpretation, represent European artefacts appropriated into African, slave and recaptive society. They provide an insight into a culture in flux, reinventing itself in response to traumatic and perspective-shifting events.

Notes

1   Half Tree Hollow lies to the south-west of Jamestown, on a large flat expanse of ground between James Valley and Breakneck Valley: in 1860 it was only sparsely occupied, but in recent decades it has grown into a major settlement.

2   The Liberated African Cemetery in Half Tree Hollow is shown on the 1872 revision of Palmer's map, within the area known as Dallas: it is now occupied by an area of scrub and a playground.

3   Silver is a soft metal and therefore silver coinage is very prone to wear. There is no published information on this subject, but unpublished studies of wear associated with Roman *denarii* indicate rates of loss peaking at 0.01g per annum. These peak losses occur around AD 200–210, when there was an interruption in the money supply (J Creighton, pers comm). Owing to the extent of corrosion on the coins from Rupert's Valley, no such analysis is possible for these artefacts. Even if it were, the amount of research required to reach even a tentative (and ultimately unprovable) conclusion about the length of time in circulation would not be justified by the results.

4   The exact date of the stone walls of the gaol is not certain. No design drawing for the gaol has yet been found, but the correspondence in the early 1850s consistently describes an 'iron gaol', whilst the report on the fire of 1867 not only describes the building's complete destruction but comments that it was predominantly made of wood. This creates some uncertainty about the nature of the masonry walls that now occupy the site of the gaol: were they an original part of the building, or a slightly later addition? Historical records in the CO 247 series make no mention of the rebuilding of the gaol after the fire; rather, it was relocated back in Jamestown, where it is still located. The 1872 Palmer revision labels the structure as 'Prison (ruins of)'.

5   Due to the inaccuracy of GPS handsets on the island, the 2007 evaluation trenches were marked with stone cairns. When attempts were made to relocate them in 2008, most could not be found.

6   The naturalist Hans Sloane commented about Jamaica in 1689: 'The air here being so hot and brisk as to corrupt and spoil meat in four hours after 'tis killed, no wonder if a deceased Body must be soon buried. They usually bury within twelve hours after death at all times of the day and night' (Sloane 1707, xlviii). The environment in Rupert's Valley must have enforced similar burial practices.

7   There is evidence for other contemporary seafarers having been buried in the graveyard of the Church of St Paul, in the centre of the island. Here, a number of wooden grave markers commemorate sailors from a variety of nations, including Britain, France and Holland. No markers for Portuguese, Brazilian or Spanish mariners were found during our cursory examination of this large graveyard. Of course, it is quite possible that slave crew were buried in consecrated ground at St Paul's or elsewhere, but in unmarked pauper's graves.

8   In the 17th and 18th centuries there is a great deal of evidence to show that both the slave traders and plantation owners could distinguish between different tribes and ethnic groups – see for example Trotter (1785) and Crow (1830).

9   It was common practice for slaves to be shaved prior to embarkation. However, many of the individuals from the excavation had either not

been shaved, or had survived long enough for their hair to regrow.

10 An example of such a whip survives in the National Maritime Museum, London: catalogue number ZBA 2485.

11 'Barracoon' was a contemporary term for a barracks in which slaves or convicts were held in temporary confinement.

12 By way of a caveat, there does exist a letter from 1841 regarding a liberated African woman who absconded from quarantine in Lemon Valley and who returned to the depot with a musket wound to the arm. No such incident was ever recorded in Rupert's Valley, however.

13 See Webster 2005 for ongoing research into this subject. See also Hamilton and Blyth (2007) for a discussion of art, artefacts and archival material relating to slavery in the National Maritime Museum.

14 See Brown (2008, 244–6) for a discussion of the use of coffins for the burial of slaves in the Caribbean. The archaeological record suggests that Africans and their descendents in the West Indies began to use coffins during the 18th century. However, coffin burials were not common, generally reserved by the plantation masters as a reward for highly valued slaves. Brown further comments that 'the wealthiest whites were sometimes wound in silk sheets, whilst enslaved Africans often went to their graves naked. Coffins were generally reserved for whites' (Brown 2008, 82).

8   Conclusion

The transatlantic slave trade, which in the later 18th and 19th century was an issue of such great contention, is now accepted as an evil. Modern scholarship, therefore, tends to discuss the subject in dispassionate terms – a distinct departure from earlier studies, which often combined historical narrative with moral condemnation.

In many respects this report has adopted the same model, presenting and analysing the data from the excavations in an objective manner. Clearly there is much to be gained from such an approach: this site is unique, providing an insight into the Atlantic crossing and its aftermath that is not currently offered by any other archaeological assemblage.

As noted in the Introduction, this report is seen as a necessary first stage in the presentation and study of this site. Although Chapter 2 places the Rupert's Valley graveyards within their broad historical context, the other reference points of the analysis are largely internal. Whilst a limited contextual discussion has been undertaken in Chapter 5 in relation to the artefacts and textiles, the remainder of the study has neither sought (nor sought to create) comparative data sets. However, this is a clearly a logical next step, and one which applies to the historical, osteological and artefactual aspects of the site.

Although the academic potential of the Rupert's Valley graveyards is beyond doubt, they also have a cultural significance that extends beyond such research agendas. Macroscopic studies of slavery, dealing with unimaginable numbers and observing large-scale trends must, by necessity, work on an impersonal level (eg Curtin 1969). The archaeology of Rupert's Valley, however, is bound up with the individual victims: despite the institutional character of the graveyards, it is possible to obtain a picture of people with a clear sense of their identity and culture. As such, the data from this site complement that from the small number of excavated New World slave cemeteries, and the equally limited number of Middle Passage narratives written by the Africans themselves.

The transatlantic slave trade had effectively ended by 1870, although slavery itself remained in place for some years in the New World and the parallel trade in the Indian Ocean was not suppressed until the close of the 19th century. However, it remains the case that slavery has yet to be universally condemned, continuing today in both old and novel forms (Bales and Trodd 2007). Rupert's Valley provides tangible evidence for the slave trade, of a predominantly young population who died as a direct result of their capture and transportation. In so doing it serves not only as a visceral reminder of past cruelties, but also of evils which still persist in the modern world.

Figure 8.1 Skeletons 422 and 424 (Group 2449). A young child buried in association with a mature adult female, plausibly its mother

164

Appendix 1   *Visits to Slave-Ships*: an account by Dr George McHenry

The following text was published as a pamphlet by the British and Foreign Anti-Slavery Society in 1863.

VISITS TO SLAVE-SHIPS

The subjoined narrative has been contributed by Mr George McHenry, formerly Surgeon and Superintendent of the Liberated African Establishment at St Helena, as the result of his own experience of the spectacle presented to view on boarding slave-ships.

On the arrival of a slaver at the quarantine station in Lemon Valley (St Helena), it was my custom immediately to order my boat, manned by four rowers, and board the vessel. This is generally a schooner of about 200 tons, having on board a British officer, a lieutenant, or a master's mate, assisted by three or four seamen, in charge of the prize, also the original crew of about half a dozen Spaniards, Portuguese, or Brazilians, sometimes mixed with the Mulattoes or Negroes. The cargo consists of as many Africans as can be stowed away, often so closely packed that it would be difficult to squeeze in another human bale.

On coming alongside, and springing on the deck, a shocking spectacle is presented to the view. A crowd of slaves, of both sexes, and of all ages from infancy to mature manhood, with very few instances, however, of old age, may be perceived, squatting, reclining, extended, or standing, in all directions. Many are completely naked, the males almost always so; but some few women are sometimes provided with a cloth tied round the loins, and a favoured one or two with a calico gown, and a gaudy kerchief: these, in addition, may be decorated with ample necklaces made of glass beads, and small circular pieces of bone or ostriches' egg-shells, while bracelets and anklets of thick, polished brass rings, jingle with every motion of their arms and legs. Some exhibit huge scabs, the result of blows, over different parts of the body; or thick crusts, formed from the drying of the humours of the craw-craw, a loathsome cutaneous eruption. A few, still able to crawl, may be marked with the incipient pustules of the smallpox; while others are conspicuous from the size of the scorbutic tumours with which they are affected, or hideous and repulsive from the extent of the gangrenous sores eating into their flesh. Among the throng are to be found a few unable to move, from the rack of rheumatism, the stab of pleurisy, or the tortures of a broken bone; or in the last stage of emaciation, oozing out their lives with the constant flux of dysentery; or perhaps just dead. Such are the sights of physical suffering that meet the eye on board a slaver.

As to the moral agonies they are fated to endure, how can I properly describe them? Their separation from what they have loved and cherished, the loss of home, and absence from their country, the forfeiture of personal liberty, the degradation of servitude, their cruel imprisonment, the abject wretchedness of their present lot, the lack of hope for the future, the blank despair: each and all of these sentiments must have been felt by some throbbing human breast there; and the nobler the heart the more terribly it must have realized the horrors of that abyss of misery.

Scattered about the deck may be observed tin-pans, with the remains of their repasts, consisting of farina mixed with boiling water, scalded beans, and salted fish or jerked beef; and, lashed to the bulwarks on each side, a range of tubs, continually in requisition – especially by such as are ill of dysentery – amidst scolding, and jostling, and fighting.

The officer in charge furnishes information respecting the sort of voyage they have experienced, whether favourable or otherwise; the number of slaves when captured, and the amount of deaths that have occurred since; also what diseases have prevailed, and if any are of an infectious character.

A muster is then called. All who are able to quit the hold are urged, or driven, or carried up, and ranged along the deck, the males being placed on one side, and the females on the other. Then may be seen many who have been manacled in couples, generally such as have exhibited a refractory or indignant disposition, and who are thus chained to prevent them from inflicting punishment upon their captors, and revenging the indignities they have suffered, or from committing suicide by leaping into the sea; a frequent occurrence on board a slaver. An accurate account of them is taken, divided into males and females, adults and children.

It next becomes necessary to ascertain the number below, who are unable from weakness or disease to ascend upon deck. Accompanied by the officer in charge, or a deputy among the British sailors, appointed by him, the ladder is descended into what may be considered a lower depth of misery.

In the hold, sometimes boarded with deals, but generally devoid of that convenience and comparative comfort, lying upon the water-barrels, or upon a few tattered rush-mats spread over them, with no covering whatever, are found about a third of the human cargo. Reduced by the pestiferous effects of putrid fever, scurvy, dysentery, and small-pox, these are to be seen in all states of emaciation, and, I may add, of decomposition. Several absolutely rotten, already smell as intolerably as if they had been dead some days. The heavy acid odour from those who are still living, mingling with the intolerable stench from the dead, and from tubs similar to those already described, of which there is generally a sufficient provision here, but which, perhaps, have never been removed since the beginning of the voyage from the coast of Africa, rendered more overpowering by a suffocating atmosphere, ranging from 100 to 120 degrees Fahrenheit, constitute together what must be the quintessence of miasmata, the most destructive weapon in the armoury of death.

A lazar-house it seems, wherein are laid
Numbers of all diseased, all maladies
Of ghastly spasm or rocking torture, qualms
Of heart-sick agony, all feverous kinds,
Demoniac frenzy, moping melancholy,
And moon-struck madness, pining atrophy,
Marasmus, and wide-wasting pestilence,
Dropsies, and asthmas, and joint-racking rheums.
Dire is the tossing, deep the groans: Despair
Tends on the sick, busiest from couch to couch
And over them triumphant Death his dart
Shakes, but delays to strike, though oft invoked
With vows, as their chief good, and final hope.

I will candidly confess, though ever fearless in my attendance upon the sick; regardless – perhaps too much so – of any precaution in the presence of contagious and infectious maladies, that I have felt a shudder creep over me, a sinking of the heart, a loathing of the stomach, and a momentary terror of the mind, when obliged by my duty to examine the hold of a slave-ship. I envy not that state of insensibility that could behold so sad a sight without emotion.

Here let me remark, that I have seen in some small vessels – not the height between decks, for a lower deck is out of the question, but the space between the water-barrels and the deck, or what I may call the roof of the hold – not to exceed four feet. The slaves, unable to stand erect, or even to sit upright, are compelled to preserve continually a recumbent position, and to remain during the voyage on the same spot where they were placed at starting, not free to move until such as are nearer the hatchway are brought upon deck. Chained together in pairs, in that hideous dungeon, they are necessitated to perform all the functions of nature beneath them. The condition of their own bodies, and of the mats and water-casks, may then be conceived, but cannot be described without a shock to decency. Sometimes the bungs of the barrels are removed by the slaves themselves, in order to get at the water to quench their intolerable thirst: perhaps the bungs have dropped between the barrels, and thus been lost, allowing the flow from these diseased bodies to mix with the water, rendering its use pestiferous, and aggravating fearfully the horrors of the situation. In some vessels, where the casks have been loosely stowed, I have found corpses below the barrels, fallen down there in the struggles of dissolution, or jammed to death; the living reclining over them, perhaps sleeping above them, unconscious or careless of their propinquity, so little seemed the difference between the quick and the dead.

Separated from the hold by a bulk-head of thin boards, with many gaps and rents between, so constructed, perhaps, to watch what the inmates within are doing, is the cabin, furnished with two, four, or six berths, according to its dimensions, where the slaver's crew couch, if they do not repose; for slumber can scarcely visit their eyelids when the ear must be annoyed with groans and curses, and the nostrils offended with the reeking stenches. Here their knives, pikes, pistols, muskets, and ammunition, are deposited. Here is indeed, "the den of Murder, the iron bedchambers of the Furies, and frantic Discord, with her viper's locks bound with bloody fillets".

The muster-roll, after repeated investigations, having been verified, a receipt is signed for the number found, and is delivered to the prize-officer. Then some jack-tar, in the exuberance of gaiety, possibly from anticipation of the pleasures awaiting him on shore, will perhaps call upon the slaves for a song. These unfortunate and degraded creatures – unlike the Jews in their captivity, who hung their harps on the willows of the Euphrates, and refused to sing of Zion in a strange land – accustomed to implicit submission and obedience, will then strike up with loud voices a whining monotonous string of notes, accompanied with clapping of hands, repeating the same tune many a time without the least variation. The vessel, with all its contents, excepting the British and foreign crews and their property, is then handed over to the care of the Superintendent. They, with their clothes and trunks, are landed at Lemon Valley, to undergo a quarantine of three days, previously to being allowed access to Jamestown, the capital of the island.

George McHenry
Formerly Surgeon and Superintendent of the
Liberated African Establishment at St Helena.
Liverpool, May 1862.

Appendix 2   Contents of the digital volume, digital appendices and project archive

Digital volume

The digital volume forms an integral part of this published report. It contains material that can be considered as data appendices: these enable a more detailed examination of the site, including cross-referencing between burial groups, skeletons and finds. The digital volume comprises the following:

Appendix D1. Structural catalogue
Description of natural and archaeological features; plans of all archaeological groups

Appendix D2. Finds catalogue
Description and photographs of the artefacts recovered from the excavation

Appendix D3. Catalogue of glass bead varieties

Appendix D4. Osteological catalogue
Tables detailing age and sex, dental modifications and pathology groups (sorted by skeleton number)

Appendix D5. The disarticulated human remains

Appendix D6. Supplementary photographs
Images of St Helena pertaining to the excavation, the historical context, and of the island as a whole

Digital appendices

The digital appendices contain primary data, generated during the excavation and post-excavation phases of the project.

Where possible the archive conforms to standards set out by *MAP2* (English Heritage 1991) and the Institute for Archaeologists' *Standards and Guidance for the creation, compilation, transfer and deposition of archaeological archives* (2009). However, some customisation of these standards has been necessary in order to take account of the unusual project circumstances.

The digital volume and digital appendices have been deposited with the Archaeology Data Service (ADS; http://archaeologydataservice.ac.uk/). The ADS Digital Object Identifier for the project is doi:10.5284/1011174.

Site record

Scanned paper record

Context index and register
Burial index and register
Small finds register
Photographic register
Plan and drawing register
Site plans and drawings
Sample index and register
Evaluation trench register

Material generated during post-excavation

Project documentation

Post-excavation research design
Press releases

Finds conservation and analysis

Conservation assessment
Treatment records
X-ray analysis

Project archive

The physical archive for the project is held by the St Helena Government Archives, The Castle, Jamestown, St Helena Island, South Atlantic Ocean, STHL 1ZZ.

This archive comprises the primary site documents, plans and drawings. Due to concerns about the stability of the photographic negatives in the humid conditions on St Helena, these remain in the possession of the authors of this report.

Bibliography

Adderley, R M, 2006 *New Negroes from Africa: Slave Trade Abolition and Free African Settlement in the Nineteenth-Century Caribbean*. Indiana: University Press

Admiralty, 2004 *Ocean Passages for the World: NP136* (5th edn). Taunton: United Kingdom Hydrographic Office

Aitken W C, 1866 *The early history of brass and the brass manufacturers of Birmingham*. Birmingham: Martin Billing Son and Company

Alden, D, and Miller, J C, 1987 Out of Africa: The Slave Trade and the Transmission of Smallpox to Brazil, 1560-1831, *J Interdisciplinary Hist*, **18 (2)**, 195–224

Allan, J, 1956 *Cowry Shells of World Seas*. Melbourne: The Griffin Press

Anderson, D L, Thompson, G W, and Popovitch, F, 1976 Age of attainment of mineralisation stages of the permanent dentition, *J Forensic Sci*, **21**, 191–200

Anon, 1832 *The Englishman's Almanack and Commercial Directory of St Helier*. Jersey

Anon, 1862 *The Baptism of Slaves on St Helena*. London: Bell and Daldy

Anon, 1865 *St Helena; by a 'Bird of Passage'*. London: Houlston and Wright

Appleyard, H M, 1978 *Guide to the Identification of Animal Fibres*. Leeds: WIRA

Ashley, G T, 1956 The relationship between the pattern of ossification and the definitive shape of the mesosternum in man, *J Anat*, **90**(1), 87–105

Ashmole, P, and Ashmole, M, 2000 *St Helena and Ascension Island: A Natural History*. Oswestry: Anthony Nelson

Asiegbu, J U, 1976 The Dynamics of Freedom: A Study of Liberated African Emigration and British Antislavery Policy, *J Black Studies*, **7** (1), 95–106

Aufderheide, A C, and Rodríguez-Martín, C, 1998 *The Cambridge encyclopedia of human paleopathology*. Cambridge: Cambridge University Press

Baker, I, 1969 Petrology of the volcanic rocks of St Helena Island, South Atlantic, *Geol Soc America Bulletin*, **80**, 1283–1310

Baker, I, 2004 St Helena: *One Man's Island*. Windsor: Wilton 65

Bales, K, and Trodd, Z, 2007 All of It Is Now, in E Christopher, C Pybus and M Rediker (eds) *Many Middle Passages: forced migration and the making of the modern world*. Berkeley: University of California Press, 222–34

Barnes, A, 2008 Congenital anomalies, in R Pinhasi and S Mays (eds) *Advances in Human Palaeopathology*. Chichester: John Wiley and Sons Ltd, 329–62

Beck, H C, 1928 Classification and Nomenclature of Beads and Pendants, *Soc Antiq Lond*, **77**, 1–76

Behrendt, S D, 1997 Crew mortality in the Transatlantic Slave Trade in the eighteenth century, *Slavery and Abolition*, **18**, 49–71

Bekvalac, J 2005 MPY 86, Palaeopathology. Available: http://www.museumoflondon.org.uk/NR/rdonlyres/814F0BFF-020E-4EAF-B6F2-603F57100E6C/0/MPY865104.doc. Accessed: 24 May 2010

Bennon, E, 1979 *Antique Medical Instruments*. London: Sotheby Parke Bernet

Bergad, L W, Garcia, F E, and Carmen Barcia, M, 2003 *The Cuban Slave Market, 1790–1880*. Cambridge: University Press

Berry, C A, and Berry, R J, 1967 Epigenetic variation in the human cranium, *J Anat*, **101**, 361–79

Bertram, J M, 1852 *St Helena and the Cape of Good Hope: or, Incidents in the Missionary Life or Rev James McGregor Bertram, of St Helena*. New York: E H Fletcher

Bethell, L, 1966 The Mixed Commissions for the Suppression of the Transatlantic Slave Trade in the Nineteenth Century, *J African Hist*, **7**, 79–89

Bevan, G P, 1878 *British manufacturing industries*. London: E. Stanford

Black, S, and Scheuer, L, 1997 The ontogenetic development of the cervical rib, *Internat J Osteoarchaeol*, **7**, 2–10

Blackburn, J, 2000 *The Emperor's Last Island: Journey to St Helena*. London: Vintage

Blankenship, J A, Mincer, H H, Anderson, K M, Woods, M A, and Burton, E L, 2007 Third molar development in the estimation of chronologic age in American blacks compared to whites, *J Forensic Sci*, **52**(2), 428–33

Boocock, P, Roberts, C, and Manchester, K, 1995 Maxillary sinusitis in medieval Chichester, England, *Amer J Phys Anthropol*, **98**, 483–95

Borbolla, D R, 1940 Types of tooth mutilations found in Mexico, *Amer J Phys Anthropol*, **26**(1), 349–65

Boston, C, Boyle, A, Gill, J, and Witkin, A, 2009 *In the Vaults Beneath: Archaeological Recording at St George's Church, Bloomsbury*. Oxford: Oxbow

Boston, C, Witkin, A, Boyle, A, and Wilkinson, D R P, 2008 *Safe Moor'd in Greenwich Tier: A study of the skeletons of Royal Navy Sailors and Marines excavated at the Royal Hospital Greenwich*. Oxford: Oxbow

Boulter, S, Robertson, D J, and Start, H, 1998 *The Newcastle Infirmary at the Forth, Newcastle*

Upon Tyne. Volume II. The osteology: People, disease and surgery. Unpublished report, Archaeological Research and Consultancy at the University of Sheffield

Brickley, M, 2000 The diagnosis of metabolic disease in archaeological bone, in M Cox and S Mays (eds) *Human osteology in archaeology and forensic science*. London: Greenwich Medical Media Ltd, 183–98

Brickley, M, 2006 Rib fractures in the archaeological record: A useful source of sociocultural information? *Internat J Osteoarch*, **16**, 61–75

Brickley, M, and Ives, R 2008 *The bioarchaeology of metabolic bone disease*. London: Elsevier

Brickley, M, and Miles, A, 1999 *The Cross Bones burial ground, Redcross Way, Southwark, London. Archaeological excavations (1991–1998) for the London Underground Limited Jubilee Line Extension Project*. London: Museum of London Archaeological Service

Brickley, M, Buteau, S, Adams, J, and Cherrington, R, 2006 *St Martin's Uncovered: Investigations in the Churchyard of St Martin's in-the-Bull Ring, Birmingham 2001*. Oxford: Oxbow

Brooks, S, and Suchey, J M, 1990 Skeletal age determination based on the os pubis: a comparison of the Acsádi-Nemeskéri and Suchey-Brooks method, *Human Evolution*, **5**, 227–38

Brothwell, D, 1981 *Digging up bones*. New York: Cornell University Press

Brothwell, D, and Zakrzewski, S, 2004 Metric and non-metric studies of archaeological human bone, in M Brickley and J I McKinley (eds) *Guideline to the standards of recording human remains*. Reading: Institute of Field Archaeologists, Paper **7**, 27–33 (available on line: http://www.babao.org.uk)

Brown, V, 2008 *The Reaper's Garden: Death and Power in the World of Atlantic Slavery*. Cambridge, MA: Harvard University Press

Brunello, F, 1973 The *Art of Dyeing in the History of Mankind*. Vicenza: Neri Pozza

Bryson, A, 1847 *Report on the Climate and Principal Diseases of the African Station, compiled from Documents in the Office of the Director-General of the Medical Department, and from other sources*. London: William Cloves and Son

Bubenik G A, and Bubenik, A B, 1990 *Horns, Pronghorns, and Antlers*. New York: Springer-Verlag

Buikstra, J E, and Ubelaker, D H, 1994 *Standards for data collection from human skeletal remains*. Arkansas: Arkansas archaeological survey research series No. **44**

Burnside, M H, 2002, The Henrietta Marie, in Macmillan, B C (ed) *Captive Passage: the trans-atlantic slave trade and the making of the Americas*. Newport News, VA: The Mariners' Museum, 77–98

Burroughs, R, 2010 Eyes on the Prize: Journeys in Slave Ships Taken as Prizes by the Royal Navy, *Slavery and Abolition*, **31 (1)**, 99–115

Buxton, T F, 1838 *Slave Mortality after Captures of Vessels, 1828–1837*. MS Brit. Emp. s 444, vol. 28 CL (1–4). Papers of Sir Thomas Foxwell Buxton, 1786–1845, Rhodes House, Oxford

Canney, D A, 2006 *Africa Squadron: the US Navy and the Slave Trade, 1842–1861*. Dulles, Virginia: Potomac Books

Carlile, J, 1859 *Journal of a voyage with Coolie emigrants, from Calcutta to Trinidad. By Captain and Mrs Swinton, late of the Ship Salsette*. London: Alfred Bennett

Case, D T, and Heilman, J, 2005 Pedal symphalangism in modern American and Japanese skeletons, *HOMO* **55**, 251–62

Chagula, W K, 1960 The age of eruption of the third permanent molars in the male East Africans, *Amer J Phys Anthropol*, **18**, 77–82

Chamier, F, 1832 The Life of a Sailor, by a Captain in the Navy. London: Richard Bentley

Christopher, E, 2006 *Slave Ship Sailors and their Captive Cargoes, 1730–1807*. Cambridge: University Press

Cook, J G, 1968 Handbook of Textile Fibres, I: Natural Fibres. Watford

Corwin, A F, 1967 Spain and the abolition of slavery in Cuba, 1817–1886. Austin: University of Texas Press

Cowie, R, Bekvalae, J, and Kausmally, T, 2008 *Late 17th–19th century burial and earlier occupation at All Saints Chelsea Old Church, Royal Borough of Kensington and Chelsea*. London: Museum of London Archaeological Service

Crow, H, 1830 *Memoirs of the Late Captain Hugh Crow of Liverpool*. London: Longman, Rees, Ormes and Brown

Curtin, P D, 1968 Epidemiology and the Slave Trade, *Political Sci Quarterly*, **83**, 190–216

Curtin, P D, 1969 *The Atlantic Slave Trade: a census*. Madison: University of Milwaukee Press

Debret, J B, 1834–39 *Voyage Pittoresque et Historique au Brésil ou Séjour d'un artiste français au Brésil depuis 1816 jusqu'en 1831 inclusivement*. Paris: Firmin Didot

DeCorse, C R, 2001 *An archaeology of Elmina: Africans and Europeans on the Gold Coast, 1400–1900*. Washington, DC: Smithsonian Institution Press

DeCorse, C R, Richard, F G, and Thiaw, I, 2003 Towards a systematic bead description system: a view from the Lower Falemme, Senegal, *J African Archaeol*, **1**, 77–109

Denholm, K, 1994 *From Signal Gun to Satellite: a history of communications on the island of St Helena*. Unpublished report, Jamestown Library

Devereux, W C, 1869 *A Cruise in the 'Gorgon'. Or Eighteen Months on HMS Gorgon, Engaged in the Suppression of the Slave Trade on the East Coast of Africa. Including a Trip Up the Zambezi with Dr Livingstone*. London: Bell and Daldy

Diouf, S A, 2009 *Dreams of Africa in Alabama: the slave ship Clotilda and the story of the last*

Africans brought to America. Oxford: University Press

Dottridge Brothers Ltd, *c* 1925 *General Catalogue of Coffins and Mortuary Fittings*. London: S.N.

Du Bois, W E B, 1896 *The Suppression of the Slave-Trade to the United States of America, 1638–1870*. New York: Longmans, Green and Co

Dumbrell, R, 1983 *Understanding Antique Wine Bottles*. Woodbridge, Suffolk: Baron Publishing

Edwards, B, 2007 *Royal Navy versus the Slave Traders: Enforcing Abolition at Sea 1808–1898*. Barnsley: Pen and Sword Maritime

Edwards, P, 1988 *Last Voyages: Cavendish, Hudson, Raleigh. The Original Narratives*. London: Clarendon Press

Eltis, D, 1984 Mortality and Voyage Length in the Middle Passage: New Evidence from the Nineteenth Century, *J Econom Hist*, **44 (2)**, 301–8

Eltis, D, 1986 Fluctuations in the Age and Sex Ratios of Slaves in the Nineteenth Century Transatlantic Slave Traffic, *Slavery and Abolition*, **7**, 257–72

Eltis, D, and Engerman, S L, 1992 Was the Slave Trade Dominated by Men?, *J Interdisc Hist*, **23** (2), 237–57

Eltis, D, and Engerman, S L, 1993 Fluctuations in the Age and Sex Ratios of Slaves in the Transatlantic Slave Traffic, 1663–1864, *Economic Hist Rev*, **46**, 308–23

Eltis, D, and Richardson, D, 2010 *Atlas of the Transatlantic Slave Trade*. Yale: University Press

Eltis, D, Behrendt, S D, Richardson, D, and Klein, H S, 1999 *The Transatlantic Slave Trade: a database on CD ROM*. Cambridge: University Press

English Heritage, 1991 *Management of Archaeological Projects (MAP2)*. London: HBMCE

English Heritage, 2009 *Metric Survey Specifications for Cultural Heritage*. Swindon: English Heritage

Falconbridge, A, 1788 *An Account of the Slave Trade on the Coast of Africa*. London: J Phillips

Fazecas, I G, and Kósa, F, 1978 *Forensic fetal osteology*. Budapest: Akadémiai Kiadó

Fellner, E, 2011 *African ancestry of African-American quilters*. Available: http://hartcottagequilts.com/africantextiles1.htm Accessed 8 April 2011

Finnegan, M, 1978 Non-metric variation of the infracranial skeleton, *J Anat*, **25**, 23–37

Finucane, B C, Manning, K, and Touré, M 2008 Prehistoric dental modification in West Africa – Early evidence from Karkarichinkat Nord, Mali, *Internat J Osteoarch*, **18**, 632–40

Fyfe, C, 1993 *A History of Sierra Leone*. London: Gregg Revivals

Galera, V, Ubelaker, D H, and Hayek, L, 1998 Comparison of macroscopic cranial methods of age estimation applied to skeletons from the Terry collection. *J Forensic Sci*, **43**(5), 933–9

Geggus, D, 1989 Sex Ratio, Age and Ethnicity in the Atlantic Slave Trade: Data from French

Shipping and Plantation Records, *J African Hist*, **30** (1), 23–44

George, B, 1999 *Boer Prisoners on St Helena 1900–1902*. Unpublished document

Gill, R, and Teale, P L, 1999 *St Helena 500: a chronological history of the island*. St Helena: St Helena Heritage Society

Glanville, E V, 1967 Perforation of the coronoid-olecranon septum. Humero-ulnar relationships in Netherlands and African populations, *Amer J Phys Anthropol*, **26**, 85–92

Goodman, A, Jones, J, Reid, M, Mack, M, Blakey, M L, Amarasiriwardena, D, Burton, P, and Coleman, D, 2006 Isotopic and elemental chemistry of teeth: Implications for places of birth, forced migration patterns, nutritional status, and pollution, in *The New York African Burial Ground. Skeletal biology final report. Volume 1*. Available: http://www.africanburialground.gov/FinalReports/HUsbrABG_Ch6_Rvsd.pdf Accessed: 20 May 2010

Goose, D H, 1963 Tooth-mutilation in West Africans, *Man*, **63**, 91–3

Gosse, P, 1938 *St Helena 1502–1938*. Oswestry: Anthony Nelson

Grant, B, 1883 *A few notes on St Helena and descriptive guide*. Jamestown: Benjamin Grant

Gray, R, 1849 *Diocese of Cape Town – Part 1. A journal of the bishop's visitation tour through the Cape Colony, in 1848, with an account of his visit to the island of St Helena in 1849*. London: Society for Promoting Christian Knowledge

Hamilton, D, and Blyth, R J, 2007 *Representing Slavery: Art, Artefacts and Archives in the collections of the National Maritime Museum*. Hampshire: Lund Humphries

Handler, J S, 1994 Determining African birth from skeletal remains: A note on tooth mutilation, *Historical Archaeol*, **28**(3), 113–19

Handler, J S, 2006 On the Transportation of Material Goods by Enslaved Africans during the Middle Passage: preliminary findings from documentary sources, *African Diaspora Archaeological Network*, December 2006 Newsletter

Handler, J S, 2008 Aspects of the Atlantic Slave Trade: Smoking Pipes, Tobacco and the Middle Passage, *African Diaspora Archaeological Network*, June 2008 Newsletter

Handler, J S, 2009 The Middle Passage and the Material Culture of Captive Africans, *Slavery and Abolition*, **30** (1), 1–26

Handler, J S, and Lange, F W, 1999 *Plantation Slavery in Barbados: An Archaeological and Historical Investigation* (2nd edn). Lincoln: iUniverse Inc.

Handler, J S, Corruccini, R S, and Mutaw, R J, 1982 Tooth mutilation in the Caribbean: Evidence from the slave burial ground in Barbados, *J Human Evolution*, **11**, 297–313

Haour, A, and Pearson, J A, 2005 An instance of dental modification of a human skeleton from

Niger, West Africa, *Oxford J Archaeol* **24**(4), 427–33

Hart-Davis, D, 1972 *Ascension: The Story of a South Atlantic Island*. London: Constable

Harvie, D I, 2002 *Limeys: the conquest of scurvy*. Stroud: Sutton

Hassanali, J, 1995 The third permanent molar eruption in Kenyan Africans and Asians, *Annals of Human Biology*, **12**(6), 517–23

Hassanali, J, and Amwayi, P, 1993 Biometric analysis of the dental casts of Maasai following traditional extraction of mandibular central incisors and of Kikuyu children, *European J Orthodontics*, **15**, 513–18

Helfman, T, 2006 The Court of Vice Admiralty at Sierra Leone and the Abolition of the West African Slave Trade, *Yale Law Journal*, **115** (5), 1122–56

Higman, B W, 1979 Growth in Afro-Caribbean slave populations, *Amer J Phys Anthropol*, **50** (3), 373–86

Hillson, S W, 1996 *Dental anthropology*. Cambridge: Cambridge University Press

Hillson, S W, 2000 Dental pathology, in M A Katzenberg and S R Saunders (eds), *Biological anthropology of the human skeleton*. New York: Wiley-Liss

Hodges, E R, Hood, J, Canham, J E, Sauberlich, H E, and Baker, E M, 1971 Clinical manifestations of ascorbic acid deficiency in man, *Amer J Clinical Nutrition*, **24**, 432–43

Hoffman, J M, 1979 Age estimations from diaphyseal lengths: two months to twelve years, *J Forensic Sci*; **24**, 461–9

Holick, M F, 2003 Vitamin D: A millennium perspective, *J Cellular Biochem*, **88**, 296–307

Holick, M F, 2006 Resurrection of vitamin D deficiency and rickets, *J Clinical Investigation*, **16**(8), 2062–72

Houart, V, 1977 *Buttons: A Collectors' Guide*. London: Souvenir Press

House of Commons Paper; Accounts and Papers Number 643. *Emigration. Return to an address of the Honourable the House of Commons, dated 8 April 1850; for, 'copies or extracts of any correspondence with the Secretary of State for the Colonies, relative to the emigration of labourers from Sierra Leone and St Helena to the West Indies'*

Hu-DeHart, E, 2007 The 'Yellow Trade' and the Middle Passage, 1847–1884, in E Christopher, C Pybus and M Rediker (eds) *Many Middle Passages: forced migration and the making of the modern world*. Berkeley: University of California Press, 166–83

Ingall, Parsons, Clive and Co, *c* 1890 *Illustrated Catalogue and Net Price of Mortuary Fittings*. Birmingham

Inoue, N, Sakashita, R, Inoue, M, Kamegai, T, Ohashi, K, and Katsivo M, 1995 Ritual ablation of front teeth in modern and recent Kenyans, *Anthropol Sci*, **103** (3), 263–77

Institute for Archaeologists, 2009 *Standard and guidance for the compilation, transfer and deposition of archaeological archives*

Iscan, M Y, Loth, S R, and Wright, R K, 1984 Age estimation from the ribs by phase analysis: White males. *J Forensic Sci*, **29**, 1094–104

Iscan, M Y, Loth, S R, and Wright, R K, 1985 Age estimation from the ribs by phase analysis: White females, *J Forensic Sci*, **30**, 853–63

Jackson, E L, 1902 *A pictorial and descriptive souvenir of St Helena*. New York: Ward Lock and Co. Ltd

Jackson, E L, 1903 *St Helena: the historic island from its discovery to the present date*. Melbourne: Ward Lock and Company

Jakes, K A, and Sibley, L R, 1983 Survival of cellulosic fibres in the archaeological context, *Sci and Archaeol*, **25**, 31–8

Jamieson, R W, 1995 Material Culture and Social Death: African-American Burial Practices, *Historical Archaeol*, **29** (4), 39–58

Janaway, R C, 1985 Dust to dust: the preservation of textile materials in metal artefact corrosion products with reference to inhumation graves, *Sci and Archaeol*, **27**, 29–34

Janaway, R C, 1989 Corrosion preserved textile evidence: mechanism, bias and interpretation, Evidence preserved in Corrosion Products: New Fields in Artefact Studies, *UKIC Occasional Papers*, **8**, 21–9

Janaway, R C, 1993 The textiles, in J Reeve and M Adams (eds) *The Spitalfields Project, Volume I: Across the Styx*, CBA Research Report **85**, 93–119. London: Council for British Archaeology

Janaway, R C, 1998 An introductory guide to textiles from 18th and 19th century burials, in M Cox (ed) *Grave Concerns: Death and Burial in England 1700–1850*, CBA Research Report **113**, 17–36. York: Council for British Archaeology

Janisch, H R, 1908 *Extracts from the St Helena records*. St Helena: Benjamin Grant

Jans, M M F, Nielsen-March, C M, Smith, C I, Collin, M J, and Kars, H, 2004 Characterisations of microbial attacks on archaeological bones, *J Archaeol Sci*, **31**(1), 87–95

Jeffs, B, and Pearson A F, 2011 *Lemon Valley Conservation Management Plan*. Unpublished report in Jamestown Archives, Blackfreighter Archaeology and Pearson Archaeology Ltd

Jones, A, 1992 Tooth mutilations in Angola, *Brit Dental J*, **173**, 177–9

Karklins, K, 1985 *Glass beads: Guide to the description and classification of glass beads*. Ottawa: National Historic Parks and Sites Branch, Parks Canada, Environment Canada

Karklins, K, 1993 The *A Speo* method of heat rounding drawn glass beads and its archaeological manifestations, *Beads*, **5**, 27–36

Karklins, K, 2004 The Levin catalogue of mid 19th century beads, *Beads*, **16**, 39–50

Kerr, N W, 1988 A method for assessing periodontal status in archaeological derived material, *J Paleopathol*, **2**, 67–78

Kidd, K E, and Kidd, M A, 1970 A classification system for glass beads for the use of field archaeologists, *Canadian Historic Sites: Occasional Papers in Archaeology and History*, **1**, 45–89

Kinahan, J, 2000 Cattle for beads, the archaeology of historical contact and trade on the Namib Coast, *Studies in African Archaeology* **17**. Uppsala: Department of Archaeology and Ancient History

Kiple, K, and Higgins, B, 1989 Mortality caused by dehydration during the Middle Passage, *Social Sci Hist*, **13** (4), 421–37

Kiple, K, and Higgins, B, 1992 Mortality caused by dehydration during the Middle Passage, in J Inikori and S L Engerman (eds) *The Atlantic Slave Trade: effects on economies, societies and peoples in Africa, the Americas and Europe.* Durham, NC: Duke University Press, 322–31

Klein, H S, 1978 *The Middle Passage: comparative studies in the Atlantic Slave Trade.* Princeton: University Press

Klein, H S, Engerman, S, Haines, R, and Shlomowitz, R, 2001 Transoceanic Mortality: The Slave Trade in Comparative Perspective, *William and Mary Quarterly*, **58** (1), 93–117

Knüsel, C, 2000 Activity-related skeletal change, in V Fiorato, A Boylston and C Knüsel (eds) *Blood red roses. The archaeology of a mass grave from the battle of Towton AD 1461.* Oxford: Oxbow books, 103–18

Kriger, C E, 2006 *Cloth in West African History.* Lanham: AltaMira

Krogman, W M, and Işcan, M Y, 1986 *The human skeleton in forensic medicine,* 2nd edn. Illinois: Charles C Thomas

Kroon, D F, Lawson, M L, Derkay, C S, Hoffman, K and McCook, J, 2002 Surfer's ear: External auditory exostose are more prevalent in cold water surfers. *Otolaryngology Head Neck Surgery*, **126**, 499–504

LaGamma, A, 2000 *Art and Oracle – African Art and Rituals of Divination.* New York: Metropolitan Museum of Art

Laurie, R, 1799 *The African Pilot: Being a Collection of New and Accurate Charts, On a Large Scale of the Coasts, Islands, and Harbours of Africa.* London

Lefroy, J H, 1895 *Autobiography of General Sir J H Lefroy.* London: Pardon and Sons Ltd

Lewis, M E, 2004 Endocranial lesions in non-adult skeletons: understanding their aetiology, *Internat J Osteoarchaeol*, **14**, 82–97

Litten, J, 1991 *The English Way of Death – the Common funeral since 1450.* London: Robert Hale

Lloyd, C, 1949 *The Navy and the Slave Trade: the suppression of the African slave trade in the nineteenth century.* London: Longman

Lobel, R, Davidson, M, Hailstone, A, and Calligas, E, 1995 *Coincraft's Standard Catalogue of English and UK coins, 1066 to date.* London: Coincraft

Lovejoy C O, Meindl, R S, Pryzbeck, T R, Mensforth R P, 1985 Chronological metamorphosis of the auricular surface of the ilium: a new method for the determination of adult skeletal age at death. *Amer J Phys Anthropol*, **68**, 15–28

Lovejoy, P E, 2000 *Transformations in Slavery: a history of slavery in Africa.* Cambridge: University Press

Lovejoy, P E, 2006 The Children of Slavery – the transatlantic phase, *Slavery and Abolition*, **27**, 197–217

Lovell, N C, 1997 Trauma analysis in palaeopathology, *Yearbook of Phys Anthropol*, **40**, 139–70

Lukacs, J R, 1989 Dental pathology: Methods for reconstructing dietary patterns, in M Y Işcan and K A R Kennedy (eds) *Reconstruction of life from the skeleton.* New York: Alan R Liss, 261–86

Luscomb, S C, 1967 *The encyclopaedia of buttons.* New York: Bonanza Books

Maat, G J R 2004 Scurvy in adults and youngsters: The Dutch experience. A review of the history and the pathology of a disregarded disease, *Internat J Osteoarchaeol*, **14**, 77–81

MacQuarrie, H C, 2010 *Prize Possessions: personal adornment from a Liberated African cemetery, St Helena.* Unpublished MPhil Dissertation, University of Bristol

Manchester, K, 1983 *The archaeology of disease.* Bradford: Bradford University Pres

Martinez, J S, 2007 Anti-Slavery Courts and the Dawn of International Human Rights Law, *Yale Law J*, **117**, 1–98

Martrille, L, Ubelaker, D H, Cattaneo, C, Seguret, F, Tremblay, M, and Baccino, E, 2007 Comparison of four skeletal methods for the estimation of age at death on white and black adults, *J Forensic Sci*, **52**(2), 302–7

Mathieson, W L, 1929 *Great Britain and the Slave Trade, 1839–1865.* London: Longman

Mayhew, H, 1861 *London labour and the London poor. Volume 3.* London: Griffin, Bohn, and Company

Mays, S, 1998 *The archaeology of human bones.* London: Routledge

Mays, S, 2008 Septal aperture of the humerus in a mediaeval human skeletal population. *Amer J Phys Anthropol*, **136**, 432–40

McCormick, W F 1981 Sternal foramena in man, *Amer J Forensic Medicine and Pathol*, **2**(3), 249–52

McHenry, G, 1845–46 *An Account of the Liberated African Establishment on St Helena.* Published in seven instalments in *Simmond's Colonial Magazine and Foreign Miscellany*, **5 (18** and **20), 6 (22, 23** and **24), 7 (25** and **26)**

McHenry, G, 1863 *Visits to Slave Ships.* London: British and Foreign Anti-Slavery Society

McKinley, J, 2004 Compiling a skeletal inventory: disarticulated co-mingled remains, in M

Brickley and J I McKinley (eds) *Guideline to the standards of recording human remains*. Reading: Institute of Field Archaeologists, Paper **7**, 14–17. Available: http://www.babao.org.uk

Melliss, J C, 1875 *A Physical, Historical, and Topographical Description of the Island, Including its Geology, Fauna, Flora and Geology*. London: L Reeve and Co

Miles, A, Powers, N, Wroe-Brown, R, and Walker D, 2008 *St Marylebone Church and burial ground in the 18th–19th centuries: Excavations at St Marylebone School, 1992 and 2004–6*. London: Museum of London Archaeological Service

Miller, J C, 1981 Mortality in the Atlantic Slave Trade: statistical evidence on causality, *J Interdisciplinary Hist*, **11**, 385–423

Miller, J C, 1988 *Way of Death: Merchant Capitalism and the Angolan Slave Trade 1730–1830*. Madison: University of Wisconsin Press

Moore, W R G, 1980 *Northamptonshire Clay Tobacco-Pipes and Pipemakers*. Northampton: Northampton Museums and Art Gallery

Moorees, C F A, Fanning, E A, and Hunt, E E, 1963a Age variation of formation stages for ten permanent teeth, *J Dental Research*, **42**, 1490–1502

Moorees, C F A, Fanning, E. A, and Hunt, E E, 1963b Formation and resorption of three deciduous teeth in children, *Amer J Phys Anthropol*, **21**, 205–13

Munsell Color Division, 1966 *Munsell book of color. Glossy finish collection*. New York: Kollmorgen Corporation

Murray, A C, 1845, Narrative of a Voyage from Accra to Sierra Leone, from August 12th 1840 to January 5th 1841, in the Dores, a captured slaver, to HMS Dolphin, *United Service Magazine*, **1**, 512–21

Neer, R M, 1975 The evolutionary significance of vitamin D, skin pigment and ultraviolet light, *Amer J Phys Anthropol*, **43**(3), 409–16

Ogden, A, 2008 Advances in the palaeopathology of teeth and jaws, in R Pinhasi and S Mays (eds) *Advances in human palaeopathology*. Chichester: John Wiley and Sons Ltd, 283–307

Okumura, M, Boyadjian, C H C, and Eggers, S, 2007 Auditory exostoses as an aquatic activity marker. A comparison of coastal and inland skeletal remains from tropical and subtropical regions of Brazil, *Amer J Phys Anthropol*, **132**, 558–67

Oppert, F, 1867 *Hospitals, Infirmaries and Dispensaries. Their construction, interior arrangement and management*. London: John Churchill and Sons

Ortner, D J, 1966 A recent occurrence of an African type tooth mutilation in Florida, *Amer J Phys Anthropol*, **25**, 177–80

Ortner, D J, 2003 *Identifications of pathological conditions in human skeletal remains*, 2nd edn. New York: Academic Press

Ortner, D J, and Ericksen, M F, 1997 Bone changes in the human skull probably resulting from scurvy in infancy and childhood, *Internat J Osteoarchaeol*, **7**, 212–20

Ortner, D J, Butler, W, Cafarella, J, and Milligan, L, 2001 Evidence of probable scurvy in subadults from archaeological sites in North America. *Amer J Phys Anthropol*, **114**, 343–51

Ortner, D J, Kimmerle, E H, Diez, M, 1999 Probable evidence of scurvy in subadults from archaeological sites in Peru, *Amer J Phys Anthropol*, **108**, 321–31

Oswald, A, 1975 *Clay Pipes for the Archaeologist*, BAR, British Series, **14**. Oxford: British Archaeological Reports

Parra, E J, 2007 Human pigmentation variation: Evolution, genetic basis and implications for public health, *Yearbook of Phys Anthropol*, **50**, 85–105

Peacock, P, 1972 *Buttons for Collectors*. Newton Abbot: David and Charles

Perry, W R, Howson, J, and Bianco, B A (eds), 2006 *New York African Burial Ground, Archaeology Final Report Volume 1*. Howard University for the United States General Services Administration, Northeastern and Caribbean Region. Available: http://www.africanburialground.gov/FinalReports/Archaeology/ABG_FRONTFEB.pdf Accessed: 22 July 2011

Picard, J, 1987 Fancy Beads from the West African Trade, *Beads from the West African Trade*, **3**

Picard J, 1988 White hearts, feather and eye beads from the West African Trade, *Beads from the West African Trade*, **4**

Picard J, 1989 Russian blues, faceted and fancy beads from the West African Trade, *Beads from the West African Trade*, **5**

Pindborg, J J, 1969 Dental mutilation and associated abnormalities in Uganda, *Amer J Phys Anthropol* **31**(3), 383–9

Plume, S, *c* 1900 *Coffins and Coffin Making*. London: Undertakers Journal

Postma, J, 1975 Mortality in the Dutch slave trade 1675–1795, in H A Gemery and J S Hogendorn (eds) *The Uncommon Market: essays in the economic history of the Atlantic slave trade*. New York: Academic, 239–60

Ramdin, R, 1994 *The Other Middle Passage: Journal of a Voyage from Calcutta to Trinidad, 1858*. London: Hansib

Rediker, M, 2007 *The slave ship: a human history*. London: John Murray

Rees, S, 2009 *Sweet Water and Bitter: the ships that stopped the slave trade*. London: Chatto and Windus

Reeve, J, and Adams, M, 1993 *The Spitalfields Project: Volume 1, The Archaeology*. York: Council for British Archaeology

Reichart, P A, Creutz, U, and Scheifele, C, 2008 Dental mutilations and associated alveolar bone pathology in African skulls of the anthropology skull collection, Charité, Berlin, *J Oral Pathol Med*, **37**, 50–5

Richardson, D, 2001 Shipboard Revolts, African

Authority and the Atlantic Slave Trade, *William and Mary Quarterly*, **58**, 70–93

Roberts, C, 2007 A bioarchaeological study of maxillary sinusitis, *Amer J Phys Anthropol*, **133**, 792–807

Roberts, C A, 2009 *Human Remains in Archaeology: a handbook*. CBA Practical Handbook **19**. York: Council for British Archaeology

Roberts, C, and Connell, B, 2004 Guidance on recording palaeopatholgy, in M Brickley and J I McKinley (eds) *Guideline to the standards of recording human remains*. Reading: Institute of Field Archaeologists, Paper **7**, 14–17 (available on line: http://www.babao.org.uk)

Roberts, C, and Manchester, K, 1995 *The archaeology of disease*, 2nd edn. Stroud: Sutton Publishing Limited

Roberts, C, Lucy, D, and Manchester, K, 1994 Inflammatory lesions of ribs: An analysis of the Terry collection, *Amer J Phys Anthropol*, **95**, 169–82

Robins, A H, 2009 The evolution of light skin colour: The role of vitamin D disputed, *Amer J Phys Anthropol*, **139**, 447–50

Rogers, J, and Waldron, T, 1995 *A field guide to joint disease in archaeology*. Chichester: John Wiley and Sons Ltd

Royle, S, 2006 St Helena as a Boer Prisoner of War Camp, 1900–2: Information from the Alice Stopford Green Papers, *J Hist Geog*, **24** (1)

Rulau, R, 2001 *Standard Catalog of Hard Times Tokens 1832–1844*. Iola, Wisconsin: Krausse Publications

Ryder, M L, 1987 *Cashmere, Mohair and other Luxury Animal Fibres for the Breeder and Spinner*. Southampton: White Rose II

Ryder, M L, 1993 The use of goat hair: an introductory historical review, *Anthropozoologica*, **17**, 37–46

Scheuer, J L, and Black, S, 2000a *Developmental juvenile osteology*. London: Academic Press

Scheuer, J L, and Black, S, 2000b Development and ageing of the juvenile skeleton, in M Cox and S Mays (eds) *Human osteology in archaeology and forensic science*. London: Greenwich Medical Media Ltd, 9–21

Scheuer, J L, Musgrave, J H and Evans, S P, 1980 The estimation of late fetal and perinatal age from limb bone length by linear and logarithmic regression, *Annals of Human Biology* **7**(3), 257–65

Schulenburg, A H, 2003 Aspects of the Lives of the 'Liberated Africans' on St Helena, *Wirebird*, **26**, 18–27

Schuler, M, 1980 *Alas, Alas, Kongo: A Social History of Indentured African Immigration into Jamaica, 1841–1865*. Baltimore: John Hopkins University Press

Schuler, M, 2000 Liberated Central Africans in Nineteenth-Century Guyana. Harriet Tubman Seminar, 24 January 2000. Available: www.yorku.ca/nhp/seminars/seminars/schuler.doc Accessed: 4 May 2010

Schuler, M, 2002 Liberated Central Africans in Nineteenth Century Guyana, in L M Heywood (ed) *Central Africans and Cultural Transformations in the American Diaspora*. Cambridge: University Press, 319–52

Schwartz, J H, 1995 *Skeleton keys. An introduction to human morphology, development and analysis*. Oxford: Oxford University Press

Schweppe, H, 1992 *Handbuch der Naturfarbstoffe: Vorkommen, Verwendung, Nachweis*. Landsberg/Lech: Ecomed

Scott, R J, 1985 *Slave Emancipation in Cuba. The Transition to Free Labor, 1860–1899*. Pittsburgh: University Press

Sherr, L, 1987 *A history of beads from 30,000 BC to the present*. Dublin: Thames and Hudson

Sibley, L R, and Jakes, K A, 1984 Survival of protein fibres in archaeological contexts, *Sci and Archaeol*, **26**, 17–27

Sloane, H, 1707 *A Voyage to the Islands Madera, Barbados, Nieves, S. Christophers and Jamaica, with the Natural History of the Herbs and Trees, Four-footed Beasts, Fishes, Birds, Insects, Reptiles, etc. of the Last of those Islands*. London: Benjamin Motte

Smith, B, 1995 *A guide to the manuscript sources for the history of St Helena*. Todmorton: Altair

Stearns, P N, 1977 Slave child mortality: Some nutritional answers to a perennial puzzle, *J Social Hist*, **10**(3), 284–309

Steckel, R H, and Jensen, R A, 1986 New evidence on the causes of slave and crew mortality in the Atlantic Slave Trade, *J Econ Hist*, **46**, 55–77

Steckel, R H, Larsen, C S, Sciulli, P W, and Walker, P L 2006 *Data collection codebook*. Available: http://global.sbs.ohio-state.edu/

Stewart, T D, and Groome, J R, 1968 The African custom of tooth mutilation in America, *Amer J Phys Anthropol*, **28**, 31–42

Stirland, A J, 2000 *Raising the dead. The skeleton crew of King Henry VIII's great ship, the Mary Rose*. Chichester: John Wiley and Sons Ltd

Stuart-Macadam, P, 1991 Anaemia in Roman Britain, in H Bush and M Zvelebil (eds) *Health in Past Societies*. BAR International Series **567**. Oxford: Tempus Reparatum

Suzuki, T, Kusumoto, A, Fujita, H and Shi, C D, 1995 The fourth molar in a mandible found in a Jomon skeleton in Japan, *Internat J Osteoarchaeol*, **5**, 174–80

Svalesen, L, 2000 *The Slave Ship Fredensborg*. Indianapolis: Indiana University Press

Teale, P L, 1974 *Saint Helena: A History of the Development of the Island*. Unpublished document (3 volumes)

Teale, P L, 1979 *A Brief History of the Development of the Island of St Helena*. Jamestown: Thorpe and Sons

Thomas, H, 1997 *The Slave Trade: The History of the Atlantic Slave Trade 1440–1870*. London: Picador

Tiesler, V, 2002 New cases of an African tooth decoration from colonial Campeche, Mexico. *Homo*, **52**(3), 277–82

Tinker, H, 1991 *A New System of Slavery: The Export of Indian Labour Overseas, 1830–1920*. London: Hansib

Todd, T W, 1920 Age changes to the pubic bone: 1 The male white pubis, *Amer J Phys Anthropol*, **3**(3), 285–334

Todd, T W, 1921 Age changes in the pubic bone, *Amer J Phys Anthropol*, **4**(1), 1–70

Trotter, M, 1970 Estimations of stature from intact long limb bones, in T D Stewart (ed) *Personal identification in Mass Disasters*. Washington: National Museum of Natural History, 71–83

Trotter, T, 1785 *Observations on the Scurvy, with a Review of the Theories lately advanced on that Disease; and the Theories of Dr Milman refuted from Practice*. London

Tyrrell, A, 2000 Skeletal non-metric traits and the assessment of inter- and intra-population diversity: past problems and future potential, in M Cox and S Mays (eds) *Human osteology in archaeology and forensic science*. London: Greenwich Medical Media Ltd, 289–306

Van de Velde, S, 2007 An island of freedom, *St Helena Herald*, **6** (37), 10

Van de Velde, S, n.d *The end of slavery and the Liberated Africans' Depot in Rupert's Valley*. Unpublished document

Van der Merwe, A E, Steyn, M, and Maat, G J R, 2010 Adult scurvy in skeletal remains of late 19th mineworkers in Kimberley, South Africa, *Internat J Osteoarchaeol*, **20**, 307–16

Van der Sleen, W G N, 1967 *A handbook on beads*. Paris: Journées internationalles du Verre Liege

Van Rippen, B, 1918 Practices and customs of the African natives involving dental procedure, *Amer Anthropologist*, **20**(4), 461–3

Vice, D, 1983 *The Coinage of British West Africa and St Helena 1684–1958*. Birmingham: Peter Ireland

Vukovic, A, Bajsman, A, Zukic, S, and Secic, S, 2009 Cosmetic dentistry in ancient times – a short review, *Bull Internat Assoc Paleodont*, **3**(2),9–13

Waldron, T, 2009 *Palaeopathlogy*. Cambridge: Cambridge University Press

Walker, L P, Bathurst, R R, Richman, R, Gjerdrum, T, and Andrushko, V A, 2009 The cause of porotic hyperostosis and cribra orbitalia: A reappraisal of the iron-deficiency-anemia hypothesis, *Amer J Phys Anthropol*, **139**, 109–25

Walton Rogers, P, 2006 Textiles, in Brickley *et al* 2006, 163–78

Walton Rogers, P, 2011 Internal textiles and fibres from burials, in W Rodwell, *St Peter's Barton-upon-Humber, Lincolnshire: a Parish Church and its Community, Volume 1: History, Archaeology and Architecture (part 2)*. Oxford & Oakville: Oxbow, 177–13

Walton Rogers, P, unpublished a Garments, Coffin Covers and Coffin linings from All Saints, Pavement, York, Site 1995.47, TRA Report to Map Archaeology, 20 July 1998

Walton Rogers, P, unpublished b Textiles from the City of Lincoln 1972–1989, TRA Report to City of Lincoln Archaeology Unit, 22 January 1993

Walton, P, and Taylor, G W, 1991 The characterisation of dyes in textiles from archaeological excavations, *Chromatography and Analysis*, **17**, 5–7

Walvin, J, 2006 *Atlas of Slavery*. London: Longman

Ward, W E F, 1969 *The Royal Navy and the Slavers*. London: George Allen and Unwin Co

Webster, J, 2005 Looking for the material culture of the Middle Passage, *J Maritime Res*. Available: http://www.jmr.nmm.ac.uk/server/show/ConJmrArticle.209 Accessed: 10 June 2010

Weston, D A, 2008 Investigating the specificity of periosteal reactions in pathology museum specimens, *Amer J Phys Anthropol*, **137**, 48–59

White, T D, and Folkens, P A, 2005 *The human bone manual*. Oxford: Elsevier Academic Press

Wildman, A B, 1954 *The Microscopy of Animal Textile Fibres*. Leeds: WIRA

Witkin, A V, 2011 The health of the labouring poor. Surgical and post-mortem procedures at the Bristol Royal Infirmary, 1757–1854: A biocultural approach. Unpublished PhD thesis, University of Bristol.

Index

Entries in bold refer to the figures